SO-BJG-263

PHILOSOPHY IN THE 20TH CENTURY: CATHOLIC AND CHRISTIAN

PHILOSOPHY IN THE 20TH CENTURY:
CATHOLIC AND CHRISTIAN

Volume II:

A BIBLIOGRAPHY OF CHRISTIAN PHILOSOPHY AND CONTEMPORARY ISSUES

Edited by George F. McLean, O.M.I.

FREDERICK UNGAR PUBLISHING CO.
NEW YORK

Copyright © 1967 by
Frederick Ungar Publishing Co., Inc.

Printed in the United States of America

Library of Congress Catalog Card Number: 67-24186

MAY 2 5 1982

Reference
Z
7821
.M26

PREFACE

Today's culture, with its unprecedented possibilities for human development and repression, has brought the resources of Western man's religious philosophy into vital dialogue with other contemporary philosophical currents concerning such central themes as man, person, love, freedom, culture, value, ethics, language, law, and God. This select bibliography is organized to aid in the identification of materials relevant to these themes.

To accomplish this, selected books and articles of the last thirty years have been compiled in eight chapters. Their topics are: Christian Philosophy; Contemporary Philosophies; Philosophy and Technology; Philosophy of Man and God; The Problem of God in a Secular Culture; Religious Knowledge and Language; Moral Philosophy; and Teaching Philosophy. Included in these chapters are the special sub-themes cited above. The division within the individual chapters is included in the separate chapter introductions.

An appendix lists the philosophy doctoral dissertations presented in Catholic universities of the United States and Canada. They constitute a rich source of the research devoted to the above issues on this continent.

In compiling these lists, the editor has been aided by the suggestions of outstanding philosophers from the United States and Canada, many of whom served as lecturers and seminar directors of the philosophy workshops on these subjects held under his direction at The Catholic University of America between 1961 and 1966.

G.F.M.

CONTENTS

I   Christian Philosophy   1
    A.   Christian Philosophy   1
    B.   Perennial Philosophy   17
    C.   Scholastic Thought   21
II Contemporary Philosophies   35
    A.   Evolutionary Trends   35
    B.   Existential Phenomenology   39
    C.   Linguistic Analysis   45
    D.   Naturalism   49
    E.   General   51
III Philosophy and Technology   54
    A.   Technology   54
    B.   Technology and Philosophy   57
    C.   Technology and Man   60
    D.   Technology and Culture   65
    E.   Technology and Religion   71
    F.   Technology and Ethics   74
IV Philosophy of Man and God   76
    A.   Person   76
    B.   Love   83
    C.   God   89
    D.   Religious Renewal   99
    E.   Ecumenism   103
V   The Problem of God in a Secular Culture   107
    A.   The Problem of God   107
    B.   Contemporary Atheism and the Death of God   111
    C.   Reality and the Existence of God   117
    D.   Divine Immanence and Transcendence   120
    E.   Religion and Philosophy of Religion   123
    F.   Culture and Religion   127
    G.   Christian Thought   130
    H.   Scientific Naturalism and Humanism   134
    I.   The Religious and the Secular   139

VI   Religious Knowledge and Language   146
  A. Belief and Faith   146
  B. Faith and Reason; Philosophy and Theology   152
  C. Metaphysics and Theodicy   155
  D. Knowledge of God   156
  E. Religious Language   160
  F. Myth, Symbol, and Analogy   167

VII   Moral Philosophy   173
  A. Freedom   173
  B. Value   184
  C. Ethics   190
  D. Law   197
  E. Natural Law   202

VIII   Teaching Philosophy   208
  A. Teaching Philosophy   208
  B. Teaching Christian Philosophy   219
  C. The Church on Teaching Philosophy   222

APPENDIX   230
  A. The Catholic University of America   231
  B. Fordham University   244
  C. Georgetown University   250
  D. Laval University   252
  E. Loyola University   258
  F. Marquette University   258
  G. Notre Dame University   259
  H. Pontifical Institute of Mediaeval Studies   264
  I. St. John's University   270
  J. Saint Louis University   270
  K. Studium Generale of Saint Thomas   275
  L. University of Montreal   276
  M. The University of Ottawa   280

INDEX   283

CHAPTER I

Christian Philosophy

This chapter comprises selected books and articles since 1934 on the relation between philosophy and religious thought, which in Western philosophy, especially since 1930, generally has been identified as the problem of Christian philosophy. The chapter is divided into three sections:

A. Christian Philosophy
B. Perennial Philosophy
C. Scholastic Thought

In this sequence section A treats the development of philosophy within the broad context of Christian culture; section B concerns the general problem of continuity in philosophic thought; while section C is on the systematization of these insights and their transmission through scholastic thought.

It is suggested that the reader familiarize himself with Chapter I and Chapters XIV to XVI of *An Annotated Bibliography of Philosophy in Catholic Thought*, the companion volume by the same editor.

A. CHRISTIAN PHILOSOPHY

ARMSTRONG, A. H., and MARKUS, R. A. *Christian Faith and Greek Philosophy*. New York: Sheed and Ward, 1964.

COHEN, M. A. *Reason and Nature*. Glencoe, Ill.: Free Press, 1953.

CONRADIE, Anna L. *The Neo-Calvinistic Concept of Philosophy: A Study in the Problem of Philosophic Communication*. Pietermaritzburg: Univ. of Natal Press, 1960.

DINGLE, Herbert, and SAMUEL, Herbert L. *A Threefold Cord: Philosophy, Science, Religion: A Discussion*. London: Allen, 1961.

DODDS, E. R. *Pagan and Christian in an Age of Anxiety*. Cambridge: Univ. Press, 1965.

DONDEYNE, A. *Contemporary European Thought and Christian Faith*. Pittsburgh: Duquesne Univ. Press, 1958.

GILSON, Etienne. *Christianity and Philosophy*. Translated by R. MacDonald. New York: Sheed and Ward, 1939.

————. *The Philosopher and Theology*. New York: Random House, 1962.

JAMES, F. *Christian Philosophy*. London: Burns, Oates and Washbourne, 1939.

KAUFMANN, W. *Critique of Religion and Philosophy*. New York: Harper, 1958.

LANGMEAD CASSERLEY, J. V. *The Christian in Philosophy*. London: Faber and Faber, 1949.

MARITAIN, Jacques. *An Essay on Christian Philosophy*. Translated by E. Flannery. New York: Philosophical Library, 1955.

NÉDONCELLE, Maurice. *Is There a Christian Philosophy?* Translated by I. Trethowan. Vol. X of the *Twentieth Century Encyclopedia of Catholicism*. Englewood Cliffs, N.J.: Hawthorn Books, 1960.

PEGIS, Anton C. *Christian Philosophy and Intellectual Freedom*. Milwaukee: Bruce, 1960.

PRESTIGE, G. L. *God in Patristic Thought*. London: S.P.C.K., 1959.

The Role of the Christian Philosopher. The Proceedings of the American Catholic Philosophical Association, XXXII (1958).

SCHNEIDER, H. W. *Meditations in Season on the Elements of Christian Philosophy*. New York: Oxford Univ. Press, 1938.

TRESMONTANT, Claude. *The Origins of Christian Philosophy*. New York: Hawthorn, 1963.

TRETHOWAN, Illtyd. *An Essay in Christian Philosophy.* London: Longmans, Green, 1954.

WAGERS, Herndon. *Christian Faith and Philosophical Inquiry.* Lexington: College of the Bible, 1961.

ASHLEY, Benedict M. "Theology and Faith: The Ultimate Objective and Subjective Integration of Catholic Education," in *Philosophy and the Integration of Contemporary Catholic Education.* Edited by G. McLean. Washington, D.C.: Catholic Univ. of America Press, 1962. Pp. 266-86.

BROPHY, Thomas. "Is There a Christian Philosophy?" *Philosophical Studies,* I (1951), 59-67.

BURCH, George B. "The Place of Revelation in Philosophical Thought," *Review of Metaphysics,* XV (1961-62), 396-408.

BURKE, Eugene M. "Dialogue with Protestants," in *Philosophy and the Integration of Contemporary Catholic Education.* Edited by G. McLean. Washington, D.C.: The Catholic Univ. of America Press, 1962. Pp. 205-27.

CHUBB, J. N. "Faith and Philosophy," *Philosophical Quarterly,* (Amalner, India), XXVI (1954), 215-21.

COLLINS, James. "Philosophy in Catholic Life," *Religion in Life,* XXIX (1960), 179-88.

———. "The Religious Theme in Existentialism," in *Philosophy and the Modern Mind.* Edited by F. Canfield. Detroit: Sacred Heart Seminary, 1961. Pp. 20-48.

COPLESTON, F. C. "In the Clothing of Sheep: Philosophy and Religion," *Month* (1962), 219-28.

CORKEY, R. "A Christian Philosophy for Today," *Hibbert Journal,* LVII (1958-59), 20-30.

DESCH, Paul. "The Possibility of a Christian Philosophy," *Duns Scotus Philosophical Association Proceedings,* XXVI (1962), 1-19.

DURFEE, Harold A. "The Relationship of Philosophy, Theology and Religion," *Journal of Religion,* XXXII (1952), 188-97.

FERRÉ, Nels F. S. "Philosophy and Religion Face the Future Together," *Journal of Religion,* XXXIII (1953), 245-53.

FREEMAN, David H. "A New School of Christian Philosophy," *Journal of Religion,* XXXVIII (1958), 46-53.

GILSON, Etienne. "Concerning Christian Philosophy. The Distinctiveness of the Philosophic Order," in *Philosophy and History.* Edited by R. Klibansky and H. J. Paton. Oxford: Clarendon Press, 1936. Pp. 61-76.

———. "Science, Philosophy and Religious Wisdom," in *Proceedings of the American Catholic Philosophical Association,* XXVI (1952), 5-13.

GRISEZ, Germain G. "The 'Four Meanings' of 'Christian Philosophy,'" *Journal of Religion,* XLII (1962), 103-18.

GUTHRIE, H. "Problem of Christian Philosophy," *Thought,* XIV (1939), 88-94.

HAROUTUNIAN, Joseph. "Christian Faith and Metaphysics," *Journal of Religion,* XXXIII (1953), 103-12.

HOLMES, Arthur F. "The Methodology of Christian Philosophy," *Journal of Religion,* XLII (1962), 215-24.

HUG, Pacific L. "The Place and Function of the Catholic Philosopher in the World Today," in *Proceedings of the American Catholic Philosophical Association,* XXXII (1958), 34-53.

KELLY, J. "Was There or Is There a 'Christian' Philosophy?" in *Proceedings of the American Catholic Philosophical Asociation,* XII (1936), 17-30.

McCORMICK, J. F. "Must There Be a Christian Philosophy?" in *Proceedings of the American Catholic Philosophical Association,* XII (1936), 30-37.

McNEIL, H. "Can There Be a Christian Philosophy?" in *Proceedings of the American Catholic Philosophical Association,* XII (1936), 37-45.

MALEVEZ, L. "The Believer and the Philosopher," *Philosophy Today,* V (1962), 14-30.

MÜLLER-THYM, B. J. "The Christian Philosophy," *The Ecclesiastical Review,* XCVI (1936), 357-74.

NIELSEN, Kai. "'Christian Positivism' and the Appeal to Religious Experience," *Journal of Religion,* XLII (1962), 248-61.

PARSONS, Howard L. "A Reformulation of the Philosophical Presuppositions of Religion," *Journal of Religion*, XLII (1962), 119-32.

PATTERSON, Robert L. "Philosophy and Christianity," *The Review of Religion*, XI (1947), 132-49.

PENELHUM, Terence. "Faith, Fact and Philosophy," *University of Toronto Quarterly*, XXVI (1956), 92-104.

RAHNER, Karl. "Philosophy and Theology," *Theological Digest*, XII (1964), 118-22.

REINHARDT, Kurt F. "Contemporary Philosophy and Christian Faith," *New Scholasticism*, XXIX (1955), 82-88.

ROBERTS, David E. "Is a Christian Philosophy a Contradiction in Terms?" *Journal of Religion*, XIX (1939), 110-33.

RUCH, E. A. "Problem of Christian Philosophy," *Philosophy Today*, VI (1962), 133-45.

RYAN, John K. "Philosophy and Theology in a Discourse of St. Thomas on the Incarnation and the Kingship of Christ," in *Studies in Philosophy and the History of Philosophy*, I (1961), 194-215.

SCHRAG, O. O. "Faith and Reason: Still Shifting for First Place," *Journal of Bible and of Religion*, XXIII (1955), 197-201.

SILLEM, E. A. "Perspectives on Christian Philosophy," *Philosophy Today*, V (1961), 3-13.

SONTAG, F. and CORBISHLEY, T. "Philosophy, Theology, and Metaphysics: A Protestant-Catholic Dialogue," *Heythrop Journal*, II (1961), 299-317.

VAN ACKEREN, Gerald. "Reflections on the Relation between Philosophy and Theology," *Theological Studies*, XIV (1953), 527-50.

WEISS, Paul. "Philosophy and Faith," *Journal of Religion*, XXVI (1946), 278-82.

WU, John C. H. "The Natural Law and Christian Civilization," in *Philosophy and the Integration of Contemporary Catholic Education*. Edited by G. McLean. Washington, D.C.: Catholic Univ. of America Press, 1962. Pp. 158-75.

BARTH, Karl. *Philosophie et théologie.* Genève: Labor et Fides, 1960.

BLONDEL, M. *La philosohie et l'esprit chrétien.* Paris: Presses Univ. de France, 1944.

BOGLIOLO, Luigi. *Il problema della filosofia cristiana.* Brescia: Morcelliana, 1959.

BOISSET, J. *Le problème de la philosophie chrétienne.* Paris: Presses Univ. de France, 1949.

BUCHENBACHER, Hans. *Natur und Geist. Grundzüge einer christlichen Philosophie.* Bern: Haupt, 1954.

DEMPF, A. *Christliche Philosophie. Der Mensch zwischen Gott und der Welt.* Bonn: Buchgemeinde, 1938.

DERISI, O. N. *Concetto della filosofia cristiana.* Buenos-Aires: Gotelli, 1935.

DOOYEWEERD, Herman. *La prétendue autonomie de la pensée philosophique.* Saint-Germain-en-Laye: Société Calviniste, 1959.

Filosofia e cristianesimo. Atti del II convegno italiano di studi filosofici cristiani (Gallarate, 1946). Milano: Marzorati, 1947.

Foi et réflexion philosophique. Mélanges Franz Grégoire. Van Waeyenbergh, H., *et al.* Louvain: Publ. Universitaires, 1961.

GARCIA MARTINEZ, Fidel. *De l'authenticité d'une philosophie à l'intérieur de la pensée chrétienne.* Ona, Burgos: Sociedad Internacional "Francesco Suarez," 1955.

GEIGER, L.-B. *Philosophie et spiritualité.* Paris: Cerf., 1963.

GILSON, Etienne. *Christianisme et philosophie.* Paris: Vrin, 1936.

————, and BÖHNER, Ph. *Die Geschichte der christlichen Philosophie von ihren Anfängen bis Nikolaus von Cues.* Paderborn: Schöningh, 1937.

————. *Introduction à la philosophie chrétienne.* Paris: Vrin, 1960.

————. *Le philosophe et la théologie.* Paris: Fayard, 1960.

GUNTHER, G., and SCHELSKY, H. *Christliche Metaphysik und das Schicksal des modernen Bewusstseins.* Leipzig: Hirzel, 1937.

HENNEMANN, Gerhard. *Philosophie, Religion, moderne Naturwissenschaft.* Witten: Luther-Verlag, 1955.

HOFFMAN, E. *Platonismus und christliche Philosophie.* Zürich: Artemis, 1960.

INCARDONA, Nunzio. *Filosofia e rivelazione.* Palermo: Palumbo. 1960.

JASPERS, Karl. *Der philosophische Glaube angesichts der Offenbarung.* München: Pieper, 1962.

LACOMBE, O. *Chemins de l'Inde et philosophie chrétienne.* Paris: Alsatia, 1956.

MADARIAGA, Bernardo. *La filosofia al interior de la teologia.* Madrid: Cisneros, 1961.

MARITAIN, J. *De la philosophie chrétienne.* Rio de Janeiro: Atlantica, 1945.

MASNOVO, Amato. *La filosofia verso la religione.* Milano: "Vita e Pensiero," 1960.

MEHL, Roger. *La condition du philosophe chrétien.* Paris: Neuchâtel et Niestlé, 1947.

MEKKES, J. P. *Scheppingsopenbaring en wijsbegeerte.* Kampen: Kok, 1961.

MUÑOZ ALONSO, Adolfo. *Valores filosóficos del catolicismo.* Barcelona: Juan Flors, 1954.

NAUD, André. *Le problème de la philosophie chrétienne: éléments d'une solution thomiste.* Montreal: Faculté de Théologie, 1960.

PADOVANI, Umberto A. *Filosofia e religione.* Brescia: La Scuola, 1956.

PERRIOLLAT, C. *Le chemin du philosophe chrétien.* Versailles: Aubert, 1938.

La philosophie chrétienne. Journées de la société thomiste. Juvisy: Cerf, 1934.

Philosophies chrétiennes. Vol. X of *Recherches et Débats.* Paris: Fayard, 1955.

PLATZECK, Erhard W. *El pensar armónico, como problema de la filosofía cristiana.* Madrid: Verdad y Vida, 1945.

Quaestio de philosophia christiana. Roma: Pioda, 1937.

RAHNER, K. *Hörer des Wortes: Zur Grundlegung einer Religionsphilosophie.* München: Kösel-Pustet, 1940.

Religione e filosofia. Relazioni e comunicazioni all'XI Congresso nazionale di filosofia, Genova, Settembre, 1936. *Rivista di Filosofia Neo-Scolastica,* XIV (1936), Suppl.

SERTILLANGES, A.-D. *Le christianisme et les philosophies.* Paris: Aubier, 1939. 2 vols.

THIBEAUD, Henri. *A Dieu et à Jésus-Christ par la philosophie.* Paris: Lethielleux, 1956.

TRESMONTANT, C. *Les origines de la philosophie chrétienne.* Paris: Fayard, 1962.

VALORI, P. M. *Blondel e il problema d'una filosofia cristiana.* Roma: La Civiltà Cattolica, 1951.

VANCOURT, R. *Pensée moderne et philosophie chrétienne.* Paris: Fayard, 1957.

AJA, Pedro V. "La religiosidad en el vivir filosófico," in *Atti XII Congresso internazionale di Filosofia,* VIII (1960), 7-14.

AMORE, Benedetto d'. "La filosofia e il Vangelo," *Sapienza,* VIII (1955), 266-85.

————. "Filosofia ed esperienza religiosa," *Filosofia e Vita.* I (n. 4; 1960), 84-91.

ANZ, W. "Warum kann unsere Kirche die philosophische Arbeit nicht entbehren?" *Evangelische Theologie,* XVI (1956), 145-62.

ARÉVALO BILBAO, Pedro-José, "Actas de un coloquio sobre 'Filosofía cristiana,'" *Revista de Filosofía,* XVIII (1959), 113-16.

BARALE, P. e VIGLINO, C. "Si può parlare di flosofia 'cristiana'?" *Rivista Rosminiana di Filosofia e di Cultura,* XXVIII (1934), 81-86.

BARON, Roger. "Philosophies chrétiennes, humanismes chrétiens et Incarnation," *Nouvelle Revue Théologique*, LXXVIII (1956), 63-72.

BARTH, Karl. "Philosophie und Theologie," in *Philosophie und christliche Existenz*. Hsrg. von Gerhard Huber. Basel: Helbing & Lichtenhahn, 1960. Pp. 93-106.

BARTOLOMEI, T. M. "Esiste una 'filosofia cristiana'? L'incontro della ragione con la fede determina la formazione lenta e progressiva della filosofia cristiana," *Rivista di Filosofia Neo-Scolastica*, XXVI (1934), 14-52.

BASILI DE RUBI, B. "El concepto de filosofía cristiana," *Criterio*, XI (1935), 238-53.

BAUDOUX, B. "Philosophia 'ancilla theologiae,' " *Antonianum* XII (1937), 293-326.

———. "Quaestio de philosophia christiana," *Antonianum*, XI (1936), 487-552.

BECKER, A. "Discours de philosophie chrétienne," *Recueil de l'Académie des Jeux Floraux* (1937), 67-107.

BESCHIN, Giuseppe. "Il problema della filosofia cristiana," *Filosofia e Vita*, I (1960), 30-32.

BETANCUR, Cayetano. "El cristianesimo ante la filosofía actual," *Univ. de Antioquia*, XXXV (1959), 167-90.

BETTAZZI, Luigi. "Filosofia e teologia," *Filosofia e Vita*, I (1960), 17-25.

BLIC, J. de. "Quonam sensu recta sit locutio 'philosophia christiana'?" in *Acta Secundi Congressus Thomistici Internationalis, Acta Pont. Acad. Rom. S. Thomae Aquinatis et Religionis Catholicae*, n.s. III (1937), 450-53.

BÖHNER, P. "Christentum und Philosophie," *Catholica*, VII (1938), 67-72.

BOYER, C. "La philosophie chrétienne au Congrès Descartes," *Gregorianum*, XVIII (1937), 591-95.

BRUNI, G. "Ancora a proposito di 'filosofia cristiana,' " *Bollettino Filosofico*, I (1935), 49-62.

BURGELIN, Pierre. "La recontre de la théologie et de la philosophie," *Revue d'Histoire et de Philosophie Religieuse,* XXXVIII (1958), 160-70.

CAMPO, Mariano. "Cristianesimo, religione e categorie," *Rivista di Filosofia Neo-Scolastica,* XXVIII (1936), suppl., 37-47.

CANAL GÓMEZ, M. "La controversia intorno a una 'filosofia cristiana,'" *Bollettino Filosofico,* I (1935), 30-44.

CARLINI, A. "In qual senso la filosofia moderna è una filosofia cristiana," *Studium,* LV (1959), 231-46.

————. "S. Tommaso e la filosofia moderna," in *Filosofia e cristianesimo.* Milano: Marzorati, 1947. Pp. 43-58; 71-74.

CASTELLI, E. "Philosophie et religion. Le problème de la philosophie chrétienne," *Actes du VIII Congrès International de Philosophie à Prague,* (1936), pp. 457-63.

CERIANI, G. "Religione e filosofia nel pensiero idealistico e nella gnoseologia tomistica," *Rivista di Filosofia Neo-Scolastica,* XXIV (1937), 16-43.

CHENU, M. D. "Ratio superior et inferior, un cas de philosophie chrétienne," *Laval Théologique et Philosophique,* I (1945), 119-23.

CHIAVACCI, Gaetano. "Filosofia e religione," *Giornale Critico della Filosofia Italiana,* XLIX (1960), 461-73.

CHISERI, S. "La 'filosofia cristiana' alla seconda giornata tomista di Juvisy," *La Civiltà Cattolica,* I (1935), 280-86.

COCHET, L.-P. "En vue d'une philosophie chrétienne," *Revue Apologétique,* LVIII, (1934), 257-69; LIX (1934), 129-49; LX (1935), 272-95.

COLOMBO, C. "Intorno alla 'filosofia cristiana'," *Rivista di Filosofia Neo-Scolastica,* XXVIII (1936), 510-17.

COLOMER POUS, Eusebio. "Nuevas precisiones en torno al problema de la filosofía cristiana," *Espíritu,* VIII (1959), 165-77.

CORTS GRAU, J. "La filosofía cristiana y su coyuntura actual," *Cisneros,* VI (1943), 7-24.

DEMPF, Alois. "Um die Zukunft der christlichen Philosophie," *Hochland,* XXXVI (1938-39), 89-98.

DERISI, O. N. "Filosofía y religión," *Veritas,* IV (1959), 159-67.

———. "Filosofía y teología," *Veritas,* IV (1959), 144-58.

DIEZ ALEGRIA, José M. "Ciencia, metafísica y fe en la estructuración del saber del hombre," *Orbis Catholicus,* III (1960), 97-117.

———. "Filosofía y concepcion del mundo en relacion con el problema de una filosofía catolica," *Pensamiento* VII (1951), 503-18.

DOOYEWEERD, H. "La base religieuse de la philosophie scolastique," *Revue Réformée,* X (1959), 35-47.

FABRO, Cornelio. "S. Tommaso e la filosofia cristiana nel tempo presente," *Filosofia e Vita,* I (1960), 46-65.

FAZIO-ALLMAYER, Vito. "Religione e filosofia," *Giornale Critico della Filosofia Italiana,* XXXII (1953), 281-91.

FELLERMEIER, Jakob. "Das Problem der christlichen Philosophie, *Freiburger Zeitschrift für Philosophie und Theologie.* VII (1960), 375-90.

FERNANDEZ ALONSO, Aniceto. "El concepto antiguo y tradicional de filosofía," *Rivista di Filosofia Neo-Scolastica,* XIX (1937), 353-74.

FOREST, Aimé. "La formation intellectuelle de l'enseignement chrétien," *Bulletin Joseph Lotte* (1936), 51-76.

———. "La philosophie dans l'ordre du salut," *Lumière et Vie,* XXXII (1955), 103-24.

FRAILE, Guillermo. "El cristianismo y la filosofía," *Estudios Franciscanos,* III (1954), 33-81.

GARRIGOU-LAGRANGE, R. "De relationibus inter philosophiam et religionem," in *Acta Secundi Congressus Thomistici Internationalis.* Romae, 23-28 novembris, 1936. Romae: Marietti, 1937. Pp. 379-94.

GAYO, F. J. "Filosofía cristiana," *Unitas,* XXV (1952), 883-89.

GENTILE, Marino. "Metafisica e sovrannaturale; chiarimento alla distinzione dei due concetti," *Rivista di Filosofia Neo-Scolastica,* XXVIII (1936), suppl., 31-35.

GIANNINI, Giorgio. "Filosofia e teologia in un recente volume del Gilson," *Doctor Communis*, XIII (1960), 131-42.

GILLON, Ludovico. "Cattolicesimo e pensiero moderno," *Sapienza*, VIII (1955), 158-73.

GILSON, E. "La possibilité philosophique de la philosophie chrétienne," *Recherches de Science Religieuse*, XXXII (1958), 168-96.

GOOSSENS, W. "Les controverses récentes touchant 'la philosophie chrétienne.' A propos d'une Journée d'etudes de la Société thomiste," *Collationes Gandavenses*, XXI (1934), 241-45.

GOUHIER, H. "Digression sur la philosophie à propos de la philosophie chrétienne," *Recherches Philosophiques*, III (1933-34), 211-36.

GRÉGOIRE, Franz. "Foi chrétienne et pensée contemporaine," *Revue Philosophique de Louvain*, L (1952), 305-21.

GUÉRIN, P. "A propos de la philosophie chrétienne," *Revue d'Histoire de la Philosophie Religieuse*, XV (1935), 210-42.

HÄBERLIN, Paul. "Christliche Theologie und Philosophie," *Zeitschrift für Philosophische Forschung*, XI (1957), 20-36.

HENNIG, Johannes. "Zum Problem der christlichen Philosophie," *Hochland*, XXXV (1937-38), 495-98.

HENRY, André. "La querelle de la philosophie chrétienne. Histoire et bilan d'un débat," in *Philosophies chrétiennes*. Edited by H. Bedarida, *et al.* Paris: Fayard, 1955. Pp. 35-68.

HERING, H. S. "La philosophie et la pratique de la science chrétienne," *La Nouvelle Revue*, LIX (1937), 123-41.

HILCKMAN, A. "Christliche Philosophie," *Philosophisches Jarhbuch*, LX (1950), 457-63.

INNOCENTI, U. degl'. "Osservazioni sulla filosofia cristiana," *Angelicum*, XVIII (1941), 357-78.

IRIARTE, Joaquín. "La controversia sobre la noción de filosofía cristiana," *Estudios Eclesiásticos*, XVII (1943), 289-302.

―――. "La controversia sobre la noción de filosofía cristiana," *Pensamiento*, I (1945), 7-29; 275-98.

————. "El filósofo cristiano en su ser y actitud, en su impulso y consistencia," *Pensamiento*, VII (1951), 481-502.

JANSEN, B. "Christliche Philosophie," *Stimmen der Zeit*, CXXVIII (1935), 229-38; CXXXI (1936), 31-38.

JOLIVET, R. "Philosophie chrétienne et bergsonisme," *Revue des Sciences Religieuses*, XV (1935), 28-43.

KLAMP, Gerhard. "Philosophie und 'dialektische' Theologie," *Zeitschrift für Philosophische Forschung*, II (1947-48), 84-110.

LACOMBE, O. "La pluralité des philosophies est-elle une richesse?" *Nova et Vetera*, XXXIV (1959), 10-25.

LANDGREBE, Ludwig. "Philosophie und Theologie," *Neue Zeitschrift für systematische Theologie*, V (1963), 3-15.

LUBAC, Henri de. "Sur la philosophie chrétienne. Réflexions à la suite d'un débat," *Nouvelle Revue Théologique*, LXIII (1936), 225-53.

MALEVEZ, L. "Le croyant et le philosophe," *Nouvelle Revue Théologique*, LXXXII (1960), 897-917.

MANSER, G. M. "Gibt es eine 'christliche' Philosophie?" *Divus Thomas* (Fr.), XIV (1936), 19-51; 123-41.

MARTINEZ, Elías. "¿Dos teologías y dos filosofías: una teologia de la adoración y metafísica del ser, una teología de la conversión y dialéctica del obrar?" *Las Ciencias*, XXIV (1959), 905-25.

MASI, Roberto. "Il significato storico di S. Tommaso d'Aquino per la sintesi cristiana del mondo moderno," *Aquinas*, III (1960), 328-42.

MASNOVO, Amato. "Filosofia cristiana," *Rivista di Filosofia Neo-Scolastica*, XXVI (1934), suppl., 21-27.

————. "La filosofia verso la religione," *Rivista di Filosofia Neo-Scolastica*, XXVIII (1936), suppl., 1-29.

MAYDIEU, J.-J. "Le bilan d'un débat philosophique. Réflexions sur la philosophie chrétienne," *Bulletin de Littérature Ecclesiastique*, XXXVI (1935), 193-222.

MAZZANTINI, C. "Il concetto filosofico della realtà creaturale e il suo significato religioso," *Rivista di Filosofia Neo-Scolastica*, XXVIII (1936), suppl., 49-54.

MEHL, R. "Pensée chrétienne et pensée philosophique," *Dieu Vivant*, XIV (1948), 95-107.

————. "Die Philosophie vor der Theologie," *Theologische Literaturzeitung*, LXXV (1950), 585-90.

MERLEAU-PONTY, M. "Christianisme et philosophie," in *Les philosophes célèbres*. Paris: L. Mazenod, 1956. Pp. 104-9.

MEYER, H. "Christliche Philosophie?" *Münchener Theologische Zeitschrift*, II (1951), 390-430.

MIANO, V. "Il filosofo e la teologia," *Euntes Docete*, XIV (1961), 157-77.

MIQUEL i MACAYA, J. "La filosofia cristiana," *Criterion*, XI (1935), 261.

MIRANDA, D. "Boletín de filosofía. Alrededor de 'la filosofía cristiana'," *La Ciencia Tomista*, XLIX (1934), 359-72.

MOTTE, A.-R. "Le problème de la 'Philosophie chrétienne'," *Bulletin Thomiste*, V (1937), 230-55.

NOEL, L. "La notion de philosophie chrétienne," *Revue Néoscolastique de Philosophie*, XXXVII (1934), 337-44.

OLGIATI, Francesco. "Il problema della 'filosofia cristiana' e la metafisica," in *La metafisica classica*. Atti del Congresso di Filosofia promosso dalla Società italiana per gli Studi Filosofici e Religiosi. Milano, 25-27 ottobre, 1953. Milano: Vita e Pensiero, 1954. Pp. 129-48.

PADOVANI, Umberto A. "Filosofia e cristianesimo al secondo convegno di studi cristiani," *Rivista di Filosofia Neo-Scolastica*, XXXIX (1947), 352-57.

"Para el desarrollo de la filosofía cristiana," Resumen de la discussión del primero tema, Reuniones Filosóficas, mayo de 1955, Instituto Filosófico de Balmesiana, *Espíritu*, V (1956), 54-63.

PELLEGRINO, Ubaldo. "Teologia e metafisica," *La Scuola Cattolica*, LXXXIX (1961), 290-95.

PELSTER, Franz. "Die Berechtigung einer Philosophie im Innern des christlichen Gedankens," *Scholastik*, XXXI (1956), 404-12.

PENIDO, M. T. "Sur le problème historique de la philosophie chrétienne," *Revue Thomiste*, XVII (1934), 103-108.

"Pensiero cristiano e pensiero metafisico." *Filosofia e Vita*, IV (1963), 3-6.

PERINI, Giuseppe. "La posizione del filosofo cristiano," *Divus Thomas*, LXV (1962), 214-21.

PETERS, Thomas. "Die Krankheit der christlichen Philosophie. Der Neothomismus und die Sprache der Zeit," *Wort und Wahrheit*, VII (1952), 85-92.

PEURSEN, C. A. van. "Philosophie et théologie," *Revue de Theologie et de Philosophie*, V (1955), 106-10.

PIEMONTESE, Filippo. "Il problema della filosofia cristiana," *Humanitas*, XIV (1959), 697-704.

———. "Sul concetto di filosofia cristiana," *Salesianum*, XXII (1960), 107-13.

PIEPER, J. "Sobre el dilema de una filosofía no cristiana," *Criterio*, XXVIII (1955), 906-909.

"Presupposti filosofici di un Concilio ecumenico." *Filosofia e Vita*, II (1961), 3-6.

PRZYWARA, E. "Das Christliche im Denken," *Stimmen der Zeit*, CXXX (1936), 493-97.

QUESTIAUX, F. "Théologie et philosophie chrétienne," *Collationes Namurcenses*, XXX (1936), 397-413.

QUILES, Ismael. "Filosofía y cristianismo," *Ciencia y Fe*, I (1944), 92-100.

RAEYMAEKER, L. de. "Le climat doctrinal chrétien et la philosophie," *Revue Philosophique de Louvain*, XLVI (1948), 448-62.

REISNER, E. "Spekulation, Erkenntniskritik und christliche Metaphysik," *Zeitschrift für Theologie und Kirche*, XV (1934), 343-57.

ROBLES, Laureano. "Ambivalencias sobre el tema: filosofía cristiana," *Estudios Filosóficos*, XI (1962), 491-504.

ROIG GIRONELLA, J. "La filosofía cristiana entre el racionalismo y el existencialismo," *Las Ciencias*, XVIII (1953), 345-61.

ROMEYER, B. "Autour du problème de la philosophie chrétienne. Essai critique et positif," *Archives de Philosophie*, X (1934), 1-64; 419-82.

ROSSI, Opilio. "La importancia de la filosofía cristiana," *Estudios tomistas*, I (1959), 93-101.

ROSSI, P. "Le moderne teorie fisiche e la filosofia cristiana," *Studium*, XXXI (1935), 644-54.

RUSSO, F. "L'entreprise scientifique moderne et la foi chrétienne," *Sciences ecclésiastiques* XIII (1961), 137-45.

SCIMÉ, S. "Filosofia e cristianesimo," *La Civiltà Cattolica*, XCIX (1948), 62-66.

SEVER de Montsonís. "La filosofia cristiana," *Criterion*, X (1934), 87-95.

SIMON, Y. "Philosophie chrétienne. Notes complémentaires," *Études Carmélitaines*, XIX (1934), 107-19.

SIRCHIA, Franco. "Esiste una filosofia cristiana? A proposito dell'opera omonima di M. Nédoncelle," *Rivista di Filosofia Neo-Scolastica*, L (1958), 268-75.

SQUADRINI, I. "S. Bonaventura, christianus philosophus," *Antonianum*, XVI (1941), 103-30; 253-304.

STEENBERGHEN, Fernand, van. "La philosophie en chrétienté," *Revue Philosophique de Louvain*, LXL (1963), 561-82.

STEFANINI, Luigi. "Filosofia e religione," *Studia Patavina*, I, (1954), 65-84.

THIEL, M. "Über die Aufteilung der christlichen Philosophie nach verschiedenen Ordensidealen," *Divus Thomas* (Fr.), XXIII (1945), 345-78.

————. "Weltanschauung, Philosophie und System," *Divus Thomas* (Fr.), XX (1942), 319-34.

THIRY, A. "Le philosophe et la théologie," *Nouvelle Revue Théologique,* LXXXIV (1962), 337-64.

TILLICH, Paul. "Philosophie et théologie," *Revue de Théologie et de Philosophie,* V (1955), 82-119.

TINELLO, Francesco. "Tradizione, rinnovamento, validità della filosofia cristiana," *Filosofia e Vita,* IV (1963), 7-16.

TOCCAFONDI, E. T. "La religiosità della filosofia e l'importanza del problema della conoscenza per l'affermazione dei valori religiosi," *Angelicum,* XXV (1948), 329-42.

———. "Aspetti odierni del problema dei rapporti fra verità filosofica e verita rivelata," *Doctor Communis,* IV (1951), 123-37.

VERNEAUX, R. "Doute et croyance. Critique du fidéisme néocriticiste," *Revue Philosophique de Louvain,* XLV (1947), 21-44.

VIA, Vincenzo La. "La interna apertura della 'filosofia' alla 'fede cristiana'?" *Teoresi,* XVI (1961), 79-82.

VOGEL, Cornelia J. de. " 'Ego sum qui sum' et sa signification pour une philosophie chrétienne," *Revue des Sciences Religieuses,* XXXV (1961), 337-55.

VRIES, J. de. "Christliche Philosophie," *Scholastik,* XII (1937), 1-16.

ZARAGÜETA BENGOECHEA, Juan. "Escolástica y Filosofía cristiana," *Revista de Filosofía,* VI (1947), 589-646.

———. "Santo Tomás de Aquino en su tiempo y en el nuestro," in *Estudios filosóficos* XII (1963), 335-74.

B. PERENNIAL PHILOSOPHY

BOSLEY, Harold A. *The Philosophical Heritage of the Christian Faith.* Chicago: Clark, 1944.

Philosophy in a Pluralistic Society. The Proceedings of the American Catholic Philosophical Association, XXXVII (1963).

COLLINS, James. "The Problem of the Philosophia Perennis," *Thought,* XXVIII (1953-54), 571-97.

COPLESTON, F. C. "The Value of Different Philosophical Systems," *Month*, XXV (1961), 276-84, 337-45.

CORBETT, J. P. "Innovation and Philosophy," *Mind*, LXVIII (1959), 289-308.

DANIELOU, J. "Pluralism within Christian Thought," *Theology Digest*, X (1962), 67-70.

GERBER, William. "The Significance of Disagreement among Philosophers," *Hibbert Journal*, LVII (1958-59), 368-74.

HEINEMANN, F. H. "Is Philosophy Finished?" *Hibbert Journal*, LVII (1958-59), 279-85.

HENDERSON, Edgar H. "Should We Undertake Systems Today?" *International Philosophical Quarterly*, III (1963), 418-27.

HINNERS, Richard. "Are There Eternal Truths?" *Continuum*, II (1964), 17-26.

McCOOL, Gerald. "Philosophical Pluralism and an Evolving Thomism," *Continuum*, II (1964). 3-16.

McLEAN, George F. "The Unity of Truth: Context of an Education," in *Philosophy and the Integration of Contemporary Catholic Education*. Edited by G. McLean. Washington, D.C.: Catholic Univ. of America Press, 1962. Pp. 3-30.

MELAND, B. E. "The Retreat to Tradition," *The Personalist*, XXIV (1943), 40-45.

PORRECO, Rocco E. "Philosophical Pluralism and the Teaching of Philosophy," in *Proceedings of the American Catholic Philosophical Association*, XXXVII (1963), 153-59.

RÉGNÉLL, Hans. "Why Do Interpreters of Philosophy Disagree?" in *Philosophical Essays Dedicated to Gunnar Aspelin*. Lund: Gleerup, 1963.

REIN'L, Robert L. "Comparative Philosophy and Intellectual Tolerance," *Philosophy East and West*, II (1953), 333-39.

SARTON, George. "The Historical Basis of Philosophical Unification," *Journal of Unified Science*, IX (1939), 90-93.

L'attualità dei filosofi classici: età moderna. A cura di Augusto Guzzo. Milano: Bocca, 1940.

BARION, J. *Philosophia perennis als Problem und als Aufgabe.* München: Hueber, 1936.

GARCÍA MARTÍNEZ, Fidel. *Algunas consideraciones sobre la vuelta a la filosofía perenne.* Santander: Comillas, 1945.

HARTMANN, Albert. *Vraie et fausse tolérance.* Paris: Cerf, 1958.

MAZZANTINI, Carlo. *Filosofia perenne e personalità filosofiche.* Padova: CEDAM, 1942.

SCIACCA, M. F. *Studi sulla filosofia medioevale e moderna.* Napoli: Perella, 1938.

Temi e problemi di filosofia classica . . . alla memoria di Agostino Gemelli. Milano: Vita e Pensiero, 1960.

TERAN, S. *Aproximaciones a la doctrina tradicional.* Buenos Aires: La faculdad, 1935.

WAELKENS, R. *Adaptation et tradition.* Louvain: Nova et Vetera, 1947.

ABBAGNANO, N., and MAZZANTINI, C. "Il concetto di 'attualità' dei filosofi del passato," in *L'attualità dei filosofi classici: antichità.* A cura di Augusto Guzzo. Milano: Bocca, 1940. Pp. 1-20.

BLONDEL, M. "Fidélité conservée par la croissance même de la tradition," *Revue Thomiste,* XVIII (1935), 611-26. (Réponse de R. Garrigou-Lagrange, 626-28.)

———. "La pérennité de la philosophie et le discernement progressif d'une constante et indispensable médiation," *Revue de Métaphysique et de Morale,* XLVII (1940), 349-62.

CECCATO, Silvio. "Avvertimento ai filosofi che intendono modificare la perenne situazione filosofica," *Methodos,* VI (1954), 149-52.

CRISTALDI, Mariano. "Il valore della 'filosofia perenne,'" *Humanitas,* IX (1954), 563-69.

CROCE, Benedetto. "Lo storicismo e l'idea tradizionale della filosofia," *Quaderni della Critica,* XIII (1949), 83-87.

DERISI, O. N. "La realidad y el conocimiento histórico en relación con la filosofía," *Veritas,* IV (1959), 61-92.

————. "Verdad, filosofía e historia," *Veritas,* IV (1959), 130-43.

DUFRENNE, Mikel. "Note sur la tradition," *Cahiers Internationaux de Sociologie,* III (1947), 158-69.

FEBRER, M. "Aproximaciones a la doctrina tradicional," *Contemporánea,* IV (1936), 262-66.

FILIASI CARCANO, Paolo. "Metodologia odierna e filosofia tradizionale," *Giornale Critico della Filosofia Italiana,* XXXVIII (1959), 429-41.

GAMBRA CIUDAD, R. "El concepto de la tradicíon en la filosofía actual," *Arbor,* IV (1945), 545-73.

GARCÍA ASENSIO, Pedro. "Hacia la unidad de la escolástica," *Pensamiento,* XIII (1957), 263-96.

GARIEPY, Benoît. "De l'utilité des erreurs," *Laval Théologique et Philosophique,* XIX (1963), 179-205.

HUFNAGEL, A. "Philosophia perennis heute," *Lebendige Seelsorge,* IX (1958), 140-44.

LACOMBE, Olivier. "Réflexions thomistes sur la pluralité des philosophies chrétiennes," *Recherches et Débats,* X (1955), 69-81.

LINERA, A. A. de. "Las tesis fundamentales de la filosofía perenne," *Las Ciencias,* XXIV (1959), 109-20.

LOMBARDI, R. "Orizzonti di filosofia cattolica," in *Concetto e programma della filosofia d'oggi.* Milano: Bocca, 1941. Pp. 147-57.

MADARIAGA, Bernardo. "La filosofía al interior de la teología," *Verdad y Vida,* XIX (1961), 193-267.

————. "La filosofía y la teología en el dinamismo del intelectual creyente," *Verdad y Vida,* XIX (1961), 665-83.

MARIAS, Julián. "La escolástica en su mundo y en el nuestro," *Revista de Psicología General y Aplicada,* II (1947), 79-131.

MAZZANTINI, Carlo. "In che consiste, e quale valore possiede, l'attualità dei filosofi classici?" in *L'attualità dei filosofi classici: età moderna.* A cura di Augusto Guzzo. Milano: Bocca, 1940.

"Misión perenne y misión actual de la filosofía," *Sapientia,* VII (1952), 83-89.

ORESTANO, F. "Stoicismo filosofico e filosofia vivente," *Sophia*, III (1935), 510-30.

PIEPER, Josef. "Ueber den Begriff der Tradition," *Tijdschrift voor Philosophie*, XIX (1957), 21-52.

POMPA, K. J. "Philosophia perennis," *Philosophia Reformata*, XX (1955), 64-86.

ZAMBONI, Giuseppe. "Filosofia medioevale, filosofia moderna e filosofia perenne," in *Filosofia e cristianesimo. Atti del II convegno italiano di studi filosofici cristiani* (Gallarate, 1946). Pp. 318-45.

C. SCHOLASTIC THOUGHT

ADLER, M. J. *St. Thomas and the Gentiles*. Milwaukee: Marquette Univ. Press, 1938.

ARDLEY, G. *Aquinas and Kant. The Foundations of Modern Science*. London: Longmans, 1950.

ARMSTRONG, A. H. *Aristotle, Plotinus and St. Thomas*. Oxford: Blackfriars, 1946.

DOOLAN, A. *Revival of Thomism*. Dublin: Conmore and Reynolds, 1951.

GARRIGOU-LAGRANGE, Reginald. *Reality. A Synthesis of Thomistic Thought*. Translated by P. Cummins. St. Louis: Herder, 1950.

GILSON, Etienne. *The Christian Philosophy of St. Thomas Aquinas*. Translated by L. K. Shook, with a catalogue of St. Thomas's works by I. T. Eschmann. New York: Random House, 1956.

LITTLE, Arthur. *The Platonic Heritage of Thomism*. Dublin: Golden Eagle, 1950.

MEYER, Hans. *The Philosophy of St. Thomas Aquinas*. Translated by F. Eckhoff. St. Louis: Herder, 1944.

PERRIER, J. L. *Revival of Scholastic Philosophy*. New York: Columbia Univ. Press., 1948.

STAUNTON, J. A. *Scholasticism, the Philosophy of Common Sense*. Notre Dame: Notre Dame Univ. Press, 1937.

STEINER, K. *Redemption of Thinking. A Study in the Philosophy of St. Thomas Aquinas.* Translated by A. Shepherd and M. Nicoll. London: Hodder, 1956.

ALIMWRUNG, M. M. "The Thomasian Spirit of the Future," *Unitas,* XXX (1957), 419-23.

ANDERSON, James F. "Is Scholastic Philosophy Philosophical?" *Philosophy and Phenomenological Research,* X (1949-50), 251-59.

————. "Remarks on Professor Cunningham's 'Reply,'" *Philosophy and Phenomenological Research,* X (1949-50), 262.

ASHLEY, Benedict M. "The Thomistic Synthesis," in *Teaching Thomism Today.* Edited by George F. McLean. Washington, D.C.: The Catholic Univ. of America Press, 1963. Pp. 39-63.

BASTABLE, J. D. "Thomism and Modern European Philosophy," *Philosophical Studies,* I (1951), 3-16.

BÖHNER, Philotheus. "A Milestone of Research in Scholasticism," *Franciscan Studies,* VIII (1948), 295-300.

BRAUER, Theodore. "Thomism and Modern Philosophy," in *Thomistic Principles in a Catholic School.* Edited by T. Brauer. St. Louis: Herder, 1943. Pp. 69-108.

BRENNAN, R. E. "The Mansions of Thomistic Philosophy," *Thomist,* I (1939), 62-79.

BROAD, C. D. "Some Basic Notions in the Philosophy of St. Thomas," *Philosophy Today,* III (1959), 199-211.

CALLUS, D. "The Philosophy of St. Bonaventure and of St. Thomas," *Blackfriars,* XXI (1940), 151-64; 249-67.

COLLINS, James. "Thomists in Transition," *America,* CIV (1960), 371-74.

————. "Toward a Philosophically Ordered Thomism," *New Scholasticism,* XXXII (1958), 301-26.

CUNNINGHAM, G. W. "Is Scholastic Philosophy Philosophical? A Reply," *Philosophy and Phenomenological Research,* X (1949-50), 260-61.

————. "Must We All Be Thomists?" *The Philosophical Review*, V (1948), 493-504.

DAVIS, H. F. "Thomism and the Unity of Christian Thought," *Dominican Studies*, I (1948), 99-112.

DONCEEL, J. "A Thomistic Misapprehension," *Thought*, XXXII (1957) 189-98.

EGAN, J. M. "Notes on the Relations of Reason and Culture in the Philosophy of St. Thomas," *Angelicum*, XV (1938), 110-20.

GARCÍA MARTÍNEZ, Fidel. "The Place of St. Thomas in Catholic Philosophy," *Cross Currents*, VIII (1958), 43-66.

HARVANEK, R. F. "The Pursuit of Truth, Thomist and Pragmatist," *Thought*, XXX (1955), 214-30.

————. "Suarezianism," in *Teaching Thomism Today*. Edited by George F. McLean. Washington, D.C.: The Catholic Univ. of America Press, 1963. Pp. 81-96.

KREYCHE, G. "Is Thomism Relevant to the 20th Century?" *Catholic Messenger*, LXXXI (1963), 5-6.

LAWSON, W. "Neo-Thomism," in *Education and the Philosophic Mind*. Edited by A. V. Judges. London: Harrap, 1957. Pp. 43-59.

McLEAN, George F. "Philosophic Continuity and Thomism," in *Teaching Thomism Today*. Edited by George F. McLean, Washington, D.C.: The Catholic Univ. of America Press, 1963. Pp. 3-38.

MANN, J. A. "Neo-Scholastic Philosophy in the United States," *Proceedings of the American Catholic Philosophical Association*, XXXIII (1959), 127-36.

MORRISON, C. C. "Thomism and the Rebirth of Protestant Philosophy," *Christendom*, II (1937), 110-25.

MULLANEY, James V. "Developmental Thomism," *Thomist*, XIX (1956), 1-21.

————. "On Being Thomistic. The Authority of St. Thomas in Philosophy," in *Proceedings of the American Catholic Philosophical Association*, XXV (1951), 141-47. (Commentary by H. DuLac, 147-51.)

O'GRADY, Daniel C. "Thomism as a Frame of Reference," *Thomist*, I (1939), 213-36.

PIEPER, J. "The Contemporary Character of Saint Thomas," *Philosophy Today*, III (1959), 73-75.

———. "The Timeliness of Thomism," in *Modern Catholic Thinkers*. Edited by A. Caponigri. New York: Harper, 1960. Pp. 538-47.

RAHNER, Karl. "The Nature of Truth in Aquinas," *Continuum*, II (1964), 60-72.

REILLY, George C. "The Objective Validity of Truth," in *Philosophy and the Integration of Contemporary Catholic Education*. Edited by George McLean. Washington, D.C.: Catholic Univ. of America Press, 1962. Pp. 31-43.

TEMPLE, William. "Thomism and Modern Needs," *Blackfriars*, XXV (1944), 86-93.

TOUT, T. F. "The Place of St. Thomas in History," in *St. Thomas. Papers Read at Manchester, 1924*. Oxford: Blackwell, 1925. Pp. 1-32.

VAN STEENBERGHEN, Fernand. "Thomism in a Changing World," *New Scholasticism*, XXVI (1952), 37-48.

WOLTER, Allan B. "Scotism," in *Teaching Thomism Today*. Edited by G. McLean. Washington, D.C.: The Catholic Univ. of America Press, 1963. Pp. 64-80.

ALBANESE, Francesco. *La filosofia di S. Tommaso e gli sviluppi della scienza moderna*. Palermo: Stella, 1934.

———. *Svolgimenti di filosofia tomistica in armonia colla scienza moderna*. Palermo: Ausonia, 1949.

BARALE, P., and MUZIO, G. *Torniamo a San Tommaso! Fedeltà ai testi tomistici essentiali. Interpretazioni neoscolastiche e interpretazione rosminiana*. Roma: Salesiana, 1962.

BARTOLOMEI, T. *San Tommaso d'Aquino alla luce della critica moderna*. 2 vols. Napoli: Rondinella, 1939-40.

BONET, A. *Santo Tomás renovador del pensamiento medieval*. Madrid: Acción Católica Española, 1952.

CASAS, M. G. *Santo Tomás y la filosofía existencial con otros ensayos*. Córdoba: Meteoro, 1948.

CHENU, M.-D. *Introduction à l'étude de saint Thomas d'Aquin*. Montréal: Inst. d'Études Médiévales, 1950.

DERISI, O. M. *Filosofía moderna y filosofía tomista*. 2 vols. Buenos Aires: Guadalupe, 1947.

DESCOQS, P. *Thomisme et scolastique. A propos de M. Rougier*. Paris: Beauchesne, 1935.

De WULF, M. *Initiation à la philosophie thomiste*. Louvain: Nauwelaerts, 1949.

DUPONCHEL, P. *Hypothèses pour l'interprétation de l'axiomatique thomiste*. Paris: Vrin, 1953.

GARRIGOU-LAGRANGE, R. *Essenza e attualità del tomismo*. Brescia: La Scuola, 1947.

GELINAS, J.-P. *La restauration du thomisme sous Léon XIII et les philosophies nouvelles. Etude de la pensée de Maurice Blondel et du Père Laberthonniere à la lumière de "Aeterni Patris."* Washington, D.C.: Catholic Univ. of America Press, 1959.

GIACON, Carlo. *L'attualità di S. Tommaso*. Milano: Bocca, 1941.

———. *Le grandi tesi del tomismo*. Como: Masorati, 1945.

GONSETH, F. (ed.) *Philosophie néo-scolastique et philosophie ouverte*. Paris: Presses Univ. de France, 1954.

HESSEN, J. *Thomas von Aquin und wir*. Basel: Reinhardt, 1955.

JUGNET, J. *Pour connaître la pensée de saint Thomas d'Aquin*. Paris: Bordas, 1949.

MANSER, G. M. *Das Wesen des Thomismus*. Freiburg: Paulusverlag, 1949.

MARCESCA, M. *S. Tommaso d'Aquino e la scolastica*. Milano: Garzanti, 1943.

MARIAS AGUILERA, Julián. *La escolástica en su mundo y en el nuestro*. Pontevedra: Huguin, 1951.

MARKOVICS, R. *Grundsätzliche Vorfragen einer methodischen Thomasdeutung*. Rom: Herder, 1956.

MASNOVO, A. *S. Agostino e S. Tommaso: concordanze e sviluppi.* Milano: Vita e Pensiero, 1942.

QUILES, Ismael. *La esencia de la filosofía tomista.* Buenos Aires: La Colmena, 1947.

ROSANAS, J. *Tomistas y tomistas.* Buenos Aires: Espasa-Calpe, 1942.

SAITTA, G. *Il carattere della filosofia tomista.* Firenze: Sansoni, 1947.

SANCHEZ-MARIN, F. and OROMI, M. *La filosofía escolástica y el intelectual católico.* Madrid: Macional, 1955.

SERTILLANGES, A.-D. *La philosophie de S. Thomas d'Aquin.* 2 vols. Paris: Aubier, 1940.

SILVA-TAROUCA, A. *Thomas heute. Zehn Vorträge zum Aufbau einer existentiellen Ordnungs-Metaphysik nach Thomas von Aquin.* Wien: Herder, 1947.

WEBERT, J. *Saint Thomas d'Aquin. Le génie de l'ordre.* Paris: Denoël et Steele, 1934.

ZARAGÜETA BENGOECHEA, Juan. *Una introducción moderna a la filosofía escolástica.* Granada: Suarez, 1946.

————. *Santo Tomás de Aquino en su tiempo y en el nuestro.* Madrid: Univ. de Madrid, 1942.

"Actualidad y perennidad del tomismo," *Sapientia,* III (1948), 101-10.

ADAMCZYK, S. "De systematis tomistici convenientia interna," *Collectanea Theologica,* XIX (1938), 47-58.

ALMEIDA, Enrique D. "El tomismo contemporáneo," *Estudios Tomistas,* I (1959), 9-29.

ALMEIDA, Paulo Bessa de. "A estruttura critica do pensamento tomista," *Kriterion,* VIII (1955), 164-85.

AMORE, Benedetto d'. "Scienza e filosofia nei contemporanei neo-scolastici," *Sapienza,* I (1948), 167-85.

BALIC, C. "De relatione S. Thomae Aquinatis ad alios doctores scolasticos," *Bogoslovska Smotra,* XXV (1937), 133-60 and 261-90.

————. "Sanctus Thomas et alii doctores," *Bogoslovska Smotra,* XXVI (1938), 94-99.

BASABE, Fernando M. de. "Trayectoria sistemática del tomismo," *Revista de Filosofía,* X (1951), 641-86.

BAUMGARTNER, M. "La filosofía tomista," *Revista Dominicana de Filosofía,* V (1959), 41-57.

BELMOND, S. "A propos d'une critique néo-thomiste du scotisme," *Revue de Philosophie,* XXXVI (1936), 57-67.

BONAFEDE, Giulio. "L'incontro tra la filosofia scolastica e la filosofia moderna," in *Filosofia e Cristianesimo. Atti del II convegno italiano di studi filosofici cristiani* (Gallarate, 1946). Milano: Marzorati, 1947. Pp. 77-95.

BONTADINI, Gustavo. "L'incontro della filosofia scolastica con la filosofia moderna," in *Filosofia e Cristianiesimo. Atti del II convegno italiano di studi filosofici cristiani* (Gallarate, 1946). Milano: Marzorati, 1947. Pp. 145-49.

BORDOY-TORRENTS, P. "Intorno alla restaurazione della filosofia di S. Tommaso d'Aquino," in *Xenia Thomistica.* Edited by Sadoc Szabó. Roma: Typ. Pol. Vaticana, 1925. I, 87-104.

BORTOLASO, G. "Il metodo della filosofia scolastica e l'accusa di razionalismo," *La Civiltà Cattolica,* CIV (1953), 396-407.

BOYER, C. "Saint Thomas et certaines tendances de la pensée moderne," *Doctor Communis,* V (1952), 1-10.

BRETON, V.-M. "Augustinisme et thomisme," *France Franciscaine,* XVIII (1936), 493-96.

CARLINI, Armando. "Il mio scolasticismo," *Rivista di Filosofia Neo-Scolastica,* XLII (1950), 365-69.

————. "S. Tommaso e il pensiero moderno," *Giornale di Metafisica,* II (1947), 1-13.

CASOTTI, M. "Pregiudizi contro la scolastica," *Rivista di Filosofia Neo-Scolastica,* XXXI (1939), 358-67.

CAUSSIMON, J. "L'intuition métaphysique de l'existence chez saint Thomas et l'existentialisme contemporain," *Revue de Métaphysique et de Morale,* LV (1950), 392-407.

CHENU, M.-D. "L'équilibre de la scolastique médiévale," *Revue des Sciences Philosophiques et Théologiques*, XXIX (1940), 304-12.

CILENTO, V. "San Tommaso d'Aquino umanista," *Rassegna di Scienze Filosofiche*, XIII (1960), 148-64.

COMTE-LIME, V. "Le mouvement scotiste de 1900 à 1914 d'après les publications de langue française," *France Franciscaine*, XVII (1935), 249-91.

CONRAD-MARTIUS, H. "Thomistische Perspektiven," *Catholica*, VI (1937), 33-40.

DERISI, Octavio N. "Agustinismo y Tomismo," *Augustinus*, IV (1959), 67-82.

————. "La esencia del tomismo. En torno al libro de P. G. M. Manser," *Sapientia*, III (1948), 174-81.

————. "Para una vigencia actual del tomismo," *Sapientia*, XVII (1962), 83-88.

————. "Reflexiones acerca del sentido del *esse* en Santo Tomás frente a la concepción respectiva en Aristóteles, en la Escolástica y en Heidegger," *Sapientia*, XIV (1959), 289-92.

————. "*Sapientia*, tomismo y actualidad filosófica," *Sapientia*, VII (1952), 291-95.

————. "Tomismo y existencialismo," *Sapientia*, II (1947), 197-203.

DROUIN, Paul E. "L'entitatif et l'intentionnel. Etude comparée de la doctrine thomiste et de l'enseignement Suarézien," *Laval Théologique et Philosophique*, VI (1950), 249-313.

ELL, J. "Das Existenzproblem in der Scholastik," *Divus Thomas* (Fr.), XIX (1941), 81-107.

ELSWIJK, H. C. Van. "De filosofische methode van Sint Thomas," *Studia Catholica*, XXXV (1960), 43-62

FABRO, Cornelio. "Le grandi correnti della scolastica e S. Tommaso d'Aquino," *Rivista di Filosofia Neo-Scolastica*, XXXI (1939), 329-40.

————. "Intorno al fondamento della metafisica Tomistica," *Aquinas*, III (1960), 83-135.

———. "Santo Tomás y la filosofía cristiana actual," *Sapientia,* XV (1960), 86-106.

———. "S. Tommaso e il pensiero moderno," *Osservatore Romano.* 7 Marzo, 1963.

———. "Tomismo e pensiero moderno," *Rassegna di Filosofia,* II (1953), 339-43.

FESSARD, G. "Thomisme et philosophie moderne," *Recherches de Science Religieuse,* XXXVI (1949), 310-20.

FINANCE, Joseph de. "Valeur et tâches actuelles du Thomisme," *Aquinas,* III (1960), 136-50.

FONT PUIG, P. "El sistema tomista como dechado doctrinal," *Estudios Filosóficos,* VIII (1959), 453-58.

FUENTES CASTELLANOS, F. "Actualidad del Tomismo," *Eca,* VI (1951), 357-61; 422-26.

GALLUCCI, G. "Il tema Agostiniano e il tema Tomistico nella speculazione filosofica," *Sophia,* II (1934), 39-53.

GARCÍA ASENSIO, P. "Hacia la unidad de la escolástica," *Pensamiento,* XIII (1957), 263-96.

GARCÍA MARTÍNEZ, Fidel. "Algunos principios diferenciales de la metafísica Suareciana frente al Tomismo tradicional," *Pensamiento,* IV (1948), 11*-20*.

GARRIGOU-LAGRANGE, Réginald. "La puissance d'assimilation du thomisme," *Revue Thomiste,* XLV (1939), 271-84.

———. "Thomisme et éclectisme chrétien," *Revue Thomiste,* XLII (1937), 3-15.

GEIGER, L.-B. "Quelques aspects du thomisme contemporain à propos de publications récentes," *Revue des Sciences Philosophiques et Théologiques,* XXXIV (1950), 315-57.

———. "Saint Thomas peut-il être actuel?" *Revue Dominicaine,* LVII (1951), 152-64.

GIANNINI, G. "A proposito del *Thomas von Aquin und wir* di J. Hessen," *Aquinas,* I (1958), 40-74.

———. "Attualità della filosofia di S. Tommaso," *Aquinas,* III (1960), 153-70.

GILSON, Etienne. "Le thomisme et les philosophies existentielles," *La Vie Intellectuelle,* XIII (1945), 144-55.

GISZTER, W. "Saint Thomas d'Aquin: un penseur non moye-nâgeux," *Ateneum Kaplanskie* (1958-59). Pp. 246-54.

GRABMANN, M. "La vitalità intellettuale della filosofia medioe-vale," *Rivista di Filosofia Neo-Scolastica*, XXX (1938), 109-31.

GRENET, Paul. "Situation du thomisme dans le monde contem-porain," *Bulletin du Cercle Thomiste Saint-Nicolas de Caen*, VII (1954), n. 1, 1-4; n. 3, 1-7; VIII (1955), n. 4, 2-6.

HERNANZ, Francisco. "Aspecto polémico del renacimiento esco-lástico-Tomista," *Cristiandad*, III (1946), 120-23.

INNOCENTI, Humbertus Degl'. "Cur sanctus Thomas," *Aquinas*, III (1960), 47-57.

————. "Ritorniamo a San Tommaso," *Salesianum*, XXIII (1961), 340-50.

"La inquietud del filósofo católico," *Razón y Fe*, CLIII (1956), 729-31.

JIMÉNEZ FERNÁNDEZ, Manuel. "Coyuntura actual de la filo-sofía Aquiniana," *Anales de la Universidad Hispalense*, XI (1950), 27-94.

JOLIVET, J. "Remarques sur l'esprit scolastique," in *Aspects de la dialectique. Recherches de Philosophie*, II. Paris: Desclée de Brouwer, 1956. Pp. 303-14.

KITCHANOVA, I. M. "La philosophie de Thomas d'Aquin," *Voprossi Filozofii* (USSR) (1958), 104-17.

LENZ, Joseph. "Thomistische Philosophie als Lebensweisheit," *Pastor Bonus*, XLIX (1939), 323-37.

MARC, A. "Orientations actuelles de la psychologie métaphysique néo-thomiste," *Sciences Ecclésiastiques*, X (1958), 226-32.

MARITAIN, J. "Coopération philosophique et justice intellec-tuelle," *Giornale di Metafisica*, II (1947), 93-102; 205-14.

MARTINI, A. "S. Tommaso e gli altri dottori," *Segni dei Tempi*, I (1934), n. 1.

MASNOVO, A. "Il significato storico di S. Tommaso d'Aquino," *Acta Pontificia Academiae Romanae S. Thomae*, I (1934), 9-32.

————. "S. Agostino e S. Tommaso," *Rivista di Filosofia Neo-Scolastica*, XXXIII (1941), 44-55.

MAZZARELLA, P. "Contraddizioni neoscolastiche," *Sophia*, XXVII (1959), 304-10.

MEYER, H. "Thomas von Aquin als Interpret der aristotelischen Gottleslehre," in *Aus der Geistwelt des Mittelalters*. Edited by A. Lang, J. Lechner, and M. Schmaus. Münster: Aschendorff, 1935. Pp. 682-87.

MITTERER, A. "Formen und Missformen des Heutigen Thomismus," *Philosophisches Jahrbuch*, LXV (1957), 87-105.

————. "Weltbildvergleichende Thomasforschung und Kritischer Thomismus," *Theologische Quartalschrift*, CXXXIV (1954), 148-90.

————. "Wissenschaftliche Wege zu Thomas von Aquin," *Gloria Dei*, III (1948), 1-24.

MORÓN ARROYO, Ciriaco. "Posibilidad y hecho de un tomismo existencial," *Salmanticensis*, IV (1957), 395-430.

MUNOS ALONSO, A. "La existencia en el tomismo y en el existencialismo," *Crisis*, III (1956), 79-82.

OLGIATI, F. "Assalti innocui al tomismo," *Rivista di Filosofia Neo-Scolastica*, XLIX (1957), 191-96.

————. "Il tramonto di S. Tommaso e la sua resurrezione," in *S. Tommaso d'Aquino*. A cura della Fac. di Filos. dell'Univ. Catt. del Sacro Cuore, Milano. Milano: Vita e Pensiero, 1923. Pp. 302-17.

PADOVANI, Umberto A. "Dalla filosofia neoscolastica alla metafisica classica," *Rassegna di Scienze Filosofiche*, IV (1951), 32-47.

————. "S. Tommaso e la cultura moderna," *Giornale di Metafisica*, I (1946), 17-24.

PARENTE, P. "Vitalità di S. Tommaso," *Aquinas*, I (1958), 171-84.

PÉCANTET, J. "A restauração tomista e o espírito científico," *Broteria*, LXX (1960), 167-74.

PERA, Ceslao. "Il tomismo di fronte alle correnti platoniche e neo-platoniche," *Aquinas*, III (1960), 279-306.

PETRUZZELLIS, N. "S. Tommaso e il pensiero moderno," *Logos*, XXI (1938), 136-37.

PIEPER, Josef. "Aktualität der Scholastik," *Wort und Wahreit*, XIV (1959), 733-39.

PIZZORNI, R. "Necessità di un ritorno alla dottrina Tomistica del diritto naturale," *Aquinas*, III (1960), 244-76.

PRA, Mario del. "Filosofia scolastica e filosofia autonoma," *Rivista di Storia della Filosofia*, V (1950), 135-37.

PRINI, P. "Aspetti e ragioni del realismo nella neo-scolastica," *Studium*, LIV (1958), 571-76.

PRUCHE, Benoît. "Le thomisme peut-il se présenter comme 'Philosophie existentielle'?" *Revue Philosophique de Louvain*, XLVIII (1950), 329-53.

PRZYWARA, E. "Thomas v. Aq., Ignatius v. Loyola, Fried. Nietzsche," *Zeitschrift für Aszese und Mystik*, XI (1936), 257-95.

PUNTEL, L. B. "S. Tomás de Aquino e o nosso tempo," *Estudos*, XX (1960), 17-23.

QUEIROLO, A. "La perenne vitalità del pensiero fondamentale di S. Tommaso d'Aquino," *Osservatore Romano*, 30 Apr., 1954.

QUILES, Ismael. "Para una demarcación doctrinal e histórica de la filosofía escolástica," *Ciencia y Fe*, VII (1951), 7-36.

RAEYMAEKER, Louis de. "L'idée inspiratrice de la métaphysique thomiste," *Aquinas*, III (1960), 61-82.

————. "Tomismo, neotomismo e il problema della molteplicità delle dottrine," *Humanitas*, XII (1957), 91-104.

REATZ, A. "Die Kulturkrisis der Gegenwart und Thomas von Aquin," *Beiträge zur Christlichen Philosophie*, II (1947) 3-11.

RODRIGUEZ-BACHILLER, A. "La personalidad de Santo Tomás desde el punto de vista filosófico," *Contemporanea*, VII (1935), 456-65; VIII (1935), 92-102.

SANCHEZ, J. F. "La vigencia de Sto. Tomás," *Revista Dominicana de Filosofía*, I (1956), 65-75.

SANTOS, P. dos. "Originalidade do Sistema Tomista," *Alma Mater*, II (1960), 9-24.

SCOTTI, P. "Il tomismo e la cultura moderna," *La Scuola Cattolica*, LXV (1937), 297-403.

SERTILLANGES, A.-D. "Actualité du thomisme," *Synthèses*, II (1947), 20-30.

SIMARD, G. "Les thomistes et saint Augustin," *Revue de l'Université d'Ottawa*, VI (1936), 5*-21*.

SOLAGES, B. de. "S. Thomas d'Aquin, champion de l'autonomie de la raison," *Bulletin de Littérature Ecclésiastique*, XXXVII (1936), 49-62.

STAFFA, Dino., 'Il tomismo é vivo," *Angelicum*, XL (1963), 145-72.

———. "Tomisticae doctrinae perennis valor," *Aquinas*, IV (1961), 251-55.

STEENBERGHEN, Fernand Van. "L'avenir du thomisme," *Revue Philosophique de Louvain*, LIV (1956), 201-18.

THONNARD, F.-J. "Augustinisme et thomisme comme philosophies chrétiennes," *Revue des Etudes Augustiniennes*, VI (1960), 255.

———. "Philosophie augustinienne et philosophie thomiste," *L'Année Théologique Augustinienne*, X (1949), 343-54.

TOCCAFONDI, Eugenio. "Valore perenne della gnoseologia tomistica," *Aquinas*, III (1960), 214-38.

URMENETA, F. de. "Características del tomismo según Grabmann y Sertillanges," *La Ciencia Tomista*, LXXVII (1950), 227-36.

VALORI, Paolo. "Problemi morali dell'ora e risposta tomista," *Aquinas* III (1960), 239-43.

VANNI ROVIGHI, Sofia. "Perenne validità delle 'cinque vie' di S. Tommaso." *Aquinas*, III (1960), 198-213.

———. "Tesi fondamentali della scolastica e loro vitalità," *Rivista di Filosofia Neo-Scolastica*, XXVI, suppl. (1934), 29-41.

VANSTEENKISTE, Clemente. "Il posto del tomismo nella storia del pensiero medioevale," *Aquinas*, III (1960), 307-27.

VILLENEUVE, J.-M.-R. "Ite ad Thomam!" *Angelicum*, XIII (1936), 3-23.

————. "La vraie culture thomiste," *Revue de l'Université d'Ottawa*, VI (1936), 225*-42*.

VLEESCHAUWER, J. H. de. "La scolatica. Saggio di una definizione," *Filosofia*, XI (1960), 377-403.

WOESTYNE, Z. Van de. "Augustinismus in gnoseologia S. Bonaventurae et S. Thomae," *Antonianum*, VIII (1933), 281-306; IX (1934), 383-404.

WUST, P. "Das augustinisch-franziskanische Denken in seiner Bedeutung für die Philosophie unserer Zeit," *Wissenschaft und Weisheit*, I (1934), 3-7.

CHAPTER II

Contemporary Philosophies

This chapter comprises selected books and articles concerning the main orientations of contemporary philosophy, with special attention to the implications of these directions for religious perspectives. The areas are divided as follows:

A. Evolutionary Trends
B. Existential Phenomenology
C. Linguistic Analysis
D. Naturalism
E. General

The reader is referred to Chapters II and XVII of *An Annotated Bibliography of Philosophy in Catholic Thought* by the same editor.

A. EVOLUTIONARY TRENDS

COLEN, Remy, *Evolution*. New York: Hawthorn, 1959.

DANIELOU, J. *The Lord of History*. London: Longmans, 1958.

DESAN, W. *The Planetary Man*. Washington, D.C.: Georgetown Univ. Press, 1961.

Duquesne University Symposium on Evolution. Pittsburgh: Duquesne Univ. Press, 1959.

EWING, J. Franklin. *Human Evolution*. Washington, D.C.: Catholic Univ. of America Press, 1956.

FRANCOEUR, R. *The World of Teilhard*. Baltimore: Helicon, 1961.

HUXLEY, Julian. *Man in the Modern World*. New York: New American Library, 1952.

KROEBER, A. (ed.) *Anthropology Today*. Chicago: Univ. of Chicago Press, 1953.

MacMURRAY, John. *Interpreting the Universe*. London: Faber and Faber, 1956.

MESSENGER, Ernest C. (ed.) *Theology and Evolution*. Westminster, Md.: Newman, 1952.

MURRAY, Desmond. *Species Revalued*. London: Blackfriars, 1955.

O'BRIEN, J. *God and Evolution*. Notre Dame: Univ. of Notre Dame Press, 1961.

ONG, W. *Darwin's Vision and Christian Perspectives*. New York: Macmillan, 1960.

RUFFINI, E. *Theory of Evolution Judged by Reason and Faith*. New York: Wagner, 1959.

SMITH, V. E. *Philosophy of Biology*. Jamaica, N.Y.: St. John's Univ. Press, 1962.

TEILHARD DE CHARDIN, Pierre. *The Divine Milieu*. New York: Harper, 1960.

———. *The Phenomenon of Man*. New York: Harper, 1959.

BETTS, J. R. "Darwinism, Evolution, and American Catholic Thought," *Catholic Historical Review*, XLV (1959), 161-85.

BLONDEL, M. and TEILHARD DE CHARDIN, P. "An Exchange of Letters," *Thought*, XXXVII (1962), 543-62.

BOSIO, G. "Reflections on Darwinism," *American Ecclesiastical Review*, CXLIII (1960), 1-17.

BRENNAN, M. "The Phenomenon of Man," *Studies*, XLIX (1960), 117-30.

BRUNNER, A. "Pierre Teilhard de Chardin: a Critique," *Theology Digest*, VIII (1960), 143-47.

COLLINS, J. "Darwin's Impact on Philosophy," *Thought*, XXXIV (1959), 185-248.

DOOLAN, A. "When Human Life Begins: Animation Theories; Was St. Thomas Wrong?" *Irish Ecclesiastical Review*, XLIV (1960), 228-33.

ELLIOTT, F. "World Vision of Teilhard de Chardin," *International Philosophical Quarterly*, I (1961), 620-47.

EWING, J. "The Human Phenomenon: Critical Review of the Phenomenon of Man," *Theological Studies*, XXII (1961), 86-101.

FRANCOEUR, R. "Evolution and Panpsychism in Teilhard de Chardin," *American Benedictine Review*, XII (1961), 206-19.

HOPKINS, V. "Darwinism and America," *Thought*, XXXIV (1959), 259-68.

JOHANN, R. "The Logic of Evolution," *Thought*, XXXVI (1961), 595-612.

MORRISON, J. "Orestes Brownson and the Catholic Reaction to Darwinism," *Duquesne Review*, VI (1961), 75-87.

NOGAR, R. "Darwin Centennial: a Philosophical Intrusion," *New Scholasticism*, XXXIII (1959), 411-15.

———. "From the Fact of Evolution to the Philosophy of Evolutionism," *Thomist*, XXIV (1961), 463-501.

NORTH, R. "Teilhard and the Problem of Creation," *Theological Studies*, XXIV (1963), 577-601.

PONTET, M. "Evolution According to Teilhard de Chardin," *Thought*, XXXVI (1961), 167-89.

ROTH, R. "The Importance of Matter; an Assessment of Pierre T. de Chardin's Appeal for the American Mind," *America*, CIX (1963), 792-94.

RUSSELL, J. "Principle of Finality in the Philosophy of Aristotle and Teilhard de Chardin," *Heythrop Journal*, III (1962), 347-57; IV (1963), 32-41.

SCHRAG, C. "Whitehead and Heidegger; Process Philosophy and Existential Philosophy," *Philosophy Today*, IV (1960), 26-35.

SHEED, W. "Père Teilhard's View of Evolution," *Jubilee*, VII (1959), 7-42.

SHEERIN, John B. "Huxley's New Religion," *Catholic World*, CXC (1960), 206-207.

SMITH, V. E. "Evolution and Entropy," *Thomist*, XXIV (1961), 441-62.

STOCK, M. "Scientific vs. Phenomenological Evolution: a Critique of Teilhard de Chardin," *New Scholasticism*, XXXIV (1962), 368-80.

TEILHARD DE CHARDIN, P. "Building the Earth," *Cross Currents*, IX (1959), 315-30.

TOWERS, B. "The Phenomenon of Man; Père Teilhard de Chardin in Translation," *Tablet*, CCXIII (1959), 962.

VOLLERT, C. "Toward Omega: Man in the Vision of Teilhard de Chardin," *Month*, XXIII (1960), 261-69.

WALLACE, W. A. "The Cosmogony of Teilhard," *New Scholasticism*, XXXVI (1962), 353-67.

DENIS, Paul. *Les origines du monde et de l'humanité.* Liège: La Pensée catholique, 1950.

KUHN, Oskar. *Die Deszendenz theorie.* München: Kösel, 1951.

LEONARDI, P. *L'evoluzione dei viventi.* Brescia: Morcelliana, 1950.

OLIVA, Antonio. *Possibilità ed impossibilità metafisica a proposito di ipotetici gradi di vita.* Roma: Gregoriana, 1956.

OTIS, Louis-Eugêne. *La doctrine de l'évolution.* Montréal: Fides, 1950.

TEILLARD DE CHARDIN, Pierre. *L'apparition de l'homme.* Paris: Seuil, 1956.

――――. *L'avenir de l'homme.* Paris: Seuil, 1959.

――――. *Construire de terre.* Paris: Seuil, 1958.

――――. *Vision du passé.* Paris: Seuil, 1957.

TERRIER, H. *Le transformisme et la penseé catholique.* Paris: Cèdre, 1950.

BOSIO, G. "Il presénte stato del problema dell'evoluzione," *Civiltà Cattolica*, III (1949), 479-92.

CECCHINI, Augusto. "Difficoltà metodologiche del concetto di evoluzione," *Filosofia*, II (1950), 191-212.

DE KONINCK, Charles. "Le problème de l'evolution," *Laval Théologique et Philosophique*, VI (1950), 363-67.

MALVEZ, L. "La philosophie chrétienne du progrès," *Nouvelle Revue Théologique*, LXIV (1937), 377-85.

B. EXISTENTIAL PHENOMENOLOGY

BROWN, James. *Kierkegaard, Heidegger, Buber, and Barth.* New York: Collier Books, 1962.

DESAN, W. *The Tragic Finale: An Essay on the Philosophy of Jean-Paul Sartre.* New York: Harper, 1960.

DONDEYNE, A. *Contemporary European Thought and Christian Faith.* Pittsburgh: Duquesne Univ. Press, 1958.

FARBER, Marvin. *The Foundation of Phenomenology.* New York: Paine-Whitman, 1965.

――――. *Naturalism and Subjectivism.* Springfield, Ill.: Thomas, 1959.

――――. (ed.) *Philosophical Essays in Memory of Edmund Husserl.* Cambridge, Mass.: Harvard Univ. Press, 1940.

FROMM, Erich. *Beyond the Chains of Illusion.* New York: Simon and Schuster, 1962.

GALLAGHER, Kenneth. *The Philosophy of Gabriel Marcel.* New York: Fordham Univ. Press, 1962.

HEIDEGGER, Martin. *Being and Time.* Translated by J. Macquarrie and Edward Robinson. New York: Harper and Row, 1962.

――――. *Introduction to Metaphysics.* Garden City, N.Y.: Doubleday, 1961.

HERBERG, W. *Four Existentialist Theologians.* Garden City, N.Y.: Doubleday, 1958.

HUSSERL, Edmund. *Cartesian Meditations: An Introduction to Phenomenology.* Translated by D. Cairns. The Hague: Nijhoff, 1960.

――――. *The Idea of Phenomenology.* Translated by W. Alston and G. Nakhnikian. The Hague: Nijhoff, 1964.

————. *Ideas: A General Introduction to Pure Phenomenology.* Translated by W. Gibson. New York: Macmillan, 1958.

————. *The Paris Lectures.* Translated by P. Koestenbaum. The Hague: Nijhoff, 1964.

————. *The Phenomenology of Internal Time-Consciousness.* Edited by M. Heidegger; translated by J. Churchill. The Hague: Nijhoff, 1964.

JOLIVET, Régis. *Introduction to Kierkegaard.* Translated by W. H. Barber. New York: Dutton, 1951.

KIERKEGAARD, S. *A Kierkegaard Anthology.* Edited by Robert Bretall. Princeton, N.J.: Princeton Univ. Press, 1946.

————. *Concluding Unscientific Postscript to the* PHILOSOPHICAL FRAGMENTS. Translated by D. F. Swenson. Princeton, N.J.: Princeton Univ. Press, 1941.

————. *Fear and Trembling and The Sickness Unto Death.* Garden City, N.Y.: Doubleday, 1954.

————. *Philosophical Fragments.* Translated by D. F. Swenson. Princeton, N.J.: Princeton Univ. Press, 1936.

KREYCHE, G. F. *Kiekegaardian Existentialism.* Ottawa: Univ. of Ottawa Press, 1958.

KWANT, T. *Encounter.* Pittsburgh: Duquesne Univ. Press, 1960.

LANGAN, Thomas. *Meaning of Heidegger.* New York: Columbia Univ. Press, 1963.

LAUER, Quentin. *The Triumph of Subjectivity.* New York: Fordham Univ. Press, 1958.

LUIJPEN, W. *Existential Phenomenology.* Pittsburgh: Duquesne Univ. Press, 1960.

MARCEL, Gabriel. *Creative Fidelity.* New York: Farrar, Straus, 1964.

————. *Homo Viator.* Translated by Emma Craufurd. New York: Harper, 1961.

————. *The Mystery of Being.* Volumes I and II. Chicago: Regnery, 1950-1951.

————. *The Philosophy of Existentialism.* New York: Citadel, 1961.

MERLEAU-PONTY, Maurice. *In Praise of Philosophy*. Evanston, Ill.: Northwestern Univ. Press, 1963.

―――. *Sense and Non-Sense*. Evanston, Ill.: Northwestern Univ. Press, 1964.

―――. *Signs*. Evanston, Ill.: Northwestern Univ. Press, 1964.

MICHALSON, C., (ed.) *Christianity and the Existentialists*. New York: Scribner's, 1956.

MIHALICH, J. *Existentialism and Thomism*. New York: Philosophical Library, 1960.

RICOEUR, Paul. *Fallible Man*. Chicago: Regnery, 1965.

―――. *History and Truth*. Evanston, Ill.: Northwestern Univ. Press, 1965.

ROBERTS, D. and ROGER, H. (eds.) *Existentialism and Religious Belief*. New York: Oxford Univ. Press, 1957.

SPIEGELBERG, Herbert. *The Phenomenological Movement: A Historical Introduction*. 2 vols. The Hague: Nijhoff, 1960.

TILLICH, Paul. *The Shaking of the Foundations*. New York: Scribner's, 1948.

―――. *Systematic Theology*. 3 vols. Chicago: Univ. of Chicago Press, 1951-1963.

TROISFONTAINES, Roger. *Existentialism and Christian Thought*. Translated by M. Jarret-Kerr. London: Dacre, 1950.

BEDNARSKY, J. "Two Aspects of Husserl's Reduction: Bracketing and Reflection," *Philosophy Today,* IV (1960), 208-23.

BRETON, S. "From Phenomenology to Ontology," *Philosophy Today,* IV (1960), 227-37; V (1961), 65-78.

BURKILL, T. A. "Romanticism, Existentialism and Religion," *Philosophy,* XXX (1955), 318-32.

CAIRNS, Dorion. "Phenomenology," in *A History of Philosophical Systems*. Edited by Vergilius Ferm. New York: Philosophical Library, 1950. Pp. 353-64.

CREAVEN, John A. "The Doctrine of God in Personalism," *Thomist,* XIV (1951), 161-216.

DE WAELHENS, A. "The Outlook for Phenomenology," *International Philosophical Quarterly*, II (1962), 458-73.

FOSTER, K. "Paul Tillich and Saint Thomas. *Blackfriars*, XLI (1960), 306-13.

GOULET, D. A. "Kierkegaard, Aquinas and the Dilemma of Abraham," *Thought*, XXXII (1957), 165-88.

HASSETT, J. "Heidegger, Being, and a World of Turmoil," *Thought*, XXXVI (1961), 537-54.

HEINEMANN, F. H. "Existentialism, Religion and Theology," *The Hibbert Journal*, XXVII (1960), 387-93.

HESCHEL, L. "Depth-Theology," *Cross-Currents*, X (1960), 317-25.

HESS, M. "Paul Tillich: the Last of the German Idealists," *Catholic World*, CLXXXIX (1959), 421-26.

McNICHOLL, A. J. "Some Positive Contributions of Existentialism," *Hibernia*, III (1955), 31-41.

MANN, J. "Role of Reflective Intelligence According to the American Pragmatists," *Proceedings of the American Catholic Philosophical Association*, XXXV (1961), 117-24.

PIEPER, J. "The Contemporary Aquinas: Existentialism," *Philosophy Today*, V (1959), 73-75.

RENARD, Henri. "Introduction to the Philosophy of the Existential Moral Act," *The New Scholasticism*, XXVIII (1954), 145-69.

RICHARDSON, W. J. "Heidegger and the Problem of Thought," *Revue Philosophique de Louvain*, LX (1962), 58-78.

———. "Heidegger and the Origin of Language," *International Philosophical Quarterly*, II (1962), 404-11.

SPIEGELBERG, H. "How Subjective Is Phenomenology?" *Proceedings of the American Catholic Philosophical Association*, XXXIII (1959), 28-36.

STALKNECHT, Newton P. "Mysticism and Existentialism," in *Mysticism and the Modern Mind*. Edited by Alfred Stiernotte. New York: Liberal Arts, 1959. Pp. 138-56.

VAN PEURSON, C. A. "Phenomenology and Ontology," *Philosophy Today*, III (1959), 35-42.

WILDER, AMOS N. "Christian Social Action and Existentialism," *The Journal of Religion*, XL (1960), 155-60.

BRETON, Stanislas. *Approches phénoménologiques de l'idée d'être.* Paris: Vitte, 1959.

DERISI, O. N. *Tratado de Existencialismo y Tomismo.* Buenos Aires: Emecé, 1956.

DUMÉRY, Henry. *Phénoménologie et religion.* Paris: Presses Univ. de France, 1958.

GABRIEL, Leo. *Existenzphilosophie von Kierkegaard bis Sartre.* Wien: Herold, 1951.

HOLLENBACH, J. M. *Sein und Gewissen:* Ueber den Ursprung der Gewissensregung. Eine Begegnung zwischen Martin Heidegger und thomistischer Philosophie. Baden-Baden: Kunst und Wissenschaft, 1954.

JOLIVET, Régis. *Aux sources de l'existentialisme chrétien: Kierkegaard.* Paris: Fayard, 1957.

———. *Le problème de la mort chez M. Heidegger et J. P. Sartre.* Paris: Fontenelle, 1950.

LAUER, Quentin, *La Phénoménologie de Husserl.* Paris: Presses Univ. de France, 1955.

LENZ, Joseph. *Der moderne deutsche und französische Existentialismus.* Trier: Paulinusverlag, 1951.

LEPP, Ignace. *L'existence authentique.* Paris: La Colombe, 1950.

———. *Existence et existentialismes.* Paris: Témoignage Chrétien, 1954.

LEEUW, G. van der. *Fenomenologia della religione.* Trad. V. Vacca. Torino: Boringhieri, 1960.

QUILES, Ismael. *Más allá del existencialismo.* Barcelona: Miracle, 1958.

STEIN, E. *Endliches und Ewiges.* Freiburg: Herder, 1950.

STRASSER, S. *Das Gemüt.* Freiburg: Herder, 1956.

VANCOURT, Raymond. *La phénoménologie et la foi.* Tournai: Desclée, 1953.

WAELHENS, Alphonse de. *Existence et signification.* Louvain. Nauwelaerts, 1958.

44   CONTEMPORARY PHILOSOPHIES

——. *Phénoménologie et vérité.* Paris: Presses Univ. de France, 1953.

——. *Philosophie et les expériences naturelles.* Hague: Nijhoff, 1961.

WUST, Peter. *Ungewissheit und Wagnis.* München: Kösel, 1950.

ALVES DE CAMPOS, A. "O problema de Deus na filosofia existencial," *Estudos,* XXX (1952), 447-63.

BOUILLARD, Henri. "La position d'une théologie réformée en face de l'interprétation existentielle," *Archivio di Filosofia* (1961), 307-10.

BRETON, S. "Etudes phénoménologiques. Conscience et intentionnalité selon saint Thomas et Brentano," *Archives de Philosophie,* XIX (1956), 63-87.

DIAZ, J. C. "Existencialismo y metafísica," *Sapientia Aquinatis,* II (1956), 214-21.

FABRO, C. "Kierkegaard e S. Tommaso," *Sapienza,* IX (1956), 292-308.

GOMEZ NOGALES, Salvador. "Unidad y multiplicidad de las formas hilemórfica y existencial en el ámbito del ser," *Pensamiento,* XIV (1958), 217-24.

HILDEBRAND, Dietrich von. "Die geistigen Formen der Affektivität," *Philosophisches Jahrbuch,* LXVIII (1960), 180-90.

JOLIVET, R. "La méthode thomiste et la phénoménologie existentielle," *Sapientia Aquinatis,* I (1956), 499-508.

MOREAU, C. " 'Veritas intellectus' et 'veritas rei' selon saint Thomas et Heidegger," *Sapientia Aquinatis,* I (1956), 528-36.

MUÑOZ, Alonso A. "La existencia en Santo Tomas' y en el Existencialismo," *Sapientia Aquinatis,* II (1956), 180-83.

PASSERI PIGNONI, Vera. "Considerazioni sull'angoscia," *Sapienza,* XII (1959), 272-86.

REINER, Hans. "Thomistische und phänomenologische Ethik," *Zeitschrift für Philosophische Forschung,* XIV (1960), 247-63.

RICARD, L. "La relation à autrui dans l'existentialisme et la philosophie de saint Thomas," *Sapientia Aquinatis,* I (1956), 554-61.

RUBERT CANDAU, José María. "La raíz fenomenológica de la vida," *Verdad y Vida,* XIII (1955), 5-21.

SANTINELLO, Giovanni. "Il fenomeno della morte e la fenomenologia religiosa," in *Atti del Centro di Studi Filosofici* (Gallarate, 1960). Pp. 134-37.

C. LINGUISTIC ANALYSIS

Analytic Philosophy. Proceedings of the American Catholic Philosophical Association, XXXIV (1962).

AUSTIN, J. L. *Philosophical Papers.* Oxford: Clarendon, 1961.

AYER, A. J. *Logical Positivism.* Glencoe: Free Press, 1959.

———— *et al. The Revolution in Philosophy.* London: Macmillan, 1956.

BENDALL, Kent, and FERRÉ, F. *Exploring the Logic of Faith.* New York: Association, 1962.

BLACKSTONE, W. T. *The Problem of Religious Knowledge.* Englewood Cliffs, N.J.: Prentice-Hall, 1963.

BRAITHWAITE, R. *An Empiricist's View of the Nature of Religious Belief.* Cambridge: Univ. Press, 1955.

CATON, C. E. (ed.) *Philosophy and Ordinary Language.* Urbana, Ill.: Univ. of Illinois Press, 1963.

CHARLESWORTH, M. *Philosophy and Linguistic Analysis.* Pittsburgh: Duquesne Univ. Press, 1959.

FERRÉ, Fred. *Language, Logic and God.* New York: Harper, 1961.

FLEW, Antony. (ed.) *Essays in Conceptual Analysis.* New York: St. Martin's, 1960.

————. (ed.) *Essays on Logic and Language.* 2 vols. New York: Philosophical Library, 1951.

————, and MacINTYRE, A. *New Essays in Philosophical Theology.* London: S. C. M., 1955.

HEPBURN, Ronald. *Christianity and Paradox*. London: Watts, 1958.

HICK, John. *Faith and Knowledge*. Ithaca, N.Y.: Cornell Univ. Press, 1957.

KIMPEL, Ben F. *Language and Religion*. New York: Philosophical Library, 1957.

LEWIS, H. D. (ed.) *Clarity Is Not Enough: Essays in Criticism of Linguistic Philosophy*. New York: Humanities, 1963.

MacINTYRE, A. *Difficulties in Religious Belief*. London: S.C.M., 1959.

———. (ed.) *Metaphysical Beliefs*. London: S.C.M., 1957.

MARTIN, C. *Religious Belief*. Ithaca, N.Y.: Cornell Univ. Press, 1961.

MASCALL, E. L. *Words and Images*. London: Longmans, Green, 1957.

MITCHELL, B. (ed.) *Faith and Logic*. London: Allen and Unwin, 1957.

PEARS, D. (ed.) *The Nature of Metaphysics*. London: Macmillan, 1957.

RAMSEY, I. *Religious Language*. London: S.C.M. Press, 1957.

Religious Experience and Truth. Edited by Sidney Hook. New York: New York Univ. Press, 1961.

RYLE, Gilbert. *The Concept of Mind*. New York: Barnes and Noble, 1949.

———. *Dilemmas*. Cambridge: Univ. Press, 1954.

STRAWSON, P. F. *Individuals: An Essay in Descriptive Metaphysics*. Garden City, N.Y.: Doubleday, 1959.

URMSON, J. *Philosophical Analysis*. Oxford: Clarendon, 1956.

WILSON, John. *Philosophy and Religion: Logic of Religious Belief*. Cambridge: Univ. Press, 1961.

WITTGENSTEIN, Ludwig. *Blue and Brown Books: Or Preliminary Studies for Philosophical Investigations*. New York: St. Martin's, 1960.

———. *Philosophical Investigations*. Translated by G. E. M. Anscombe. New York: Macmillan, 1953.

ZUURDEEG, Willem. *An Analytical Philosophy of Religion.* London: Allen and Unwin, 1959.

CHARLESWORTH, M. "Linguistic Analysis and Language About God," *International Philosophical Quarterly,* I (1961), 139-67.

CLARKE, W. N. "Linguistic Analysis and Natural Theology," *Proceedings of the American Catholic Philosophical Association,* XXXIV (1960), 110-26.

COLLINS, J. "Analytic Theism and Demonstrative Inference," *International Philosophical Quarterly,* I (1961), 139-67.

COLOMBO, C. G. "The Analysis of Belief," *Downside Review,* LXXVII (1958-1959), 18-37.

DALY, C. B. "The Knowableness of God," *Philosophical Studies,* IX (1959), 90-137.

DUCASSE, C. J. "Concerning the Language of Religion," *The Philosophical Review,* LXV (1956), 401-402.

FOSTER, M. "Contemporary British Philosophy and Christian Belief," *Cross Currents,* X (1960), 375-85.

GRIESBACH, M. F. "The Analysts and the Nature of Philosophy," *Proceedings of the American Catholic Philosophical Association,* XXXIV (1960), 210-15.

HARTSHORNE, C. "John Wisdom on Gods," *Downside Review,* LXXVII (1959), 5-17.

HARVANEK, R. F. "The Pursuit of Truth (Thomists and Pragmatists, II)," *Thought,* XXX (1955), 214-30.

HICK, J. "Necessary Being," *Scottish Journal of Theology,* XIV (1961), 353-69.

HOLMER, Paul L. "The Nature of Religious Propositions," *The Review of Religion,* XIX (1955), 136-49.

KENNICK, W. E. "The Language of Religion," *Philosophical Review,* LXV (1956), 56-71.

KENNY, A. "Aquinas and Wittgenstein," *Downside Review,* LXXVII (1959), 217-35.

LAWLER, R. D. "The Nature of Analytical Ethics," *Proceedings of the American Catholic Philosophical Association,* XXXIV (1960), 151-57.

LEON, Philip. "The Meaning of Religious Propositions," *The Hibbert Journal,* LIII (1954), 51-61.

McGLYNN, J. V. "Philosophy and Analysis," *Downside Review,* LXXVIII (1960), 25-35.

McMULLEN, E. "The Analytic Approach to Philosophy," *Proceedings of the American Catholic Philosophical Association,* XXXIV (1960), 50-79.

MALCOLM, Norman, "Anselm's Ontological Arguments," *Philosophical Review,* XLVII (1960), 41-62.

MORRIS, V. C. "Deaf Men's Quarrels (Thomists and Pragmatists, I)," *Thought,* XXX (1955), 199-213.

NEMETZ, A. "The Problem of Philosophic Communication," *International Philosophical Quarterly,* I (1961), 193-213.

PENELHUM, T. "Divine Necessity," *Mind,* LXIX (1960), 175-86.

RORTY, R. "Realism, Categories, and the 'Linguistic Turn,'" *International Philosophical Quarterly,* II (1962), 307-22.

ROSS, J. "God and Logical Necessity," *Philosophical Quarterly,* XI (1961), 22-27.

"Symposium on God and Philosophy," *Philosophy,* XXXII (1957), 193-252.

"Symposium on the Concept of God," *Journal of Philosophy,* LVII (1960), 689-734.

TRETHOWAN, Iltyd. "God and Logical Analysis," *Downside Review,* LXXIV (1956), 185-98.

WARNOCK, G. "Verification and the Use of Language," *Revue Internationale de Philosophie,* V (1951), 307-22.

WEITZ, Morris. "Oxford Philosophy," *Philosophical Review,* LXXII (1953), 187-234.

WILLIAMS, C. J. "The Marriage of Aquinas and Wittgenstein," *Downside Review,* LXXVIII (1960), 203-12.

ZABEEH, F. "Oxford and Metaphysics: a New Page in Contemporary Philosophy," *International Philosophical Quarterly,* III (1963), 307-20.

D. NATURALISM

BLEWETT, J. (ed.) *John Dewey: His Thought and Influence.* New York: Fordham Univ. Press, 1960.

BRAITHWAITE, R. B. *An Empiricist's View of the Nature of Religious Belief.* Cambridge: Univ. Press, 1955.

DEWEY, John. *A Common Faith.* New Haven: Yale Univ. Press, 1934.

————. *Experience and Nature.* Chicago: Open Court, 1925.

————. *The Quest for Certainty: A Study of the Relation of Knowledge and Action.* New York: Minton, Balch, 1929.

EDEL, Abraham. *Ethical Judgment: The Use of Science in Ethics.* New York: Free Press of Glencoe, 1964.

FRANK, P. *Philosophy of Science.* New York: Prentice-Hall, 1957.

GEIGER, G. *John Dewey in Perspective.* New York: Oxford Univ. Press, 1958.

HARTSHORNE, Charles and REESE, William L. (eds.) *Philosophers Speak of God.* Chicago: Univ. of Chicago Press, 1953.

HOOK, Sidney. *John Dewey. An Intellectual Portrait.* New York: Day, 1939.

————. *The Quest for Being, and Other Studies in Naturalism and Humanism.* New York: St. Martin's, 1961.

JAMES, William. *The Varieties of Religious Experience.* New York: Longmans, Green, 1902.

————. *The Will to Believe.* New York, Dover, 1956.

KRIKORIAN, Y. (ed.) *Naturalism and the Human Spirit.* New York: Columbia Univ. Press, 1944.

KURTZ, Paul. (ed.) *American Philosophy in the Twentieth Century.* New York: Macmillan, 1966.

————. *Decision and the Condition of Man.* Seattle: Univ. of Washington Press, 1965.

LAMPRECHT, Sterling. *Nature and History.* New York: Columbia, 1950.

MacQUARRIE, John. *Twentieth-Century Religious Thought.* New York: Harper and Row, 1963.

ONG, W. *Frontiers in American Catholicism; Essays on Ideology and Culture.* New York: Macmillan, 1961.

RANDALL, John H., Jr. *Nature and Historical Experience: Essays in Naturalism and in the Theory of History.* New York: Columbia, 1959.

ROTH, R. *John Dewey and Self-Realization.* Englewood Cliffs, N.J.: Prentice-Hall, 1962.

RUSSO, F. and ROTH, R. *The Meaning of Teilhard de Chardin.* New York: America Press, n.d.

SCHNEIDER, Herbert W. *Ways of Being: Elements of Analytic Ontology.* New York: Columbia, 1962.

WOODBRIDGE, F. J. E. *An Essay on Nature.* New York: Columbia, 1961.

———. *Nature and Mind.* New York: Russell, 1965.

AUBREY, Edwin. "Naturalism and Religious Thought," *Journal of Philosophy,* XLVIII (1951), 57-66.

BERNARD, A. "Is Our Technical Civilization Open to the Gospel?" *Lumen,* XIII (1958), 600-21.

BLEWETT, J. "John Dewey's Case Against Religion," *Catholic World,* CLXXXIX (1959), 16-21.

CHENU, M. D. "Towards a Theology of Work," *Cross Currents,* VII (1957), 175-83.

CLARKE, W. N. "Christian Humanism for Today," *Social Order,* III (1953), 269-88.

———. "Christians Confront Technology," *America,* CI (1959), 761-62.

———. "The End of the Modern World," *America,* XCIX (1958), 106-108.

———. "Modern World: End or Beginning?" *America* XCIX (1958), 311-12.

DANIÉLOU, J. "A Dialogue With Time," *Cross Currents,* I (1951), 78-90.

LA FARGE, J. "American Humanist Climate," *Social Order,* III (1953), 260-68.

MATHRANI, G. N. "A Positivist Approach to Religion," *Philosophical Quarterly,* XXVIII (1956), 255-62.

MURRAY, J. C. "Christian Humanism in America," *Social Order,* III (1953), 233-44.

O'CONNELL, F. "C. S. Peirce's Conception of Philosophy," *Downside Review,* LXXVII (1959), 277-95.

ROTH, R. "The Importance of Matter," *America,* CIX (1963), 792-94.

SMITH, F. "A Thomistic Appraisal of the Philosophy of John Dewey," *Thomist,* XVIII (1955), 127-85.

SMITH, J. E. "Purpose in American Philosophy," *International Philosophical Quarterly,* I (1961), 390-406.

WILHELMSEN, F. "Modern World: End or Beginning?" *America,* XCIX (1958), 310-11.

E. GENERAL

BOCHENSKI, Innocentius. *Contemporary European Philosophy.* Translated by D. Nicholl and K. Aschenbrenner. Berkeley: Univ. of California Press, 1956.

BURR, Nelson. *A Critical Bibliography of Religion in America.* Princeton, N.J.: Princeton Univ. Press, 1961.

CANFIELD, F. *Philosophy and the Modern Mind.* Detroit: Sacred Heart Seminary, 1961.

COPLESTON, F. *Contemporary Philosophy.* Westminster, Md.: Newman, 1956.

DONDEYNE, A. *Contemporary European Thought.* Pittsburgh: Duquesne Univ. Press, 1958.

————. *Contemporary European Thought and the Christian Faith.* Pittsburgh: Duquesne Univ. Press, 1958.

FIRKEL, E. *Woman in the Modern World.* Notre Dame: Fides, 1959.

GUARDINI, R. *The End of the Modern World.* New York: Sheed and Ward, 1957.

HAWKINS, D. J. B. *Crucial Problems in Modern Philosophy.* Notre Dame, Ind.: Univ. of Notre Dame Press, 1957.

MARITAIN, J. *On the Use of Philosophy.* Princeton, N.J.: Princeton Univ. Press: 1961.

O'DEA, Thomas F. *American Catholic Dilemma.* New York: Sheed and Ward, 1958.

ORTEGA y GASSET, J. *The Modern Theme.* New York: Harper, 1961.

COLLINS, J. "Thomists in Transition," *America,* CIV (1960), 371-74.

COPLESTON, F. C. "Value of Different Philosophical Systems," *Month,* XXV (1961), 276-84; (June, 1961), 337-45.

DOUGHERTY, J. "The Metaphysical Roots of Contemporary Restlessness," *Proceedings of the American Catholic Philosophical Association,* XXXI (1963), 187-96.

HARTSHORNE, C. "Hume's Metaphysics and Its Present-Day Influence," *New Scholasticism,* XXXV (1961), 152-71.

HENDERSON, E. "Should We Undertake Systems Today?" *International Philosophical Quarterly,* III (1963), 418-27.

KRYCHE, G. "Is Thomism Relevant to the 20th Century?" *Catholic Messenger* (March 14, 1963), 5-6.

MOELLER, J. "Metaphysics Today," *Philosophy Today,* V (1961), 227-41.

STOKES, W. E. "Communist Broadside at Neo-Thomists," *America,* CIII (1960), 273.

BLONDEL, Maurice. *La philosophie et l'esprit chrétien.* Paris: Presses Univ. de France, 1944.

————. *Lettre sur les exigences de la penseé contemporaine en matière d'apologétique et sur la méthode de la philosophie dans l'étude du problème religieux.* Paris: Presses Univ. de France, 1956.

BOUTHILLIER, Yves. *Réalisme ou idolâtrie.* Paris: Cèdre, 1956.

BRETON, Stanislas. *Situation de la philosophie contemporaine.* Paris: Vitte, 1959.

DAUJAT, Jean. *L'église et le monde moderne.* Paris: La Colombe, 1950.

DONDEYNE, Albert. *Foi chrétienne et pensée contemporaine.* Louvain: Univ. de Louvain, 1951.

Monde moderne et sens de Dieu. Recherches et Débats, VII (1954).

I problemi filosofici del mondo moderno. Roma: Studium Christi, 1949.

SCIACCA, Michele. *Le problème de Dieu et de la religion dans la philosophie contemporaine.* Translated by J. Chaix-Riup. Paris: Aubier, 1951.

———. "El problema de Dios en la Filosofía actual," *Orbis Catolicus,* IV (1961), 1-20.

CHAPTER III

Philosophy and Technology

This chapter comprises books and articles on the philosophical issues raised by technology. In contemporary culture, technology is having a profound influence on man's understanding of himself and is changing his relation to his universe. At the same time, this technology is creating an increasingly urgent demand for orientation toward goals worthy of the understanding which Christian philosophy provides concerning man, his God, and his world. To bring into focus the materials available for the accomplishment of these tasks, relevant works have been drawn together and arranged under the following topics:

A. Technology
B. Technology and Philosophy
C. Technology and Man
D. Technology and Culture
E. Technology and Religion
F. Technology and Ethics

Particularly pertinent to these issues would be Chapter X of *An Annotated Bibliography of Philosophy in Catholic Thought* by the same editor.

A. TECHNOLOGY

BELL, D. A. *Intelligent Machines: An Introduction to Cybernetics*. New York: Random House, 1962.

CLAGETT, Marshall. *The Science of Mechanics in the Middle Ages*. Madison, Wis.: Univ. of Wisconsin Press, 1959.

DUNLOP, John T. (ed.) *Automation and Technological Change.* Englewood Cliffs, N.J.: Prentice-Hall, 1962.

ENGLEBARDT, Stanley, L. *Computers.* New York: Pyramid, 1962.

ELBERS, Gerald W. and DUNCAN, Paul (eds.) *The Scientific Revolution: Challenge and Promise.* Washington, D.C.: Public Affairs, 1959.

FOURASTIE, Jean. *The Causes of Wealth.* Translated by T. Caplow. Glencoe, Ill.: Free Press, 1960.

Hearings on Automation and Technological Change. Washington, D.C.: U.S. Government Printing Office, 1955.

KLEMM, Friedrich. *A History of Western Technology.* Translated by D. Singer. New York: Scribner's, 1959.

POKROVSKY, G. I. *Science and Technology in Contemporary War.* Translated by R. Garthoff. New York: Praeger, 1959.

SINGER, Charles, *et al.* (eds.) A History of Technology. 5 Vols. London: Oxford Univ. Press, 1955-58.

TAUBE, Mortimer. *Computers and Common Sense, the Myth of Thinking Machines.* New York: Columbia Univ. Press, 1961.

WIENER, Norbert. *Cybernetics; or Control and Communication in the Animal and the Machine.* Cambridge, Mass.: MIT Press, 1961.

COHEN, Robert S. "Alternative Interpretations of the History of Science," *The Scientific Monthly,* LXXX (1955), 111-16.

ELLUL, Jacques. "Technological Order," *Technology and Culture,* III (1962), 394-421.

FIEBLEMAN, James K. "Pure Science, Applied Science, Technology, Engineering: an Attempt at Definitions," *Technology and Culture,* II (1961), 305-17.

FINCH, James K. "Engineering and Science," *Technology and Culture,* II (1961), 318-32.

HALL, A. Rupert. "Engineering and the Scientific Revolution," *Technology and Culture,* II (1961), 333-41.

HEINEMANN, F. H. "Beyond Technology?" *The Hibbert Journal*, LI (1952-53), 37-46.

JONES, Howard M. "Ideas, History, Technology," *Technology and Culture*, I (1959), 20-27.

KURTH, Edmund. "Experts Look at Automation," *Social Order*, VI (1956), 264-73.

ONG, Walter. "Ideas of Technology: Commentary," *Technology and Culture*, III (1962), 459-62.

PIUS XII. "Problems of Automation: Letter to the *Semaines Sociales de France*," *Catholic Mind*, LIV (1956), 661-62.

RAE, John B. "The 'Know-How' Tradition: Technology in American History," *Technology and Culture*, I (1960), 139-50.

ZVORIKINE, A. "The History of Technology as a Science and a Branch of Learning," *Technology and Culture*, II (1961), 1-4.

BOUDIER, F., *et al. L'Invention humaine*. Technique, morale, science, leurs rapports au cours de l'évolution. Paris: Michel, 1954.

BURCKHARDT, Georg. *Weltbild der werkschaffenden Menschheit in Grundzuegen*. München-Basel: Reinhardt, 1959.

DAUMAS, Maurice. *Histoire générale des techniques*. 4 vols. Paris: Presses Univ. de France, 1960.

FORTI, Umberto. *Storia della Tecnica dal Medioevo al Rinascimento*. Firenze: Sansoni, 1957.

RATHENOU, Walter. *Die Mechanisierung der Welt*. Schwenningen: Neckar-Verlag, 1948.

CHEVALLIER, Louis. "Nature et diversité des fonctions techniques," in *La technique et l'homme. Recherches et Débats*, XXXI (1960), 45-53.

DESSAUER, Friedrich. "Technik, Wirtschaft und Gesellschaft," *Theologische Quartalschrift*, CXXXIII (1953), 257-77.

GERMAIN, Paul. "Idéal scientifique et idéal technique," *La technique et l'homme. Recherches et Débats*, XXXI (1960), 96-105.

MORRIS, Bertram. *Philosophical Aspects of Culture*. Yellow Springs, Ohio: Antioch, 1961.

RUSSELL, John. *Science and Metaphysics*. New York: Sheed and Ward, 1958.

UPTON, Cyril. *What Is Wisdom? The World's Oldest Question Posed in the Light of Contemporary Perplexity*. London: Linden, 1959.

WEISHEIPL, James A. *Dignity of Science:* Studies in the Philosophy of Science Presented to William H. Kane, O.P. Washington, D.C.: Thomist, 1961.

FRANK, Philipp. "Contemporary Science and the Contemporary World View," *Daedalus,* LXXXVII (1958), 57-66.

HUGHES, H. Stuart. "Technology and the History of Ideas," *Technology and Culture,* II (1961), 237-39.

JORAVSKY, David. "The History of Technology in Soviet Russia and Marxist Doctrine," *Technology and Culture,* II (1961), 5-10.

KOYRÉ, A. "Influence of Philosophic Trends on the Formulation of Scientific Theories," *Scientific Monthly,* LXXX (1955), 107-11.

MOLL, Jan A.M. Van. "Philosophy and the Progress of Cultural Endeavor" in *Atti XII Congresso Internazionale di Filosofia,* VIII (1960), 269-76.

NEILL, Thomas P. "Automation and Christian Culture," in *Technology and Christian Culture*. Edited by R. Mohan. Washington, D.C.: Catholic Univ. of America Press, 1960. Pp. 47-71.

SCHLIPP, Paul A. "A Challenge to Philosophers in the Atomic Age," *Philosophy,* XXIV (1949), 56-58.

———. "Does Philosophy Have Anything to Say to Our Atomic Age?" in *Atti XII Congresso Internazionale di Filosofia,* VIII (1960), 239-45.

WALLACE, William A. "Natural Philosophy and the Physical Sciences," in *Philosophy and the Integration of Contemporary Catholic Education*. Edited by G. McLean. Washington, D.C.: Catholic Univ. of America Press, 1962. Pp. 130-57.

GUZZO, Augusto. " 'Techne' e tecnica," *Filosofia,* XII (196 108.

KÖSSLER, P. "Natur und Technik," *Studium Generale* (1954), 308-11.

LALANDE, André. "Technique et science," *Journal de F logie Normale et Pathologique,* XLI (1948), 79-88.

LEROI-GOURHAM, André. "L'illusion technologique," *technique et l'homme. Recherches et Débats,* XXXI 65-74.

RALEA, Mihail. "Dialectique du donné et du construit *XII Congresso Internazionale di Filosofia,* VIII (196 13.

RIESSEN, I. H. van. "De structuur der technik," *Phil Reformata,* XXVI (1961), 114-30.

RÖPKE, Wilhelm. "Die Technik in der Gesellschaftsk Gegenwart," *Universitas,* VII (1952), 673-79.

RUSSO, François. "La création scientifique et technique," CCCV (1960), 28-40.

B. TECHNOLOGY AND PHILOS

CONNOLLY, Frederick G. *Science Versus Philosop* York: Philosophical Library, 1957.

FOLEY, Leo A. *Cosmology, Philosophical and Scien* waukee: Bruce, 1962.

FRIEDRICK, Lawrence W. (ed.) *The Nature of Physic edge.* Milwaukee: Marquette Univ. Press, 1960.

KWANT, Remy C. *Encounter.* Translated by R. Ad burgh: Duquesne Univ. Press, 1960.

MELSEN, Andrew G. van. *Science and Technology.* F Duquesne Univ. Press, 1961.

MOHAN, Robert P. (ed.) *Technology and Christia* Washington, D.C.: Catholic Univ. of America P

MOREUX, Theophile. *Modern Science and the Trut* Translated by M. Fitzsimon. New York: Benzige

————. "Place of Science in the Liberal Arts Curriculum," *The Catholic Educational Review*, LX (1962), 371-76.

————. "The Thomistic Order of Development in Natural Philosophy," *Teaching Thomism Today*. Edited by G. McLean. Washington, D.C.: Catholic Univ. of America Press, 1963. Pp. 247-70.

BENSE, Max. *Technische Existenz*. Stuttgart: Deutsche, 1949.

BULLE, G. *Die Technik als philosophisches Problem*. Erfurt: Koenig, 1934.

DESSAUER, Frederico. *Filosofia della tecnica*. Trad. di M. Bendiscioli. 2ª ed. Brescia: Morcelliana, 1947.

FREYER, Hans. *Theorie des gegenwärtigen Zeitalters*. Stuttgart: Deutsche, 1955.

MEYER, Hermann J. *Die Technisierung der Welt; Herkunft, Wesen und Gefahren*. Tübingen: Niemeyer, 1961.

SCHADEWALDT, Wolfgang. *Natur, Technik, Kunst*. Göttingen: Musterschmidt, 1960.

SCHRÖTER, M. *Philosophie der Technik*. München: Oldenbourg, 1934.

WENZL, Aloys. *Wissenschaft und Weltanschauung*. 2 Aufl. Leipzig: Felix-Meiner-Verlag, 1949.

ZSCHIMMER, E. *Deutsche Philosophen der Technik*. Stuttgart: Enke, 1937.

BRUIN, P. de. "Philosophie der Technik," *Studia Catholica*, XIII (1937), 436-64.

COSTABEL, Pierre. "L'histoire des sciences propose-t-elle une philosophie des sciences?" in *La Science peut-elle former l'homme? Recherches et Débats*, XII (1955), 100-109.

DUCASSE, P. "Les techniques et la philosophie contemporaine," in *Proceedings of the Tenth International Congress of Philosophy*, 1048-50.

————. "Technocratie ou sagesse?" *Revue de Synthèse*, LXXIV (1953), 69-74.

FABRO, Cornelio. "El humanismo y la filosofía moderna," in *Humanismo y mundo moderno.* Trad. José Oroz. Madrid: Augustinus, 1960. Pp. 65-95.

GIACON, Carlo. "La ciencia y la filosofía en un humanismo cristiano," in *Humanismo y mundo moderno.* Trad. by José Oroz. Madrid: Augustinus, 1960. Pp. 271-93.

LADRIÈRE, Jean. "La science dans une philosophie de la culture," in *La Science peut-elle former l'homme? Recherches et Débats,* XII (1955), 13-25.

MARTI DEL CASTILLO, Rubén. "Para una gnoseología de la automacion," in *Atti XII Congresso Internazionale di Filosofia,* VIII (1960), 153-59.

POHL, Heinrich. "Das Wesen der Technik," in *Atti XII Congresso Internazionale di Filosofia,* VIII (1960), 195-200.

POIRIER, René. "Sur la crise de la philosophie des sciences" in *La Science peut-elle former l'homme? Recherches et Débats,* XII (1955), 110-23.

RIESSEN, I. H. van. "Philosophie der Technik," *Philosophia Reformata,* III (1938), 202-24.

ROSSMANN, Kurt. "Die Philosophen und die Technik." *Studium Generale,* IV (1951), 59-64.

SOUCY, Claude. "Technique et philosophie," in *La technique et l'homme. Recherches et Débats,* XXXI (1960), 109-23.

C. TECHNOLOGY AND MAN

ANDERSON, Harold H. (ed.) *Creativity and Its Cultivation.* New York: Harper, 1959.

CONANT, James B. *Modern Science and Modern Man.* New York: Columbia Univ. Press, 1952.

CRONAN, Edward, P. *The Dignity of the Human Person.* New York: Philosophical Library, 1955.

DOHERTY, Richard T. *The Relation of the Individual to Society in the Light of Christian Principles as Expounded by the Angelic Doctor.* Rome: Officium Libri Catholici, 1957.

EYKEN, Albert. *The Status of Man in the Universe.* London: Longmans, Green, 1956.

FORBES, R. J. *Man the Maker.* New York: Schuman, 1950.

FRANKEL, Charles. *The Case for Modern Man.* New York: Harper, 1956.

HEARD, Gerald. *Human Venture.* New York: Harper, 1955.

JASPERS, Karl. *Man in the Modern Age.* Translated by Eden and Cedar Paul. Garden City, N.Y.: Doubleday, 1957.

LEWIS, C. S. *The Abolition of Man.* New York: Macmillan, 1947.

MacMURRAY, John. *Persons in Relation.* London: Faber and Faber, 1957.

Man in Contemporary Society. A source book prepared by the Contemporary Civilization Staff of Columbia College, Columbia University. Vols. I and II. New York: Columbia Univ. Press, 1955-56.

Men and Machines. (Aristotelian Society for the Systematic Study of Philosophy. Supplementary Vol. 26.) London: Harrison, 1952.

MOUROUX, Jean. *The Meaning of Man.* Translated by A. Downes. New York: Sheed and Ward, 1948.

TYRRELL, G. N. M. *Man the Maker.* New York: Dutton, 1952.

WIENER, Norbert. *The Human Use of Human Beings: Cybernetics and Society.* Garden City, N. Y.: Doubleday, 1954.

WINGATE, M. *Human Problems of Today.* London: Hutchinson, 1954.

ZEHRER, Hans. *Man in this World.* New York: University Press, 1955.

ABBAGNANO, Nicola. "Contemporary Science and Freedom," *Review of Metaphysics,* V (1952), 361-78.

ALLERS, Rudolf. "Technology and the Human Person," in *Technology and Christian Culture.* Edited by R. Mohan. Washington, D.C.: Catholic Univ. of America Press, 1960. Pp. 10-46.

CHAKRAVARTI, K. C. "Man, the Maker of the Universe," *Prabuddha Bharata*, LVII (1952), 341-44.

CLARKE, W. Norris. "Technology and Man: a Christian Vision," *Catholic Mind*, LXI (1963), 4-20.

HILDEBRAND, D. von. "Technology and Its Dangers," in *Technology and Christian Culture*. Edited by R. Mohan. Washington, D.C.: Catholic Univ. of America Press, 1960. Pp. 72-98.

BERDIAEV, Nikolai. *Der Mensch und die Technik*. Luzern: Vita Nova, 1948.

BIANCA, Omero D. *Umanesimo della tecnica e umanesimo delle lettere*. Alesandria: Novesi, 1954.

BRINKMANN, Donald. *Mensch und Technik*. Bern: Francke, 1946.

CHAUCHARD, Paul. *L'humanisme et la science*. Paris: Spes, 1961.

CHOPARD, Edmond. *Mission de l'esprit dans notre civilisation technique*. Neuchâtel: Messeiller, 1959.

CONANT, James B. *La scienza moderna e l'uomo moderno*. Trad. di Andrea Damiano. Milano: Aldo Martello, 1955.

ENGELHARDT, Wolf von. *Der Mensch in der technischen Welt*. Köln-Graz: Böhlau, 1957.

GIRARDEAU, Emile. *Le progrès technique et la personnalité humaine*. Paris: Plon, 1955.

HAIDANT, Paul. *L'homme et la machine. La grande angoisse du temps présent*. Paris: Béranger, 1950.

Humanismus und Technik. Hrsg. von der Gesellschaft von Freunden d. Technischen Universität Berlin-Charlottenburg. Frankfurt: Vahlen, 1954.

LALOUP, Jean. *La science et l'humain*. Paris: Casterman, 1959.

————, and NELIS, Jean. *Hommes et machines. Initiation à l'humanisme technique*. 2e ed. Paris-Tournai: Casterman, 1957.

LEROI-GOURHAN, André. *Evolution et techniques: l'homme et la matière*. Paris: Michel, 1943.

LERSCH, Philipp. *Der Mensch in der Gegenwart.* Basel: Reinhardt, 1955.

LITT, Theodor. *Le scienze e l'uomo.* Trad. Carlo d'Altavilla. Roma: Armando, 1960.

MARCEL, Gabriel. *La condición del intelectual en el mundo contemporáneo.* Madrid: Ateneo, 1960.

Mensch und Technik. Hrsg. von H. Schwippert. Darmstadt: Neue Darmstädter Verlagsanstalt, 1952.

ORTEGA y GASSET, José. *Betrachtungen über die Technik. Der Intellektuelle und der Andere.* Stuttgart: Deutsche Verlagsanstalt, 1949.

PARIS, Carlos. *Mundo técnico y existencia auténtica.* Madrid: Guadarrama, 1959.

SCHWARZ, Ernst. *Am Wendepunkt. Weltbild und Mensch im Atomzeitalter.* Stuttgart: Klett, 1960.

La science peut-elle former l'homme? Recherches et Débats, XII (1955).

ALEJANDRO, José M. "Técnica y humanismo," *Razón y Fé,* CLIX (1959), 253-70.

BARDET, Gaston. "Die Sackgasse der Technik; der Arbeiter als Funktion und als Mensch," *Wort und Wahrheit,* V (1950), 673-84.

BRINKMANN, Donald. "L'homme et la technique," in *Actes du XIe Congres International de Philosophie,* VIII, 149-50.

———. "Der Mensch im Zeitalter der Automation," in *Festschr. H. J. de Vleeschauwer.* Pretoria, So. Africa: Publications Committee of the Univ. of So. Africa, 1960. Pp. 96-113.

BRUNNER, August. "Geist im technischen Zeitalter," *Stimmen der Zeit,* CLXI (1957-1958), 161-72.

CAPOCACCIA, Antonio. "Umanesimo della macchina," *Humanitas,* VII (1953), 165-75.

CARUSO, Igor A. "Crise du monde technique et psychologie," in *La technique et l'homme. Recherches et Débats,* XXX (1960), 54-64.

COLONNETTI, G. "La tecnica e la sua influenza nel regno dello spirito," *Studium*, XXXI (1935), 517-34.

―――. "La tecnica, strumento di elevazione dell'uomo," *Studium*, XLVII (1950), 604-17.

DRACAULIDES, N. N. "Les répercussions déshumanisantes du machinisme d'aujourd'hui," *Psyché*, V (1951), 729-32.

DUCATILLON, V. "Le progrès scientifique et technique, phénomène de maturation," in *Espoir humain et espérance chrétienne*. Paris: Flore, 1951. Pp. 148-66.

GEORGE, André. "Pour une vulgarisation au service de la science," in *La science peut-elle former l'homme? Recherches et Débats*, XII (1955), 34-43.

―――. "Science et technique, espoir de l'humanité?" in *Espoir humain et espérance chrétienne*. Paris: Flore, 1951. Pp. 135-48.

GONSETH, Ferdinand. "De l'humanisation de la technique," *Dialectica*, X (1956), 99-112.

GRASSI, Ernesto. "Il tempo umano. L'umanesimo contro la 'techne,'" in *Umanesimo e scienza politica*. Milano: Marzorati, 1951. Pp. 201-206.

GUARDINI, Romano. "Die Situation des Menschen," in *Die Künste im technischen Zeitalter*. Edited by Clemens G. Podervils. München: Oldenbourg, 1954.

JAVILLIER, Maurice. "Science et technique, espoir de l'humanité?" in *Espoir humain et espérance chrétienne*. Paris: Flore, 1951. Pp. 183-87.

LEPRINCE-RINGUET, Louis. "Science et techniques, espoir de l'humanite?" in *Espoir humain et espérance chrètienne*. Paris: Flore, 1951. Pp. 166-70.

LERSCH, Philipp. "Das Bild des Menschen in der Sicht der Gegenwart," *Universität*, XIII (1958), 1-10.

OBERT, Elisa. "Natura, tecnica, umanesimo," *Atti XII Congresso iternazionale di Filosofia*, VIII (1960), 169-76.

PERRIN, R.; LEVARD, G.; DEMONQUE, M.; DEVAUH, L. "Automation et avenir humain," in *Automation et Avenir Humain. Recherches et Débats*, XX (1957), 77-98.

PICARD, Max. "Die Atomisierung der Person," *Universitas,* XIII (1958), 367-80.

RIDEAU, E. "Technique et avènement de l'homme," *Revue de l'Action Populaire,* (1951), 293-302.

ROTH, Paul. "Mensch und Technik," *Stimmen der Zeit,* CXLIX (1951), 1-10.

SAUERBRUCH, Ferdinand. "Mensch und Technik," *Die Erziehung,* XIV (1938), 65-78.

SCHUHL, Pierce-Maxime. "L'homme et le progrès scientifique et technique," *Revue Philosophique de la France et de l'Etranger,* LXXXIV (1959), 113-14.

SCHELER, Hermann. "Ueber das Verhältnis von Mensch und Technik," in *Atti XII congresso internazionale di Filosofia,* VIII (1960), 231-38.

SIMONDON, G. "Les limites du progrès humain," *Revue de Métaphysique et de Morale,* LXIV (1959), 370-76.

SUSINOS, Francisco. "Técnica y humanismo," *Revista de Filosofía,* XIX (1960), 213-29.

THEUBET, Louis. "L'homme et le spécialiste," *Revue de l'Université d'Ottawa,* XXIX (1959), 385-412.

TOURNIER, Gilbert. "L'automation, espoir ou menace pour l'homme," in *Automation et Avenir Humain. Recherches et Débats,* XX (1957), 99-108.

WASMUTH, E. "Der Mensch und die zweite technische Revolution," *Wissenschaft und Weltbild,* VIII (1955), 248-57.

D. TECHNOLOGY AND CULTURE

BARANSKI, Leo J. *Scientific Basis for World Civilization.* Boston: Christopher, 1960.

BURCHARD, John E. *Mid-Century: The Social Implications of Scientific Progress.* New York: Technology Press, 1950.

BUSIJ, J. B. *The Idea of Progress: An Inquiry into Its Origin and Growth.* New York: Dover, 1955.

BRUSHOVSKY, Meyer N. *Cosmic Design: Man's Inner Urge for Progress.* New York: Vantage, 1955.

BURKHARDT, Frederick (ed.) *The Cleavage in Our Culture.* Boston: Beacon, 1952.

DUBARLE, Dominque. *Scientific Humanism and Christian Thought.* Translated by R. Trevett. New York: Philosophical Library, 1956.

Essays in the Science of Culture. Edited by G. Dole and R. Carneiro. New York: Crowell, 1960.

HOSELITZ, Bert F. *Sociological Aspects of Economic Growth.* Glencoe, Ill.: Free Press, 1960.

KAPLAN, Max. *Leisure in America: A Social Inquiry.* New York: Wiley, 1960.

LOVELL, Bernard. *Science and Civilization.* London: Nelson, 1939.

MARCEL, Gabriel. *Man Against Mass Society.* Chicago: Regnery, 1952.

MEADOWS, Paul. *The Culture of Industrial Man.* Lincoln: Univ. of Nebraska Press, 1950.

MUMFORD, L. *Technics and Civilization.* New York: Harcourt, Brace, 1934.

NOLTE, Fred. *The Life of the Spirit, the Immediacy of Meaning.* I: *Science and Civilization.* Lancaster, Pa.: Lancaster, 1950.

PIEPER, Josef. *Leisure, the Basis of Culture.* Translated by A. Dru. New York: Pantheon, 1952.

RUSSELL, Bertrand. *The Impact of Science on Society.* New York: Columbia University Press, 1950.

SCHILPP, Paul A. *Human Nature and Progress.* Stockton, Calif.: College of the Pacific, 1954.

Science and Life in the World. Vol. I: Science and Civilization. The Future of Atomic Energy. Vol. II: Transportation. A Measurement of Civilization. Light, Life and Man. Vol. III: A Challenge to the World. The George Westinghouse Centennial Forum, May 16, 17, 18, 1946. New York: McGraw-Hill, 1946.

SMITH, Alan Gordon. *The Western Dilemma.* London: Longmans, Green, 1954.

STAUFFER, Robert C. (ed.) *Science and Civilization.* Madison, Wis.: Univ. of Wisconsin Press, 1949.

STEELE, George, and KIRCHER, Paul. *The Crisis We Face: Automation and the Cold War.* New York: McGraw-Hill, 1960.

STILL, Joseph W. *Science and Education at the Crossroads: A View from the Laboratory.* Washington, D.C.: Public Affairs, 1958.

WHITEHEAD, Alfred. *Science and the Modern World.* New York: Macmillan, 1925.

ALLEN, Francis R. "Technology and Social Change: Current Status and Outlook," *Technology and Culture,* I (1959), 48-60.

AYRES, C. E. "Technology and Progress," *Antioch Review,* III (n. 1, 1943), 6-20.

BURLINGAME, Roger. "Technology: Neglected Clue to Historical Change," *Technology and Culture,* II (1961), 219-29.

CALDIN, E. F. "The Place of Science in Modern Culture," *Blackfriars* XXVI (1945), 142-49.

COLLIER, K. G. "The Impact of Science on the Western View of Life," *The Hibbert Journal,* XLVII (1949), 160-65.

DRUCKER, Peter F. "The Technological Revolution: Notes on the Relationship of Technology, Science, and Culture," *Technology and Culture,* II (1961), 342-51.

HALPERN, B. "The Dynamic Elements of Culture," *Ethics,* LXV (1955), 235-49.

LAGUNA, Grace A. de. "The Lebenswelt and the Cultural World," *Journal of Philosophy,* LVII (1960), 777-91.

McKINNEY, Richard D. "Science and the Humanities in a Space Age," in *Atti XII Congresso Internazionale di Filosofia,* VIII (1960), 161-67.

MELSEN, H. van. "The Impact of Science on Culture," *International Philosophical Quarterly,* I (1961), 503-12.

MUMFORD, Lewis. "History: Neglected Clue to Technological Change," *Technology and Culture,* II (1961), 230-36.

OPPENHEIMER, Robert. "The Growth of Science and the Structure of Culture. Comments on Dr. Frank's Paper," *Daedalus,* LXXXVII (1958), 67-76.

SCHMIDT, Paul F. "Some Criticisms of Cultural Relativism," *Journal of Philosophy,* LII (1955), 780-91.

WU, John C. H. "Technology and Christian Culture: an Oriental View," in *Technology and Christian Culture.* Edited by R. Mohan. Washington, D.C.: Catholic University of America Press, 1960. Pp. 99-118.

AGUIRRE BELTRAN, Gonzalo. *Teoría de la investigación intercultural* (Suplementos del Seminario de Problemas Científicos y Filosóficos. No. 7.) Mexico: Univ. de Mexico, 1956.

BADEN, Hans Jürgen. *Ende und Anfang der Humanität.* Gütersloh: Bertelsmann, 1955.

BÉRARD, Léon, and PASTEUR, Vallery-Radot. *Science et humanisme.* Paris: Flammarion, 1956.

Confort et technocratie, Témoignages, XXXV (1952). Saint-Leger-Vauban, Yonne: Abbaye de la Pierre-qui-Vire, 1952.

DAGONET, F. *Sciences de la vie et de la culture.* Paris: Hachette, 1953.

DESSAUER, Friedrich. *Kultur, Technik, und Gesellschaft.* Wolfshagen-Scharbeutz: Westphal, 1954.

———. *Streit um die Technik.* Freiburg: Herder, 1959.

DUCHET, René. *Bilan de la civilisation technique.* Toulouse: Privat, 1955.

ELLUL, Jacques. *La technique ou l'enjeu du siècle.* Paris: Colin, 1954.

FRANCHINI, Raffaello. *L'idea di progresso.* Napoli: Giannini, 1960.

FRIEDMANN, Georges. *Humanisme du travail et humanités.* Paris: Colin, 1950.

FUDALLA, Siegfried G. *Die Gegenwart als Patient.* Wien: Scherz, 1960.

HANTEL, Erika. *Verborgenes Kräftespiel. Die Pflege des Menschlichen als Aufgabe von Industrie und Wirtschaft.* 2 Aufl. Stuttgart: Klett, 1953.

LITT, Theodor. *Technisches Denken und menschliche Bildung.* Heidelberg: Quelle und Meyer, 1957.

ROSTENNE, Paul. *La barbarie des élites.* Tournai: Desclée, 1954.

SAMUEL, Otto. *Die Ontologie der Kultur.* Berlin: Gruyter, 1956.

SPIRITO, Ugo. *Significato del nostro tempo.* Firenze: Sansoni, 1955.

THIEL, Manfred. *Die Umstilisierung der Wissenschaft und die Krise der Welt.* Heidelberg: Winter, 1958.

TOYNBEE, A. J. *Kultur am Scheidewege.* Frankfurt: Ullstein Taschenbucher-Verl, 1958.

BAUHOFER, Oscar. "Technik und Kultur," *Gloria Dei,* IV (1949-50), 232-38.

BRUNNER, August, "Die Gefahren des technischen Denkens," *Stimmen der Zeit,* CLVII (1956), 335-46.

DAINVILLE, François de et RUSSO, François. "Culture, technique et spécialisation," *Etudes,* CCLXXVIII (1953), 158-71; CCLXXIX (1953), 45-54.

DUBARLE, Dominique. "El mundo de la cultura y el pensamiento científico," *Arbor,* XXVI (1953), 218-34.

———. "Técnicas modernas y problemas de civilización," *Cuadernos hispanoamericanos,* VII (1951), 39-51.

———. "Technique et avenir," *Vie Intellectuelle,* XVIII (1950), 142-63.

FINANCE, Joseph de. "Réflexions sur le 'prométhéisme' contemporain," *Doctor Communis,* V (1952), 46-51.

GONZALES RIOS, Francisco. "Quelques conclusions sur l'aporie entre humanisme et technique," in *Actes: II* Congrès Inter-

national de l'Union Internationale de Philosophie des Sciences, IV. Neuchâtel: Griffon, 1955. Pp. 78-85.

GUARDINI, Romano. "La cultura e l'uomo," *Humanitas,* IX (1954), 431-35.

GUZZO, Augusto. "Mondo ringiovanito," *Filosofia,* XII (1961), 3-14.

HEIDEGGER, Martin. "Die Frage nach der Technik," in *Die Künste im technischen Zeitalter.* Edited by Clemens Podewils. München: Oldenbourg, 1954.

KAHN, Jean-Louis. "La valeur culturelle de la technique," in *La technique et l'homme. Recherches et Débats,* XXXI (1960), 75-95.

KAUTZ, Heinrich. "Weltgespräch um die Technik," *Die Neue Ordnung,* XI (1957), 100-105.

LECLERQ, Jacques. "L'ideé de civilisation; la révolution du XXe siècle," *La Revue Nouvelle,* XXX (1959), 148-60.

LICHNEROWICZ, André. "Une civilisation méconnue, notre civilisation scientifique et technique," *Vie intellectuelle,* XXI (1953), 81-87.

PERROUX, François. "Travail et civilisation," *Esprit,* XXIV (1954), 481-97.

RIEGER, Ladislau. "Le travail comme base de la civilisation," *Proceedings of the Tenth International Congress of Philosophy,* pp. 1222-34.

RUSSO, François. "De l'inculture d'une culture scientifique," *La science peut-elle former l'homme? Recherches et Débats,* XII (1955), 26-33.

SALVINIEN, J. "Science et humanisme," *Bulletin de l'Association Guillaume Budé,* III (1947), 46-57.

SCHRÖDER, E. F. "Techniek, economie, cultuur," *Studien,* CXXVIII (1937), 56-64.

TEUCHER, W. "Wirtschaft und Kultur," *Politica,* II (1950), 74-80.

VAZQUEZ, Juan A. "Una metafísica de la cultura," in *Metafísica y cultura.* Buenos Aires: Sudamericana, 1954.

E. TECHNOLOGY AND RELIGION

BALTHASAR, Hans U. von. *Science, Religion and Christianity*. Translated by H. Graeff. Westminster, Md.: Newman Press, 1958.

BRUNNER, Emil. *Christianity and Civilization*. Part I, *Foundations*. New York: Scribner, 1948.

CHAUVIN, Remy. *God of the Scientists, God of the Experiment*. Translated by S. Attanasio. Baltimore: Helicon, 1960.

Christian Humanism in Letters. West Hartford, Conn.: St. Joseph College, 1954.

DAWSON, Christopher. *Enquiries into Religion and Culture*. London: Sheed and Ward, 1933.

———. *Religion and Culture*. London: Sheed and Ward, 1948.

JOHN XXIII, *Mater et Magistra*. Letter of His Holiness Pope John XXIII on Christianity and Social Progress. Washington, D.C.: National Catholic Welfare Conference, 1961.

———. *Pacem in Terris*. Washington, D.C.: National Catholic Welfare Conference, 1963.

KNOX, Ronald A. *God and the Atom*. New York: Sheed and Ward, 1945.

LINDSAY, Alexander D. *Religion, Science and Society in the Modern World*. New Haven: Yale Univ. Press, 1943.

NEILL, Thomas P. *Religion and Culture: the Christian Idea of Man in Contemporary Society*. Milwaukee: Bruce, 1952.

Pius XII and Technology. Edited by L. Haigerty. Milwaukee: Bruce, 1962.

WARD, Leo. *God and World Order: A Study of Nature*. St. Louis: Herder, 1961.

WESTFALL, Richard S. *Science and Religion in Seventeenth Century England*. New Haven: Yale Univ. Press, 1958.

WHITTAKER, Edmund T. *Space and Spirit: Theories of the Universe and the Arguments for the Existence of God*. Chicago: Regnery, 1948.

CONNELL, Francis J. "Technology and the Mystical Body of Christ," in *Technology and Christian Culture*. Edited by R. Mohan. Washington, D.C.: Catholic Univ. of America Press, 1960. Pp. 119-40.

FEYNMAN, Richard P. "The Relation of Science and Religion," in *Frontiers in Science*. Edited by E. Hutchings, Jr. New York: Basic Books, 1958. Pp. 260-67.

LOWRY, Charles W. "The State of Christian Civilization To-day," in *Civiltà e pace. Atti del primo Convegno internazionale per la civilta e la pace cristiana*, Firenze, 23-28 guigno 1952. Firenze: L'impronta, 1953. Pp. 87-97.

McMULLIN, Ernan. "Natural Science and Christian Thought," *Irish Theological Quarterly*, XXVI (1959), 1-22.

WALLACE, William A. "Science and Religion in the Twentieth Century," *The Homiletic and Pastoral Review*, LXIII (1962), 23-31.

————. "Theology and the Natural Sciences," in *Theology in the Catholic College*. Edited by R. Masterson. Dubuque: Priory Press, 1961. Pp. 167-204.

BANGERTER, O. *Der "Geist der Technik" und das Evangelium. Ein Beitrag zur Frage nach der religiösen Krisis des "modernen" Menschen*. Heidelberg: Evangelischer Verlag, 1939.

CRÉMER, P. *L'humanisme scientifique devant la foi*. Bruxelles: La Pensée Catholique, 1955.

SCHLEMMER, H. *Die Technik und das Evangelium*. Leipzig: Hinrichs, 1941.

SCIACCA, Michele Federico. *La hora de Cristo. Actitudes claras frente a compromisos equivocos*. Trad. de J. Ruiz Cuevas. Barcelona: Editorial Miracle, 1954.

BOVIS, André de. "Le sens catholique du travail et de la civilisation," *Nouvelle Revue Théologique*, LXXII (1950), 357-71.

CHENU, Marie-Dominique. "Vers une théologie de la technique," in *La technique et l'homme. Recherches et Débats*, XXXI (1960), 157-66.

CHEVALLIER, Louis. "Athéisme du monde technique?" in *La Technique et l'homme. Recherches et Débats*, XXXI (1960), 136-43.

DONDEYNE, Albert. "Technique et religion," in *La technique et l'homme. Recherches et Débats*, XXXI (1960), 124-35.

GIACON, Carlo. "Scienze e filosofia in un umanesimo cristiano," *Giornale di Metafisica*, IX (1954), 198-210.

MASI, Roberto. "Il volo nello spazio: scienza, filosofia, religione," *Filosofia e Vita*, II (1961), 47-55.

PASTORE, Annibale. "La spiritualitá della tecnica." *Rivista di Filosofia*, XLIII (1952), 289-300.

PERROUX, François. "Christianisme et civilisation," in *Les désordres de l'homme*. Paris: Pierre Horay, 1961. Pp. 121-30.

ROTUREAU, Gaston. "Conscience religieuse et mentalité technique," in *La technique et l'homme. Recherches et Débats*, XXXI, (1960), 144-56.

SPIAZZI, Raimundo. "La síntesis cristiana de los valores del hombre moderno," in *Humanismo y mundo moderno*. Trad. José Oroz. Madrid: Augustinus, 1960. Pp. 295-319.

COMES, Salvatore. *Responsabilità della cultura*. Firenze: Vallechi, 1961.

FOURASTIÉ, J. *Machinisme et bien-être*. Paris: Minuit, 1950.

FRIEDMANN, Georges. *Dove va il lavoro umano?* Trad. di. B. Abbina. Milano: Communità, 1955.

LOSSIER, Jean-G. *Les civilisations et le service du prochain*. Paris: Vieux-Colombier, 1958.

POZZO, Gianni M. *L'umanesimo del lavoro*. Padova: CEDAM, 1960.

RABUT, Olivier A. *La Vérité de L'Action*. Paris: Les Editions du Cerf, 1962.

VIALATROUX, J. *Signification humaine du travail*. Paris: Ouvrières, 1953.

POZZO, Gianni M. "Il concetto dell 'umanesimo del lavoro,'" *Giornale di Metafisica*, XVI (1961), 225-43.

———. "Tecnicismo e morale: crisi del mondo moderno," *Humanitas,* VI (1961), 861-69.

ROVASENDA, E. Di. "I valori della tecnica," *Sapienza,* XIII (1960), 161-80.

F. TECHNOLOGY AND ETHICS

BORNE, Etienne and HENRY, François. *The Philosophy of Work.* Translated by F. Jackson. New York: Sheed and Ward, 1938.

CRONIN, John F. *Social Principles and Economic Life.* Milwaukee: Bruce, 1959.

DEPLOIGE, Simon. *The Conflict between Ethics and Sociology.* Translated by C. Miltner. St. Louis: Herder, 1938.

GUARDINI, Romano. *The End of the Modern World.* Translated by J. Theman and H. Burke. New York: Sheed and Ward, 1956.

———. *Power and Responsibility. A Course of Action for the New Age.* Translated by E. Briefs. Chicago: Regnery, 1961.

KILLEEN, Sylvester M. *The Philosophy of Labor According to St. Thomas Aquinas.* Washington: Catholic Univ. of America Press, 1939.

KWANT, Remy C. *Philosophy of Labor.* Pittsburgh: Duquesne Univ. Press, 1960.

MICHEL, Virgil. *Christian Social Reconstruction: Some Fundamentals of the* QUADRAGESIMO ANNO. Milwaukee: Bruce, 1938.

NELL-BREUNING, Oswald von. *Reorganization of Social Economy: The Social Encyclical Developed and Explained.* Translated by B. Dempsey. Milwaukee: Bruce, 1936.

QUINN, Francis S. (ed.) *The Ethical Aftermath of Automation.* Westminster, Md.: Newman, 1962.

ROPP, Theodore. *War in the Modern World.* Durham: Duke Univ. Press, 1959.

RYAN, John K. *Modern War and Basic Ethics.* Milwaukee: Bruce, 1940.

TANNENBAUM, Frank. *A Philosophy of Labor.* New York: Knopf, 1951.

AMES, Van Meter. "Science and the Reconstruction of Value," *The Humanist,* V (1945), 8-16.

CREEGAN, Robert F. "The Category of Work," *Philosophy and Phenomenological Research,* XI (1951), 418-20.

"Physical Science and Human Values," *Nature,* CLXII (1948), 751-52.

ARVON, Henri. *La philosophie du travail.* Paris: Presses Univ. de France, 1960.

BATTAGLIA, Felice. *Filosofia del lavoro.* Bologna: Zuffi, 1951.

CHAPTER IV

Philosophy of Man and God

This chapter comprises selected books and articles on central philosophical issues involved in recent discussions concerning the dignity of man which have taken place within the context of religious renewal. The particular stress on the dignity of the person in modern philosophy has led to new insights concerning the dignity of man, love, personal relationship to God, and the possibilities of a renewed social dialogue concerning religion. It is the intent of this chapter to identify the philosophical issues essential to these developments.

The material has been arranged under the following topics:

A. Person

B. Love

C. God

D. Religious Renewal

E. Ecumenism

Particularly pertinent to these issues would be Chapters VI to VIII of *an Annotated Bibliography of Philosophy In Catholic Thought* by the same editor.

A. PERSON

ARNOLD, Magda B. *et al. An Approach to an Integral Theory of Personality.* New York: Ronald, 1954.

————, and GASSON, J. *The Human Person.* New York: Ronald 1954.

BERTOCCI, Peter, and MILLARD, Richard. *Personality and the Good.* New York: McKay, 1963.

BRIGHTMAN, E. S. *Person and Reality*. New York: Ronald, 1958.

BUBER, Martin. *Between Man and Man*. Boston: Beacon, 1955.

———. *I and Thou*. New York: Scribner's, 1958.

CRONAN, E. P. *The Dignity of the Human Person*. New York: Philosophical Library, 1955.

CUSKELLY, E. J. *A Heart to Know Thee*. Westminster, Md.: Newman, 1963.

DESAN, Wilfred. *The Planetary Man*. Washington, D.C.: Georgetown Univ. Press, 1961.

FOLEY, Sr. M. *Authority and Personality Development According to St. Thomas Aquinas*. Washington, D.C.: Catholic Univ. of America Press, 1956.

GOLDBRUNNER, J. *Individuation*. New York: Pantheon, 1956.

HENRY, Paul. *Augustine on Personality*. New York: Macmillan, 1960.

HILDEBRAND, D. Von. *Christian Ethics*. New York: McKay, 1953.

———. *Liturgy and Personality*. New York: Longmans, Green, 1943.

———. *Transformation in Christ*. Baltimore, Md.: Helicon, 1948.

JASPERS, Karl. *Man in the Modern Age*. Trans. by E. and C. Paul. Garden City, N.Y.: Doubleday, 1957.

LAUER, Quentin. *The Triumph of Subjectivity*. New York: Fordham Univ. Press, 1958.

LAWLOR, Monica. *Personal Responsibility*. New York: Hawthorn, 1962.

LECLERCQ, Jacques. *Christian in the World*. New York: Sheed and Ward, 1961.

LOMBARDI, R. *Hope of a Better World*. New York: St. Paul, 1957.

MacMURRAY, John. *Interpreting the Universe*. London: Faber, 1956.

———. *Persons in Relation*. London: Faber, 1956.

———. *The Self As Agent*. London: Faber, 1956.

MARIAN, Sr. Dolores. *The Creative Personality in the Religious Life*. Westminster, Md.: Newman, 1963.

MARIAS, J. *Reason and Life*. New Haven: Yale Univ. Press, 1956.

MOUNIER, E. *Be Not Afraid*. New York: Sheed and Ward, 1962.

————. *Personalism*. New York: Grove, 1952.

MURRAY, J. C. *We Hold These Truths*. New York: Sheed and Ward, 1960.

NELSON, J. *Wisdom for our Time*. New York: Norton, 1961.

NEUMANN, Erich. *The Origins and History of Consciousness*. New York: Pantheon, 1954.

ORTEGA y GASSET, J. *Man and People*. New York: Norton, 1957.

REISMAN, David. *Constraint and Variety in American Education*. New York: Doubleday, 1958.

————. *The Lonely Crowd*. New York: Doubleday, 1950.

ROGERS, Carl. *On Becoming a Person*. London: Constable, 1959.

SCHELER, M. *Man's Place in Nature*. Toronto: Beacon, 1961.

————. *On the Eternal in Man*. New York: Harper, 1961.

SCHWARZ, Baldwin. *The Human Person and the World of Values*. New York: Fordham Univ. Press, 1960.

SIMEC, Sr. M. Sophie. *Philosophical Bases for Human Dignity and Change*. Washington, D.C.: Catholic Univ. of America Press, 1953.

STAAB, Giles. *The Dignity of Man in Modern Papal Doctrine*. Washington, D.C.: Catholic Univ. of America Press, 1957.

STRASSER, Stephen. *Phenonenology and the Human Sciences*. Pittsburgh: Duquesne Univ. Press, 1958.

————.*The Soul in Empirical Psychology and Metaphysics*. Pittsburgh: Duquesne Univ. Press, 1963.

SULLIVAN, John. *The Image of God; the Doctrine of St. Augustine and Its Influence*. Dubuque: Priory Press, 1963.

TODD, J. M. *Work; Christian Thought and Practice, a Symposium*. Baltimore: Helicon, 1960.

TOURNIER, P. *The Meaning of the Person*. New York: Harper, 1958.

TROQUER, R. le. *What Is Man?* New York: Hawthorn, 1961.

WALTERS, Sr. Annette. *Readings in Psychology*. Westminster, Md.: Newman, 1963.

WHYTE, William H. *The Organization Man*. New York: Doubleday, 1956.

ZAVALLONI, Roberto. *Self-Determination*. Chicago: Forum, 1962.

ZILBOORG, Gregory. *Psychoanalysis and Religion*. New York: Farrar, 1962.

BALTHASAR, H. Urs von. "The Freedom of the Subject," *Cross Currents*, XII (1962), 13-30.

BARUK, H. "Personality: A Psychological and Metaphysical Problem," *Philosophy Today*, I (1957), 122-27.

COPLESTON, F. "The Human Person in Contemporary Philosophy," *Philosophy*, XXV (1950), 3-19.

———. "The World, Person, and God," *Month*, XXII (1959), 22-32.

DeGEORGE, R. T. "Psychonalysis, Metaphysics and Self-Knowledge," *Proceedings of the American Catholic Philosophical Association*, XXXV (1961), 197-204.

DUHRSSEN, Alfred. "The Self and the Body," *Review of Metaphysics*, X (1956), 28-34.

FAY, C. "Human Evolution: a Challenge to Thomistic Ethics," *International Philosophical Quarterly*, II (1962), 50-80.

———. "Toward a Thomistic-Anthropological View of the Evolution of Obligation," *Natural Law Forum*, VII (1962), 38-53.

FINANCE, J. de. "Being and Subjectivity," *Cross Currents*, XII (1956), 163-78.

GEIGER, L. "Morality According to St. Thomas and Depth Psychology," *Philosophy Today*, VI (1962), 227-38.

LANIGAN, J. "Knowledges of Person Implied in the Thomistic Doctrine of Love," *Proceedings of the American Catholic Philosophical Association*, XXXI (1957), 179-87.

LÉONARD, Augustine. "Psychology and Mature Spiritual Life," *Cross and Crown*, IX (1957), 189-94.

LUYTEN, Norbert. "The Significance of The Body in a Thomistic Anthropology," *Philosophy Today*, VII (1963), 175-93.

McCOOL, G. "The Primacy of Intuition," *Thought*, XXXVII (1962), 57-73.

MULLANEY, Thomas U. "Created Personality: the Unity of Thomistic Tradition," *The New Scholasticism*, XXIX (1955), 369-402.

O'DOHERTY, E. F. "Toward a Dynamic Psychology: Freud and St. Thomas," *Studies*, XLIX (1960), 341-54.

RESAN, J. "External World and the Self," *Review of Metaphysics*, VI (1953), 539-50.

RICOEUR, Paul. "The 'Image of God' and the Epic of Man," *Cross Currents*, XI (1961), 37-50.

———. "Mass and Person," *Cross Currents*, II (1952), 59-66.

———. " 'Morality Without Sin' or Sin Without Moralism?" *Cross Currents*, V (1955), 339-52.

STEVENS, G. "Thomistic Morality and Openness to Being," *Thomist*, XXVI (1963), 67-99.

STOCK, M. "Thomistic Analysis of the Concept of Repression," *Thomist*, XXV (1962), 463-94.

VAN KAAM, A. "A Psychology of Falling-away-from-the-Faith," *Insight*, II (1963), 3-16.

VOGEL, C. J. de. "The Concept of Personality in Greek and Christian Thought," in J. Ryan, ed. *Studies in Philosophy and the History of Philosophy*, II. Washington, D.C.: Catholic Univ. of America Press, 1963. Pp. 20-60.

BRUNNER, Auguste. *La personne incarnée*. Paris: Beauchesne, 1947.

CASEL, Odo. *Vom wahren Menschenbild.* Regensburg: Pustet, 1953.

CARBONARA, Cleto. *Persona e libertà.* Napoli: Scientifica, 1959.

CHARMOT, F. *L'humanisme et l'humain.* Paris: Spes, 1934.

CROTEAU, Jacques. *Les fondements thomistes du personnalisme de Maritain.* Ottawa: Ed. de l'Univ. d'Ottawa, 1955.

DAVENPORT, Russell W. *La dignidad del hombre.* Buenos Aires: Raigal, 1957.

DERISI, O. *La Persona.* La Plata: Univ. Nacional, 1950.

DESMARAIS, Marcel. *L'amour à l'âge atomique.* Montréal: Lévrier, 1957.

GUARDINI, Romano. *Welt und Person.* Würzburg: Werkbund, 1955.

HÄCKER, Theodor. *Was ist der Mensch?* Frankfurt/M: Ullstein Taschenbücher-Verlag, 1959.

JOLIVET, Régis. *L'homme métaphysique.* Paris: Fayard, 1958.

LACROIX, Jean. *Personne et amour.* Paris: Seuil, 1956.

LUSIGNANI, Gildo. *Dignità e vocazione della persona umana.* Milano: Gioventù Italiana di Azione Cattolica, 1954.

MARTANO, Giuseppe. *Considerazioni sulla "Persona."* Napoli: Scientifica, 1958.

PENDE, Nicola. *La scienza moderna della persona umana.* Milano: Garzanti, 1949.

Qu'est-ce que l'homme? Recherches et Débats (1955).

SEMMELROTH, Otto. *Das geistliche Amt.* Frankfurt: Knecht, 1958.

SOUKUP, L. *Grundzüge einer Ethik der Persönlichkeit.* Wien: Pustet, 1951.

BRUNING, W. "Individualismo y personalismo en la imagen del hombre," *Revista de la Universidad Católica de S. Paulo,* V (1954), 49-59.

DALMAU, José M. "La analogía en el concepto de persona," *Estudios Eclesiásticos,* XXVIII (1954), 195-210.

DEBUISSON, Damien. "A la recherche de la personne," *Témoignages* (n. 52, 1955), 559-63.

DERISI, Octavio F. "Fenomenología y ontología de la persona," in *Actas del Primer Congreso Nacional de Filosofía.* Mendoza, Argentina, I (1950), 281-99.

DUQUESNE, M. "Personne et existence." *Revue des Sciences Philosophiques et Théologiques,* XXXVI (1952), 418-35; 626-55.

FABRO, C. "La verità integrale dell'uomo integrale," *Divus Thomas,* LIII (1950), 511-19.

FORTI, Edgard. "Aspects psychologiques de la reprise de soi," *Revue Philosophique de la France et de l'Etranger,* CXLVIII (1958), 223-37.

GEFFRÉ, C. J. "Structure de la personne et rapports interpersonnels," *Revue Thomiste,* LVII (1957), 672-92.

INNOCENTI, Humbertus degl'. "De actu essendi substantiali et constitutione personae," *Sapientia Aquinatis,* I (1955), 459-64.

MARC, André. "Personne, société communauté," *Revue Philosophique de Louvain,* LII (1954), 447-61.

NIETO ARTETA, Luis. "La persona humana y la vida," in *Actas del Primer Congreso Nacional de Filosofía,* Mendoza, Argentina, 1949. II, 1070-78.

PAREYSON, Luigi. "L'affermazione cristiana del concetto di persona," in *Filosofia e Cristianesimo,* LVII (1955), 253-63.

"La personnalité," *Revue Internationale de Philosophie,* X (n. 35, 1956), fasc. 1.

POZZO, Gianni M. "Il concetto di 'persona' nell'umanesimo del lavoro," *Humanitas,* VI (1951), 265-67.

QUADRI, Goffredo. "Uomo e persona," *Rivista Internazionale di Filosofia del Diritto,* XXX (1953), 51-79.

ROBILLIARD, J. A. "Personne et société," *La Vie Spirituelle,* Supplément (n. 35, 1955), 428-43.

RONCO, Albino. "Considerazioni sopra una teoria fenomenologica della personalità," *Salesianum,* XXII (1960), 326-54.

RÜFNER, V. "Sein, Person und das Absolute," *Tijdschrift voor Philosophie,* XIX (1957), 273-93.

SCIACCA, Michele. "Persona umana ed interiorita oggettiva," *Giornale di Metafisica,* VI (1951), 40-56.

STEFANINI, Luigi. "Persona e società," in *Atti del VI convegno di studi filosofici cristiani* (Gallarate, 1950). Pp. 37-66.

B. LOVE

AQUINAS, Thomas, St. *On Charity.* Milwaukee: Marquette Univ. Press, 1960.

ASHLEY, Montague. *The Meaning of Love.* New York: Julian, 1953.

BAYLEY, John. *The Characters of Love: A Study in the Literature of Personality.* New York: Collier, 1961.

BENOIT, Hubert. *The Many Faces of Love.* New York: Pantheon, 1955.

BERDIAEV, Nikolai. *The Meaning of the Creative Act.* New York: Collier, 1962.

BUBER, Martin. *I and Thou.* New York: Scribner's, 1958.

BUCKLER, R. *The Perfection of Man by Charity.* London: Blackfriars, 1954.

CARY-ELWES, Columba. *Law, Liberty, and Love.* New York: Devin-Adair, 1951.

D'ARCY, M. *The Mind and Heart of Love: A Study of Eros and Agape.* New York: Holt, 1947.

DE FERRARI, Sr. T. M. *The Problem of Charity for Self.* Washington, D.C.: The Catholic Univ. of America Press, 1962.

DIGGS, B. *Love and Being: An Investigation into the Metaphysics of St. Thomas Aquinas.* New York: Vanni, 1947.

FARAON, M. *The Metaphysical and Psychological Principles of Love.* River Forest: Albertus Magnus Institute, 1952.

FROMME, Allan. *The Ability to Love.* New York: Farrar, Straus, and Giroux, 1965.

GILLEMAN, G. *Primacy of Charity in Moral Theology.* Westminster, Md.: Newman, 1959.

GILSON, Etienne. *Wisdom and Love in St. Thomas Aquinas.* Milwaukee: Marquette Univ. Press, 1951.

GRAHAM, Aelred. *Love of God.* Garden City, N.Y.: Doubleday, 1959.

GUITTON, Jean. *Essay on Human Love.* London: Rockliff, 1951.

JOHANN, R. *The Meaning of Love.* Westminster, Md.: Newman Press, 1955.

JOHN XXIII. *Pacem in Terris.* Washington, D.C.: National Catholic Welfare Conference, 1963.

KNOX, R. *Enthusiasm.* New York: Oxford Univ. Press, 1950.

LEPP, Ignace. *The Psychology of Loving.* Baltimore: Helicon, 1963.

LEWIS, C. S. *The Four Loves.* New York: Harcourt-Brace, 1960.

McGINNIS, R. *The Wisdom of Love.* Roma: Officium Libri Cattolici, 1951.

MEHL, Roger. *Society and Love: Ethical Problems of Family Life.* Philadelphia: Westminster, 1964.

MURRY, John Middleton. *Love, Freedom, and Society.* London: Cape, 1957.

NAPOLEON, I. *Law, Love and Religion.* New York: Carlton, 1961.

NYGREN, Anders. *Agape and Eros.* Translated by P. Watson. London: S.P.C.K., 1953.

ORAISON, M. *Love or Constraint? Some Psychological Aspects of Religious Training.* New York: Paulist, 1961.

ORTEGA y GASSET, Jose. *On Love.* New York: Meridian, 1959.

PIEPER, J. *Love and Inspiration.* Translated by R. and C. Winston. London: Faber and Faber, 1965.

PRENTICE, Robert. *The Psychology of Love According to St. Bonaventure.* St. Bonaventure, N.Y.: Franciscan Institute, 1957.

ROUGEMONT, Denis de. *Love Declared: Essays on the Myths of Love*. New York: Pantheon, 1963.

————. *Love in the Western World*. New York: Pantheon, 1940.

SCHELER, Max F. *On the Eternal in Man*. New York: Harper, 1961.

TILLICH, Paul. *Love, Power, and Justice. Ontological Analyses and Ethical Applications*. New York: Oxford Univ. Press, 1960.

WILHELMSEN, Frederick. *Metaphysics of Love*. New York: Sheed and Ward, 1962.

BERTOCCI, Peter A. "Does the Concept of Christian Love Add Anything to Moral Philosophy?" *The Journal of Religion*, XXXVIII (1958), 1-11.

BRETON, S. "Metaphysics of Charity; the Thought of Laberthonnière," *Philosophy Today*, VI (1962), 295-300.

CUSHING, R. J. "Fullness of One Law Is Love," *Jurist*, XV (1955), 4-10.

FULLMAN, Christopher. "The Energetics of Love," in *The World of Teilhard*. Edited by R. T. Francoeur. Baltimore: Helicon, 1961. Pp. 146-55.

GARNETT, A. C. "Charity and Natural Law," *Ethics*, LXVI (1956), 117-22.

GLEASON, Robert. "Law and Love," *American Ecclesiastical Review*, CXXXIX (1958), 176-83.

————. "Reason and Revelation on the Subject of Charity," in *The Human Person and the World*. Edited by Baldwin Schwarz, New York: Fordham Univ. Press, 1960. Pp. 132-42.

GUITTON, Jean. "Love as an Oblation," in *Modern Catholic Thinkers*. Edited by Aloysius Caponigri. New York: Harper, 1960.

JOHANN, Robert O. "Charity and Time," *Cross Currents*, IX (1959), 140-49.

————. "Permanence and Change," *America*, CIX (1963), 359.

————. "The Problem of Love," *Review of Metaphysics,* VIII (1954), 225-45.

JOLIVET, Régis. "Neighbor: Communication to Communion," *Philosophy Today,* II (1958), 113-18.

LAVELLE, L. "In the Presence of Being," in *Modern Catholic Thinkers.* Edited by Aloysius Caponigri. New York: Harper, 1960. Pp. 43-64.

O'BRIEN, James F. "Gravity and Love as Unifying Principles," *Thomist,* XXI (1958), 184-93.

PIUS XII. "The World Community and Religious Tolerance," in *Discorsi e Radio Messagi,* XV (1953-54), 481-92.

PLÉ, A. "The Church and Charity," *Life of the Spirit,* VII (1953), 283-90.

QUITO, E. S. "The Will and Its Relation to Divine Causality and Knowledge," *Unitas,* XXIX (1956), 5-79.

RYAN, J. K. "St. Francis de Sales' THE LOVE OF GOD and the Modern World," *American Ecclesiastical Review,* CXLIX (1963), 289-92.

SCHULTZ, N. "Toward a Philosophy of Love," *Duns Scotus Philosophical Association Proceedings,* XXV (1961), 60-86.

SMITH, F. J. "Phenomenology of Encounter," *Philosophy Today,* VII (1963), 194-208.

TANER, J. "Focus for Contemporary Ethics: Love," *Thought,* XXXIX (1964), 5-19.

WALSH, John V. "Love and Philosophy," in *The Human Person and the World of Values.* Edited by Baldwin Schwarz. New York: Fordham Univ. Press, 1960. Pp. 36-48.

BUSTI, M. *Il primato della carità.* Milano: Vita e pensiero, 1960.

CARROUGES, M. *et al. L'Amour du prochain.* Paris: Cerf, 1954.

CRUZ, Tomás, de la. *El amor y su fundamento ontológico según Santo Tomás.* Roma: Angelicum, 1956.

GEIGER, L. B. *Le problème de l'amour chez Saint Thomas d'Aquin.* Montréal: Institut d'Etudes Médiévales, 1952.

GUITTON, Jean. *L'amour humain.* Paris: Aubier, 1955.

HAMM, Johann. *Die Macht der Liebe.* Luzern: Caritas-Verlag, 1950.

HÉRIS, C. *Spiritualité de l'amour.* Paris: Siloé, 1951.

LACROIX, J. *Personne et amour.* Paris: Aubier, 1943.

LEMAITRE, G. *L'amour, est-il un plaisir?* Paris: Familiales, 1957.

LINSSEN, Robert. *De l'amour humain à l'amour divin.* Lyon: Derain, 1953.

MADINIER, Gaston. *Conscience et amour.* Paris: Presses Univ. de France, 1938.

MIÉVILLE, Henri. *Condition de l'homme.* Genève: Droz, 1959.

NÉDONCELLE, M. *Vers une philosophie de l'amour et de la personne.* Paris: Aubier, 1957.

OTTENSMEYER, Hilary. *Le thème de l'amour dans l'oeuvre de Simone Weil.* Paris: Les Lettres Modernes, 1958.

OUWERKERK, C. A. J. van. *Caritas et ratio.* Nijmegen: Janssen, 1956.

PÉPIN, Adrien. *La charité envers Dieu.* Paris: Nouv. ed. latines, 1952.

PEURSEN, Cornelis van. *Leib, Seele, Geist.* Gütersloh: Mohn, 1959.

REGINA, G. *La carità e le virtù morali.* Roma: Pontificia Opera di Assistenza, 1957.

SERTILLANGES, Antonin. *L'amour chrétien.* Paris: Lecoffre, 1919.

SPICQ, C. *Agapè dans le Nouveau Testament.* 3 vols. Paris: Gabalda, 1958-60.

SUENENS, Léon. *Un problème crucial.* Bruges: Desclée, 1960.

VOLK, Hermann. *Schöpfungsglaube und Entwicklung.* Münster: Aschendorf, 1958.

WARNACH, V. *Agape; Die Liebe als Grundmotiv der neutestamentlichen Theologie.* Düsseldorf: Patmos-Verlag, 1951.

BRUNEAU, A. J. "Amour et connaissance," *Revue Thomiste,* LIV (1954), 608-13.

――――. "Réalité spirituelle de l'amour," *Revue Thomiste,* LX (1960), 381-416.

CAPORALE, V. "Il dovere e l'amore nella vita morale," *Civiltà Cattolica,* CXII (1961), 153-66.

CARPENTIER, R. "Le primat de l'amour dans la vie morale," *Nouvelle Revue Théologique,* LXXXIII (1960), 3-24, 255-71.

――――. "Vers une morale de la charité," *Gregorianum,* XXXIV (1953), 32-55.

FINANCE, J. de. "Amour, volonté, causalité," *Giornale di Metafisica,* XIII (1958), 1-22.

FLACELIERE, R. "Les Epicuriens et l'amour," *Revue des Etudes Grecques,* LXVII (1954), 69-81.

GIARDINI, Fabio. "L'essenza dell'amore," *Sapienza,* XII (1959), 35-56.

JEROME, J. "Psychologie Aristotélicienne et psychologie contemporaine de la volonté," *Vie Spirituelle,* VI (1953), 446-68.

LUIJPEN, Guillaume. "Amour et justice," in *Communicationes V. Congressus Thomistici Internationalis, Bibliotheca Pontificiae Academiae Romanae S. Thomae Aquinatis,* III (1960), 126-34.

MARCEL, Gabriel. "Notes pour une philosophie de l'amour," *Revue de Métaphysique et de Morale,* LIX (1954), 374-79.

NOTHOMB, D. "La charité fraternelle at les autres amours humains," *Revue Thomiste,* LII (1952), 361-77.

RAMIREZ, J. Roland. "L'amour de soi base de l'amour d'autrui," *Laval Théologique et Philosophique,* XIV (1958), 77-88.

RICOEUR, P. "Sympathie et respect," *Revue de métaphysique et de morale,* LIX (1954), 381-84.

VEN, J. J. M. van der. "Recht, Gerechtigkeit und Liebe," *Hochland,* XLVII (1955), 297-309.

C. GOD

BERDIAEV, N. *Slavery and Freedom.* New York: Scribner's, 1961.

COLLINS, J. *God in Modern Philosophy.* Chicago: Regnery, 1959.

DANIELOU, J. *God and the Ways of Knowing.* New York: Meridian, 1957.

D'ARCY, Martin. *No Absent God.* New York: Harper, 1962.

The Existence and Nature of God. Proceedings of the American Catholic Philosophical Association, XXIX (1954).

GILSON, Etienne. *God and Philosophy.* New Haven: Yale Univ. Press, 1959.

GREELEY, Andrew. *Strangers in the House.* New York: Sheed and Ward, 1961.

GUARDINI, Romano. *The Living God.* Translated by S. Goodman, New York: Pantheon, 1957.

HARTSHORNE, Charles. *The Divine Relativity.* New Haven: Yale Univ. Press, 1948.

————. *Man's Vision of God.* Chicago: Willett, Clark, 1941.

————, and REESE, W. L., editors. *Philosophers Speak of God.* Chicago: Univ. of Chicago Press, 1953.

HAWKINS, Denis. *The Essentials of Theism.* New York: Sheed and Ward, 1950.

HOCKING, William E. *Meaning of God in Human Experience.* New Haven: Yale Univ. Press, 1964.

HOOK, Sidney. *Religious Experience and Truth.* New York: New York Univ. Press, 1961.

JOLIVET, R. *God of Reason.* New York: Hawthorn, 1958.

JOURNET, Charles. *The Dark Knowledge of God.* Trans. by J. Anderson. New York: Sheed and Ward, 1948.

KIMPEL, B. *The Symbols of Religious Faith.* New York: Philosophical Library, 1954.

LEWIS, Hywell D. *Our Experience of God*. London: Allen and Unwin, 1959.

LUBAC, Henri de. *The Discovery of God*. Trans. by A. Dru. London: Darton, Longman and Todd, 1960.

———. *Drama of Atheistic Humanism*. New York: Meridian, 1964.

McLAUGHLIN, P. J. *Modern Science and God*. Dublin: Clonmore and Reynolds, 1952.

MARITAIN, J. *Approaches to God*. New York: Collier, 1962.

MAZZEI, Alfredo, M. *Does God Exist?* Trans. by D. Fornacca. Boston: St. Paul, 1956.

MOUROUX, Jean. *I Believe: The Personal Structure of Faith*. New York: Sheed and Ward, 1959.

New Essays in Philosophical Theology. Ed. by A. Few and A. MacIntyre. New York: Macmillan, 1955.

PICARD, Max. *The Flight From God*. Trans. by M. Kuschnitzsky and J. Cameron. Chicago: Regnery, 1951.

RAHNER, Karl. *Theological Investigations*. Baltimore: Helicon, 1961.

SHEEN, Fulton J. *God and Intelligence in Modern Philosophy*. New York: Doubleday, 1958.

SILLEM, Edward. *Ways of Thinking About God*. London: Darton, 1961.

SMART, Ninian. *Reasons and Faiths*. New York: Humanities, 1959.

TOULMIN, S.; HEPBURN, R.; and MacINTYRE, A. *Metaphysical Beliefs*. London: S.C.M. Press, 1957.

TRESMONTANT, C. *Toward the Knowledge of God*. Baltimore: Helicon, 1961.

WEIGEL, G. *Knowledge, Its Value and Limits*. New York: Prentice-Hall, 1961.

———. *Religion and the Knowledge of God*. New York: Prentice-Hall, 1961.

WHITE, Victor. *God and the Unconscious*. New York: Harper, 1956.

ZUNDEL, Maurice. *In Search of the Unknown God.* New York: Herder, 1959.

ALSTON, William P. "The Ontological Argument Revisited," *The Philosophical Review,* LXIX (1960), 452-74.

ANDERSON, James F. "Is God's Knowledge Scientific?" in *An Etienne Gilson Tribute.* Edited by Charles J. O'Neil. Milwaukee: Marquette University Press, 1959. Pp. 1-19.

ANNICE, Sr. Mary. "Logic and Mystery in the Quarta via of St. Thomas," *Thomist,* XIX (1956), 22-58.

BOBIK, J. "Some Disputable Points Apropos of St. Thomas and Metaphysics," *New Scholasticism,* XXXVII (1963), 411-30.

BOURKE, Vernon J. "Invalid Proofs for God's Existence," *Proceedings of the American Catholic Philosophical Association,* XXVIII (1954), 36-54.

COLLINS, J. D. "Analytic Theism and Demonstrative Inference," *International Philosophical Quarterly,* I (1961), 235-63.

COLLINS, Joseph P. "God's Eternal Law," *Thomist,* XXIII (1960), 497-532.

CONNOLLY, Thomas K. "The Basis of the Third Proof for the Existence of God," *The Thomist,* XVII (1954), 281-349.

DALY, C. B. "The Knowableness of God," *Philosophical Studies,* IX (1959), 90-137.

DANIELOU, J. "God and Existentialism," *Perspectives,* IV (1959), 4-9.

DESCH, Paul. "The Transcendence of God in Whitehead's Philosophy," *Philosophical Studies,* XI (1961), 7-27.

FINILI, Antoninus. "Is There a Philosophical Approach to God?" *Dominican Studies,* IV (1951), 80-101.

FITCH, R. E. "Morality Without Religion? The Inadequacies of a Humanist Ethic," *Southwest Review,* XLI (1956), 24-38.

GLASGOW, W. D. "Knowledge of God," *Philosophy,* XXXII (1957), 229-40.

GREEN-ARMYTAGE, A. H. "Argument from Design," *The Downside Review*, LXXIX (1961), 1-9.

HART, Charles A. "Participation and the Thomistic Five Ways," *The New Scholasticism*, XXVI (1952), 267-82.

HAWKINS, D. J. "What Do the Proofs of the Existence of God Purport to Do?" *The Clergy Review*, XXXVII (1952), 321-32.

JOLIVET, R. "The Problem of God in the Philosophy of Merleau-Ponty," *Philosophy Today*, VII (1963), 150-64.

KENNICK, William E. "The Language of Religion," *The Philosophical Review*, LXV (1956), 56-71.

KLUBERTANZ, G. P. "Being and God," *Modern Schoolman*, XXXII (1954), 1-17.

LINEHAN, J. "Modern Science and the Proof From Motion of the Existence of a Theistic God," *Fransciscan Studies*, XIX (1959), 128-41.

McPHERSON, Thomas. "The Argument from Design," *Philosophy*, XXXII (1957), 219-28.

McWILLIAMS, J. A. "Metaphysics of Knowledge," *Proceedings of the American Catholic Philosophical Association*, XXXV (1961), 14-20.

MARCEL, Gabriel. "Philosophical Atheism," *International Philosophical Quarterly*, II (1962), 501-14.

NASH, Peter W. "Ordinary Knowledge of God and Philosophical Demonstration," *Proceedings of the American Catholic Philosophical Association*, XXVIII (1954), 55-77.

O'CONNELL, J. "C. S. Peirce and the Problem of God," *Philosophical Studies*, VIII (1958), 24-45.

PONTIFEX, M. "The Crucial Point in the Argument for God's Existence," *Downside Review*, LXXIX (1961), 317-33.

ROCK, J. P. "The Value of the Moral Argument for God's Existence," *Proceedings of the American Catholic Philosophical Association*, XXVIII (1954), 183-94.

RYAN, Columba. "The Reach of Analogical Argument," *Dominican Studies*, IV (1951), 102-18.

RYLE, G. "Back to the Ontological Argument," *Mind*, 46 (1937) 53-57.

SALAMUCHA, J. "The Proof 'ex motu' for the Existence of God: Logical Analysis of St. Thomas' Arguments," *New Scholasticism*, XXXII (1958), 327-72.

SMITH, J. M. "Can Science Prove that God Exists?" *Heythrop Journal*, III (1962), 126-38.

————. "How Do We Prove that God Exists?" *Downside Review*, LXX (1961), 217-31.

TRETHOWAN, I. "Antimetaphysical Theology: The Status of Metaphysical Conclusions About God." *Downside Review*, LXXX (1962), 319-32.

————. "The Basis of Religion," *The Downside Review*, LXXVIII (1960), 79-92.

————. "Do We Infer God's Existence?" *The Church Quarterly Review*, CL (1950), 100-11.

WHITE, Victor and SILLEM, Edward. "The Knowledge of God," *Downside Review*, LXXVI (1958), 41-63.

WILLIAMS, C. J. "Existence and the Meaning of the Word God," *Downside Review*, LXXVII (1958), 53-71.

WINTERS, F. X. "Note on St. Augustine's View of Man's Knowledge of God During Life," *Modern Schoolman*, XXXIX (1962), 383-85.

BORNE, E. *Dieu n'est pas mort*. Paris: Fayard, 1959.

DAFFARA, M. *Dio: Esposizione e valutazione delle prove*. Torino: S.E.I., 1952.

DEFEVER, Joseph. *La preuve réelle de Dieu*. Paris: Desclée de Brouwer, 1953.

Dieu, Les Etudes Philosophiques, XIV (n.3, 1959), 275-416.

CAYRÉ, Fulbert. *Dieu présent dans la vie de l'esprit*. Paris: Desclée de Brouwer, 1951.

GARRIGOU-LAGRANGE, R. *Dieu: son existence, sa nature*. Paris: Beauchesne, 1950.

GUITTON, Jean. *Difficultés de croire*. Paris: Plon, 1960.

HORVATH, Alexander M. *Studien zum Gottesbegriff.* Freiburg: Paulusverlag, 1954.

JOLIVET, Régis. *Le dieu des philosophes et des savants.* Paris: Fayard, 1956.

LUBAC, Henri de. *Sur les chemins de Dieu.* Paris: Aubier, 1956.

MOELLER, Joseph. *Der Geist und das Absolute.* Paderborn: Schöningh, 1951.

MORE-PONTGIBAUD, Charles de. *Du fini à l'infini.* Paris: Aubier, 1957.

PIUS XII. *Le prove dell'esistenza di Dio alla luce della scienza naturale moderna.* Firenze: Fiorentina, 1951.

PRZYWARA, Eric. *Was ist Gott?* Nürnberg: Glock, 1953.

RAST, M. *Welt und Gott.* Freiburg: Herder, 1952.

SCIACCA, M. F. *L'existence de Dieu.* Trans. by R. Jolivet. Paris: Aubier, 1951.

SIEGMUND, G. *Naturordnung als Quelle der Gotteserkenntnis.* Freiburg: Herder, 1950.

SILVA TAROUCA, Amadeo van. *Praxis und Theorie des Gottesbeweises.* Wien: Herder, 1950.

STEENBERGHEN, Fernand van. *Dieu caché.* Paris: Béatrice-Nauwelaerts, 1961.

TRESMONTANT, Claude. *Essai sur la connaissance de Dieu.* Paris: Cerf, 1960.

WHITE, V. *Dieu l'inconnu.* Tournai: Casterman, 1958.

ADALBERTUS A POSTIOMA, P. "Cognitio existentiae Dei, quonam sensu dici potest omnibus naturaliter inserta," *Divus Thomas (Pi.),* LXIII (1960), 80-84.

AMERIO, Franco. "Intorno alla dimostrazione dell'esistenza di Dio," *Giornale di Metafisica,* VI (1951), 168-86.

ARATA, Carlo. "Evidenza logica ed evidenza religiosa," in *Atti del Centro di Studi Filosofici* (Gallarate, 1960). Brescia: Morcelliana, 1961. Pp. 380-88.

AUBERT, Roger. "Le Concile du Vatican et la connaissance naturelle de Dieu," *Lumière et Vie* (n. 14, 1954), 21-52.

BENDIEK, J. "Ueber ein Argument der natürlichen Theologie," *Franziskanische Studien*, XLII (1960), 130-52.

―――. "Zur logischen Struktur der Gottesbeweise," *Franziskanische Studien*, XXXVIII (1956), 1-38; 296-321.

BORNE, Etienne. "Quatre propositions sur l'athéisme," *Les Etudes Philosophiques*, XIV (1959), 275-81.

BON, H. "La connaissance scientifique de Dieu," *Pensée Catholique* (n. 28, 1953), 70-83.

BRUGGER, Walter. "La funzione significante dell'idea di 'mondo' nella scienza filosofica di Dio," *Studia Patavina*, VI (1959), 441-49.

BUSA, Roberto S. "Saggio di derivazione della Teologia naturale dalla problematica del 'Consenso Universale sulla Divinità,' " in *Miscellanea Adriano Gassana*, Milano: C. Marzorati, 1960. Pp. 329-48.

CAMPOREALE, Ignazio. "Valore assoluto e valori relativi: il contenuto dell'intuizione mistica," *Sapienza*, XIII (1960), 360-81.

CASULA, M. "L'argomento cosmologico: confutazione kantiana e contraconfutazioni scolastiche," *Gregorianum*, XXXVII (1956), 634-43.

CAYRÉ, F. "Dieu prouvé par la vie de l'esprit: avantages de cette position," *L'Année Théologique*, XII (1951), 13-24.

COLOMBO, Giuseppe. "La conoscibilità naturale di Dio nell'insegnamento del Magistero ecclesiastico," *La Scuola Cattolica*, LXXXV (1957), 325-91.

CORVEZ, M. "Foi en Dieu et connaissance naturelle de l'existence de Dieu," *Lumière et Vie* (n. 14, 1954), 9-20.

―――. "L'idée et l'affirmation de Dieu," *Revue Thomiste*, LVII (1957), 301-22.

COTTIER, M. M. "L'athéisme moderne," *Nova et Vetera*, XXXV (1960), 20-51.

CREUS VITAL, L. "Las pruebas de la existencia de Dios a la luz de la física moderna," *Cristiandad*, IX (1952), 84-85.

CRISTALDI, Mariano. "Sulla condizione religiosa," in *Atti del Centro di Studi Filosofici* (Gallarate, 1960). Pp. 449-59.

DERISI, Octavio Nicolás. "Carácter existencial de la demonstración de la existencia de Dios," *Sapientia*, VI (1951), 27-35.

DUMÉRY, Nicholas. "Foi et connaissance," *Revue Thomiste*, LX (1960), 419-24.

FAZIO ALLMAYER, Vito. "Il problema della dimostrazione dell' esistenza di Dio," *Giornale Critico della Filosofia Italiana*, 1961. Pp. 123-28.

FILLIASI CARCANO, Paolo. "Sopra la dimensione dinamica della fenomenologia religiosa," in *Atti del XV Convegno del Centro di Studi Filosofici* (Gallarate, 1960). Pp. 123-28.

FLORES D'ARCAIS, Giuseppe. "Pedagogia ed esperienza religiosa," in *Atti del Centro di Studi Filosofici* (Gallarate, 1960). Pp. 188-89.

GIACON, Carlo. "L'esperienza religiosa: illusione o verità?" in *Atti del Centro di Studi Filosofici* (Gallarate, 1960). Pp. 278-93.

GRÉGOIRE, Franz. "La preuve réelle de Dieu," *Revue Philosophique de Louvain*, LIV (1956), 112-29.

GUARDINI, Romano. "La fenomenologia dell'esperienza religiosa," in *Atti del XV Convegno del Centro di Studi Filosofici* (Gallarate 1960). Pp. 27-30.

———. "Das Phaenomen der religiösen Erfahrung" in *Atti del XV Convegno del Centro di Studi Filosofici* (Gallarate, 1960). Pp. 41-50.

GUITTON, Jean. "Dieu et le temps," *Les Etudes Philosophiques*, XIV (1959), 283-90.

———. "La psychologie de l'expérience religieuse," in *Atti del XV Convegno del Centro di Studi Filosofici* (Gallarate, 1960). Pp. 27-30.

GUZZO, Augusto. "L'esperienza religiosa vissuta," in *Atti del XV Convegno del Centro di Studi Filosofici* (Gallarate, 1960). Pp. 106-14.

HAMELIN, O. "Valeur de la preuve ontologique," *Les Etudes Philosophiques*, XII (1957), 144-50.

HARTSHORNE, Charles. "Ob göttliches Wissen um die welt-liche Existenz notwendig sein kann," *Philosophisches Jahrbuch*, LX (1950), 469-71.

INNOCENTI, H. degl'. "Animadversiones in argumentum deontologicum pro existentia Dei," in *Thomistica Morum Principia; Communicationes V Congressus Thomistici Internationalis*. Romae: Officium Libri Catholica, 1960. I, 44-47.

KEILBACH, Wilhelm. "Ist der 'historische' Gottesbeweis ein Zirkelschluss?" *Scholastik*, XXIX (1954), 506-19.

LAGAZ y LACAMBRA, Luis. "La experiencia religiosa y la experiencia jurídica," in *Atti del XV Convegno del Centro di Studi Filosofici* (Gallarate, 1960). Pp. 93-105.

LAZZARINI, Renato. "La fenomenologia dell'esperienza metafisica in relazione all'esperienza religiosa," in *Atti del XV Convegno del Centro di Studi Filosofici* (Gallarate, 1960). Pp. 51-73.

LECLERCQ, Jacques. "Preuve de Dieu et conscience de Dieu," *Lumière et Vie* (n. 14, 1954), 107-22.

LIEBHART, L. "Wege der natürlichen Gotteserkenntnis," *Theologisch-praktische Quartalschrift*, CVIII (1960) 81-94, 161-72.

LÓPEZ SALGADO, Cesáreo. "La prueba de la existencia de Dios 'por la verdad' según el Prof. Sciacca," *Sapientia*, XIV (1959), 121-35.

LOTTIN, O. "La preuve de la liberté humaine chez saint Thomas d'Aquin," *Recherches de théologie ancienne et médievale*, XXIII (1956), 323-30.

LOTZ, Giovanni B. "La filosofia dell'esperienza religiosa, *Sapienza*, XIII (1960), 568-73.

———. "Zur philosophischen Klärung der religiösen Erfahrung," in *Atti del Centro di Studi Filosofici* (Gallarate, 1960). Pp. 259-77.

MASI, Giuseppe. "Esperienza personalistica e religiosa," in *Atti del Centro di Studi Filosofici* (Gallarate, 1960). Pp. 422-25.

MASI, R. "L'esistenza di Dio alla luce della cosmogonia moderna," *Divinitas*, I (1957), 252-90.

MATHIEU, Vittorio. "L'autenticità dell'esperienza religiosa," in *Atti del Centro di Studi Filosofici* (Gallarate, 1960). Pp. 203-207.

MOREAU, Joseph. " 'Expérience' religieuse," in *Atti del Centro di Studi Filosofici* (Gallarate, 1960). Pp. 344-46.

MORRA, Gianfranco. "Il problema dell'esperienza religiosa nel neopositivismo," in *Atti del Centro di Studi Filosofici* (Gallarate, 1960). Pp. 218-28.

MOSCHETTI, A. M. "Filosofia e religione naturale, precorrimenti del 'Mistero' cristiano," in *Atti del Centro di Studi Filosofici* (Gallarate, 1960). Pp. 463-69.

MUNOZ ALONSO, Adolfo. "Experiencia religiosa y experiencia ética," in *Atti del XV Convegno del Centro di Studi Filosofici* (Gallarate, 1960). Pp. 74-77.

NABERT, Jean. "Le divin et Dieu," *Les Etudes Philosophiques,* XIV (1959), 321-32.

NAVRATIL, Michel. "La phénoménologie de l'expérience esthétique dans ses rapports avec l'expérience religieuse," in *Atti del XV Convegno del Centro di Studi Filosofici* (Gallarate, 1960). Pp. 78-92.

NÉDONCELLE, M. "Un chemin philosophique vers Dieu," *Tijdschrift voor Philosophie,* XXII (1960), 425-40.

PAGGIARO, Luigi. "L'esperienza religiosa," in *Atti del Centro di Studi Filosofici* (Gallarate, 1960). Pp. 238-43.

PAISSAC, Hyacinthe. "Existence de Dieu et connaissance habituelle," *Doctor Communis,* IV (1951), 84-90.

———. "Les preuves de Dieu," *Lumière et Vie* (n. 14, 1954), 81-106.

"Perfection de Dieu, étude de la Somme Théologique, II, q. 4, aa. 1-3," *Bulletin du Cercle Thomiste* (1951), pp. 13-19.

PHILIPPE DE LA TRINITÉ. "Les cinq voies de saint Thomas d'Aquin," *Divinitas,* II (1958), 268-338.

PIEMONTESE, Filippo. "L'esperienza religiosa e l'incomprensibilità dell'esistenza," in *Atti del XV Convegno del Centro di Studi Filosofici* (Gallarate, 1960). Pp. 229-31.

PIUS XII. "Die Gottesbeweise im Licht der modernen Natur-wissenschaft," *Universitas*, VII (1952), 1103-1109.

RAEMAEKER, L. de. "Le caractère spécial de la preuve de Dieu," in *Studi filosofici intorno all' "esistenza," al mondo, al trascendente. Analecta Gregoriana; Studi Filosofici*, LXVII. Roma: Pontificia Univ. Gregoriana, 1954. Pp. 243-56.

REDANO, Ugo. "Coscienza religiosa e situazione-limite," in *Atti del Centro di Studi Filosofici* (Gallarate, 1960). Pp. 359-63.

RINTELEN, Fritz-Joachim. "Nuove vie per la transcendenza," *Sophia*, XIX (1951), 141-59.

RIVETTI, Barbo. "La struttura logica della prima via per pro-vare l'esistenza di Dio," *Rivista di Filosofia Neo-Scolastica*, LII (1960), 241-318.

ROBERT, Jean-Dominique. "Dieu, fondement ultime du vrai scientifique," *Nouvelle Revue Théologique*, XXCII (1960), 840-51.

ROSTENNE, Paul. "Dieu sensible à l'intelligence," *La Revue Nouvelle*, XIII (1951), 100-103.

SELVAGGI, Filippo. "L'esperienza religiosa dello scienziato," in *Atti del XV Convegno del Centro di Studi Filosofici* (Gallarate, 1960). Pp. 129-33.

STEENBERGHEN, Fernand van. "Como presentar a nuestros contemporaneos la prueba de la existencia de Dios?" *Orbis Catholicus*, IV (1961), 21-37.

―――. "Sciences positives et existence de Dieu," *Revue Philoso-phique de Louvain*, LVII (1959), 397-414.

D. RELIGIOUS RENEWAL

BEDOYERE, Michael de la. *The Layman in the Church*. Lon-don: Burns, Oates and Washbourne, 1955.

BULTMANN, Rudolf. *Primitive Christianity in Its Contempo-rary Setting*. London: Thames and Hudson, 1956.

CALLAHAN, D. (ed.). *Christianity Divided; Protestant and Roman Catholic Theological Issues.* New York: Sheed and Ward, 1961.

———. *The Mind of the Catholic Layman.* New York: Scribner's, 1963.

CONGAR, Yves. *Laity, Church and World.* Baltimore: Helicon, 1961.

———. *Lay People in the Church, a Study for a Theology of the Laity.* Westminster, Md.: Newman, 1956.

———. *The Mystery of the Church,* Baltimore: Helicon, 1960.

COULSON, C. A. *Christianity in an Age of Science.* London: Oxford Univ. Press, 1953.

DANIELOU, J. *From Shadows to Reality.* Westminster, Md.: Newman, 1960.

———. *The Lord of History.* London: Longmans, 1958.

DIETRICH, S. *God's Unfolding Purpose.* Westminster, Md.: Newman, 1958.

GRAHAM, Aelred. *Catholicism and the World Today.* New York: McKay, 1952.

GUARDINI, Romano. *The End of the Modern World.* New York: Sheed and Ward, 1956.

GREELEY, Andrew. *Religion and Career.* New York: Sheed and Ward, 1961.

HARDON, Leonard, *et al. On the Authority of the Bible.* London: S.P.C.K., 1960.

HUEDON, John. *Christianity in Conflict.* Westminster, Md.: Newman, 1959.

JENKINS, Daniel. *Tradition, Freedom and the Spirit.* Philadelphia: Westminster Press, 1951.

JUNGMANN, Joseph. *Mass of the Roman Rite.* New York: Benziger, 1959.

KÜNG, Hans. *The Council: Reform and Reunion.* New York: Sheed and Ward, 1962.

LECLERCQ, Jacques. *Christians in the World.* New York: Sheed and Ward, 1961.

LOCHET, Louis. *Son of the Church*. New York: Fides, 1956.

McKENZIE, John. *The Living Church: Reflections on the Second Vatican Council*. London: Sheed and Ward, 1963.

————. *The Two-Edged Sword*. Milwaukee: Bruce, 1956.

MALONE, E. F. *Apostolic Zeal According to the Principles of St. Thomas Aquinas*. New York: Maryknoll, 1957.

RAHNER, Karl. *Free Speech in the Church*. New York: Sheed and Ward, 1959.

————. *Theological Investigations*. Baltimore: Helicon, 1961.

SCHEPERS, Maurice. *The Church of Christ*. Englewood Cliffs, N.J.: Prentice-Hall, 1963.

SCHILLEBEECKX, E. *Christ, the Sacrament of the Encounter with God*. New York: Sheed and Ward, 1963.

SLOYAN, Gerard. *Modern Catechetics; Message and Method in Religious Formation*. New York: Macmillan, 1963.

BÉVENOT, M. "Tradition, Church, and Dogma," *Heythrop Journal*, I (1960), 34-47.

CLARKE, W. Norris. "Christian Humanism for Today," *Social Order*, III (1953), 269-88.

————. "A Dialogue with Time," *Cross Currents*, I (1951), 78-90.

————. "The End of the Modern World?", *America*, XCIX (1958), 106-8.

————. "Modern World: End or Beginning?", *America*, XCIX (1958), 311-12.

DANIELOU, J. "Pluralism Within Christian Thought," *Theology Digest*, X (1962), 67-70.

DEURINCK, G. "Authority and the Laity," *Perspectives*, VI (1961), 17-19.

ELLIS, J. T. "American Catholic Laity: Role of the Laity Today," *Way*, XVIII (1962), 13-17.

GREELEY, A. M. "Psychology of Worship," *Worship*, XXXIV (1960), 118-95.

HAAS, W. P. "Phenomenology and the Sacraments," *North American Liturgical Week*, XXI (1960), 130-34.

HOVDA, R. W. "The Layman: Victim of Reaction?" *Commonweal*, LXXVI (1962), 249-52.

JOUVE, Raymond. "Two Approaches to Progress," *America*, LXXIX (1948), 387-89.

LEONARD, A. P. "Freedom of the Laity," *Perspectives*, VI (1961), 8-12.

————. "Theological Foundation of the Lay Apostolate," *Thomist*, XXVII (1963), 284-306.

McNALLY, R. E. "Crisis and Criticism in the Church," *America*, CVII (1962), 1088-90.

MESSNER, Johannes. "Freedom as a Principle of Social Order," *Modern Schoolman*, XXVIII (1951), 97-110.

MOULD, D. D. "St. Thomas and the Apostolate," *Furrow*, X (1959), 643-54.

O'GARA, J. "Theology of the Laity: Need to Define their Function," *Critic*, XXI (1962), 15-18.

O'MALLEY, F. "The Thinker in the Church; the Spirit of Newman," *Review of Politics*, XXI (1959), 5-23.

L'ascèse chrétienne et l'homme contemporain. Paris: Cerf, 1951.

FOLLIET, Joseph. *Le catholicisme mondial aujourd'hui*. Paris: Cerf, 1958.

Les intellectuelles dans la chrétienté. Rome: Pax Romana, 1949.

LABOURDETTE, M. *Foi catholique et problèmes modernes*. Paris: Desclée, 1954.

LECLERCQ, Jacques. *Christliche Moral in der Krise der Zeit*. Einsiedeln-Köln: Benziger Verlag, 1954.

MARC, André. *Raison et conversion chrétienne*. Bruges: Desclée de Brouwer, 1961.

TIBERGHIEN, P. *Sens chrétien et vie sociale*. Paris: Ouvrières, 1954.

AUBERT, R. "Discussions récentes autour de la théologie de l'histoire," *Collectanea Mechliniensia*, XVIII (1948), 129-49.

BOUYER, L. "Christianisme et eschatologie," *La Vie Intellectuelle*, XVI (1948), 6-38.

BRUNELLO, Bruno. "Religione e sociologia," in *Atti del Centro di Studi Filosofici* (Gallarate, 1960). Pp. 232-37.

DANIELOU, Jean. "Christianisme et histoire," *Etudes*, CCLIV (1947), 166-84.

———. "Christianisme et progrès," *Etudes*, CCV (1947), 399-402.

MALEVEZ, L. "La vision chrétienne de l'histoire: II. Dans la théologie catholique," *Nouvelle Revue Théologique*, LXXI (1949), 244-64.

E. ECUMENISM

BAUM, Gregory. *Progress and Perspectives*. New York: Sheed and Ward, 1962.

———. *That They May Be One*. Westminster, Md.: Newman, 1958.

BELL, George. *Documents on Christian Unity*. New York: Oxford Univ. Press, 1948.

CONWAY, John. *Time of Decision*. Notre Dame, Indiana: Fides, 1962.

DOTY, W. *Trends and Counter Trends Among American Catholics*. St. Louis: Herder, 1962.

DUMONT, Christopher. *Approaches to Christian Unity*. Translated by Henry St. John. Baltimore: Helicon Press, 1959.

LECLERC, Joseph. *Toleration and the Reformation*. New York: Association Press, 1960.

LEEMING, Bernard. *The Churches and the Church; a Study of Ecumenism*. Westminster, Md.: Newman, 1960.

LUBAC, Henri de. *Catholicism. A Study of Dogma in Relation to the Corporate Destiny of Mankind*. New York: Sheed and Ward, 1958.

MINEAR, Paul. (ed.) *The Nature of the Unity We Seek*. St. Louis: Bethany, 1958.

ONG, W. *American Catholic Crossroads; Religious-Secular Encounters in the Modern World*. New York: Collier, 1962.

ST. JOHN, Henry. *Essays In Christian Unity*. Westminster, Md.: Newman, 1955.

SUENENS, Léon J. *The Gospel to Every Creature*. Translated by L. G. Duffy. Westminster, Md.: Newman, 1957.

TAVARD, Georges H. *Two Centuries of Ecumenism*. Translated by R. W. Hughes. Notre Dame, Ind.: Fides, 1960.

TAYLOR, Sherwood, *et al*. *The Spirit of Unity*. London: Blackfriars, 1950.

THORMAN, D. *The Emerging Layman*. Garden City, N.Y.: Doubleday, 1962.

TODD, John, M. *Catholicism and the Ecumenical Movement*. New York: Longmans, 1956.

VILLAIN, Maurice. *Unity; A History and Some Reflections*. Translated by J. R. Foster. Baltimore: Helicon, 1963.

WEIGEL, G. and BROWN, R. M. *An American Dialogue*. Garden City, N.Y.: Doubleday, 1960.

————. *Faith and Understanding in America*. New York: Macmillan, 1959.

WHITE, Victor. *God and the Unconscious*. Cleveland: World, 1961.

BROWN, R. M. "Rules for the Dialogue," *Commonweal*, LXXI (1960), 563-66.

COLLINS, J. "The Philosopher's Responsibility," *America*, CII (1959), 188-89.

COWLEY, R. "The Causes of the World Ecumenical Movement," *Thomist*, XXVII (1963), 551-69.

DUFF, E. "Church and State in the American Environment: An Historical and Legal Survey," *Studies*, XLIX (1960), 229-48.

EUSTACE, C. J. "Catholics and Protestants in a Secularized World," *Culture*, XXI (1960), 13-31.

GALLAGHER, D. "The Task of the American Catholic Philosopher in a Pluralistic Society," *Proceedings of the American Catholic Philosophical Society*, XXXVII (1963), 1-15.

GRISEZ, G. "Toward a Metaphilosophy; How to Explain Lack of Consensus Among Philosophers," *Proceedings of the*

American Catholic Philosophical Association, XXXVII (1963), 47-70.

HANELL, P. J. "The Ecumenical Movement; a Survey," *Irish Ecclesiastical Review,* XCVI (1961), 356-74.

HOWELL, C. "Select Bibliography on Ecumenism," *Worship,* XXXIII (1959), 551-60.

MAGUIRE, J. J. "New Look in Comparative Religion," *Perspectives,* V (1960), 8-10.

O'DEA, T. F. "Ideologists and the Missing Dialog: Catholic-Protestant Issues in the United States," *Catholic Mind,* LVII (1959), 392-98.

PIEPER, J. "Concept of Tradition," *Theology Digest,* VIII (1960), 3-7.

ROTENSTREICH, N. "Some Problems in Buber's Dialogical Philosophy," *Philosophy Today,* III (1959), 151-67.

ST. JOHN, H. "Ecumenical Survey," *Blackfriars,* XLII (1961), 25-29.

———. "The Laity and Ecumenism," *Thomist,* XXVII (1963), 307-16.

SIMON, Y. R. "Common Good and Common Action," *Review of Politics,* XXII (1960), 202-44.

STEPHENSON, A. "Notes on Recent Work: Ecumenical Writing," *Clergy Review,* XLVII (1962), 29-33.

TAVARD, G. "Laity and Ecumenism," *Perspectives,* VIII (1963), 4-8.

THALHAMMER, D. "Christian Maturity; Qualities of the Layman," *Cross and Crown,* XIV (1962), 29-34.

———. "The Layman in Modern Times," *Cross and Crown,* XII (1960), 281-91.

WRIGHT, J. J. "The Church and the Intellectual," *Catholic Mind,* LVIII (1960), 518-20.

AUBERT, Roger. *Problèmes de l'unité chrétienne.* Chevetogne: Chevetogne, 1953.

BOYER, Charles. *Unus pastor.* Toulouse: Apos. de la prière, 1951.

CADIER, J., *et al. Unité chrétienne et tolérance religieuse.* Paris: Temps Présent, 1950.

CONGAR, Yves. *Vraie et fausse réforme dans l'Eglise.* Paris: Cerf, 1950.

KARRER, Otto. *Um die Einheit der Christen; die Petrusfrage.* Frankfurt: Knecht, 1953.

PHILIPS, Gérard and MOELLER, Charles. *Grâce et oecuménisme.* Chevetogne: Chevetogne, 1958.

ROGER, Aubert *et al. Tolérance et communauté humaine.* Paris: Casterman, 1952.

SCHMIDT, Hermann, *Brückenschlag zwischen den Konfessionen.* Paderborn: Schöningh, 1951.

SARTORY, Thomas. *Die ökumenische Bewegung und die Einheit der Kirche.* Meitungen: Kyrios, 1955.

VILLAIN, Maurice. *Introduction à l'oecuménisme.* Paris: Casterman, 1958.

CHAPTER V

The Problem of God in a Secular Culture

This chapter comprises selected books and articles on the meaning of religion, especially as related to the secular, the natural, and the profane. This problem area has a long history when considered in terms of the variegating influence of cultures on religious expression. Recently, however, the problem has been posed in the more radical terms of whether religion is a positive or destructive factor in man's cultural development. In order to focus on this later statement of the problem, the chapter has been divided into nine sections:

A. The Problem of God
B. Contemporary Atheism and the Death of God
C. Reality and the Existence of God
D. Divine Immanence and Transcendence
E. Religion and Philosophy of Religion
F. Culture and Religion
G. Christian Thought
H. Scientific Naturalism and Humanism
I. The Religious and the Secular

Also, pertinent to these issues are Chapters I, II, III E, and IV C of this volume and Chapters VIII and XVII of *An Annotated Bibliography of Philosophy in Catholic Thought* by the same editor.

A. THE PROBLEM OF GOD

BURKILL, T. A. *God and Reality in Modern Thought.* Englewood Cliffs, N. J.: Prentice-Hall, 1963.

COLLINS, James. *God in Modern Philosophy*. Chicago: Regnery, 1959.

D'ARCY, Martin. *No Absent God*. New York: Harper and Row, 1962.

DUMERY, H. *The Problem of God in Philosophy of Religion*. Evanston, Ill.: Northwestern Univ. Press, 1964.

GILSON, Etienne. *God and Philosophy*. Fairlawn, N. J.: Oxford Univ. Press, 1960.

GORNALL, T. *A Philosophy of God*. New York: Sheed and Ward, 1962.

HAMMOND, Guyton B. *A Comparison of the Thought of Paul Tillich and Erich Fromm*. Nashville, Tenn.: Vanderbilt Univ. Press, 1965.

KARRER, Otto. *The Kingdom of God Today*. New York: Herder and Herder, 1964.

KREYCHE, Robert L. *God and Contemporary Man: Reflections of a Christian Philosopher*. Milwaukee, Wisc.: Bruce, 1965.

MARTY, M. E. *The New Shape of American Religion*. New York: Harper, 1959.

MURRAY, John C. *The Problem of God, Yesterday and Today*. New Haven, Conn.: Yale Univ. Press, 1964.

PATON, H. *The Modern Predicament*. New York: Collier, 1962.

ROBINSON, John A. *The New Reformation*. Philadelphia: Westminster, 1965.

ADLER, Mortimer. "God and Modern Man," *Critic*, XXV (1966), 18-23.

ALVAREZ TURIENZO, S. "Absence of God and Man's Insecurity," *Philosophy Today*, III (1959), 135-39.

ANTOINE, R. "Bridging the Gulf: Christian and Gnostic," *Clergy Monthly Supplement*, III (1956), 18-29.

BAKER, A. E. "A Theology for Today," *Religion in Education*, XXVI (1958), 18-21.

BERTOCCI, P. "An Impasse in Philosophical Theology," *International Philosophical Quarterly*, V (1965), 379-96.

COBB, John B., Jr. "From Crisis Theology to the Post-Modern World," *The Centennial Review*, VIII (1964), 174-88.

"The Council and the Problems of the Age," *Herder Correspondence*, II (1965), 57-62.

DOUGHERTY, J. "The Metaphysical Roots of Contemporary Restlessness," *Proceedings of the American Catholic Philosophical Association*, XXXVII (1963), 187-96.

EDIE, James M. "The Absence of God," in *Christianity and Existentialism*. Edited by John Wild. Evanston, Ill.: Northwestern Univ. Press, 1963. Pp. 113-48.

EDWARDS, David. "A New Reformation," *London Quarterly and Holborn Review*, XXXIII (1964), 257-66.

FACKENHEIM, Emil. "On the Eclipse of God," *Commentary*, XXXVII (1964), 55-60.

HAZELTOP, Roger. "The Future of God," *Andover Newton Quarterly*, VI (1966), 7-14.

HOLLON, Ellis, Jr. "Beware the Antithesis!" *Christian Century*, LXXXIII (1966), 303-4.

JELLEMA, D. W. "Towards Investigating the Post-Modern Mind," *Journal for the Scientific Study of Religion*, III (1963), 81-85.

JENKINS, Daniel. "Religion and Coming of Age," in *The Honest to God Debate*. Edited by D. Edwards. Philadelphia: Westminster, 1963. Pp. 207-14.

LACHS, John. "Two Concepts of God," *The Harvard Theological Review*, LIX (1966), 227-40.

MARTINDALE, C. "Another Reformation," *Month*, XII (1954), 35-41.

MURRAY, J. "Challenge to Religion": A Review of THE MODERN PREDICAMENT, by H. J. Paton, *Clergy Review*, XLI (1956), 594-606.

———. "On the Structure of the Problem of God: Historical Analytical Summary," *Theological Studies*, XXIII (1962), 1-26.

NORRIS, Richard A. "The Existentialist Veto," *Religion in Life*, XXX (1961), 513-20.

PARKER, Francis H. "Head, Heart, and God," *Review of Metaphysics*, XXIII (1960-61), 328-52.

RYAN, M. P. "Problem of God in the World Today": A Review of SCIENCE, RELIGION, AND CHRISTIANITY, *Worship*, XXXIV (1959), 9-19.

STEVENSON, J. C. "Contemporary Views on the Doctrine of God," *Canadian Journal of Theology*, X (1964), 237-47.

BALTHASAR, H. Urs Von. *Dieu et l'homme d'aujourd'hui.* Bruges: Desclée de Brouwer, 1958.

DANIELOU, J. *Le problème de Dieu et l'existentialisme.* Montréal: Collège Jean-de-Brébeuf, 1960.

DELANGLADE, Jean. *Le problème de Dieu.* Paris: Aubier, 1960.

FLUKE, Otto. *Der letzte Gott.* Hamburg: Rütten und Heoning, 1961.

HENRICH, D. *Der ontologische Gottesbeweis: sein Problem und seine Geschichte in der Neuzeit.* Tübingen: Mohr, 1960.

KRIKOWSKI, Johannes. *Wer macht die Götter.* Wuppertal: Aussaat, 1963.

SCIACCA, Michele F. *Le problème de Dieu et de la religion dans la philosophie contemporaine.* Paris: Aubier, 1950.

COLOMBO, C. "Lo studio teologico del problema di Dio," *La Scuola Cattolica*, LXXXIV (1956), 32-60.

ECOLE, J. "Le problème de Dieu dans la philosophie de M. Sartre," *Giornale di Metafisica*, XIII (1958), 606-18.

FABRO, C. "Il problema di Dio: introduzione al problema teologico," in *Problemi e orientamenti di teologia dommatica.* Milano: Mazorati, 1957. Vol. II, 1-64.

JONAS, Hans. "Gnosis und Moderner Nihilismus," *Kerygma und Dogma*, VI (1960), 155-71.

LE BLOND, J. "L'Aspect social du problème de Dieu," *Etudes*, CCLXXXIV (1955), 3-17.

PANNEBERG, W. "Die Frage nach Gott," *Evangelische Theologie*, XXV (1965), 238-62.

PRUCHE, B. "Absence et silence de Dieu dans le monde con-temporain," *Revue de l'Université d'Ottawa,* XXVIII (1958), 145-79.

RAHNER, Karl. "Die Wirklichkeit Gottes und das heutige Weltbild," *Universitas,* XVIII (1963), 263-72.

REDANO, Ugo. "Coscienza religiosa e situazione-limite," in *Atti del centro di studi filosofici* (Gallarate, 1960). Brescia: Morcelliana, 1961. Pp. 359-63.

SCHINDLER, A. "Kann der moderne Mensch an die Existenz Gottes glauben?" *Reformatio,* XIII (1964), 139-52.

B. CONTEMPORARY ATHEISM AND THE DEATH OF GOD

ALTIZER, Thomas J. *The Gospel of Christian Atheism.* Philadelphia: Westminster, 1966.

————, and HAMILTON, William. *Radical Theology and the Death of God.* New York: Bobbs-Merrill, 1966.

BAUMER, F. L. *Religion and the Rise of Scepticism.* New York: Harcourt, Brace, 1960.

BELL, Bernard I. *God Is Not Dead.* New York: Harper, 1945.

BORNE, Etienne. *Atheism.* New York: Hawthorn, 1961.

FARRER, Austin. *God Is Not Dead.* New York: Morehouse-Barlow, 1966.

FITZGIBBON, John P. *A Survey of Modern Atheism in the Light of Thomistic Philosophy.* Washington, D. C.: The Catholic Univ. of America Press, 1950.

HAMILTON, Kenneth. *God Is Dead: The Anatomy of a Slogan.* Grand Rapids, Mich.: Eerdmans, 1966.

KOCH, Hans. *The Abolition of God: Materialistic Atheism and the Christian Religion.* Philadelphia: Fortress, 1964.

LACROIX, Jean. *The Meaning of Modern Atheism.* New York: Macmillan, 1965.

LEPP, Ignace. *Atheism in Our Time.* Translated by B. Murchland. New York: Macmillan, 1963.

LILJE, Hanns. *Atheism, Humanism and Christianity.* Minneapolis, Minn.: Augsburg, 1965.

LUIJPEN, W. *Phenomenology and Atheism.* Pittsburgh: Duquesne Univ. Press, 1964.

MARTY, Martin. *Varieties of Unbelief.* New York: Holt, Rinehart, 1964.

MATSON, Wallace I. *The Existence of God.* Ithaca, N. Y.: Cornell Univ. Press, 1965.

MILLER, Joseph H. *The Disappearance of God: Five Nineteenth-Century Writers.* Cambridge, Mass.: Harvard Univ. Press, 1963.

MORRIS, Leon. *The Abolition of Religion.* Chicago: Inter-Varsity, 1964.

PELZ, Werner. *God Is No More.* Philadelphia: Lippincott, 1964.

PHILLIPS, J. B. *Your God Is Too Small.* New York: Macmillan, 1961.

ROBINSON, Richard. *An Atheist's Values.* Oxford: Clarendon, 1964.

VAHANIAN, G. *The Death of God: The Culture of Our Post Christian Era.* New York: Braziller, 1961.
———. *Wait Without Idols.* New York: Braziller, 1964.

ALEXANDER, W. M. "Death of God or God of Death," *Christian Century,* LXXXIII (1966), 363-65.

ALTIZER, Thomas J. "Creative Negation in Theology," *Christian Century,* LXXXII (1965), 864-67.
———. "Theology and the Death of God," *The Centennial Review,* VIII (1964), 129-46.

ARMSTRONG, C. B. "Christianity Without Religion," *Church Quarterly Review,* CLXV (1964), 175-84.

BALLARD, E. G. "Use for Atheism in Ethics," *Journal of Religion and Health,* II (1963), 150-55.

BLOMME, Robert. "My Brother, the Unbeliever," *Lumen vitae,* XVI (1961), 417-25.

CAIRNS, Dorion. "Can a Truly Contemporary Person Not Be an Atheist?" *The Expository Times*, LXXXVII (1966), 296-300.

CAMUS, Albert. "The Unbeliever and Christians," in *Resistance, Rebellion and Death*. New York: Knopf, 1961. Pp. 51-56.

CHENU, M. D. and HEER, F. "Is the Modern World Atheist," *Cross Currents*, XI (1961), 5-24.

COPLESTON, F. "An Atheist's Values," *Heythrop Journal*, V (1964), 402-9.

EARLE, William. "Man Is the Impossibility of God," in *Christianity and Existentialism*. W. Earle, *et al.* Evanston, Ill.: Northwestern Univ. Press, 1963. Pp. 66-87.

————. "The Paradox and the Death of God," in *Christianity and Existentialism*. W. Earle, *et al.* Evanston, Ill.: Northwestern Univ. Press, 1963. Pp. 88-112.

EDIE, James M. "The Absence of God," in *Christianity and Existentialism*. W. Earle, *et al.* Evanston, Ill.: Northwestern Univ. Press, 1963. Pp. 113-48.

FENNELL, W. "Religion *post mortem Dei*," *Canadian Journal of Theology*, IX (1963) 287-89.

GILKEY, Langdon. " 'Is God Dead?' and 'God Is Not Dead,' " *The Voice*, LVII (1965), 4-11.

HERTZBERG, Arthur. "Jews and the Death of God," *Christianity and Crisis*, XXVI (1966), 8.

JEANNIERE, Abel. "Atheism Today," *Cross Currents*, XVI (1966), 1-14.

————. "Faith and Atheism Today," *Cross Currents*, XVI (1966), 1-13.

LE BLOND, J. M. "The Christian and Modern Atheism," *Theology Digest*, III (1955), 139-43.

McLAUGHLIN, J. "Atheism and Anti-Theism": Discussion of DRAMA OF ATHEIST HUMANISM by H. de Lubac, *Catholic Mind*, XLIX (1951), 318-25.

MARCEL, G. "Philosophical Atheism," *International Philosophical Quarterly*, II (1962), 501-14.

MARITAIN, Jacques. "On the Meaning of Contemporary Atheism," *The Review of Politics*, XI (1949), 267-80.

MOULTON, Warren L., *et al.* "Death of God: Four Views," *Christian Century*, LXXXII (1965), 1412-13.

PADOVANO, Anthony T. "God: Dead or Alive?" *Ave Maria*, CIV (1966), 22-23.

PFEIL, H. "Modern Denial of God: Its Origin and Tragedy," *Philosophy Today*, III (1959), 19-26.

RAMSEY, P. "No Morality Without Immorality: Dostoevski and the Meaning of Atheism," *Journal of Religion*, XXXVI (1956), 90-108.

RICKMAN, H. P. "The Death of God": A Discussion of Sartre's THE FLIES, *Hibbert Journal*, LIX (1961), 220-26.

THIELICKE, H. "Can the Church and Atheism Coexist?" *Theology Today*, XXI (1964), 108-11.

TROTTER, F. Thomas. "Variations on the 'Death of God' Theme in Recent Theology," *Journal of Bible and Religion*, XXXIII (1965), 42-48.

VAHANIAN, G. "Beyond the Death of God," *Dialog*, I (1962), 18-21.

———. "Kafka and the Atheist's Problem of God," *Hartford Quarterly*, IV (1964), 65-76.

———. "Swallowed Up by Godlessness," *Christian Century*, LXXXII (1965), 1505-7.

VAN BUREN, Paul. "The Dissolution of the Absolute," *Religion in Life*, XXXIV (1965), 334-42.

WILLIAMS, Boniface A. "The Death of God Phenomena," *Catholic World*, CCIV (1966), 17-19.

BISER, E. *Gott ist tot. Nietzsches Destruktion des christlichen Bewussteins.* München: Kösel, 1962.

COFFY, R. *Dieu des athées: Marx, Sartre, Camus.* Lyon: Chronique Sociale de France, 1965.

FABRO, C. *Introduzione all'ateismo moderno.* Roma: Studium, 1964.

FURSTENBERG, E. Von. *Der Selbstwiderspruch des philosophischen Atheismus.* Regensburg: Habbel, 1960.

GARAUDY, R. *Dieu est mort: étude sur Hegel.* Paris: P.U.F., 1962.

JUCHEN, Aurel Von. *Gespräch mit Atheisten.* Kirch um Mann: Gütersloh, 1962.

LACROIX, J. *Le sens de l'athéisme moderne.* Tournai: Casterman, 1958.

―――. *Wege des heutigen Atheismus.* Freiburg im Breisgau: Herder, 1960.

LUBAC, Henri de. *Le drame de l'humanisme athée.* Paris: Union Générale, 1963.

MARITAIN, Jacques. *La signification de l'athéisme contemporain,"* Paris: Desclée de Brouwer, 1949.

MAURIS, E. *et al. L'athéisme contemporain.* Genève: Labor et Fides, 1956.

MULLER-SCHWEFE, H. *Atheismus.* Stuttgart: Kreuz, 1962.

OLESCHTSCHUK, F. N. *Atheismus.* Berlin: Dietz, 1955.

PATTE, D. *L'athéisme d'un chrétien ou un chrétien à l'écoute de Sartre.* Paris: Nouvelles Éditions Latines, 1965.

PFEIL, H. *Der atheistische Humanismus der Gegenwart.* Zurich: Christiana, 1959.

REDING, M. *Der politische Atheismus.* Köln, Styria, 1957.

SOLIE, Dorothée. *Stellvertretung: ein kapitel theologie nach dem "Tode Gottes."* Stuttgart: Kreuz, 1965.

SZCZESNY, G. *Die Zukunft des Unglaubens.* München: List, 1959.

VERNEAUX, R. *Leçons sur l'athéisme contemporaine.* Paris: Téqui, 1964.

VEUILLOT, M. *L'athéisme: tentation du monde, réveil des chrétiens?* Paris: Cerf, 1963.

BABOLIN, A. "Il problema dell' ateismi," *Giornale de Metafisica*, XVII (1962), 280-94.

BISER, E. "Was besagt Nietzsches These 'Gott ist tot'?" *Wissenschaft und Weisheit*, XXV (1962), 48-63.

BORNE, E. "Quatre propositions sur l'athéisme," *Études Philosophiques*, XIV (1959), 275-81.

COTTIER, M. M. "L'athéisme moderne. Brève esquisse historique," *Nova et Vetera*, XXXV (1960), 20-51.

DONDEYNE, A. "L'athéisme contemporain et le problème des attributs de Dieu," *Ephemerides Theologicae Lovanienses*, XXXVII (1961), 462-80.

ETCHEVERRY, A. "Physionomie nouvelle de l'athéisme," *Bulletin de Littérature Ecclésiastique*, LXIV (1963), 269-83.

FABRO, C. "L'ateismo contemporaneo," *Il Fuoco*, VII (1959), 44-46.

―――. "L'ateismo costruttivo come caratteristica della irreligiosito contemporanea," *Euntes Docete*, XIII (1960), 3-39.

―――. "Le fondement théorique de l'athéisme contemporain," *Sciences Ecclésiastiques*, XIV (1962), 351-74.

GIRARDI, Jules. "Athéisme et théisme: face au problème de la valeur absolue de l'homme," *Doctor Communis*, XVIII (1965), 93-111.

JOLIF, Jean. "Remarques sur la signification philosophique de l'athéisme," in *L'existence de Dieu* (*Cahiers de l'actualité religieuse*, N. 16). Paris: Casterman, 1961. Pp. 13-18.

KAYAYAN, A. "Dieu sans Dieu," *Etudes Evangéliques*, XXIV (1964), 118-28.

LOTZ, J. "Alcuni aspetti positivi nel problema dell'ateismo," *Humanitas*, XVII (1962), 193-207.

MONTULL, T. "Anti-teismo en Sartre," *La Ciencia Tomista*, LIII (1962), 69-138.

―――. "El ateismo de Merleau-Ponty," *La Ciencia Tomista*, XLIV (1963), 115-18.

MULLER, G. "Der Mythos vom 'religionslosen' Menschen," *Lutherische Monatshefte*, III (1964), 573-76.

MUNOZ-ALONSO, A. "Il fenomeno dell'ateismo," *Humanitas*, XVII (1962), 111-18.

PRINI, Pietro. "Esperienza religiosa, ateismo e comunicazione," in *Atti del centro di studi filosofici* (Gallarate, 1960). Brescia: Morcelliana, 1961. Pp. 120-22.

RIDEAU, Emile. "La crise de la conscience contemporaine," *Nouvelle Revue Théologique*, LXXXI (1959), 251-71.

THIELICKE, Helmut. "Studie zum Atheismus Problem," *Zeitschrift für Evangelische Ethik*, IV (1960), 129-36.

THIER, E. "Zum politischen Atheismus," *Archiv für Rechts- und Sozialphilosophie*, XLV (1959), 103-10.

VANCOURT, R. "Religion naturelle et passé religieux de l'humanité," *Mélanges de Science Religieuse*, XXI (1964), 15-31.

WESTERMANN, C. "Die Illusion des Atheismus. Über das Phänomen der elementaren Verwurzelung des Menschen in Gott," *Zeitwende*, XXXIV (1963), 91-100.

C. REALITY AND THE EXISTENCE OF GOD

GANSER, Geoffrey. *Contemporary Materialism and the Existence of God*. Washington, D. C.: The Catholic Univ. of America Press, 1963.

GLEASON, R. W. *The Search for God*. New York: Sheed and Ward, 1965.

GOLLWITZER, Helmut. *The Existence of God as Confessed by Faith*. Translated by James Leitch. Philadelphia: Westminster, 1965.

LEWIS, H. D. *Our Experience of God*. New York: Macmillan, 1959.

MATSON, Wallace I. *The Existence of God*. Ithaca, N. Y.: Cornell Univ. Press, 1965.

MAZZEI, Alfredo M. *Does God Exist?* Translated by D. Fornacca. New York: Society of St. Paul, 1956.

O'BRIEN, Thomas C. *Metaphysics and the Existence of God*. Washington, D. C.: Thomist, 1960.

WEISS, Paul. *The God We Seek*. Carbondale, Ill.: Southern Illinois Univ. Press, 1964.

WHITTAKER, Edmund T. *Space and Spirit: Theories of the Universe and the Arguments for the Existence of God*. London: Nelson, 1947.

APALEK, John C. "Being and God," *Pacific Philosophy Forum*, V (1966), 2-56.

BALTHASAR, Hans Urs Von. "The Christian's Forgetfulness of God," *Theology Digest*, XIV (1966), 155-60.

FRIEND, J. A. "Can We Use the Proofs Today?" *Reformed Theological Review*, XXI (1962), 75-82.

LINEHAN, J. "Modern Science and the Proof from Motion of the Existence of a Theistic God," *Franciscan Studies*, XIX (1959), 128-41.

McLAUGHLIN, P. J. "Contemporary Approach to Demonstrating the Existence of God," *Irish Theological Quarterly*, XXXI (1964), 322-27.

NASH, P. "Ordinary Knowledge of God and Philosophical Demonstration," *Proceedings of the American Catholic Philosophical Association*, XXVIII (1964), 55-75.

PLATT, David. "Some Perplexities Concerning God's Existence," *The Journal of Bible and Religion*, XXXIV (1966), 244-52.

SILLEM, E. A. "The Alleged 'Massive Obstacle' of the Syllogism in Demonstrating the Existence of God," *Irish Theological Quarterly*, XXXI (1964), 150-59.

SMART, J. J. C. "Existence of God," *Church Quarterly Review*, CLVI (1955), 178-94.

TAUBES, S. A. "Absent God," *Journal of Religion*, XXV (1955), 6-16.

TRETHOWAN, J. "On Demonstrating God's Existence: A Reply to Father Sillem," *Irish Theological Quarterly*, XXXI (1964), 328-32.

BIRAULT, Henri, *et al*. *L'existence de Dieu*. Tournai: Casterman, 1963.

COURTOIS, R. *Des savants nous parlent de Dieu.* Bruxelles: Foyer Notre-Dame, 1958.

L'existence de Dieu (Cahiers de l'actualité religieuse, N. 16). Tournai: Casterman, 1961.

ROBERT, Jean D. *Approche contemporaine d'une affirmation de Dieu.* Bruges: Desclée de Brouwer, 1962.

STEENBERGHEN, Fernand Van. *Dieu caché: comment savons-nous que Dieu existe?* Louvain: Publications Universitaires, 1961.

CORVEZ, M. "L'idée et l'affirmation de Dieu," *Revue Thomiste,* LVII (1957), 301-25.

CRISTALDI, Giuseppe. "Il principio di verifica e l'esistenza di Dio," *Giornale di Metafisica,* XXI (1966), 31-34.

EBELING G. "Existenz zwischen Gott und Gott," *Zeitschrift für Theologie und Kirche,* LXII (1965), 86-113.

FELLERMEIER, J. "Der Beweis der Existenz Gottes aus der Kontingenz der Welt," *Münchener Theologische Zeitschrift,* X (1959), 289-94.

GILSON, E. "L'être et Dieu," *Revue Thomiste,* LVII (1962), 181-202, 398-416.

GIULIANO, Balbino. "Il problema metafisico e la dimostrazione di Dio," in *Atti del IV Convegno di Studi Filosofici.* Padova: Liviana, 1949. Pp. 70-92.

LEONARD, Augustin-Pierre. "Religion et philosophie en face de l'existence de Dieu," *Revue des Sciences Philosophiques et Théologiques,* L (1966), 51-66.

PETTER, Dominique de. "Le caractère métaphysique de la preuve de l'existence de Dieu et la pensée contemporaine," in *L'existence de Dieu (Cahiers de l'actualité religieuse,* N. 16). Paris: Casterman, 1961. Pp. 167-78.

PIRLOT, J. "La découverte de Dieu," *Mélanges de Science Religieuse,* XIV (1957), 198-212.

RINIKER, H. "Die Existenz Gottes," *Kirchenblatt für die reformierte Schweiz,* CXIX (1963), 322-26.

ROQUEPLO, P. "Approches contemporaines d'une affirmation de Dieu," *Revue des Sciences Philosophiques et Théologiques,* XLVIII (1964), 205-32.

STEENBERGHEN, F. Van. "Sciences positives et existence de Dieu," *Revue Philosophique de Louvain,* LVII (1959), 397-414.

D. DIVINE IMMANENCE AND TRANSCENDENCE

BARTH, K. *God Here and Now.* New York: Harper and Row, 1964.

DANIELOU, Jean. *The Presence of God.* Baltimore, Md.: Helicon, 1959.

D'ARCY, Martin C. *No Absent God: The Relations Between God and the Self.* New York: Harper and Row, 1962.

EDWARDS, David L. (ed.) *The Honest to God Debate.* London: SCM, 1963.

FARLEY, Edward. *Transcendence of God.* Philadelphia: Westminster, 1960.

GUELLUY, Robert. *Christian Commitment to God and to the World.* Translated by M. Bouchard. New York: Desclée, 1965.

PAGE, Robert J. *New Directions in Anglican Theology: A Survey from Temple to Robinson.* New York: Seabury, 1965.

ROBINSON, John A. *Honest to God.* Philadelphia: Westminster, 1963.

ROUTLEY, E. *The Man for Others: An Important Contribution to the Discussion Inspired by the Book* HONEST TO GOD. New York: Oxford Univ. Press, 1964.

BAUM, Gregory. "HONEST TO GOD and Traditional Theology," *The Ecumenist,* II (1963-64), 65-68.

BEKER, E. J. "The Sovereignty of God in the Thought of Reinhold Niebuhr," *Nederlands Theologisch Tijdschrift,* XV (1960), 108-30.

BOURKE, Vernon J. "Recent Approaches to a Finite God," *Doctor Communis*, I (1965), 165-68.

CORBISHLEY, T. "Light Out of Darkness: The Dangers of Bishop Robinson's HONEST TO GOD," *Tablet*, CCXVII (1963), 337.

ERNST, C. "Holy, Holy, Holy: Review of Robinson's HONEST TO GOD," *Life of the Spirit*, XVIII (1963), 12-21.

FERRÉ, N. F. S. "Honest to God," *Expository Times*, LXXIV (1963), 308-9.

FORD, Lewis. "God and the Ontic Order," *Pacific Philosophy Forum*, V (1966), 69-77.

HARTSHORNE, C. "Whitehead and Berdyaev: Is There Tragedy in God?" *Journal of Religion*, XXXVII (1957), 71-84.

HEUVEL, A. H. Van Den. "The HONEST TO GOD Debate in Ecumenical Perspective," *The Ecumenical Review*, XVI (1964), 279-94.

HOLLAND, J. A. B. "The Debate about HONEST TO GOD," *Scottish Journal of Theology*, XVII (1964), 257-78.

HOPKO, T. "The HONEST TO GOD Debate," *St. Vladimirs Seminary Quarterly*, VIII (1964), 121-30.

JENKINS, David. "Concerning Theism," in *The Honest to God Debate*. Edited by D. Edwards. Philadelphia: Westminster, 1963. Pp. 194-206.

JONES, I. T. "In the Wake of the HONEST TO GOD Debate," *Christianity Today*, IX (1964), 12-16.

KAUFMAN, Gordon D. "On the Meaning of 'God': Transcendence without Mythology," *The Harvard Theological Review*, LIX (1966), 105-32.

LOCHMAN, J. M. "From the Church to the World," in *New Theology*, No. I. Edited by M. Marty and D. Peerman. New York: Macmillan, 1964. Pp. 169-81.

McEACHRAN, F. "Ideas behind HONEST TO GOD," *Hibbert Journal*, LXII (1964), 165-69.

McTIGHE, Thomas P. "The Finite God in Contemporary Philosophy," *Proceedings of the American Catholic Philosophical Association*, XXVIII (1954), 212-36.

MAYCOCK, H. G. "HONEST TO GOD: A Footnote," *Church Quarterly Review*, CLXV (1964), 72-81.

MICHALSON, Carl. "Between Nature and God," *The Journal of Religion*, XXXV (1955), 229-41.

MITTON, C. L. "Honest to God," *Expository Times*, LXXIV (1963), 276-79.

NOGAR, Raymond. "The God of Disorder," *Continuum*, IV (1966), 102-13.

RYAN, C. "Religionless Christianity: Review of J. Robinson's HONEST TO GOD," *Blackfriars*, XLV (1964), 242-57.

SHIDELER, Emerson W. "Taking the Death-of-God Seriously," *Theology Today*, XXIII, (1966), 183-99.

SMITH, H. S. "What Have They Done with God?" *Liguorian*, XLVII (1959), 39-43.

STOKES, W. "Is God Really Related to This World," *Proceedings of the American Catholic Philosophical Association*, XXXIX (1965), 134-55.

STREIKER, L. D. "An Everyday God," *Journal of Religious Thought*, XX (1963-64), 115-22.

TAUBES, S. A. "The Absent God," *Journal of Religion*, XXXV (1955), 6-16.

TRETHOWAN, Illtyd. "A Changing God," *The Downside Review*, LXXXIV (1966), 247-61.

TROTTER, F. T. "Variations on the 'Death of God' Theme in Recent Theology," *Journal of Bible and Religion*, XXXIII (1965), 42-48.

WILD, J. "An Existential Argument for the Divine Transcendence," *Journal of Bible and Religion*, XXX (1962), 269-77.

AUGUSTIN, Hermann W. (ed.) *Diskussion zu Bischof Robinsons GOTT IST ANDERS.* München: Kaiser, 1964.

BOROS, L. *Der anwesende Gott.* Olten: Walter, 1964.

KUNNETH, W. *Von Gott reden? Eine sprachtheologische Untersuchung zu J. A. T. Robinsons Buch, GOTT IST ANDERS.* Frankfurt am Main: Brockhaus, 1965.

SCHILLEBEECKX, E. *Personale Begegnung mit Gott: Eine Antwort an John A. T. Robinson.* Mainz: Grünewald, 1964.

AVELINO, Andrés, "Fenomenología de la transcendencia," *La Nueva Democracia,* XXXIII (1953), 42-45.

CAPIZZI, Antonio. "Il tu trascendentale e il futuro eterno," *Giornale Critico della Filosofia Italiana,* XLII (1962), 154-76.

COURTHIAL, P. "K. Barth et la révélation universelle de Dieu," *Etudes Evangéliques,* XXIV (1964), 53-62.

DECLOUX, S. "Existence de Dieu et rencontre d'Autrui," *Nouvelle Revue Theologique,* LXXXVI (1964), 706-24.

FOLEY, G. "Die religiöse Religionslosigkeit des Bischofs Robinson," *Evangelische Theologie,* XXIV (1964), 178-94.

GEIGER, Louis B. "Dissimilitude, transcendance et perfection du principe divin," *Dialogue,* I (1962-63), 17-35.

MASTERSON, Patrick. "La définition du fini implique-t-elle l'infini?" *Revue Philosophique de Louvain,* LXII (1964), 39-68.

SCHRUERS, P. "Dieu et l'homme," *Revue Ecclésiastique de Liège,* LI (1965), 163-73.

E. RELIGION AND PHILOSOPHY OF RELIGION

ADLER, Mortimer. *Religion and Theology.* Chicago: Encyclopedia Brittanica, 1961.

BURR, Nelson R. *A Critical Bibliography of Religion in America.* Princeton, N. J.: Princeton Univ. Press, 1961.

DAWSON, Christopher. *Religion and the Rise of Western Culture.* New York: Sheed and Ward, 1950.

ELIADE, Mircea. *The Sacred and the Profane: The Nature of Religion.* New York: Harcourt, Brace, 1959.

GARNETT, A. *Contemporary Thought and the Return to Religion.* Washington, D. C.: College of the Bible, 1960.

HAGERSTROM, A. *Philosophy and Religion.* New York: Humanities, 1964.

HOOK, Sidney. *Religious Experience and Truth.* London: Oliver and Boyd, 1961.

JAMES, W. *The Varieties of Religious Experience.* New Hyde Park, N. Y.: University Books, 1963.

KAUFMANN, Walter A. *Critique of Religion and Philosophy.* New York: Harper, 1958.

LEE, Robert and MARTY, Martin E. *Religion and Social Conflict.* New York: Oxford Univ. Press, 1964.

NIEBUHR, R. *The Godly and the Ungodly.* London: Faber, 1959.

OVERHOLSER, James A. *A Contemporary Christian Philosophy of Religion.* Chicago: Regnery, 1964.

RADEMACHER, Arnold. *Religion and Life.* Westminster, Md.: Newman, 1962.

ROYCE, J. *The Religious Aspect of Philosophy.* New York: Harper, 1959.

STACE, W. T. *Time and Eternity: An Essay in the Philosophy of Religion.* Princeton, N. J.: Princeton Univ. Press, 1960.

TEMPLE, William. *Philosophy of Religion.* London: S.P.C.K., 1961.

TILLICH, Paul. *Theology of Culture.* New York: Oxford Univ. Press, 1959.

WILSON, John. *Philosophy and Religion: The Logic of Religious Belief.* London: Oxford Univ. Press, 1961.

WOLFSON, H. A. *Religious Philosophy.* Cambridge, Mass.: Belknap, 1961.

ADAMS, J. L. "Religion and the Ideologies," *Confluence,* IV (1955), 72-84.

ALTIZER, T. J. "Religion and Reality," *Journal of Religion,* XXXVIII (1958), 251-62.

ANGERS, W. P. "Jung's Approach to Religion," *Downside Revue,* LXXVIII (1960), 36-51.

BEARDSLEE, William. "Frontiers in the Interpretation of Religion," *Religion in Life*, XXIX (1960), 228-38.

BOWER, William Clayton. "Religion's New Frontier," *College of the Bible Quarterly*, XXXVI (1959), 1-9.

BURKILL, T. A. "The Metaphysics of Worship," *Hibbert Journal*, LVII (1960), 338-46.

BUSCHMANN, W. M. "Theology and the Non-Christian Religions," *Theology Today*, XVI (1960), 459-70.

CHRISTIAN, W. A. "Three Kinds of Philosophy of Religion," *Journal of Religion*, XXXVII (1957), 31-36.

DUFFUS, R. L., *et al.* "Faiths in a Complex World," *Discussion*, XXVII (1957-58), 134-35.

FOSTER, P. "Religion in the Modern World," *Blackfriars*, XXXIII (1952), 528.

FRANKLIN, R. L. "Worship and God," *Mind*, LXIX (1960), 555-59.

GAHRINGER, R. E. "Toward a Reorientation in the Philosophy of Religion," *Journal of Religion*, XXXVIII (1958), 175-88.

GIBSON, A. B. "Religion Minus Intelligence," *Hibbert Journal*, LVII (1958), 31-38.

HAMMOND, Phillip. "Religion and the Informing of Culture," *Theology Digest*, XIV (1966), 149-54.

HOROSZ, W. "Some Reflections in Recent Philosophy of Religion," *Philosophy and Phenomenological Research*, XX (1959-60), 397-408.

JENSON, R. W. "Wilhelm Dilthey and the Background Problem of Theology," *Lutheran Quarterly*, XV (1963), 212-22.

JUNGMANN, Josef. "The Sense of the Sacred," *Worship*, XXX (1956), 355-56.

KAUFMAN, G. D. "Philosophy of Religion and Christian Theology," *Journal of Religion*, XXXVII (1957), 233-45.

————. "Philosophy of Religion: Subjective or Objective," *Journal of Philosophy*, LV (1958), 57-70.

LEON, Philip. "Liberal Religion and the Philosopher," *Hibbert Journal*, LVIII (1960), 230-36.

McDONALD, H. D. "What Is Meant by Religious Experience," *Vox Theologica* (1963), 58-70.

MELAND, B. E. "How Is Culture a Source for Theology?" *Criterion*, III (1964), 10-21.

NELSON, Everett J. "Creativity As a Philosophic Category," *Journal of Philosophy*, XV (1958), 153-62.

NEWBIGIN, L. "Quest for Unity Through Religion," *Journal of Religion*, XXXV (1955), 17-33.

PARSONS, H. L. "Reformation of the Philosophical Presuppositions of Religion," *Journal of Religion*, XLII (1962), 119-32.

QADIR, C. A. "Contemporary Philosophy and Religion," *International Philosophical Quarterly*, V (1965), 361-78.

SCHILLEBEECKX, E. H. "Sources of Current Religious Attitudes," *Theology Digest*, IX (1961), 137-39.

THOMAS, O. C. "Reflections on the Philosophy of Religion," *Anglican Theological Review*, XL (1958), 95-102.

GUERIN, Pierre. *Vérité et religion*. Paris: P.U.F., 1962.

MARITAIN, Jacques. *Religion et culture*. Paris: Desclée de Brouwer, 1946.

MATTEUCCI, B. *Cultura religiosa e laicismo*. Alba: Ed. Paoline, 1960.

TILLICH, Paul. *Religionsphilosophie*. Stuttgart: Kohlhammer, 1962.

WACH, J. *Sociologie de la religion*. Paris: Payot, 1955.

BULTMANN, R. "Der Gottesgedanke und der moderne Mensch," *Zeitschrift für Theologie und Kirche*, LX (1963), 335-48.

GUARDINI, Romano. "La fenomenologia dell'esperienza religiasa," in *Atti del centro di studi filosofici* (Gallarate, 1960). Brescia: Morcelliana, 1961. Pp. 21-26.

KEILBACH, W. "Religionsphilosophie und 'Natürliche,' Religion," *Theologisch-praktische Quartalschrift* CIII (1955), 285-94.

SCHATZ, O. "Religionsphilosophische Aspekte bei Karl Jaspers," *Kairos*, I (1960), 23-48.

THONNARD, F. "Philosophie et religion," *Revue des Etudes Augustiniennes*, VII (1961), 252-54.

WALCH, J. "Problématique et typologie de l'expérience religieuse," *Archives de Sociologie des Religions*, VII (1962), 35-76.

WIDMER, Gabriel. "Crise de la religion chrétienne et activité créatrice," *Les Etudes Philosophiques*, XII (1957), 29-33.

F. CULTURE AND RELIGION

ADAMS, James L. *Paul Tillich's Philosophy of Culture*. New York: Harper and Row, 1965.

BENSON, Purnell H. *Religion in Contemporary Culture: A Study of Religion Through Social Science*. New York: Harper, 1960.

DAWSON, Christopher. *Enquiries into Religion and Culture*. New York: Sheed and Ward, 1936.

———. *The Historic Reality of Christian Culture*. New York: Harper, 1960.

———. *Religion and Culture*. London: Sheed and Ward, 1943.

———. *Religion and the Rise of Western Culture*. London: Sheed and Ward, 1950.

ELIOT, T. S. *Christianity and Culture*. New York: Harcourt, Brace, 1960.

GUARDINI, R. *The End of the Modern World*. New York: Sheed and Ward, 1956.

KRONER, Richard. *Culture and Faith*. Chicago: Univ. of Chicago Press, 1951.

LEEUWEN, A. Van. *Christianity in World History: The Meeting of the Faiths of East and West*. New York: Scribner's, 1965.

LEIBRECHT, W. (ed.) *Religion and Culture: Essays in Honor of Paul Tillich*. New York: Harper, 1959.

LOWITH, Karl. *Meaning in History.* Chicago: Univ. of Chicago Press, 1950.

MEAD, Margaret. (ed.) *Cultural Patterns and Technical Change.* New York: New American, 1955.

NEILL, Thomas P. *Religion and Culture.* Milwaukee, Wisc.: Bruce, 1952.

NIEBUHR, H. Richard. *Christ and Culture.* New York: Harper, 1951.

————. *Radical Monotheism and Western Culture.* New York: Harper, 1960.

NIEBUHR, Reinhold. *Faith and History.* New York: Harper, 1947.

VAHANIAN, Gabriel. *Wait Without Idols.* New York: Braziller, 1964.

AUER, A. "The Changing Character of the Christian Understanding of the World," in A. Auer, *et al., The Christian and the World: Readings in Theology.* New York: Kenedy, 1965. Pp. 3-44.

BUSCHMANN, W. "Christianity and Culture," *Lutheran Quarterly,* IX (1957), 260-65.

CHENU, M. "Consecratio Mundi," in A. Auer, *et al., The Christian and the World: Readings in Theology.* New York: Kenedy, 1965. Pp. 161-77.

CLARK, M. "Marginal Brethren: An Explanatory Study of Sectarians in Culture Conflict," *Brethren Life and Thought,* XXI (1955), 55-62.

DONDEYNE, A. "Cultural Encounters: True and False Universalism," *World Justice,* III (1961), 35-49.

FERRE, N. F. S. "(Supernatural) Christian Presuppositions for a Creative Culture," *Expository Times,* LXVIII (1956), 36-40.

FICHTER, J. H. "Religion: Integrator of the Culture?" *Thought,* XXXIII (1958), 361-82.

FLEMING, D. J. "Different Cultural Mentalities," *Religion in Life,* XXIV (1954-55), 56-65.

HEIM, Karl. "Christianity and Culture," *Lutheran Quarterly*, VI (1954), 207-19.

HENRY, C. "Christian Education and the World of Culture," *Mennonite Quarterly Review*, XXXII (1958), 307-13.

KRAFT, C. H. "Christian Conversion or Cultural Conversion?" *Practical Anthropology*, X (1963), 179-87.

MOELLER, C. "Sense of God in Contemporary Literature," *Lumen*, VII (1952), 407-22.

OLFORD, J. E. "History, Theology and Faith," *Theology Today*, XIV (1957), 15-28.

ONG, W. J. "Secular Knowledge, Revealed Religion, and History," *Theology Digest*, VI (1958), 87-90.

RAHNER, K. "The Order of Redemption within the Order of Creation," in *The Christian Commitment*. New York: Sheed and Ward, 1936. Pp. 38-74.

————. "World History and Salvation History," in A. Auer, *et al.*, *The Christian and the World: Readings in Theology*. New York: Kenedy, 1965. Pp. 45-67.

RUETHER, R. "Vahanian: The Worldly Church and the Churchly World," *Continuum*, IV (1966), 50-62.

RUSHDOONY, R. J. "Christianity and the Cultural Problem," *Westminster Theological Journal*, XX (1958), 133-45.

SMITH, E. A. "Historicity of God," *Journal of Religion*, XLIII (1963), 20-34.

VAN BUREN, Paul. "Theology in the Context of Culture," *Christian Century*, LXII (April 7, 1965), 428-29.

ANTONELLI, M. *Cultura, vida y cristianismo*. Madrid: Augustinus, 1960.

BIROU, A. *Sociologie et religion*. Paris: Ed. Ouvrières, 1959.

————. *L'église et le monde*. Lumière et Vie, XIV (N. 73, 1965).

MARITAIN, Jacques. *Religion et culture*. Paris: Desclée de Brouwer, 1930.

MOURGUE, G. *Dieu dans la littérature d'aujourd'hui*. Paris: France-Empire, 1961.

PIEPER, J. *Muss und Kult*. München: Kösel, 1961.

ZUBIRI, Xavier. *Naturaleza, historia, Dios*. Madrid: Nacional, 1955.

VANCOURT, R. "Religion naturelle et passé religieux de l'humanité," *Mélanges des Science Religieuse*, XXI (1964), 15-31.

G. CHRISTIAN THOUGHT

AUER, Alfons, *et al. The Christian and the World: Readings in Theology*. New York: Kenedy, 1965.

BRUNNER, Emil. *Christianity and Civilization*. New York: Scribner's, 1949.

BULTMANN, Rudolf. *Primitive Christianity in Its Contemporary Setting*. New York: Meridian, 1956.

CASSERLEY, Julian V. *The Christian in Philosophy*. New York: Scribner's, 1951.

DOBERSTEIN, J. W. *Between Heaven and Earth: Conversations with American Christians*. New York: Harper and Row, 1965.

FERRÉ, N. S. F. *Christianity and Society*. New York: Harper, 1960.

GILSON, Etienne. *Christianity and Philosophy*. New York: Sheed and Ward, 1939.

HARNACK, Adolf. *What Is Christianity?* New York: Harper, 1959.

HUBBELING, H. G. *Is the Christian God-conception Philosophically Inferior?* Assen: Van Gorcum, 1963.

KERR, H. T. *Mystery and Meaning in the Christian Faith*. Toronto: Ryerson, 1958.

LANGE, Joseph. *A Christian Understanding of Existence*. Westminster, Md.: Newman, 1965.

MEHL, R. *The Condition of the Christian Philosopher*. Translated by E. Kushner. Philadelphia: Fortress, 1964.

MURPHY, Joseph S. *Christianity and Culture*. Baltimore: Helicon, 1960.

NEDONCELLE, M. *Is There a Christian Philosophy?* New York: Hawthorn, 1960.

NEILL, S. C. *Twentieth Century Christianity.* New York: Doubleday, 1963.

ROBINSON, John A. *A New Quest of the Historical Jesus.* London: S.C.M., 1959.

————. *The New Reformation.* Philadelphia: Westminster, 1965.

THILS, G. *Christian Attitudes.* Dublin: Scepter, 1959.

TILLICH, Paul. *Biblical Religion and the Search for Ultimate Reality.* Chicago: Univ. of Chicago Press, 1955.

————. *Christianity and the Encounter of the World Religions.* New York: Columbia Univ. Press, 1963.

VAN DUSEN, H. P. (ed.) *The Christian Answer.* New York: Scribner's, 1946.

VOGEL, Arthur A. *The Next Christian Epoch.* New York: Harper and Row, 1966.

BERRIGAN, D. "The Christian and His Times," *Perspectives,* VII (1962), 159-63.

BEST, Ernest E. "Max Weber and the Christian Criticism of Life," *Theology Today,* XVI (1959), 203-14.

BISER, E. "Are We Post Christian?" *America,* CVIII (1963), 394.

BLONDEL, Maurice. "Philosophy Fulfilled in Christianity," *Theology Digest,* XI (1963), 27-32.

CAMERON, Bruce G. "The Historical Problem in Paul Tillich's Christology," *Southwestern Journal of Theology,* XVIII (1965), 257-72.

CELESTIN, G. "Kierkegaard and Christian Renewal," *Dominicana,* XLIX (1964), 149-57.

CLARKE, T. "The World Is Already Christic," *America,* CXII (1965), 800-803.

CORKEY, R. "A Christian Philosophy for Today," *Hibbert Journal,* LVII (1958), 20-30.

CUNNINGHAM, Justin M. "The Christian and Philosophy," *Dominicana,* XLV (1960), 56-62.

DONDEYNE, A. "The Christian in Face of the World Today," *Lumen*, XIII (1959), 591-99.

EVANS, Donald. "Three Philosophers Analyse Christianity," *Scottish Journal of Theology*, XIII (1960), 137-48.

GRAY, D. "A New Perspective on Christian Life in the World," *North American Liturgical Week*, XXV (1964), 226-28.

HAMILTON, K. "Paul Tillich and the Idealistic Appraisal of Christianity," *Scottish Journal of Theology*, XIII (1960), 33-44.

HATCHETT, Marion J. "Hartshorne's Critique of Christian Theology," *Anglican Theological Review*, XLVIII (1966), 264-76.

HAZELTON, R. "Pascal and Jesus Christ: Reflections on the MYSTÈRE DE JÉSUS," *Journal of Religion*, XXXV (1955), 65-73.

HOLSOMB, Harmon R. "Christology Without God: A Critical Review of THE SECULAR MEANING OF THE GOSPEL," *Foundations*, VIII (1965), 49-61.

JACOBSON, N. P., and WINN, W. E. "Christianity's Debt to Its Cultured Despisers," *Journal of Religious Thought*, XX (1963-64), 53-60.

———. "Christianity Without Christ," *South East Asia Journal of Theology*, III (1964), 6-12.

JERSILD, P. T. "Neitzsche's Attack on Christiandom," *Lutheran Quarterly*, XVI (1964), 231-38.

KLEMKE, E. D. "Logicality versus Alogicality in the Christian Faith," *Journal of Religion*, XXXVIII (1958), 107-15.

MARTY, M. "What Ever Happened to Christianity?" *Ave Maria*, CI (June 29, 1965), 5-8.

MOELLER, C. "Bible and Modern Man," *Lumen*, X (1955), 51-64.

———. "Jesus Christ in the Minds of Moderns," *Lumen*, VII (1952), 509-27.

NIELSEN, Kai. "Christian Positivism," *Journal of Religion*, XLII (1962), 248-61.

RAMSEY, A. "Christian Spirituality and the Modern World," *Eastern Churches Quarterly*, XV (1963), 15-24.

ROBERTS, T. A. "The Relevance of Liberal Christianity," *Hibbert Journal*, LIX (1961), 320-30.

TAVARD, G. H. "Christianity and the Philosophies of Existence," *Theological Studies*, XVIII (1957), 1-16.

VAHANIAN, Gabriel. "The Future of Christianity in a Post-Christian Era," *The Centennial Review*, VIII (1964), 160-73.

―――. "The Lost Iconoclasm of Christianity," *The Nation*, CXCII (1961), 354-57.

CASSERLEY, J. *Absence du christianisme.* Bruges: Desclée de Brouwer, 1957.

DAUJAT, Jean. *Idées modernes: réponses chrétiennes.* Paris: Téqui, 1956.

GEBSATTEL, Viktor E. *Christentum und Humanismus.* Stuttgart: Klett, 1947.

GUITTON, J. *Jesus und wir Menschen des XX. Jahrhunderts.* Wien: Styria, 1961.

HIRSCH, E. *Hauptfragen christlicher Religionsphilosophie.* Berlin: de Gruyter, 1963.

LEPP, I. *Le monde chrétien et ses malfaçons.* Paris: Aubier, 1956.

MARCOZZI, V. *Le christianisme face aux théories modernes.* Paris: Laffont, 1959.

NADE, S. *Matérialisme philosophique dans le christianisme.* Paris: Marx, 1958.

PAGGIARO, L. *Mentalitá contemporanea e cristianesimo.* Roma: Mame, 1961.

SCHNEIDER, J. *Die Frage nach dem historischen Jesus in der Neutestamentlichen Forschung der Gegenwart.* Berlin: Evangelische, 1958.

TRESMONTANT, C. *Les idées maîtresses de la métaphysique chrétienne.* Paris: Seuil, 1962.

BOURG D'IRE, Marie-Benoit du. "La philosophie chrétienne," *Etudes Franciscaines*, XXX (1963), 33-41.

CROTEAU, J. "Dimensions existentielles du christianisme," *Sciences Ecclésiastiques*, XI (1959), 81-97.

GOUHIER, H. "Bergson et la philosophie du christianisme," *Revue de Théologie et de Philosophie*, I (1960), 1-22.

LAFFOUCRIERE, Odette. "Le christianisme est-il devenu un platonisme pour le peuple?" *Foi et Vie*, LV (1957), 98-115.

NAUD, A. "Le problème de la philosophie chrétienne," *Studia Montis Regii*, III (1960), 221-45.

H. SCIENTIFIC NATURALISM AND HUMANISM

BALTHASAR, H. Urs Von. *Science, Religion and Christ*. Philadelphia: Westminster, 1965.

BLACKHAM, H. J. *Objections to Humanism*. London: Constable, 1963.

———. *Religion in a Modern Society*. New York: Frederick Ungar, 1966.

BOUYER, Louis. *Christian Humanism*. Westminster, Md.: Newman, 1959.

CHAUVIN, R. *God of the Scientists, God of the Experiment*. Translated by S. Attanasio. Baltimore, Md.: Helicon, 1960.

COULSON, Charles Alfred. *Science and the Idea of God*. Cambridge: University Press, 1958.

DENNES, William R. *Some Dilemmas of Naturalism*. New York: Columbia Univ. Press, 1960.

DEWEY, John. *A Common Faith*. New Haven, Conn.: Yale Univ. Press, 1964.

DOUGHERTY, Jude P. *Recent American Naturalism: An Exposition and Critique*. Washington, D. C.: The Catholic Univ. of America Press, 1960.

DUBARLE, D. *Scientific Humanism and Christian Thought*. Translated by R. Trevett. New York: Philosophical Library, 1956.

FEUERBACH, Ludwig. *The Essence of Christianity.* New York: Harper, 1957.

FROMM, Erich. *Marx's Concept of Man.* New York: Frederick Ungar, 1961.

HADAS, Moses. *Humanism: The Greek Ideal and Its Survival.* London: Allen and Unwin, 1960.

HOLBROOK, Clyde A. *Religion: A Humanistic Field.* Englewood Cliffs, N. J.: Prentice-Hall, 1963.

HUXLEY, Julian. *Religion Without Revelation.* New York: Mentor, 1958.

JARRETT-KERR, Martin. *The Secular Promise: Christian Presence Amid Contemporary Humanism.* Philadelphia: Fortress, 1964.

KRIKORIAN, Yervant. *Naturalism and the Human Spirit.* New York: Columbia Univ. Press, 1944.

LEANDER, Folke. *Humanism and Naturalism.* Göteborg: Elanders Boktryckeri Aktiebolag, 1937.

LEWIS, J. *Science, Faith and Scepticism.* London: Lawrence, 1959.

MacGREGOR, G. *The Hemlock and the Cross: Humanism, Socrates and Christ.* Philadelphia: Lippincott, 1963.

MARX, Karl, and ENGELS, Friedrich. *On Religion.* New York: Schocken, 1964.

MASCALL, E. *Christian Theology and Natural Science.* New York: Ronald, 1957.

ROTENSTREICH, Nathan. *Humanism in the Contemporary Era.* New York: Humanities, 1963.

SANTAYANA, George. *Reason in Religion.* New York: Scribner's, 1906.

SARTON, George A. *The History and the New Humanism.* Bloomington, Ind.: Indiana Univ. Press, 1962.

SMITH, Ronald G. *The New Man.* London: S.C.M., 1956.

TUCKER, Robert. *Philosophy and Myth in Karl Marx.* New York: Cambridge, 1964.

WEIZSACKER, C. F. Von. *The Relevance of Science.* New York: Harper, 1965.

WHITE, H. C. *Christians in a Technological Era.* Toronto: Seabury, 1964.

WHITEHEAD, Alfred N. *Science and the Modern World.* New York: New American, 1952.

YARNOLD, G. D. *The Spiritual Crisis of the Scientific Age.* London: Allen and Unwin, 1960.

YOUNG, William F. *The New Philosophy of Pantheistic Humanism: A Thomistic Critique.* Washington, D. C.: The Catholic Univ. of America Press, 1952.

ANDERSON, D. "Images of Man in Sartre and Camus," *Modern Church,* VIII (1964), 33-45.

ANNAN, N. "People," *Twentieth Century,* CLVII (1955), 128-37.

BROWN, E. "Science and 'Post Christian' Man," *Social Justice Review,* LVI (1964), 148-52.

CLARKE, W. N. "Christian Humanism for Today," *Social Order,* III (1953), 269-88.

DAVIE, D. "Men Without God," *Twentieth Century,* CLVII (1955), 593-94.

DAWSON, C. "Christianity and the Humanist Tradition," *Dublin Review,* XXII (1952), 1-11.

"Dialogue Between Catholics and Communists," *Herder Correspondence,* II (1965), 325-30.

DODSON, E. O. "Some Comments on Science and Religion," *Revue de l'Université d'Ottawa,* XXIX (1959), 199-214.

EBERT, Hermann. "Man as the Way to God," *Philosophy Today,* X (1966), 88-106.

ETCHEVERRY, A. "The Present Diversity among Humanisms," *Philosophy Today,* III (1959), 268-76.

FORSTER, E. M. "Humanism as a Philosophy for Today," *Twentieth Century,* CLVII (1955), 157-99.

GARRARD, L. A. "Liberal Religion and the Classical Humanist," *Hibbert Journal,* LVIII (1960), 213-17.

GELBER, S. "Toward a Radical Naturalism," *Journal of Philosophy,* LVI (1959), 193-99.

GIBBS, Y. G. "A Secondary Point of Reference in Barth's Anthropology," *Southwestern Journal of Theology,* XVI (1963), 132-35.

GUINAN, A. "Scientism and Humanism in the Light of the Incarnation," *Catholic World,* CLXXXI (1955), 186-92.

GUSTAFSON, James M. "Christian Attitudes Toward a Technological Society," *Theology Today,* XVI (1959), 173-87.

HANLEY, T. "Spirituality for an Industrial Society," *Homiletic and Pastoral Review,* LIV (1954), 331-34.

HARMON, John J. "Toward a Secular Humanism," *Cross Currents,* XVI (1966), 153-66.

JOHANN, Robert O. "Creativity Without Guilt," *America,* CXIII (1965), 165.

LADRIERE, Jean. "The Integration of Scientific Research within Christian Life," *Lumen Vitae,* XV (1960), 433-50.

LAMONT, C. (ed.) "Humanist Symposium on Metaphysics," *Journal of Philosophy,* LVI (1959), 45-64.

MARCEL, G. "The Sacred in the Technological Age," *Theology Today,* XIX (1962), 27-38.

MELAND, Bernard E. "Alternatives to Absolutes," *Religion in Life,* XXXIV (1965), 345-51.

MESERVE, H. C. "What Serves Man?" *Journal of Religion and Health,* III (1964), 203-208.

MURRAY, J. C. "Christian Humanism in America," *Social Order,* III (1953), 233-44.

PAUL, R. S. "Theology and the Technological Revolution," *Hartford Quarterly,* IV (1964), 27-42.

PEACOCKE, A. R. "The Christian Faith in a Scientific Age," *Religion in Education,* XXVIII (1961), 53-59.

PRATT, O. "Science and Atheist Materialism," *Wiseman Review,* CCXXXVII (1963), 262-72.

RAMSEY, I. T. "Religion and Science: A Philosopher's Approach," *Church Quarterly Review,* CLXII (1961), 77-91.

ROBINSON, C. K. "Biblical Theism and Modern Science," *Journal of Religion,* XLIII (1963), 118-38.

SCHILLEBEECKX, E. "The Church and Mankind," in *The Church and Mankind* (*Concilium*, Dogma, Vol. I). Glen Rock, N. J.: Paulist, 1965. Pp. 69-101.

SLEEPER, R. W. "John Dewey's Empiricism and the Christian Experience," *Cross Currents*, IX (1959), 367-78.

TAVARD, G. "Theology in a Technological Age," *Integrity*, X (1955), 7-15.

TESTER, S. "Christianity and Classical Humanism," *Hibbert Journal*, LVII (1959), 133-42.

VOGEL, A. A. "On Man's Making the World and Himself," *Canadian Journal of Theology*, IX (1963), 225-30.

WEDEL, T. O. "Man Come of Age," *Union Seminary Quarterly Review*, XVIII (1963), 326-40.

WENDLAND, H. D. "Social Humanism and Christian Care," *Ecumenical Review*, LXXXI (1956), 127-42.

CORVEZ, M. *De la science à la foi: Teilhard de Chardin.* Tours: Mame, 1964.

GOGARTEN, F. *Verhängnis und Hoffnung der Neuzeit: Die Säkularisierung als theologisches Problem.* Stuttgart: Vorwerk, 1953.

LEESE, K. *Recht und Grenze der natürlichen Religion.* Zürich: Morgarten, 1954.

ALBO, X. "Materialismo y dialéctica," *Espíritu*, XI (1962), 118-34.

DIPPEL, C. J. "Christliche Existenz in der modernen wissenschaftlichen und technischen Welt," *Zeitschrift für Evangelische Ethik*, II (1958), 129-54.

DOOYEWEERD, Herman. "La base religieuse de la philosophie humaniste," *Revue Réformée*, X (1959), 48-63.

GEX, M. "Vers un humanisme cosmologique: la synthèse de Teilhard de Chardin," *Revue de Théologie et de Philosophie*, VII (1957), 186-205.

ISASI, J. M. "Teísmo y humanismo," *Lumen*, XII (1963), 41-54.

KOBEILE, A. "Gottesglaube und moderne Naturwissenschaft in der Theoligie Karl Heims," *Neue Zeitschrift für Systematische Theologie und Religionsphilosophie,* LX (1964), 115-25.

I. THE RELIGIOUS AND THE SECULAR

AUER, Ayons, *et al. The Christian and the World.* New York: Kenedy, 1965.

BONHOEFFER, D. *The Cost of Discipleship.* London: S.C.M., 1954.

COX, Harvey. *The Secular City.* New York: Macmillan, 1965.

DAWSON, Christopher H. *America and the Secularization of Modern Culture.* Houston, Tex.: Univ. of Saint Thomas, 1960.

ELIADE, Mircea. *The Sacred and the Profane.* New York: Harcourt, Brace, 1959.

FICHTER, Joseph H. *Are We Going Secular?* Milwaukee, Wisc.: Marquette Univ. Press, 1960.

GILKEY, Langdon, B. *How the Church Can Minister to the World Without Losing Itself.* New York: Harper and Row, 1964.

GODSEY, John D. *Preface to Bonhoeffer: The Man and Two of His Shorter Writings.* Philadelphia: Fortress, 1965.

JARRETT-KERR, Martin. *The Secular Promise: Christian Presence Amid Contemporary Humanism.* Philadelphia: Fortress, 1964.

KOHN, H. E. *Reflections on the Natural World and Man: Life's Values and Its Destiny.* Grand Rapids, Michigan: Eerdmans, 1963.

LEE, Robert. (ed.) *The Church and the Exploding Metropolis.* Richmond, Va.: Knox, 1965.

MASCALL, E. *The Secularization of Christianity.* London: Darton, Longman and Todd, 1965.

MICKLEM, P. *The Secular and the Sacred. An Enquiry into the Principles of a Christian Civilization.* London: Hodder and Stoughton, 1948.

MIEGGE, Giovanni. *Christian Affirmations in a Secular Age.* New York: Oxford Univ. Press, 1958.

MUNBY, D. *The Idea of a Secular Society and Its Significance for Christians.* New York: Oxford Univ. Press, 1963.

NICHOLS, James H. *History of Christianity 1650-1950.* New York: Ronald, 1956.

RAMSEY, Arthur M. *Sacred and Secular: A Study in the Other-Worldly and This-Worldly Aspects of Christianity.* New York: Harper and Row, 1965.

ROBINSON, James M. and NOTH, M. (eds.) *The Bultmann School of Biblical Interpretation: New Directions.* New York: Harper and Row, 1965.

SMITH, R. G. *Secular Christianity.* London: Collins, 1966.

VAN BUREN, Paul M. *The Secular Meaning of the Gospel, Based on an Analysis of Its Language.* New York: Macmillan, 1963.

WINTER, G. *The New Creation as Metropolis.* New York: Macmillan, 1963.

ADLER, E. "Secularization," *The Student World,* LVI (1963), 1-3.

BOHM, Anton. "Serving the World," *Theology Digest,* XII (1964), 56-59.

BULTMANN, Rudolf. "The Idea of God and Modern Man," in *Translating Theology into the Modern Age.* New York: Harper, 1965.

———. "New Testament and Mythology," in *Kerygma and Myth.* Edited by H. W. Bartsch. New York: Harper, 1961. Vol. I, 1-44.

CALLAHAN, Daniel. "Toward a Theology of Secularity," in *The Secular City Debate.* Edited by D. Callahan. New York: Macmillan, 1966. Pp. 91-100.

CLARKE, T. "The World Is Already Christic," in *That Secular City: Three Essays.* New York: America, 1966. Pp. 11-20.

COGLEY, J. "Second Coming: Question of Religious Relevance Reviewed," *Commonweal*, LXXVII (1963), 554-55.

CORBISHLEY, T. "Secularizing Christianity: Review of E. Mascall's THE SECULARIZATION OF CHRISTIANITY," *Clergy Review*, L (1965), 491-96.

COX, Harvey. "Beyond Bonhoeffer: The Future of Religionless Christianity," in *The Secular City Debate*. Edited by D. Callahan. New York: Macmillan, 1966. Pp. 205-14.

————. "Biblical Evangelism in the Twentieth Century," *Foundations*, II (1959), 101-10.

————, *et al.* "Secularization and the Secular Mentality: A New Challenge to Christian Education," *Religious Education*, LXI (1966), 83-87.

DARBY, J. H. "Christianity in the Secular State," *Catholic Mind*, LII (1954), 38-45.

DAWSON, C. "Challenge of Secularism," *Catholic World*, CLXXXII (1956), 326-30.

ELLIS, Oliver. "The Worldly Christian," *The Way*, VI (1966), 43-50.

FENNELL, William O. "Dietrich Bonhoeffer: The Man of Faith in a World Come of Age," *Canadian Journal of Theology*, XIII (1962), 172-80.

————. "Theology of True Secularity," *Theology Today*, XXII (1964), 174-83.

GILKEY, Langdon. "Critical Review of Paul M. Van Buren, THE SECULAR MEANING OF THE GOSPEL," *The Journal of Religion*, XLIV (1964), 283-343.

————. "Secularism's Impact on Contemporary Theology," *Christianity and Crisis*, XXV (1965), 64-67.

GREEN, Clifford. "Bonhoeffer's Concept of Religion," *Theology Digest*, XIII (1965), 47-51.

HAMILTON, W. H. "Bonhoeffer: Christology and Ethic United," *Christianity and Crisis*, XXIV (1965), 195-99.

————. "Secular Theology for a World Come of Age," *Theology Today*, XVIII (1962), 435-59.

————. "Thursday's Child: The Theologian Today and Tomorrow," *Theology Today*, XX (1964), 487-93.

HARDWICK, E. "The Place of Bonhoeffer," *Heythrop Journal*, V (1964), 297-98.

HERBERG, Will. "Religion in a Secularized Society: The New Shape of Religion in America," *Review of Religious Research*, III (1962), 145-58.

HOLCOMB, Harmon R. "How to Speak of God in a Secular Style," in *The Secular City Debate*. Edited by D. Callahan. New York: Macmillan, 1966. Pp. 168-78.

HOYT, R. G. "When Men Are Gods," *Grail*, XXXVII (1955), 50-55.

KELLEY, Alden D. "On Being a Christian in the World," *Religion in Life*, XXXIII (1964), 28-38.

KRUITHOF, B. "Christianity and the Rise of Secularism," *Christianity Today*, VIII (1964), 13-15.

LEHMANN, Paul. "Chalcedon in Technopolis," in *The Secular City Debate*. Edited by D. Callahan. New York: Macmillan, 1966. Pp. 64-68.

LILLIE, W. "Worldliness of Christianity," *Expository Theology*, LXXV (1964), 132-37.

LITTLE, David. "The Social Gospel Revisited," in *The Secular City Debate*. Edited by D. Callahan. New York: Macmillan, 1966. Pp. 69-74.

LOCHMAN, J. J. "From the Church to the World," in *New Theology*. Edited by M. Marty and D. Peerman. New York: Macmillan, 1964. Vol. I, 169-81.

METZ, Johannes B. "The Christian and the World," *Theology Digest*, XIII (1965), 95-100.

MYERS, C. Kilmer, "Where Is the Church?" in *The Secular City Debate*. Edited by D. Callahan. New York: Macmillan, 1966. Pp. 75-76.

MILLER, David. "False Prophets in the Secular City," *Christian Century*, LXXXII (1965), 1417-18.

MUELLNER, J. Benedict. "Cullman: The Ambivalence of the Secular," *Continuum*, IV (1966), 76-91.

MURCHLAND, Bernard. "How Do We Speak of God Without Religion?" in *The Secular City Debate*. Edited by D. Callahan. New York: Macmillan, 1966. Pp. 17-22.

NOVAK, Michael. "Secular Style and Natural Law," in *The Secular City Debate*. Edited by D. Callahan. New York: Macmillan, 1966. Pp. 81-84.

O'CONNELL, Robert. "Secular City Revisited," *America*, CXIV (1966), 545-48.

O'DEA, T. F. "Secularization of Culture," *Commonweal*, LXXI (1959), 118-19.

O'DONOVAN, Leo J. "Bultmann: The Autonomy of the Secular," *Continuum*, IV (1966), 25-38.

OGDEN, S. M. "What Sense Does It Make to Say, God Acts in History?" *Journal of Religion*, XLIII (1963), 1-19.

OGLETREE, Thomas W. "The Church's Mission to the World," *Encounter*, XXV (1964), 457-69.

PEARL, Leon. "Religious and Secular Beliefs," *Mind*, LXIX (1960), 408-12.

RAHNER, Karl. "The Christian of the Future," *Herder Correspondence*, II (1965), 227-32.

REED, L. "American Bishops' Statement on Religion and Secularism," *Lumen*, VIII (1953), 132-35.

RUBENSTEIN, Richard L. "Cox's Vision of the Secular City," in *The Secular City Debate*. Edited by D. Callahan. New York: Macmillan, 1966. Pp. 129-44.

SALISBURY, W. S. "Religion and Secularization," *Social Forces*, XXXVI (1958), 197-205.

SCHALL, James V. "The Secular City and God," *The Catholic World*, CCIV (1966), 20-26.

SCHNEIDER, E. D. "Bonhoeffer and a Secular Theology," *Lutheran Quarterly*, XV (1963), 151-55.

SCHWARZSCHILD, Steven S. "A Little Bit of a Revolution?" in *The Secular City Debate*. Edited by D. Callahan. New York: Macmillan, 1966. Pp. 145-55.

"Secularism in America: A Statement of the Hierarchy of the U.S.," *Tablet*, CC (1952), 425-26.

SHEERIN, J. B. "Second Stage of Secularism," *Catholic World,* CLXXXIX (1959), 340-43.

SHINER, Larry. "Toward a Theology of the Secular," *Journal of Religion,* XLV (1965), 279-95.

SMITH, J. MacDonald. "Towards a Christian Philosophy of Science," *Downside Review,* LXXVII (1959), 236-53.

SMITH, Ronald G. "A Theological Perspective of the Secular," *Christian Scholar,* XLIII (1960), 11-24.

SMYLIE, James H. "Sons of God in the City," in *The Secular City Debate.* Edited by D. Callahan. New York: Macmillan, 1966. Pp. 7-11.

STACKHOUSE, Max L. "Today's City: Threat or Promise?" in *The Secular City Debate.* Edited by D. Callahan. New York: Macmillan, 1966. Pp. 26-37.

TYSON, Ruel. "Urban Renewal in the Holy City," in *The Secular City Debate.* Edited by D. Callahan. New York: Macmillan, 1966. Pp. 46-55.

VAN BUREN, P. M., MELAND, B. E., and KILLINGER, J. "Secular Emphasis of Our Age: Its Values and Dangers," *Religion in Life,* XXXIV (1965), 334-64.

WALZ, H. H. "Christendom in a Secularized World," *Ecumenical Review,* X (1958), 277-85.

WELCH, Claude. "Reflections on the Problem of Speaking of God," in *The Secular City Debate.* Edited by D. Callahan. New York: Macmillan, 1966. Pp. 156-67.

WEST, Charles C. "What It Means to Be Secular," in *The Secular City Debate.* Edited by D. Callahan. New York: Macmillan, 1966. Pp. 59-63.

WICKER, B. "Secular Christianity," *New Blackfriars,* XLVII (1966), 412-21.

WICKHAM, E. R. "The Encounter of the Christian Faith and Modern Technological Society," *Ecumenical Review,* XI (1959), 259-67.

YOUNGER, George D. "Does THE SECULAR CITY Revisit the Social Gospel?" in *The Secular City Debate.* Edited by D. Callahan. New York: Macmillan, 1966. Pp. 77-80.

GOGARTEN, F. *Der Mensch zwischen Gott und Welt.* Stuttgart: Verwerk, 1956.

DUMAS, André. "Dietrich Bonhoeffer et l'interprétation du christianisme comme non-religion," *Archives de Sociologie des Religions,* XIX (1965), 5-30.

HAHN, W. "Säkularisation und Religionszerfall," *Kerygma und Dogma,* V (1959), 83-98.

LAIS, Hermann. "Das Wunder im Spannungsfeld der theologischen un profanen Wissenschaft," *Münchener Theologische Zeitschrift,* XII (1961), 294-300.

SCHLETTE, H. "Wie bewerten wir die Säkularisierung," *Zeitschrift für Missionswissenschaft und Religionswissenschaft,* L (1960), 72-88.

SEMMELROTH, O. "Die Welt als Raum der Begegnung mit Gott," *Stimmen der Zeit,* CLVII (1955-56), 444-55.

CHAPTER VI

Religious Knowledge and Language

This chapter comprises selected books and articles on religious language and its content. With the increased appreciation of the developmental character of human thought, the metaphysical and religious implications of early mythical thought have come to be valued more highly, and their importance for the full meaning of biblical, classical, and contemporary religious thought has led to new studies of the relation between faith and human knowledge and of the distinctive characteristics of religious language. Material on these issues has been collected under the following headings:

A. Belief and Faith
B. Faith and Reason; Philosophy and Theology
C. Metaphysics and Theodicy
D. Knowledge of God
E. Religious Language
F. Myth, Symbol, and Analogy

Particularly pertinent to these issues would be Chapters I, II, and IV C of the present volume as well as Chapters II, VII, and VIII of *An Annotated Bibliography of Philosophy in Catholic Thought* by the same editor.

A. BELIEF AND FAITH

BABIN, P. *Crisis in Faith*. New York: Herder and Herder, 1963.

BARS, Henry. *The Assent of Faith*. Baltimore: Helicon, 1960.

BARTH, Karl. *The Faith of the Church*. New York: Meridian, 1958.

BAVINCK, J. H. *Faith and Its Difficulties.* Grand Rapids: Eerdmans, 1959.

BENDALL, K., and FERRE, F. *Exploring the Logic of Faith.* New York: Association, 1962.

BONHOEFFER, D. *The Cost of Discipleship.* New York: Macmillan, 1963.

BRUNNER, Heinrich E. *The Scandal of Christianity: The Gospel as Stumbling Block to Modern Man.* Richmond: Knox, 1965.

BUBER, Martin, *Two Types of Faith.* New York: Harper, 1961.

BULTMANN, Rudolf. *Existence and Faith.* New York: Meridian, 1960.

D'ARCY, M. C. *The Nature of Belief.* St. Louis, Herder, 1958.

HAMILTON, F. E. *The Basis of Christian Faith.* New York: Harper and Row, 1964.

HENRY, C. F. H. *Christian Faith and Modern Theology.* Des Moines, Iowa: Meredith, 1964.

KAUFMAN, G. D. *Relativism, Knowledge and Faith.* Chicago: Univ. of Chicago Press, 1960.

MARTY, Martin E. *Varieties of Unbelief.* New York: Holt, Rinehart and Winston, 1964.

MITCHELL, B. (ed.) *Faith and Logic: Oxford Essays in Philosophical Theology.* London: Allen and Unwin, 1957.

MORE, P. E. *The Sceptical Approach to Religion.* Princeton, N. J.: Princeton Univ. Press, 1958.

NOVAK, Michael. *Belief and Unbelief.* New York: Macmillan, 1966.

OGDEN, Shubert N. *Existence and Faith: Shorter Writings of Rudolf Bultmann.* New York: Meridian, 1960.

PEARSON, R. *The Believer's Unbelief.* New York: Nelson, 1963.

PIEPER, J. *Belief and Faith: A Philosophical Tract.* New York: Pantheon, 1964.

PLANTINGA, Alvin, *Faith and Philosophy.* Grand Rapids, Mich.: Eerdmans, 1964.

SZCZESNY, G. *The Future of Unbelief.* New York: Braziller, 1961.

TILLICH, Paul. *The Dynamics of Faith.* New York: Harper, 1958.

TRETHOWAN, I. *The Basis of Belief.* New York: Hawthorn, 1961.

ALFARO, Juan. "The Supernaturality of Faith," *Theology Digest,* XIV (1966), 111-16.

ARENHOEVEL, D. "Does the Bible Suffice as the Source of Faith," *Life of the Spirit,* XIX (1964), 68-78.

AVERILL, Lloyd. "On a Certain Faithlessness," *Christian Century,* LXXXII (1965), 1087-90.

BRIEN, A. "Problem of God and Intellectual Unbelievers," *Lumen,* VII (1952), 367-72.

BROGLIE, Guy de. "The Possibility of Natural Faith," *Theology Digest,* XIV (1966), 117-23.

CAHILL, P. "Rudolf Bultmann and Post-Bultmann Tendencies," *Catholic Biblical Quarterly,* XXVI (1964), 153-78.

CIRNE-LIMA, C. "A Phenomenology of Belief," *Continuum,* I (1963), 22-31.

COLLIER, K. G. "Obstacles to Religious Belief," *Hibbert Journal,* LVI (1958), 140-47.

COLLINS, J. "Faith and Reflection in Kierkegaard," *Journal of Religion,* XXXVII (1957), 10-19.

————. "Philosophy in Catholic Life," *Religion in Life,* XXIX (1960), 179-88.

COPLESTON, F. C. "Enemy of Belief: Metaphysics and Modern Philosophers," *Month,* XVIII (1957), 292-98.

CURNOW, A. G. "Influence of Presupposition on Conviction," *London Quarterly and Holborn Review,* CLXXXI (1956), 212-17.

DUCASSE, S. "Christianity, Rationality and Faith," *Review of Religion,* XXII (1958), 121-36.

GIBSON, A. B. "Empirical Evidence and Religious Faith," *Journal of Religion,* XXXVI (1956), 24-35.

GONZÁLEZ, P. A. "The Faith of Disbelief," *Tijdschrift voor Theologie*, II (1962), 34-54.

GORRES, Ida. "The Believer's Unbelief," *Cross Currents*, XI (1961), 51-59.

HARTSHORNE, M. H. "Faith Without Doubt Is Dead," *Theology Today*, XIII (1956), 63-71.

HARVEY, V. A. "Faith and Belief in Contemporary Theology," *Theology Today*, XVIII (1962), 460-72; 506-12.

HEINEMANN, F. H. "Belief: The Mother of Philosophy," *Hibbert Journal*, LIV (1955), 70-80.

HICK, J. H. "Belief and Life: The Fundamental Nature of the Christian Ethic," *Encounter*, XX (1959), 494-516.

JOHANN, R. "Faith and Philosophy: The Catholic Philosopher," *America*, III (1964), 487.

KING, Farlow J. "Justification of Religious Belief," *Philosophical Quarterly*, XII (1962), 261-63.

KOLBE, H. E. "Faith and Philosophy: Another Look," *Journal of Bible and Religion*, XXVII (1959), 3-9.

LEVIE, Jean. "A Dialogue on the Reasons for Believing," *Theology Digest*, XIV (1966), 29-33.

LEWIS, John W. "Does Science Destroy Belief?" in *Faith, Fact and Fantasy*. C. F. D. Moule, *et al*. Philadelphia: Westminster, 1964. Pp. 9-44.

LIEGE, P. A. "Struggle of the Modern Believer," *Theology Digest*, VI (1958), 157-58.

LONERGAN, Bernard. "Openness and Religious Experience," in *Atti del Centro di Studi Filosofici* (Gallarate, 1960). Brescia: Morcelliana, 1961. Pp. 60-62.

METZ, J. B. "A Believer's Look at the World," in *The Christian and the World: Readings in Theology*. New York: Kenedy, 1965. Pp. 45-67.

MICHALSON, C. "Kierkegaard's Theology of Faith," *Religion in Life*, XXXII (1963), 225-37.

MILLER, S. H. "Help My Unbelief," *Theology Today*, XIV (1957), 13-14.

NOVAK, M. "Belief and Unbelief," *Apostolate*, X (1964), 5-23.

OGDEN, Schubert. "The Christian and Unbelievers," *Motive*, XXV (1965), 21-23.

OLBRICHT, T. M. "To Whom Shall the Church Listen?" *Christianity Today*, VIII (1963), 24-25.

OWENS, John J. "Religious Belief and Modern Demands," *Congregational Quarterly*, XXXI (1953), 227-33.

PERCY, J. D. "Today's Doubt and Unbelief," *London Quarterly and Holborn Review*, CLXXXIV (1959-60), 319-25; 345-49.

PIERSON, M. F. "The Heresy of Simple Faith," *Theology Today*, XX (1963), 339-46.

POLLOCK, S. "Validity of Faith," *Hibbert Journal*, LVII (1959), 331-37.

PRICE, H. H. "Belief 'In' and Belief 'That,' " *Religious Studies*, I (1965), 5-27.

SELLERS, J. E. "Range of Contemporary Beliefs in God," *Religion in Life*, XXVIII (1959), 202-11.

SMART, N. "Revelation and Reason," *Scottish Journal of Theology*, XI (1958), 352-61.

SMITH, R. "Faith Without Belief," in *Paul Tillich in Catholic Thought*. Chicago: Priory Press, 1964. Pp. 133-44.

SPINKS, G. S. "Significance of Disbelief," *Hibbert Journal*, LVII (1959), 107-12.

VOLLERT, Cyril. "The Commitment of Faith: A Catholic View," *The Ecumenist*, III (1965), 102-104.

WEILER, Gershon. "How Rational Is Religious Belief?" *The Philosophical Quarterly*, XII (1962), 172-77.

AUBERT, Roger. *Le problème de l'acte de foi*. Louvain: Warny, 1958.

BARS, Henry. *Introduction à la foi*. Paris: Beauchesne, 1963.

CIRNE-LIMA, C. *Der Personale Glaube*. Innsbruck: Rauch, 1959.

EBELING, G. *Wort und Glaube*. Tübingen: Mohr, 1960.

GUITTON, J. *Difficultés de croire*. Paris: Plon, 1960.

HEER, F., and SZCZESNY, G. *Glaube und Unglaube: Ein Briefwechsel.* München: List, 1959.

HOURDIN, G. *La nouvelle vague croit-elle en Dieu?* Paris: Casterman, 1960.

IWAND, H. J. *Um den rechten Glauben.* München: Kaiser, 1959.

KARISCH, R. *Naturwissenschaft und Glaube.* Donauwörth: Auer-Cassianeum, 1959.

KIRCHHOFF, R. *Wissenschaftliche Weltanschauung und religiöser Glaube.* Berlin: Wissenschaften, 1959.

LECLERCQ, J. *Il problema della fede e gli intellectuali del XX secolo.* Milano: Vita e Pensiero, 1965.

LECOMTE du NOUY, M. *Pierre Lecomte du Noüy: de l'agnosticisme à la foi.* Paris: La Colombe, 1955.

LÖWITH, K. *Fede e ricerca.* Brescia: Morcelliana, 1960.

MÖLLER, J. *Vielleicht ist alles anders? Gedanken eines gläubigen Skeptikers.* Mainz: Grünewald, 1962.

PIEPER, J. *Uber den Glauben.* München: Kössel, 1962.

PLOTZKE, U. *Aller Glaube ist Wagnis.* Frankfurt am Main: Knecht, 1963.

SPAEMANN, H. *Das Glaubenslicht.* Freiburg im Breisgau: Herder, 1963.

TRESMONTANT, C. *Die Vernunft des Glaubens.* Düsseldorf: Patmos, 1964.

ZUNDEL, Maurice. *La liberté de la foi.* Paris: Plon, 1960.

FUES, E. "Glaube und Wissen," *Kirche in der Zeit,* XV (1960), 147-52.

LEYVRAZ, J. P. "Karl Jaspers: La foi philosophique devant la révélation," *Revue de Théologie et de Philosophie,* XCVII (1964), 25-36.

LIEGE, P. A. "Le combat moderne du croyant," *Nouvelle Revue Théologique,* LXXIX (1957), 897-904.

MÄRZ, F. "Das Phänomen des Glaubens im zwischenmenschlichen Bereich als Fundament der Bildung," *Theologie und Glaube,* LV (1965), 81-95.

RAHNER, Karl. "Wissenschaft als Konfession?" *Wort und Wahrheit*, IX (1954), 809-19.

STAKEMEIER, E. "Begründung des Gottesglaubens," *Theologie und Glaube*. LIII (1963), 287-91.

THUM, B. "Glaube und Gnosis," *Kairos*, I (1959), 88-91.

WOLF, E. "Glaube, Bekenntnis, Entscheidung," *Kirche in der Zeit*, XIV (1959), 77-80.

B. FAITH AND REASON; PHILOSOPHY AND THEOLOGY

BARTH, K. and THURNEYSEN, E. *Revolutionary Theology in the Making*. Richmond, Va.: Knox, 1964.

BRUCE, Michael. *No Empty Creed*. Toronto: Seabury, 1966.

BUBER, Martin. *Eclipse of God: Studies in the Relation Between Religion and Philosophy*. New York: Harper, 1957.

BURTT, E. A. *Types of Religious Philosophy*. New York: Harper, 1951.

JOLIVET, R. *The God of Reason*. London: Burns and Oates, 1959.

KAUFMANN, Walter. *Critique of Religion and Philosophy*. New York: Harper, 1958.

MEHTA, Ved. *The New Theologian*. New York: Harper and Row, 1966.

ALTIZER, Thomas. "The Shape of a Radical Theology," *Christian Century*, LXXXII (1965), 1219-22.

BARTH, Karl. "Liberal Theology: Some Alternatives," *The Hibbert Journal*, LIX (1960-61), 213-19.

BLAKE, J. A. "Compatibility of Faith and Reason," *Journal of Religion and Health*, IV (1964), 86-103.

BRAUN, Herbert. "The Problem of a New Testament Theology," *Journal for Theology and Church*, I (1965), 169-83.

CLARK, M. T. "The DIVINE MILIEU in Philosophical Perspective," *Downside Review*, LXXX (1962), 12-25.

COLLINS, James. "The Bond of Natural Being," *Review of Metaphysics*, XV (1961-62), 539-72.

FONTINELL, Eugene. "Reflections on Faith and Metaphysics," *Cross Currents*, XVI (1966), 15-40.

FREEMAN, D. "Some Recent Trends in Philosophical Theology," *Philosphia Reformata*, XIII (1962), 58-69.

HARTSHORNE, C. "Some Empty Though Important Truths," *Review of Metaphysics*, VIII (1955), 553-68.

HIBBERT, Giles. "Christ and Philosophy," *Irish Theological Quarterly*, XXVII (1960), 228-35.

HILL, Edmund. "Remythologizing: The Key to Scripture," *Scripture*, XVI (1964), 65-75.

McCOLLOUGH, T. E. "Reinhold Niebuhr and Karl Barth on the Relevance of Theology," *Journal of Religion*, XLIII (1963), 49-55.

McINERNY, R. M. "Metaphor and Analogy," *Sciences Ecclésiastiques*, XVI (1964), 273-90.

MacINTYRE, Alasdair. "God and the Theologians," in *The Honest to God Debate*. Edited by D. Edwards. Philadelphia: Westminster, 1963. Pp. 215-28.

MACQUARRIE, J. "How Is Theology Possible?" *Union Seminary Quarterly Review*, XVIII (1963), 295-305.

MITCHELL, B. "Theology and Metaphysics," *Union Seminary Quarterly Review*, XX (1964), 9-19.

NIELSEN, N. C. "Warfare Between Philosophy and Theology," *Lutheran Quarterly*, VI (1954), 220-26.

PARSONS, H. "A Reformulation of the Philosophical Presuppositions of Religion," *Journal of Religion*, XLII (1962), 119-31.

POLANYI, M. "Faith and Reason," *Journal of Religion*, XLI (1961), 237-47.

QUINN, E. "Revelation: Propositions or Encounter?" *Downside Review*, LXXIX (1961), 10-21.

RAHNER, Karl. "Philosophy and Theology," *Theology Digest*, XII (1964), 118-22.

RAMSEY, I. T. "Contemporary Philosophy and the Christian Faith," *Religious Studies*, I (1965), 47-61.

REARDON, B. M. G. "One Problem of a Philosophical Theology," *Hibbert Journal*, LIX (1960), 30-37.

SIKES, W. W., WAGERS, H., and WILD, J. "Theologian and the Philosopher," *Religion in Life*, XXXIII (1964), 334-71.

SONTAG, F., and CORBISHLEY, T. "Philosophy, Theology and Metaphysics: A Protestant-Catholic Dialogue," *Heythrop Journal*, II (1961), 299-317.

STOKES, M. B. "Theology and the Anti-metaphysical Spirit," *Religion in Life*, XXVIII (1959), 413-25.

TILLICH, P. "The Relation of Metaphysics and Theology," *Review of Metaphysics*, X (1956), 57-63.

TRETHOWAN, I. "Anti-metaphysical Theology," *Downside Review*, LXXX (1962), 319-32.

BOUILLARD, M. "L'expérience humaine et le point de départ de la théologie fondamentale," *Concilium*, I (1965), 83-92.

DUMERY, Henry, and NICOLAS, J. H. "Foi et connaissance," *Revue Thomiste*, LX (1960), 419-24.

MIANO, Vincenzo. "Il Dio della religione e quello della filosofia," in *Atti del Central di Studi Filosofici* (Gallarate, 1960). Brescia: Morcelliana, 1961. Pp. 407-15.

MULLER, O. "Die 'Ratio' in der Theologie," *Münchener Theologische Zeitschrift*, XII (1961), 112-32.

PESCE, Domenico. "Della fede come presupposto della filosofia della religione," in *Atti del Central de Studi Filosofici* (Gallarate, 1960). Brescia: Morcelliana, 1961. Pp. 208-11.

PHILIPP, Wolfgang. "Metaphysik und Glaube: Die Grundgedanken der Physikotheologie Bernhard Nieuwentijts," *Neue Zeitschrift für Systematische Theologie*, II (1960), 90-122.

PRZYWARA, E. "Zwischen Metaphysik und Christentum," *Philosophisches Jahrbuch*, LXVI (1958), 181-93.

RIET, Georges Van. "Expérience religieuse et philosophie," in *Atti del Centro di Studi Filosofici* (Gallarate, 1960), Brescia: Morcelliana, 1961. Pp. 161-67.

——. "Foi chrétienne et réflexion philosophique," *Epheme-rides Theologicae Lovanienses,* XXXVII (1961), 417-49.

C. METAPHYSICS AND THEODICY

COBB, John B. *A Christian Natural Theology.* Philadelphia: Westminster, 1965.

McGLYNN, James V. *A Metaphysics of Being and God.* Englewood Cliffs, N. J.: Prentice-Hall, 1966.

MYERS, Gerald E. *Self, Religion, and Metaphysics.* New York: Macmillan, 1961.

TRESMONTANT, Claude. *Christian Metaphysics.* New York: Sheed and Ward, 1965.

CHERBONNIER, E. L. "Is There a Biblical Metaphysic?" *Theology Today,* XV (1958), 454-69.

De GEORGE, R. T. "Uneasy Revival of Metaphysics," *Review of Metaphysics,* XVI (1962), 68-81.

FOX, M. "Tillich's Ontology and God," *Anglican Theological Review,* XLIII (1961), 260-67.

HOLMES, Frank. "The Relevance of Metaphysics," *Hibbert Journal,* LVII (1958), 9-19.

MARIAS, J. "Metaphysics: Existence and Human Life," *Yale French Studies,* XVI (1955-56), 118-26.

MUNK, A. W. "Defense of the Metaphysical Quest," *Journal of Bible and Religion,* XXIV (1956), 31-35.

SIKES, Walter. "Current Philosophical World Views," *Encounter,* XXV (1964), 162-84.

WATTS, A. V. "Metaphysics," *Journal of Religious Thought,* X (1953), 132-43.

WERKMEISTER, W. H. "Reflections on the Possibilities of Metaphysics," *Proceedings of the American Catholic Philosophical Association,* XXXVIII (1964-65), 37-49.

CASTELLI, E., *et al. Metafisica ed esperienza religiosa.* Roma: Bocca, 1957.

GIRARDI, J. *Theologia naturalis.* Torino: Internazionale, 1961.

GRISON, M. *Théologie naturelle ou théodicée.* Paris: Beauchesne, 1959.

JOLIVET, Regis. *Man and Metaphysics.* New York: Hawthorn, 1961.

MADICKE, Horst. *Naturerkenntnis oder Gottesglaube.* Leipzig: Urania, 1961.

TRESMONTANT, Claude. *Les idées maîtresse de la métaphysique chrétienne.* Paris: Seuil, 1962.

BENDIEK, J. "Über ein Argument der natürlichen Theologie," *Franziskanische Studien,* XVI (1959), 1-18.

BRANCAFORTE, Antonio. "Metafisica e antimetafisica," *Teoresi,* XIX (1964), 86-100.

BUSA, Roberto. "Saggio di derivazione della teologia naturale dalla problematica del 'consenso universale sulla divinità,' " *Miscellanea A. Gazzana,* II (1960), 339-48.

DOIG, James C. "Science première et science universelle dans le COMMENTAIRE DE LA MÉTAPHYSIQUE de saint Thomas d'Aquin," *Revue Philosophique de Louvain,* LXIII (1965), 41-96.

DOOYEWEERD, H. "La nouvelle tâche d'une philosophie chrétienne," *La Revue Réformée,* X (1959), 64-76.

ISAYE, G. "La Metaphysique des simples," *Nouvelle Revue Théologique,* LXXXII (1960), 673-98.

SCHUTER, Dietrich. "Literaturbericht: Metaphysik," *Zeitschrift für Philosophie und Theologie,* I (1965), 120-26.

D. KNOWLEDGE OF GOD

BAILLIE, John. *Our Knowledge of God.* New York: Scribner's, 1961.

———. *The Sense of the Presence of God.* New York: Scribner's, 1962.

CALLENS, L. J. *Our Search to God.* St. Louis, Herder, 1964.

DANIELOU, Jean. *God and the Ways of Knowing*. Cleveland, Ohio: World, 1957.

GLEASON, Robert W. *The Search for God*. New York: Sheed and Ward, 1964.

GOLDMANN, Lucien. *The Hidden God*. New York: Humanities, 1965.

HARTSHORNE, Charles. *Man's Vision of God and the Logic of Theism*. Hamden, Conn.: Shoe String Press, 1941.

LEWIS, Hywel D. *Our Experience of God*. New York: Macmillan, 1960.

LOSSKY, Vladimir. *The Vision of God*. London: Faith, 1964.

LUBAC, H. de. *The Discovery of God*. New York: Kenedy, 1960.

MARITAIN, Jacques. *Approaches to God*. New York: Harper, 1954.

MATCZAK, Sebastian A. *Karl Barth on God: The Knowledge of the Divine Existence*. New York: St. Paul Publications, 1962.

SILLEM, E. A. *Ways of Thinking About God: Thomas Aquinas and Some Recent Problems*. London: Longman and Todd, 1961.

SMITH, John. *Reason and God*. New Haven: Yale Univ. Press, 1961.

TRESMONTANT, Claude. *Toward the Knowledge of God*. Baltimore: Helicon, 1961.

VOGEL, A. A. *Reality, Reason and Religion*. London: Longmans, 1959.

WEIGEL, Gustave, and MADDEN, H. G. *Religion and the Knowledge of God*. Englewood Cliffs, N.J., Prentice-Hall, 1961.

WELLS, Donald. *God, Man and the Thinker*. New York: Random House, 1962.

WIEMAN, Henry. *Intellectual Foundation of Faith*. New York: Philosophical Library, 1961.

BAUSANI, A. "Can Monotheism Be Taught?" *Numen*, X (1963), 167-201.

BOHLMANN, R. "The Natural Knowledge of God," *Concordia Theological Monthly*, XXXV (1964), 721-35.

BOND, Charles M. "How Does One Know God," *Andover Newton Quarterly*, LIII (1961), 41-45.

CHRISTIAN, W. A. "Truth Claims in Religion," *Journal of Religion*, XLII (1962), 52-62.

DICKINSON, R. "How Do We Know God?" *Journal of Bible and Religion*, XXVI (1958), 38-43.

DILLEY, F. B. "Is There Knowledge of God?" *Journal of Religion*, XXXVIII (1958), 116-26.

FERRE, N. F. S. "Definition of God in the Light of Twentieth-Century Knowledge," *Religion in Life*, XXVII (1958), 537-43.

GLASGOW, W. D. "Knowledge of God," *Philosophy*, XXXII (1957), 229-40.

HAMILTON, W. "On Doing Without Knowledge of God," *Journal of Religion*, XXXVII (1957), 37-43.

HARRISON, F. "Knowing God," *Philosophy Today*, IX (1965), 200-210.

HARTSHORNE, C. "Abstract and Concrete in God," *Review of Metaphysics*, XVII (1963), 289-95.

LEWIS, Ford. "The Loom of God," *Hibbert Journal*, LVIII (1959), 61-65.

NIELSON, K. "Christian Positivism and the Appeal to Religious Experience," *Journal of Religion*, XLII (1962), 248-61.

O'BRIEN, Ignatius. "Analogy and Our Knowledge of God," *Philosophical Studies*, VI (1956), 91-104.

O'BRIEN, Thomas. "Reflection on the Question of God's Existence in Contemporary Thomistic Metaphysics, *Thomist*, XXIII (1960), 1-89.

O'REILLY, Peter. "Knowledge of God in Metaphysics and the Philosophy of Nature," *Proceedings of the American Catholic Philosophical Association*, XXX (1956), 117-28.

SCHMIDT, P. F. "Is There Religious Knowledge?" *Journal of Philosophy*, LV (1958), 529-38.

SCHRAG, C. O. "Ontology and the Possibility of Religious Knowledge," *Journal of Religion*, XLII (1962), 87-95.

SMITH, J. E. "The Experiential Foundations of Religion," *Journal of Philosophy*, LV (1958), 538-45.

————. "The Permanent Truth in the Idea of Natural Religion," *The Harvard Theological Review*, LIV (1961), 1-19.

SMITH, Joseph J. "Primal Revelation and the Natural Knowledge of God: Brunner and Catholic Theology," *Theological Studies*, XXVII (1966), 339-57.

TRETHOWAN, I. "Antimetaphysical Theology: The Status of Metaphysical Conclusions About God," *Downside Review*, LXXX (1962), 319-32.

CHAUVIN, R. *Dieu des savants, Dieu de l'expérience*. Paris: Mame, 1958.

DELESALLE, J. *Cet étrange secret: poésie et philosophie à la recherche de Dieu*. Bruges: Desclée de Brouwer, 1957.

LE SENNE, R. *La découverte de Dieu*. Paris: Aubier, 1955.

MEURERS, Joseph. *Die Frage nach Gott und die Naturwissenschaft*. München: Pustet, 1962.

MORE-PONTGIBAUD, Charles de. *Du fini à l'infini: introduction à l'étude de la connaissance de Dieu*. Paris: Aubier, 1957.

THIBEAUD, H. *A Dieu et à Jésus-Christ par la philosophie*. Paris: Lethielleux, 1956.

TRESMONTANT, C. *Essai sur la connaissance de Dieu*. Paris: Cerf, 1959.

WHITE, V. *Dieu l'inconnu*. Tournai: Casterman, 1958.

BORDONI, M. "Note e discussioni intorno al problema della conoscenza di Dio," *Euntes Docete*, XI (1958), 274-89.

COLIN, P. "Phénoménologie et connaissance de Dieu," *Recherches Philosophiques*, III-IV (1958), 399-404.

COLOMBO, C. "La conoscibilità naturale di Dio: nell'insegnamento del Magistero Ecclesiastico," *Scuola Cattolica*, LXXXV (1957), 325-97.

GARCIA LOPEZ, J. "El conocimiento natural de Dios," *Anales de la Universidad de Murcia*, XIII (1954-55), 978-1116.

KOHLER, R. "Der 'Deus absconditus' in Philosophie und Theologie," *Zeitschrift für Religions und Geistesgeschichte*, VII (1955), 46-58.

LAMBILLIOTTE, M. "Du sens du Divin," *Revue Teilhard*, V (1961), 15-19.

LOCHET, L. "La connaissance de Dieu dans son Eglise," *Nouvelle Revue Théologique*, LXXIX (1957), 673-703.

LOTZ, J. B. "Von der Gotteserfahrung im Denken unserer Zeit," *Stimmen der Zeit*, CLXXII (1963), 321-34.

OGIERMANN, Helmut. "Die Problematik der religiösen Erfahrung," *Scholastik*, XXXVII (1963), 481-518.

ROLLAND, E. "L'intuition philosophique de Dieu," *Sciences Ecclésiastiques*, XIV (1962), 235-64.

SANTAMARIA, Carlos. "L'homme à la recherche de Dieu," in *L'homme, son oeuvre et ses âmes*. Edited by J. Leclercq. Paris: Casterman, 1961. Pp. 277-89.

SCHRUERS, P. "Notre époque à la découverte de Dieu," *Revue Ecclésiastique de Liège*, LI (1965), 3-19.

E. RELIGIOUS LANGUAGE

BANERJEE, N. V. *Language, Meaning, and Persons*. London: Allen, 1963.

BAUMER, W. H. *The Problem of Meaning in Religious Language*. Madison, Wis.: Univ. of Wisconsin, 1960.

BOCHENSKI, Innocentius M. *The Logic of Religion*. New York: New York Univ. Press, 1965.

CHRISTIAN, William A. *Meaning and Truth in Religion*. Princeton, N.J.: Princeton Univ. Press, 1964.

CRYSTAL, David. *Linguistics, Language, and Religion*. New York: Hawthorn, 1965.

DILLEY, Frank B. *Metaphysics and Religious Language*. New York: Columbia Univ. Press, 1964.

DUBA, A. D. *The Principles of Theological Language in the Writings of Horace Bushnell and Paul Tillich, and Their Implications for Christian Education Theory.* Princeton, N. J.: Princeton Theological Seminary, 1960.

EVANS, Donald D. *The Logic of Self-involvement.* London: S.C.M., 1963.

FERRE, Frederick. *Language, Logic, and God.* New York: Harper, 1961.

GREGORY, C. H. *The Problem of Descriptive Religious Statements, with Special Reference to the Thought of Paul Tillich.* Providence, R. I.: Brown Univ. Press, 1959.

HUTCHISON, J. A. *Language and Faith.* Philadelphia: Westminster, 1963.

KWANT, R. C. *Phenomenology of Language.* Pittsburgh: Duquesne Univ. Press, 1965.

MOREAU, Jules L. *Language and Religious Language.* Philadelphia: Westminster, 1960.

RAMSEY, I. F. *Religious Language.* London: S.C.M., 1957.

ROBINSON, J. M., and COBB, J. B. *New Frontiers in Theology.* Vol. I, *Later Heidegger and Theology;* Vol. II, *New Hermeneutic.* New York: Harper, 1964.

THIEL, A. Van. *Analytical Dialectic and Christian Belief.* The Hague: Boucher, 1961.

ACHTEMEIER, Paul J. "How Adequate Is the New Hermeneutic?" *Theology Today,* XXIII (1966), 101-19.

ALTIZER, Thomas J. "Word and History," *Theology Today,* XXII (1965), 380-94.

BEVENOT, M. "Terminological Problems in the Church Today," *Heythrop Journal,* V (1964), 253-58.

BIGGER, C. "Speculative Language and Theological Vision," *Anglican Theological Review,* XLIV (1962), 365-80.

BINKLEY, L. J. "What Characterizes Religious Language?" *Journal for the Scientific Study of Religion,* II (1962), 18-24.

BISMARCK, K. Von. "The Christian Vocabulary: An Obstacle to Communication?" *The Ecumenical Review*, X (1957), 1-15.

CHAPMAN, R. "Language and Religious Experience," *The Church Quarterly Review*, CLXII (1961), 323-30.

CHARLESWORTH, M. J. "Linguistic Analysis and Language About God," *International Philosophical Quarterly*, I (1961), 139-67.

CLARKE, B. L. "The Language of Revealed Theology," *Journal of Bible and Religion*, XXXII (1964), 334-41.

CLARKE, W. Norris. "Linguistic Analysis and Natural Theology," *Proceedings of the American Catholic Philosophical Association*, XXXIV (1960), 110-26.

COPLESTON, F. C. "Philosophy and Language," *Month*, V (1951), 270-78.

DEMOS, Raphael. "The Meaningfulness of Religious Language," *Philosophy and Phenomenological Research*, XVIII (1957-58), 96-106.

FEIBLEMAN, James K. "Reflections After Wittgenstein's PHILOSOPHICAL INVESTIGATIONS," *Sophia*, XXIII (1955), 322-28.

FERRE, F. "Is Language About God Fraudulent?" *Scottish Journal of Theology*, XII (1959), 33-60.

FITCH, F. B. "Universal Meta-languages for Philosophy," *Review of Metaphysics*, XVII (1964), 396-402.

FUNK, R. W. "Colloquium on Hermeneutics," *Theology Today*, XXI (1964), 287-306.

GILKEY, Langdon B. "The God Is Dead Theology and the Possibility of God-Language," *The Voice* (1965).

GILL, J. H. "Wittgenstein and Religious Language," *Theology Today*, XXI (1964), 59-72.

GREGORY, T. "Metaphysics and Language," *Tablet*, CCIII (1954), 502-3.

GUALTIERI, A. R. "Truth Claims for Religious Images," *Religious Studies*, I (1966), 151-62.

HALL, R. C. "Is There a Special Religious Language?" *Anglican Theological Review*, XLVI (1964), 88-94.

HARE, R. M., HENLE, P., and KORNER, S. "The Nature of Analysis," *Journal of Philosophy*, LIV (1954), 741-66.

HARTSHORNE, C. "How Some Speak and Yet Do Not Speak of God," *Philosophy and Phenomenological Research*, XXIII (1962-63), 274-76.

―――. "Metaphysical Statements as Non-restrictive and Existential," *Review of Metaphysics*, XII (1958), 35-47.

―――. "Some Reflections on Metaphysics and Language," *Foundations of Language*, II (1966), 20-32.

HODGSON, Leonard. "The Word, God," *Canadian Journal of Theology*, XI (1965), 83-93.

HOLMER, P. L. "Language and Theology: Some Critical Notes," *The Harvard Theological Review*, LVIII (1965), 241-61.

―――. "Scientific Language and the Language of Religion," *Journal for the Scientific Study of Religion*, I (1961), 42-60.

KELLEY, A. D. "Can We Talk About God?" *Church Quarterly Review*, CLXIII (1962), 305-17.

KENNICK, William E. "The Language of Religion," *Philosophical Review*, LXV (1956), 56-71.

KERR, F. "Language as Hermeneutics in the Later Wittgenstein," *Tijdschrift voor Filosofie*, XXVII (1965), 491-520.

JARRETT-KERR, M. "Language, Logic, and Faith," *Hibbert Journal*, LVII (1958), 39-45.

KLEINKE, E. D. "Are Religious Statements Meaningful?" *The Journal of Religion*, XL (1960), 27-39.

LYON, Mary. "Religious Language," *Hibbert Journal*, LXII (1964), 175-77.

LYON, W. "Religious Language," *Hibbert Journal*, LXII (1964), 175-77.

McGLYNN, James. "Philosophy and Analysis," *Downside Review*, LXXVIII (1960), 93-107; 125-35.

McLAUGHLIN, P. "Linguistics and Religion," *Irish Theological Quarterly*, XXXI (1964), 78-85.

McPHERSON, Thomas. "Philosophy and Language," *Church Quarterly Review*, CLVI (1955), 158-69.

MANN, W. "New Languages for Old?" *Church Quarterly Review*, CLXIV (1963), 485-91.

MARTIN, J. A. "St. Thomas and Tillich on the Names of God," *Journal of Religion*, XXXVII (1957), 253-59.

MASIH, Y. "Religious Experience and Language," *Philosophical Quarterly*, XXXIV (1961-62), 57-65.

MILLER, R. G. "Linguistic Analysis and Metaphysics," *Proceedings of the American Catholic Philosophical Association*, XXXIV (1960), 80-109.

MYERS, C. M. "Religious Belief and Conceptual Opacity," *The Personalist*, XLVII (1966), 399-410.

NAKHNIKIAN G., and SALMON, W. C. " 'Exists' as a Predicate," *Philosophical Review*, LXVI (1957), 535-42.

NIEBUHR, Reinhold. "Schleiermacher on Language and Feeling," *Theology Today*, XVII (1960), 150-67.

NIELSEN, H. A. "Language and the Philosophy of Nature," *Proceedings of the American Catholic Philosophical Association*, XXXIV (1960), 206-9.

NIELSEN, Kai. "Can Faith Validate God-Talk?" *Theology Today*, XX (1963), 158-73.

———. "On Speaking of God," *Theoria*, XXVIIII (1962), 110-37.

———. "On Talk about God," *Journal of Philosophy*, LV (1958), 888-90.

OSBORN, R. T. "Contemporary Criticism of Christian Language," *The Journal of Bible and Religion*, XXX (1962), 26-31.

PAP, A. "Belief, Synonymity, and Analysis," *Philosophical Studies*, VI (1955), 11-15.

PLANTINGA, A. "Analytic Philosophy and Christianity," *Christianity Today*, VIII (1963), 17-20.

POTEAT, William H. " 'I Will Die': An Analysis," *Philosophical Quarterly*, IX (1959), 46-58.

REESE, W. L. "Analogy, Symbolism and Linguistic Analysis," *Review of Metaphysics*, XIII (1960), 447-68.

ROSE, M. C. "The Language of Religion," *Anglican Theological Review*, XL (1958), 108-18.

ROSS, J. F. "Analogy as a Rule of Meaning for Religious Language," *International Philosophical Quarterly*, I (1961), 468-502.

ROSS, W. G., *et al.* "God and the Verification Principle," *Religion in Life*, XXXII (1962-63), 8-68.

RYAN, C. "Metaphysics and Language: An Introduction to the Problem," *Blackfriars*, XXXII (1951), 462-68.

SLEEPER, R. "Linguistic Philosophy and Religious Belief," *Cross Currents*, III (1964), 335-59.

SMITH, R. V. "Analytical Philosophy and Religious/Theological Language," *The Journal of Bible and Religion*, XXX (1962), 101-8.

SONTAG, F. "Mythical Thought and Metaphysical Language," *Journal of Religion*, XLI (1961), 109-17.

SPILKA, B., ARMATAS, P., and NUSSBAUM, J. "The Concept of God: A Factor-analytic Approach," *Review of Religious Research*, VI (1964), 28-35.

TAYLOR, W. S. "Analogical Thinking in Theology," *Scottish Journal of Theology*, XVII (1964), 279-88.

TORRANCE, T. F. "Knowledge of God and Speech About Him According to John Calvin," *Revue d'Histoire et de Philosophie Religieuses*, XLIV (1964), 402-22.

TRETHOWAN, Illtyd, and WILLIAMS, Leo. "God and Logical Analysis," *Downside Review*, LXXIV (1956), 185-98.

UNDERWOOD, Richard. "Hermes and Hermeneutics; A Viewing from the Perspectives of the Death of God and Depth Psychology," *Hartford Quarterly*, VI (1965), 34-53.

VAN BUREN, Paul M. "Christian Education *Post mortem Dei*," *Religious Education*, LX (1965), 4-10.

————, et al. "Linguistic Philosophy and Religious Education," Religious Education, LX (1965), 2-42.

VAN ROO, William A. "Talk About God," America, CXIV (1966), 601-94.

WEBER, J. C. "Language-event and Christian Faith," Theology Today, XXI (1965), 449-57.

WELLS, R. "What Has Linguistics Done for Philosophy?" The Journal of Philosophy, LIX (1962), 697-708.

WILLIAMS, C. J. F. "Existence and the Meaning of the Word 'God,'" Downside Review, LXXVII (1959), 53-71.

WOELFEL, James W. " 'Non-Metaphysical' Christian Philosophy and Linguistic Philosophy," Scottish Journal of Theology, XVII (1964), 10-20.

ZUURDEEG, W. F. "The Nature of Theological Language," Journal of Religion, XL (1960), 1-8.

NOAK, H. Sprache und Offenbarung. Gütersloh: Mohn, 1960.

SCHNEEMELCHER, W. Das Problem der Sprache in Theologie und Kirche. Berlin: Töpelmann, 1959.

SIEWERTH, Gustav. Ontologie du langage. Paris: Desclée, 1958.

VASSLER, Karl. Espíritu y cultura en el lenguaje. Madrid: Cultura Hispánica, 1959.

EBELING, G. "Wort Gottes und Hermeneutik," Zeitschrift für Theologie und Kirche, LVI (1959), 224-51.

EICKELSCHULTE, D. "Hermeneutik und Theologie bei Rudolf Bultmann. Zu den Möglichkeiten eines Gespräches mit der katholischen Theologie," Scholastik, XL (1965), 23-41.

FUNKE, G. "Krise der Hermeneutik?" Zeitschrift für Religions- und Geistesgeschichte, XLII (1961), 1-24.

HAECHT, L. Van. "Le langage de la philosophie," Revue Philosophique de Louvain, LVIII (1960), 135-64.

IMBS, P. "Du langage humain à la Parole de Dieu," Maison-Dieu, LIII (1959), 9-22.

KIMMERLE, Heinz. "Metahermeneutik, Applikation, hermeneutische Sprachbildung," *Zeitschrift für Theologie und Kirche,* LXI (1964), 221-35.

MALET, A. "Le problème des concepts et du langage dans la théologie et dans la prédication," *Foi et Vie,* LVIII (1959), 25-37.

SCHMIDT, Gerhart. "Die ethische bedeutsamkeit der sprache," *Zeitschrift für Evangelische Ethik,* III (1959), 107-13.

STUCKI, Pierre-André. "Herméneutique et dialectique," *Revue de Théologie et de Philosophie,* II (1966), 121-29.

WAELHENS, H. De. "Sur une herméneutique de l'hermémeutique," *Revue Philosophique de Louvain,* LX (1962), 573-91.

WALGRAVE, J. H. "Philosophie analytique et religion," *Archives de Philosophie,* XXIV (1961), 277-329.

F. MYTH, SYMBOL, AND ANALOGY

ALTIZER, Thomas J. *Mircea Eliade and the Dialectic of the Sacred.* Philadelphia: Westminster, 1963.

———. (ed.) *Truth, Myth, and Symbol.* Englewood Cliffs, N.J.: Prentice-Hall, 1959.

BARTISCH, H. W. (ed.) *Kerygma and Myth.* Translated by Reginald Fuller. London: S.P.C.K., 1964. 2 vols.

BEVAN, Edwin. *Symbolism and Belief.* London: Allen and Unwin, 1938.

BULTMANN, Rudolf. *Jesus Christ and Mythology.* New York: Scribner's, 1958.

CASSIRER, Ernst. *The Philosophy of Symbolic Forms.* Translated by Ralph Manheim. New Haven: Yale Univ. Press, 1953.

ELIADE, Mircea. *Images and Symbols: Studies in Religious Symbolism.* New York: Sheed and Ward, 1961.

———. *Myth and Reality.* New York: Harper and Row, 1963.

168   RELIGIOUS KNOWLEDGE AND LANGUAGE

———. *Myths, Dreams and Mysteries: The Encounter Between Contemporary Faiths and Archaic Realities*. New York: Harper, 1960.

———. *Sacred and Profane: The Nature of Religion*. New York: Harcourt, 1959.

GELLNER, Ernest. *Words and Things: A Critical Account of Linguistic Philosophy and a Study in Ideology*. London: Gollancz, 1959.

HENDERSON, Ian. *Myth in the New Testament*. Chicago: Regnery, 1952.

JASPERS, Karl. *Man in the Modern Age*. New York: Holt, 1933.

JOHNSON, Frederick. *Religious Symbolism*. New York: Institute for Religious and Social Studies, 1955.

KIMPEL, Benjamin. *The Symbols of Religious Faith*. New York: Philosophical Library, 1954.

KNOX, John. *Myth and Truth: An Essay on the Language of Faith*. Charlottesville, Va.: Univ. of Virginia Press, 1964.

LANGER, Susanne K. *Philosophy in a New Key: A Study in the Symbolism of Reason, Rite, and Art*. Cambridge, Mass.: Harvard Univ. Press, 1951.

MAY, Rollo. (ed.) *Symbolism in Religion and Literature*. New York: Braziller, 1960.

WHITEHEAD, Alfred. *Symbolism: Its Meaning and Effect*. New York: Macmillan, 1927.

ALDWINCKLE, R. F. "Tillich's Theory of Religious Symbolism," *Canadian Journal of Theology*, X (1964), 110-17.

AYERS, Robert H. " 'Myth' in Theological Discourse: A Profusion of Confusion," *Anglican Theological Review*, XLVIII (1966), 200-217.

BERGGREN, D. "Use and Abuse of Metaphor," *Review of Metaphysics*, XVI (1963), 237-58, 450-72.

BULTMANN, R. "On the Problem of Demythologizing," *Journal of Religion*, XLII (1962), 96-102.

CAHILL, J. "Bultmann's Idea of Revelation," *Theology Digest*, XI (1963), 105-8.

CASSERLEY, J. V. "Image-symbols and Event-symbols," *Cross Currents,* VIII (1958), 315-26.

CLARKE, B. L. "God and the Symbolic in Tillich," *Anglican Theological Review,* XLIII (1961), 302-11.

COPE, Gilbert. "Symbols Old and New," *Theology Today,* XVII (1961), 498-504.

DANIELOU, J. "Problem of Symbolism," *Thought,* XXV (1950), 423-40.

FENTON, J. Y. "Being-itself and Religious Symbolism," *Journal of Religion,* XLV (1965), 73-86.

FRIEDMAN, M. S. "Religious Symbolism and Universal Religion," *Journal of Religion,* XXXVIII (1958), 215-25.

GEERTZ, C. "Ethos, World View and the Analysis of Sacred Symbols," *Antioch Review,* XVII (1957-58), 421-37.

GRABAU, R. F. "Necessity of Myth: An Answer to Rudolf Bultmann," *Joural of Religion,* XLIV (1964), 113-21.

GREELEY, A. "Man's Need for Symbols," *Commonweal,* LXXIII (1961), 388-90.

————. "Myths, Symbols and Rituals in the Modern World," *Critic,* XX (1962), 18-25.

KERENYI, C. "Interpretation of Religion and Mythology," *Hibbert Journal,* LIV (1956), 124-30.

LUYSTER, Robert. "The Study of Myth: Two Approaches," *The Journal of Bible and Religion,* XXXIV (1966), 235-43.

McLEAN, George F. "Symbol and Analogy: Tillich and Thomas," in *Paul Tillich in Catholic Thought.* Edited by T. O'Meara and C. Weisser. Chicago: Priory, 1964. Pp. 145-83.

McLELLAND, J. C. "Mythology and Theological Language," *Scottish Journal of Theology,* II (1958), 13-21.

McPHERSON, Thomas. "Religion as the Inexpressible," in *New Essays in Philosophical Theology.* Edited by A. Flew and A. Macintyre. London: S.C.M., 1955. Pp. 131-43.

MARK, J. "Myth and Miracle: Or the Ambiguity of Bultmann," *Theology,* LXVI (1963), 134-40.

MATSON, W. I. "Cornford on the Birth of Metaphysics," *Review of Metaphysics*, VIII (1955), 443-54.

MILLER, David. "The Symbolizing of the Symbol," *Brethren Life and Thought*, VIII (1963), 17-24.

PARKIN, Vincent. "Bultmann and Demythologizing," *London Quarterly and Holborn Review*, XXXI (1962), 258-63.

REARDON, B. M. G. "Myth, Metaphysics and Reality," *Hibbert Journal*, LV (1957), 124-30.

RUBENSTEIN, Richard. "Person and Myth in the Judaeo-Christian Encounter," *Christian Scholar*, XLV (1963), 278-92.

SLATTERY, M. P. "Poets and Philosophers," *Franciscan Studies*, XVII (1957), 373-90.

SONTAG, F. "Mythical Thought and Metaphysical Language," *The Journal of Religion*, XLI (1961), 109-17.

STRENG, F. J. "Problem of Symbolic Structure in Religious Apprehension," *History of Religions*, IV (1964), 126-53.

TILLICH, Paul. "The Religious Symbol," in *Religious Experience and Truth: A Symposium*. New York: New York Univ. Press, 1961. Pp. 301-21.

———. "The Religious Symbol," *Daedalus*, LXXXVII (1958), 3-21.

VAHANIAN, G. "Biblical Symbolism and Man's Religious Quest," *Journal of Religion*, XXXVIII (1958), 326-39.

WEIGEL, G. "Myth, Symbol, and Analogy," in *Paul Tillich in Catholic Thought*. Edited by T. O'Meara and C. Weisser. Chicago: Priory, 1964. Pp. 184-96.

WHEELER, A. M. "God and Myth," *Hibbert Journal*, LXII (1964), 170-73.

BIANCO, Franco. *Distruzione e riconquista del mito*. Milano: Silva, 1961.

CASTELLI, E. *Umanesimo e simbolismo*. Padova: C.E.D.A.M., 1958.

DELESALLE, Jacques. *Cet étrange secret: poésie et philosophie à la recherche de Dieu*. Paris: Desclée, 1957.

Entmythologisierung und Interpretation. Kerygma und Mythos, VI (1963), 1-248.

GUSDORF, Georges. *Mythe et métaphysique.* Paris: Flammarion, 1963.

HOSTIE, R. *Du mythe à la religion: la psychologie de C. G. Jung.* Bruges: Desclée, 1955.

NOLLER, G. *Sein und Existenz: Die Überwindung des Subjekt-Objektschemas in der Philosophie Heideggers und in der Theologie der Entmythologisierung.* München: Kaiser, 1962.

SÖHNGEN, Gottlieb. *Analogie und Metaphor.* Freiburg: Alber, 1962.

THEUNIS, F. *Offenbarung und Glaube bei Rudolf Bultmann: Ergänzung zu Kerygma und Mythos, V.* Hamburg: Reich, 1960.

VONESSEN, F. *Mythos und Wahrheit.* Einsiedeln: Johannes, 1964.

WISSE, S. *Das religiöse Symbol: Versuch einer Wesensdeutung.* Essen: Ludgerus, 1963.

CARACCIOLO, Alberto. "Demitizzazione e pensiero contemporaneo," *Archivio di Filosofia* (1961), 221-29.

CASTELLI, Enrico. "La problématique de la démythisation," *Archivio di Filosofia* (1961), 13-17.

DANIELOU, J. "Symbolisme et théologie," in *Interpretation der Welt.* Hrsg. von H. Kuhn. Wurzburg: Echter, 1965. Pp. 663-74.

DONCOEUR, P. "Rôle et valeur du symbole dans l'Eglise," *Verbum Caro,* XII (1958), 160-66.

DUMERY, H., and BARTHEL, P. "Philosophie, mythe et foi chrétienne," *Revue de Théologie et de Philosophie,* XCVIII (1965), 156-71.

FRIES, H. "Mythos und Offenbarung," in *Fragen der Theologie Heute* Einsiedeln: Benziger, 1957. Pp. 11-44.

―――. "Um Bultmanns Glaubenstheologie," *Münchener Theologische Zeitschrift,* XV (1963), 65-75.

172   RELIGIOUS KNOWLEDGE AND LANGUAGE

GIANNINI, G. "A proposito di demitizzazione," *Filosofia e Vita,* IV (1963), 65-75.

GOLLWITZER, H. "La révélation et notre représentation de Dieu," *Foi et Vie,* LXIV (1965), 3-22.

GOMEZ CAFFARENA, José. "Analogía de ser y dialéctica en la afirmación humana de Dios," *Pensamiento,* XVI (1960), 143-74.

KNEVELS, W. "Wesen und Sinn des Mythos," *Studium Generale,* XV (1962), 668-706.

MANNO, M. "Filosofia e religione: introduzione allo studio del Bultmann," *Teoresi,* XII (1957), 17-84.

MARLE, René. "Y a-t-il un problème catholique de la démythisation," *Archivio di Filosofia* (1961), 157-65.

PACI, Enzo. "Funzione e significato del mito," *Giornale Critico della Filosofia Italiana,* XXXV (1956), 148-59.

PEPIN, J. "Le temps et le mythe," *Les Etudes Philosophiques,* XVII (1962), 55-68.

PRZYWARA, Erich. "Mensch, Welt, Gott, Symbol," *Archivio di Filosofia* (1958), 35-50.

THEUNIS, F. "Prolégomènes à la problématique de la démythisation," *Archivio di Filosofia* (1961), 167-74.

VALORI, Paolo. "Un convegno sull 'demitizzazione" Bultmanniana," *Gregorianum,* XLII (1962), 527-35.

VERGOTE, A. "Le symbole," *Revue Philosophique de Louvain,* LVII (1959), 197-224.

CHAPTER VII

Moral Philosophy

This chapter comprises selected books and articles on moral philosophy. The particular developments in this area in recent times have been due especially to the renewed emphasis on the dignity of the person. This emphasis has allowed for new insights into human freedom and its implications for a personal value structure. This, in turn, has raised important questions for the field of moral philosophy or ethics and its study of law. The relevant works have been drawn together and arranged under the following topics:

A. Freedom

B. Value

C. Ethics

D. Law

E. Natural Law

Also relevant to these questions is the material in the previous chapter concerning man and God as well as the material of Chapters VI, VII, IX, X, and XVII, in *An Annotated Bibliography of Philosophy in Catholic Thought* by the same editor.

A. FREEDOM

ADLER, M. *The Idea of Freedom.* New York: Doubleday, 1958-1961.

ANSHEN, Ruth. (ed.) *Freedom: Its Meaning.* New York: Harcourt, Brace, 1940.

AUGUSTINE, St. *The Problem of Free Choice.* Translated by H. Pontifex. Westminster, Md.: Newman, 1955.

BERDYAEV, N. *Freedom and the Spirit*. New York: Scribner's, 1935.

―――. *Slavery and Freedom*. New York: Scribner's; 1961.

BERGSON, Henri. *Time and Free Will*. New York: Macmillan, 1910.

CLARK, M. *Augustine, Philosopher of Freedom*. New York: Desclée, 1958.

CRANSTON, M. J. *Freedom: A New Analysis*. New York: Longmans, Green, 1953.

D'ARCY, Eric. *Conscience and its Right to Freedom*. New York: Sheed and Ward, 1962.

DEWEY, J. *On Exprience, Nature and Freedom*. New York: Liberal Arts, 1960.

EDWARDS, J. *Freedom of the Will*. New Haven: Yale Univ. Press, 1957.

FARRER, Austin. *The Freedom of the Will*. New York: Scribner's, 1960.

FROMM, E. *The Fear of Freedom*. London: K. Paul, Trench, Trubner, 1952.

GELBMANN, Frederick. *Authoritarianism and Temperament*. Washington, D.C.: The Catholic Univ. of America Press, 1958.

GRINDEL, C. W. (ed.) *The Concept of Freedom*. Chicago: Regnery, 1955.

GUARDINI, R. *Freedom, Grace, and Destiny*. New York: Pantheon, 1961.

―――. *Power and Responsibility*. Chicago: Regnery, 1961.

HÄRING, Bernhard. *The Law of Christ*. Translated by E. Kaiser. Westminster, Md.: Newman, 1961.

HAYEK, F. A. *The Constitution of Liberty*. Chicago: Univ. of Chicago Press, 1960.

HOOK, S. (ed.) *Determinism and Freedom in Age of Modern Science*. New York: Collier, 1961.

LEONI, B. *Freedom and the Law*. Princeton, N.J.: Princeton Univ. Press, 1961.

MacMURRAY, J. *Conditions of Freedom*. London: Faber and Faber, 1950.

MARITAIN, J. *Freedom in the Modern World*. London: Sheed and Ward, 1935.

MORRIS, Herbert. (ed.) *Freedom and Responsibility*. Stanford: Stanford Univ. Press, 1961.

MOUNIER, Emmanuel. *The Character of Man*. Translated by C. Rowland. New York: Harper, 1957.

O'CONNELL, David. *Christian Liberty*. Westminster, Md.: Newman, 1953.

OPPENHEIM, F. E. *Dimensions of Freedom*. New York: St. Martin's Press, 1961.

PLÉ, Albert. (ed.) *Obedience. Religious Life, III*. Westminster, Md.: Newman, 1953.

PONTIFEX, Mark. *Freedom and Providence*. New York: Hawthorn, 1960.

RAEYMAEKER, Louis de, *et al. Truth and Freedom*. Translated by H. Koren. Pittsburgh: Duquesne Univ. Press, 1954.

RAMSEY, Ian. *Freedom and Immortality*. London: Student Christian Movement Press, 1960.

RZADKIEWICZ, Arnold. *The Philosophical Bases of Human Liberty According to St. Thomas*. Washington, D.C.: The Catholic Univ. of America Press, 1949.

SCHELLING, F. W. J. *Of Human Freedom*. Chicago: Open Court, 1936.

SCHOPENHAUER, A. *Freedom of Will*. New York: Liberal Arts, 1960.

SHEEN, F. *Freedom under God*. Milwaukee: Bruce, 1940.

SIMON, Yves. *A General Theory of Authority*. Notre Dame: Univ. of Notre Dame, 1962.

SMITH, G. *The Truth That Frees*. Milwaukee: Marquette Univ. Press, 1956.

THIBON, Gustave, *et al. Christianity and Freedom: A Symposium*. London: Hollis and Carter, 1955.

TODD, John. (ed.) *Problems of Authority*. Baltimore: Helicon, 1962.

WARD, Barbara. *Faith and Freedom*. New York: Doubleday, 1958.

WILD, John. *Existence and the World of Freedom*. New York: Prentice-Hall, 1963.

ABBAGNANO, Nicola. "Intellectual Freedom," *Journal of Philosophy*, XLVIII (1951), 356-61.

BLEHL, V. F. "The Council, Newman and the Problem of Freedom and Authority," *America*, CVII (1962), 950-52.

D'ARCY, Eric. "The Logic and Meaning of the Dictum: 'Error Has No Rights,' " in *Communicationes V Congressus Thomistici Internationalis, Bibliotheca Pontificiae Academiae Romanae S. Thomas Aquinatis*, III, (1960), 287-97.

D'ARCY, M., and TURNER, Vincent. "Freedom of Choice," *Month*, XIX (1951), 69-96.

DEMPF. A. "Freedom and Value," *Philosophy Today*, III (1959), 262-67.

DISEIT, Shrinewas. "Freedom and Responsibility," *Philosophical Quarterly*, XXXIV (1961-62), 67-71.

DONCEEL, J. F. "Determinism and Freedom in the Age of Modern Science," *International Philosophical Quarterly*, I (1961), 516-32.

DUBAY, T. "Personal Integrity and Intellectual Obedience," *Review for Religious*, XXII (1963), 493-501.

EARLE, William. "Freedom and Existence," *Review of Metaphysics*, IX (1955), 45-56.

GRIMSLEY, R. "An Existentialist View of Freedom," *Filosofia*, XI (1960), 697-704.

HAMPSHIRE, S. "Spinoza and the Idea of Freedom," *Proceedings of the British Academy*, XLVI (1960), 195-215.

JOHANN, Robert. "The Way to Freedom: Responsibility," *America*, CIX (1963), 569.

KNIGHT, Thomas. "Negation and Freedom," *Review of Metaphysics*, XIII (1959-60), 407-11.

LAUER, R. Z. "St. Thomas, Theory on Intellectual Causality in Election," *New Scholasticism*, XXVIII (1954), 299-319.

LEHRER, Keith. "Can We Know that We Have Free Will by Introspection?" *The Journal of Philosophy*, LVII (1960), 145-57.

LYNCH, William F. "The Problem of Freedom," *Cross Currents*, X (1960), 96-114.

MAILLOUX, Noel. "Morality and Contemporary Psychology," *Proceedings of the Catholic Theological Society of America*, IX (1954), 47-66.

McCARTHY, D. "Freedom in the Ethics of Bertrand Russell," *Philosophical Studies*, X (1960), 100-32.

McGILL, V. J. "Conflicting Theories of Freedom," *Philosophy and Phenomenological Research*, XX (1959-60) , 437-52.

MURRAY, J. C. "The Freedom of Man in the Freedom of the Church," in *Modern Catholic Thinkers*. Edited by A. Caponigri. New York: Harper, 1960. Pp. 372-84.

———. "A Selected Bibliography on Intellectual Freedom," *The Modern Schoolman*, XXXI (1954), 117-24.

NEILSEN, K. "Examination of the Thomistic Theory of the Natural Moral Law," *Natural Law Forum*, IV (1959), 44-71.

O'NEIL, Charles. "Practical Knowledge and Liberty," *Proceedings of the American Philosophical Association*, XXIX (1955), 1-13.

QUINN, Thomas. "The True Nature of Freedom," in *Modern Myths and Popular Fancies*. Pittsburgh: Duquesne Univ. Press, 1961. Pp. 157-69.

RABBITTE, Erwin. "Liberty, Personality, Morality," *Philosophical Studies*, IX (1959), 36-48.

SAINT-HILARE, G. "Cultural Relativism and Primitive Ethics," *Modern Schoolman*, XXXVL (1959), 179-95.

SMITH, Gerard. "The Nature and Uses of Liberty," *The New Scholasticism*, XXVI (1952), 305-26.

STALLKNECT, Newton. "Freedom and Existence," *Review of Metaphysics*, IX (1955), 27-36.

178   MORAL PHILOSOPHY

URDANOZ, T. "Universal Obedience," *Cross and Crown*, IX (1957), 434-57.

WADE, Francis C. "Freedom and Existence," *Review of Metaphysics*, IX (1955), 37-45.

WEIGEL, G. "Theology and Freedom," *Thought*, XXXV (1960), 165-78.

WEISSMANN, Hans. " 'Freedom' in Ethics—a Transcausal Concept," *Philosophy and Phenomenological Research*, XX (1959), 341-53.

ANTWEILER, A. *Das Problem der Willensfreiheit*. Freiburg: Herder, 1955.

AQUINAS, Thomas von. *Die menschliche Willensfreiheit*. Düsseldorf: Schwann, 1954.

BARTOLONE, Filippo. *L'origine dell'intellettualismo nella crisi della libertà*. Palermo: Manfredi, 1959.

BERTHELEMY, J. *Structure et dimensions de la liberté*. Paris: L'Ecole, 1957.

BONTEMPS, C. *L'homme et la liberté*. Paris: Cahiers Français, 1955.

BREDOW, Gerda von. *Das Sein der Freiheit*. Düsseldorf: Schwann, 1960.

DALENCOUR, Fr. *La philosophie de la liberté comme introduction à la synthèse humaine*. Paris: Nizet, 1953.

DELESALLE, Jacques. *Liberté et valeur*. Louvain: Nauwelaerts, 1950.

L'église et la liberté. Recherches et Débats, I (1952).

FINANCE, J. de. *Existence et liberté*. Lyon: Vitte, 1955.

GRENIER, Jean. *Absolu et choix*. Paris: Presses Univ. de France, 1961.

GUSDORF, Georges. *Signification humaine de la liberté*. Paris: Payot, 1962.

HARTMANN, Albert. *Kirche und Freiheit*. Kevelaer: Butzon, 1956.

―――. *Vraie et fausse tolérance*. Paris: Cerf, 1958.

HAVARD, R. *Les problèmes de la liberté*. Paris: Desclée, 1957.

JANSSENS, L. *Droits personnels et autorité.* Louvain: Nauwe-laerts, 1954.

JERPHAGNON, Lucien. *Servitude de la liberté?* Paris: Fayard, 1958.

KIRCHER, V. *Die Freiheit des körpergebundenen Willens.* Frei-burg (Schw.): Universitätsverlag, 1957.

LEBACQZ, J. *Libre arbitre et jugement.* Bruges: Desclée, 1960.

MARCHELLO, Giuseppe. *La crisi del concetto filosofico della libertà.* Milano: A. Giuffrè, 1959.

MAUCHAUSSAT, Gaston. *La liberté spirituelle.* Paris: Presses Univ. de France, 1959.

NÉDONCELLE, Maurice. *Vers une philosophie de l'amour et de la personne.* Paris: Aubier, 1957.

L'obèissance et la religieuse d'aujourd'hui. Paris: Cerf, 1951.

PÉREZ BALLESTAR, Jorge. *La libertad.* Barcelona: Teide, 1960.

RICOEUR, P. *Philosophie de la volonté.* Paris: Aubier, 1953.

RIO, Manuel. *La liberté: choix—amour—création.* Paris: Alsatia, 1961.

ROBERTS, T. D. *Réflexions sur l'exercise de l'autorité.* Trans-lated by H. Lemaitre. Paris: Cerf, 1956.

SCHARL, E. *Freiheit und Gesetz.* Regensburg: Pustet, 1958.

SIMON, Yves. *Traité du libre arbitre.* Liège: Sciences et Lettres, 1951.

SIMONCIOLI, F. *Il problema della libértà umana in Pietro di Giovanni Olivi e Pietro de Trabibus.* Milano: Vita e Pen-siero, 1956.

Structures et liberté. Paris: Desclée, 1958.

VENNES, Gaston. *Inconscient freudien et problèmes de liberté.* Trois-Rivières: Bien Public, 1960.

Verità e libertà. Atti della settimana di studio indetta dall'Acca-demia di S. Tommaso, 1952. Roma: Officium libri Catholici, 1952.

WERNER, Charles. *L'âme et la liberté.* Paris: Payot, 1960.

ZAVALLONI, Roberto. *La libertà personale nel quadro della psicologia della condotta umana.* Milano: Vita e Pensiero, 1956.

ABBAGNANO, Nicola. "Wissenschaft und Freiheit. Möglichkeit als Grundzug der Wirkichkeit," in *Sinn und Sein.* Hrsg. Richard Wisser. Tübingen: Niemeyer, 1960. Pp. 521-37.

ALCORTA, J. I. "El valor: fundamento y expresión de la libertad," *Pensamiento,* XVI (1960), 232-37.

ALEJANDRO, José M. "Liberdade e certeza," *Revista Portuguese di Filosofia,* XVI (1960), 3-18.

AMORE, B. d'. "Verità e libertà," *Sapienza,* XIII (1960), 69-82.

ARATA, Carlo. "Verità e libertà nel personalismo cristiano," in *Communicationes V Thomistici Internationalis, Bibliotheca Pontificiae Academiae Romanae S. Thomae Aquinatis,* III (1960), 387-95.

BONTADINI, Gustavo. "Libertà e valore," in *Communicationes V Congressus Thomistici Internationalis, Bibliotheca Pontificiae Academiae Romanae S. Thomae Aquinatis,* III (1960), 256-62.

BORTOLASO, G. "La libertà come potere di scelta," *La Civiltà Cattolica,* CVII (1956), 411-20.

————. "L'atto di scelta e la libertà," *La civiltà Cattolica,* CVIII (1957), 480-90.

BOURASSA, F. "La liberté sous la grâce," *Sciences Ecclésiastiques,* IX (1957), 49-66.

BUSTAMENTO, J. "Filosofía de la libertad," *Anales* (Quito) (1954), 293-504.

CAES, P. "Déterminisme et liberté," *Synthèses,* IX (1954), 20-35.

CALVETTI, Carla. "Libertà e verità nella umana situazione," in *Communicationes V Congressus Thomistici Internationalis, Bibliotheca Pontificiae Academiae Romanae S. Thomae Aquinatis,* III (1960), 263-71.

CAMELOT, T. "Obéissance et liberté," *Vie Spirituelle,* LXXXVI (1952), 154-68.

CLARK, M. "La libertad en la filosofía contemporánea," *Augustinus,* VI (1962), 143-63.

CRISTALDI, G. "La libertà come valore esistenziale," in *Communicationes V Congressus Thomistici Internationalis, Bibliotheca Pontificiae Academiae Romanae S. Thomae Aquinatis,* III (1960), 279-86.

————. "La libertà come valore esistenziale," *Giornale di Metafisica,* XV (1960), 594-99.

CUESTA, Salvador. "La libertà come valore esistenziale," *Crisis,* V (1958), 359-66.

DECKERS, H. "De juribus veritatis ac libertatis simul servandis et componendis. These: veritas vos liberat," in *Communicationes V Congressus Thomistici Internationalis, Bibliotheca Pontificiae Romanae S. Thomae Aquinatis,* III (1960), 298-306.

DONDEYNE, A. "La signification positive de la tolérance," in *Communicationes V Congressus Thomistici Internationalis, Bibiotheca Pontificiae Academiae Romanae S. Thomae Aquinatis,* III (1960), 316-22.

EBBINGHAUS, Julius. "Über die Idee der Toleranz," *Archives de Philosophie,* IV (1950), 1-34.

FINANCE, J. de "Les plans de la liberté," *Sciences Ecclésiastiques,* XIII (1961), 295-305.

————. "Liberté et fidélité," *Gregorianum,* XLIII (1962), 12-38.

FOLZ, R. "Sur le principe de l'authorité au moyen âge," *Revue des Sciences Religieuses,* XXXVII (1963), 27-33.

GEIGER, L. B. "De la liberté," *Revue des Sciences Philosophiques et Théologiques,* XLI (1957), 601-31.

————. "Philosophie réaliste et liberté," *Revue des Sciences Philosophiques et Théologiques,* XXXIX (1965), 387-407.

GIACON, Carlo. "L'intervento della libertà nella ricerca della verità," in *Communicationes V Congressus Thomistici Internationalis, Bibliotheca Pontificiae Academiae Romanae S. Thomae Aquinatis,* III (1960), 331-40.

GLOCKNER, H. "Zum Freiheitsproblem," *Zeitschrift für Philosophische Forschung,* XIV (1960), 553-70.

GONZALEZ F. CORDERO, F. "Limitaciones de la libertad," in *Communicationes V Congressus Thomistici Internationalis, Bibliotheca Pontificiae Academiae Romanae S. Thomae Aquinatis*, III, (1960), 370-76.

HERING, Jean von. "Der kategorische Prohibitiv," *Philosophisches Jahrbuch*, LXVI (1958), 239-42.

KRUGER, G. "Christlicher Glaube und existentielles Denken," in *Festschrift R. Bultmann*. Stuttgart: Kohlhammer, 1949. Pp. 169-89.

LAURENCO de FARIA, E. "A libertade como realidade situada," *Revista filosófica*, I (1951), 54-64.

LAURETANO, Bruno. "Libertà, volontà e valori," in *Atti del XII Congresso Internazionale di Filosofia*, VII (1961), 295-302.

LOBATO, Abelardo. "El valor y la libertad humana," *Estudios Filosóficos*, VIII (1959), 117-23.

LOTTIN, O. "L'obéissance de jugement est-elle possible?" *Etudes de Morale*, XVI (1961), 329-40.

————. "La preuve de la liberté humaine chez Saint Thomas d'Aquin," *Recherches de Théologie Ancienne et Médiévale*, XXIII (1956), 323-30.

LYONNET, S. "Liberté chrétienne et loi de l'esprit selon saint Paul," *Christus*, I (1954), 6-27.

MIANO, V. "La verità della libertà," in *Communicationes V. Congressus Thomistici Internationalis, Bibliotheca Pontificiae Academiae Romanae S. Thomae Aquinatis*, III (1960), 404-11.

MURCIEGO, Pablo León. "Verdad y libertad en harmonía," in *Communicationes V. Congressus Thomistici Internationalis, Bibliotheca Pontificiae Academiae Romanae S. Thomae Aquinatis*, III (1960), 412-20.

MURRAY, J. C. "La liberté et la loi," *Relations*, XXII (1962), 179-82.

NITTEL, J. "Einige Betrachtungen über die Freiheit des Menschen," in *Actes du XI Congrès International de Philosophie*, XIV (1953), 223-27.

NUTTIN, Joseph. "Liberté et vérité psychologique," in *Liberté et vérité*. Edited by H. van Waeyenbergh. Louvain: Univ. de Louvain, 1954. Pp. 99-112.

PERTICONE, Giacomo. "Libertà e valore nella coscienza comune," *Rivista Internazionale di Filosofia del Diritto*, XXXVI (1959), 357-69.

PFAFFENWIMMER, Georgius. "De libertate prout est fundamentum moralitatis," *Doctor Communis*, XIII (1960), 143-50.

PREUSE, C. "Un pluralisme des valeurs, créateur de liberté," *Synthèses*, XIII (1958), 69-70.

PIZZORNI, Reginaldo. "Legge morale, diritto naturale e libertà," in *Communicationes V. Congressus Thomistici Internationalis, Bibliotheca Pontificiae Academiae Romanae S. Thomae Aquinatis*, III (1960), 430-41.

RODRIGUEZ, José. "La libertad como lugar natural del valor," *Crisis*, V (1958), 393-97.

ROIG GIRONELLA, Juan. "Metafísica de la libertad humana," *Pensamiento*, XII (1956), 215-23.

SANTERO, L. "L'intenzionalità fondamento metafisico della libertà," *Sapienza*, VIII (1955), 413-35.

SCIACCA, M. F. "Libertad y persona humana," *Revista de Estudios Políticos*, XXXV (1951), 103-10.

SFERRAZZA, A. "Come nasce e si evolve la libertà di scelta," *Divus Thomas*, LXI (1958), 37-49.

———. "Quando l'abitudine limita la libertà umana," *Palestra del clero*, XXXVI (1957), 831-41.

SIEWERTH, Gustav. "Les limites de la liberté et de la responsabilité humaine," in *Les désordres de l'homme; semaine des intellectuels catholiques*, (1961), 41-61.

SPIRITO, Ugo, "Verità e libertà," *Giornale Critico della Filosofia Italiana*, XXXIX (1960), 190-204.

TELLO, B. "La esencia del libre albedrío," *Sapientia*, IX (1954), 124-37.

TRINITÉ, Philippe de la. "Notre liberté devant Dieu," *Etudes Carmélitaines*, XXV (1958), 47-76.

184   MORAL PHILOSOPHY

URDANOZ, T. "La libertad en el orden moral," *Estudios Filosó-ficos*, V (1956), 3-43.

VALENSIN, A. "Du libre arbitre," *Etudes Philosophiques*, I (1953), 16-27.

VALORI, Paolo. "L'aporia verità-libertà e la sua soluzione meta-fisico-etica," in *Communicationes V. Congressus Thomistici Internationalis, Bibliotheca Pontificiae Academiae Roma-nae S. Thomae Aquinatis*, III (1960), 465-70.

VERGA, Leonardo. "De iuribus veritatis ac libertatis simul ser-vandis et componendis," in *Communicationes V. Congres-sus Thomistici Internationalis, Bibliotheca Pontificiae Aca-demiae Romanae S. Thomae Aquinatis*, III (1960), 471-77.

WIDART, Henri. "Réflexions sur la nature de l'activité libre," in *Psychologie et Pastorale*. Paris: Desclée, 1953. Pp. 47-78.

WILLMANN, Hermann. "Bemerkungen zum Freiheitsbegriff des Neothomismus," *Wissenschaftliche Zeitschrift der Karl-Marx-Universität Leipzig*, VIII (1958-1959), 561-64.

YELA, Mariano. "La libertad como experiencia y como prob-lema," *Arbor*, XXXV (1956), 209-19.

ZARAGUETA, Juan. "Liberté et valeur," *Crisis*, V (1958), 409-13.

ZAVALLONI, R. "Come si pone il problema della libertà," *An-tonianum*, XXXV (1960), 449-502.

B. VALUE

ALBERT, Ethel. *A Selected Bibliography on Values, Ethics, and Esthetics in the Behavioral Sciences and Philosophy 1920-1958*. Glencoe, Ill.: Free Press, 1959.

BARRETT, Donald N. *Values in America*. Notre Dame: Univ. of Notre Dame Press, 1961.

BRADY, Sr. Marian. *The Philosophical Basis of Human Values According to Thomistic Principles*. Washington, D.C.: Cath-olic Univ. of America Press, 1963.

CHAMBERLIN, Edward Hastings. *Towards a More General Theory of Value*. New York: Oxford Univ. Press, 1957.

COLEBURT, Russell. *The Search for Values*. New York: Sheed and Ward, 1960.

FERGUSON, J. *Moral Values in the Ancient World*. London: Methuen, 1958.

FOWLER, William F. *Values*. Lynbrook, N.Y.: 1935.

GARNETT, Arthur C. *Reality and Value*. New Haven: Yale Univ. Press, 1937.

GRAHAM, Angelus C. *The Problem of Value*. New York: Hillary House, 1961.

GRUBER, Frederick C. *Aspects of Value*. Philadelphia: Univ. of Pennsylvania Press, 1959.

HALL, Everett W. *What is Value?* London: Routledge and Paul, 1952.

KOHLER, Wolfgang. *The Place of Value in a World of Facts*. New York: Liveright, 1938.

KONVITZ, Milton R. *On the Nature of Value*. New York: King's Crown, 1946.

LAIRD, John. *The Idea of Value*. Cambridge: Cambridge Univ. Press, 1929.

LAMONT, William D. *The Value Judgment*. New York: Philosophical Library, 1955.

LEPLEY, Ray. *The Language of Value*. New York: Columbia Univ. Press, 1957.

LEWIS, Clarence I. *An Analysis of Knowledge and Valuation*. La Salle, Ill.: Open Court, 1947.

MASLOW, Abraham H. (ed.) *New Knowledge in Human Values*. New York: Harper, 1959.

MORRIS, Louis W. *Polarity: A Philosophy of Tensions Among Values*. Chicago: Regnery, 1956.

MUNSTERBERG, Hugo. *The Eternal Values*. Boston: Houghton-Mifflin, 1909.

PEPPER, Stephen C. *The Sources of Value*. Berkeley: Univ. of California Press, 1958.

SCHWARZ, Balduin V. *The Human Person and the World of Values: a Tribute to Dietrich Von Hildebrand by his Friends in Philosophy.* New York: Fordham Univ. Press, 1960.

BERTOCCI, Peter A. "The Person, Obligation, and Value," *Personalist,* XL (1959), 141-51.

BOULDING, Kenneth. "The Knowledge of Value and the Value of Knowledge," in *Ethics and the Social Sciences.* Edited by Leo Ward. Notre Dame, Ind.: Univ. of Notre Dame Press, 1959. Pp. 25-42.

COMPTON, John J. "Toward an Ontology of Value," *Philosophical Quarterly,* VIII (1958), 157-70.

FAGOTHEY, A. "Problem of Being and Value in Contemporary American Axiology," *Proceedings of the American Catholic Philosophical Association,* XXXIII (1959), 73-83.

FOX, Robert W. "Empiricist Authoritarianism versus Value," *Personalist,* XL (1959), 5-12.

GUSTAFSON, G. "Moral Values," *Priest,* XIX (1963), 21-24.

HANDY, Rollo. "A Need Definition of 'Value,'" *Philosophical Quarterly,* X (1960), 156-63.

HARRIS, Flavian. "Metaphysical Constituents of the Value Experience," *Proceedings of the Duns Scotus Philosophical Association,* XXV (1961), 29-59.

HARTMAN, Robert S. "The Relationship Between Value in General and the Specific Values," *Revista Mexicana de Filosofia,* V-VI (1963), 99-129.

HILDEBRAND, Dietrich von. "The Modes of Participation in Value," *International Philosophical Quarterly,* I (1961), 58-84.

KING-FARLOW, J. "Value and 'Essentialist' Fallacies," *Thomist,* XXI (1958), 162-70.

KLUCKHOLN, C. "Science As a Possible Source of New Moral Values," *Humanist,* V (1954), 211-14.

LE SENNE, René. "The Movement of God," in *Modern Catholic Thinkers*. Edited by Aloysius Caponigri. New York: Harper, 1960. Pp. 65-81.

MARGOLIS, Joseph. "On Value Theory, by Way of the Commonplace," *Philosophy and Phenomenological Research*, XVII (1956-57), 504-15.

MATHRANI, G. N. "A Positivist Characterization of Values," *Philosophical Quarterly*, XXIX (1956-57), 203-10.

PARKER, De Witt. "Basic Categories and Attitudes of the Value Situation," *Review of Metaphysics*, XIII (1959-60), 555-96.

ROBERTS, Louise Nisbet. "Value as Comparison—A Critique," *Tulane Studies in Philosophy*, VI (1957).

SCHNEIDERMAN, Leo. "Insubstantive Values," *Philosophy and Phenomenological Research*, XVIII (1958), 237-41.

SLEEPER, R. W. "Being and Value in the Axiology of John Dewey," *Proceedings of the American Catholic Philosophical Association*, XXXIII (1959), 83-95.

WARD, L. R. "American Rural Value Pattern," *Review of Politics*, XVII (1955), 377-91.

WASSMER, F. A. "Some Reflections on German Value Theory," *Franciscan Studies*, XIX (1959), 115-27.

WERKMEISTER, William H. "The Meaning and Being of Values Within the Framework of an Empirically Oriented Value Theory," in *Sinn und Sein*. Edited by R. Wisser. Tübingen: Niemeyer, 1960. Pp. 549-57.

CESARI, Paul. *La Valeur*. Paris: Presses Universitaires de France, 1957.

COMBÉS, Joseph. *Valeur et liberté*. Paris: Presses Universitaires de France, 1960.

DAVAL, Roger. *La valeur morale*. Paris: Presses Universitaires de France, 1950.

DELESALLE, Jacques. *Liberté et valeur*. Louvain: Louvain, 1950.

EHRLICH, Walter. *Hauptprobleme der Wertphilosophie.* Tübingen: Niemeyer, 1959.

FRONDIZI, Risieri. *¿Qué son los valores?* México: Fondo de Cultura Económica, 1958.

HARTMAN, Robert S. *La estructura del valor: fundamentos de la axiología científica.* México: Fondo de Cultura Económica, 1959.

HESSEN, Johannes. *Lehrbuch der Philosophie.* Bd. II: *Wertlehre.* München: Reinhardt, 1959.

JUHOS, Béla. *Das Wertgeschehen und Seine Erfassung.* Meisenheim: Hain, 1956.

LA PIRA, G. *Il valore della persona umana.* Firenze: Fiorentina, 1955.

LAVELLE, Louis. *Traité des valeurs.* Tome II: *Le système des différentes valeurs.* Paris: Presses Universitaires de France, 1955.

LE SENNE, René. *La découverte de Dieu.* Paris: Aubier, 1955.

MARCHELLO, Giuseppe. *Diritto e valore.* Milano: Giuffrè, 1953.

MEHL, Roger. *De l'autorité des valeurs.* Paris: Presses Universitaires de France, 1957.

PIERSOL, Wesley. *La valeur dans la philosophie de Louis Lavelle.* Paris: Vitte, 1959.

Problema del valore. Atti del Centro di Studi Filosofici (Gallarate, 1956). Brescia: Morcelliana, 1957.

PUCELLE, Jean. *Etudes sur la valeur.* Lyons: Vitte, 1959.

SINEUX, R. P. *Les valeurs de la vie.* Montpelier: Charité, 1961.

BARBUY, H. "Valor e transcendencia," *Revue Brasileira de Filosofia,* X (1960), 91-98.

BERGER, Gaston. "Valeur, Signification, Existence," *Sinn und Sein.* Hrsg. Richard Wisser. Tübingen: Niemeyer, 1960. Pp. 605-10.

BRETON, S. "Réflexions sur le fondement des valeurs," *Tijdschrift voor Filosofie*, XXII (1960), 588-607.

DUPRÉEL, E. "Consistance et valeurs," *Dialectica*, XI (1957), 345-53.

FARRÉ, L. "El sistema de valores de Max Scheler comparado con Aristóteles," *Kant-Studien*, XLVIII (1956-57), 399-403.

FINANCE, J. de. "La valeur morale et son idéal," *Sciences Ecclésiastiques*, X (1958), 296-319.

FOREST, Aimé. "La contingence et les valeurs," in *La philosophie et ses problèmes* (Recueil d'études de doctrine et d'histoire offert à Monseigneur R. Jolivet.) Paris: Vitte, 1960. Pp. 361-72.

FRONDIZI, R. "Sobre la objetividad de los valores," *Scientia*, XCIV (1959), 305-10.

GÓMEZ, Nogalez, S. "La metafísica de los valores," *Las Ciencias*, XXI (1956), 617-38.

GULIAN, C. I. "Das Problem des sittlichen Wertes," *Deutsche Zeitschrift für Philosophie*, VII (1959), 86-100.

GUTIERREZ DE LOS MONTEROS, César. "Reflexión sobre et problema del ser y los valores," *Crisis*, III (1956), 249-54.

LALANDE, André. "Valeur de la différence," *Revue Philosophique de la France et de l'Etranger*, CXLV (1955), 121-39.

MORETTI-COSTANZI, Teodorico. "I valori supremi, noi e i nostri tempi," *Kant-Studien*, LIII (1961-1962), 39-50.

RECASÉNS SICHES, Luis. "Der Sinn der Objektivität der Werte," *Sinn und Sein*. Hrsg. Richard Wisser. Tübingen: Niemeyer, 1960. Pp. 559-73.

RINTELEN, Franz Joachim von. "Valeur—existence—réalité," *La Philosophie et ses Problèmes* (Recueil: R. Jolivet). Paris: Vitte, 1960. Pp. 373-83.

THUM, Beda. "Wertphilosophie und Metaphysik," *Salzburger Jahrbuch für Philosophie*, IV (1960), 7-28.

WYLLEMAN, André. "L'homme et la création des valeurs," *Revue Philosophique de Louvain*, LVIII (1960), 88-102.

C. ETHICS

ADLER, Mortimer J. *Ethics, the Study of Moral Values.* Chicago: Encyclopedia Britannica, 1962.

BAHM, Archie. *What Makes Acts Right?* Boston: Christopher, 1958.

BAIER, Kurt. *The Moral Point of View. A Rational Basis of Ethics.* Ithaca, N.Y.: Cornell Univ. Press, 1958.

D'ARCY, E. *Human Acts. An Essay on their Moral Evaluation.* London: Oxford Univ. Press, 1963.

Ethics and other Knowledge. Proceedings of the American Catholic Philosophical Association, XXXI (1957).

FAGOTHEY, Austin. *Right and Reason.* St. Louis: Mosby, 1963.

GAEDE, Erwin A. *Reinhold Niebuhr and the Relationship of Politics and Ethics.* Ann Arbor: University Microfilms, 1960.

GREENE, Theodore M. *Moral, Aesthetic, and Religious Insight.* New Brunswick, N.J.: Rutgers Univ. Press, 1958.

HAWKINS, Denis J. B. *Man and Morals.* New York: Sheed and Ward, 1961.

HENRY, A. M. *Man and His Happiness.* Chicago: Fides, 1957.

HYTTEN, E. *The Concept of Morality and the Criteria of Legitimate Argumentation. An Examination of Some Recent Definitions of Morality.* Stockholm: Stockholms Hoegskolas Humanistiska Bibliotek, 1959.

KROOK, D. *Three Traditions of Moral Thought.* London: Cambridge Univ. Press, 1959.

LAWLER, Ronald D. *The Moral Judgment in Contemporary Analytic Philosophy.* Ann Arbor: University Microfilms, 1960.

McGLYNN, J. *Modern Ethical Theories.* Milwaukee: Bruce, 1962.

MacKINNON, D. M. *A Study in Ethical Theory.* London: Black, 1957.

MENASCE, Giovani C. de. *The Dynamics of Morality*. New York: Sheed and Ward, 1961.

MOORE, T. *Principle of Ethics*. Philadelphia: Lippincott, 1959.

OESTERLE, J. A. *Ethics: an Introduction to Moral Science*. Englewood Cliffs, N.J.: Prentice-Hall, 1957.

O'RAHILLY, Alfred. *Moral and Social Principles*. Cork: Cork Univ. Press, 1956.

————. *Philosophy and Ethics*. Nottingham: Cultural Publications, 1958.

SESONSKE, Alexander. *Value and Obligation. The Foundations of an Empiricist Ethical Theory*. Berkeley: Univ. of California Press, 1957.

Studies in Ethical Theory. Boulder: Univ. of Colorado Press, 1958.

Studies in Ethics; Tulane Studies in Philosophy, VI (1957).

THOMSON, J. A. K. *The Ethics of Aristotele*. London: Allen and Unwin, 1953.

VANN, Gerald. *The Heart of Man*. New York: Doubleday, 1960.

————. *Morals and Man*. New York: Sheed and Ward, 1960.

WELTY, Eberhard. *A Handbook of Christian Ethics*. New York: Herder and Herder, 1960.

ANSCOMBE, G. E. M. "Modern Moral Philosophy," *Philosophy*, XXXIII (1958), 1-19.

BEIS, R. "Some Contributions of Anthropology to Ethics," *Thomist*, XXVIII (1964), 174-224.

BESANCENEY, P. H. "Situation Ethics or the 'New Morality,' " *American Ecclesiastical Review*, LXXXVII (1957), 100-104.

BOUGHTON, J. S. "Concerning Moral Absolutes," *The Journal of Philosophy*, LV (1958), 309-17.

BOURKE, Vernon J. "Metaethics and Thomism" in *An Etienne Gilson Tribute*. Edited by Charles O'Neil. Milwaukee: Marquette Univ. Press, 1959. Pp. 20-32.

CARR, A. M. "The Morality of Situation Ethics," *Proceedings of the Catholic Theological Society of America*, XIII (1957), 75-100.

DALY, C. B. "Logical Positivism, Metaphysics, and Ethics," *Irish Theological Quarterly*, XXIII (1956), 111-50.

DOUGHERTY, J. P. "Recent Developments in Naturalistic Ethics," *Proceedings of the American Catholic Philosophical Association*, XXXIII (1959), 97-108.

EASTON, Burnet W. "Ethical Relativism and Popular Morality," *Theology Today*, XIV (1958), 470-77.

ENTENZA-ESCOBAR, P. "Natural and Moral Obligations," *Catholic Lawyer*, VIII (1962), 308-19.

ERNST, C. "Ethics and the Play of Intelligence," *Blackfriars*, XXXIX (1958), 324-27.

———. "Transcendence and Spontaneity in THE METAPHYSICS OF MORALS," *Dominican Studies*, VII (1954), 59-72.

ESSER, G. "Intuition in Thomistic Moral Philosophy," *Proceedings of the American Catholic Philosophical Association*, XXXI (1957), 165-77.

FINDLAY, J. N. "The Methodology of Normative Ethics," *Journal of Philosophy*, LVIII (1961), 757-64.

FORD, J. C., and KELLY, G. "The Holy See and Situation Ethics" in *Contemporary Moral Theology*. Westminster, Md.: Newman, 1958. Pp. 104-23.

FAY, C. "Toward a Thomistic-Anthropological View of the Evolution of Obligation," *Natural Law Forum*, VII (1962), 38-53.

GEWIRTH, Alan. "Meta-ethics and Normative Ethics," *Mind*, LXIX (1960), 187-205.

———. "Positive 'Ethics' and Normative 'Science,'" *The Philosophical Review*, LXIX (1960), 311-30.

GLEASON, R. W. "Charity and Ethics," *Australian Catholic Review*, XXXV (1958), 126-35.

———. "Situational Morality," *Thought*, XXXII (1957), 533-58.

HILDEBRAND, D. von. "Role of Affectivity in Morality," *Proceedings of the American Catholic Philosophical Association*, XXXII (1958), 85-95.

INAGAKI, R. "The Notion of Ethical Good in Thomas Aquinas," *Studies in Medieval Thought*, III (1960), 32-48.

JARVIS, J. "In Defense of Moral Absolutes," *Journal of Philosophy*, LV (1958), 1043-53.

JORGENSEN, Carl. "The Relation Is/Ought: Hume's Problem," *Theoria*, XXVIII (1962), 53-69.

KATTSOFF, Louis O. "Obligation and Existence," *Philosophy and Phenomenological Research*, XVIII (1957-58), 489-502.

KEMP, J. "Foundations of Morality," *Philosophical Quarterly*, VII (1957), 305-18.

KENNEDY, L. "Morality Without God," *Culture*, XXIV (1963), 343-47.

KURTZ, Paul, and MEANS, Blanchard W. "A Reassessment: Does Ethics Have Any Metaphysical Presuppositions?" *The Philosophical Quarterly*, IX (1959), 19-28.

LAUER, Quentin. "Phenomenological Ethics of Max Scheler," *International Philosophical Quarterly*, I (1961), 273-300.

LENZ, J. W. "Universalizability as a Criterion of Moral Prescriptions," *Journal of Philosophy*, LVIII (1961), 694-95.

LYNCH, J. "Situation Ethics: A Bibliographic Study," *Theological Studies*, XIX (1958), 166-70.

MacLAGEN, W. G. "Respect for Persons as a Moral Principle," *Philosophy*, XXXV (1960), 193-217, 289-305.

MAY, W. E. "Structure and Argument of the Nicomachean Ethics," *New Scholasticism*, XXXVI (1962), 1-28.

MOORE, K. "Situational Ethics," *American Ecclesiastical Review*, LXXXV (1956), 29-38.

NAKHNIKIAN, George. "Intrinsic Good and the Ethical Ought," *Journal of Philosophy*, LI (1954), 788-94.

NIELSEN, Kai. "The 'Good Reasons Approach' and 'Ontological Justification' of Morality," *The Philosophical Quarterly*, IX (1959), 116-30.

OLSON, Robert G. "Authenticity, Metaphysics, and Moral Responsibility," *Philosophy*, XXXIV (1959), 99-110.

PAPPI, A. "Background of Situation Ethics," *Philosophy Today*, I (1957), 266-77.

PHELAN, G. B. "Law and Morality" in *Progress in Philosophy*. Edited by J. McWilliams. Milwaukee: Bruce, 1955. Pp. 177-97.

RENARD, H. "Introduction to the Philosophy of the Existential Moral Act," *New Scholasticism*, XXVIII (1954), 145-69.

SAINT HILAIRE, G. "Cultural Relativism and Primitive Ethics," *Modern Schoolman*, XXXVI (1959), 179-95.

SHWAYDER, D. S. "The Sense of Duty," *Philosophical Quarterly*, VII (1957), 116-25.

SIMON, Y. "Introduction to the Study of Practical Wisdom," *New Scholasticism*, XXXV (1961), 1-40.

SUMMERS, Robert S. "The 'Is' and 'Ought' in Legal Philosophy," *Philosophical Quarterly*, XIII (1963), 157-61.

TAYLOR, Paul W. "The Normative Function of Metaethics," *The Philosophical Review*, LXVII (1958), 16-32.

WILD, John. "Ethics as a Rational Discipline and the Priority of the Good," *Journal of Philosophy*, LI (1954), 776-88.

ZAVALLONI, R. "Studying Human Conduct and Personality," *Antonianum*, XXX (1955), 45-62.

BULNES, J. P. *La filosofía del deber*. Madrid: Fax, 1954.

CARDAHI, Choucri. *Droit et morale*. Beyrouth: Université Saint Joseph de Beyrouth, 1950.

DELHAYE, P. *Problème de la conscience morale chez S. Bernard*. Namur: Godenne, 1957.

DEMAN, T. *Le traitement scientifique de la morale chrétienne selon Saint Augustin*. Paris: Vrin, 1957.

GREGOIRE, F. *Les grandes doctrines morales*. Paris: Presses Universitaires de France, 1955.

HÄRING, B. *La loi du Christ. Théologie morale à l'invention des prêtres et des laics*. Tome II: *Théologie morale spéciale. La vie en communion avec Dieu*. Paris: Desclée, 1957.

————. *Le sacré et le bien. Religion et moralité dans leur rapport mutuel*. Paris: Fleurus, 1963.

HOLLENBACH, J. M. *Sein und Gewissen. Über den Ursprung der Gewissensregung. Eine Begegnung zwischen M. Heidegger und Thomistischer Philosophie.* Baden-Baden: Grimm, 1954.

HOLTE, R. *Béatitude et sagesse. Saint Augustin et le problème de la fin de l'homme dans la philosophie ancienne.* Paris: Etudes Augustiniennes, 1962.

LECLERCQ, J. *La philosophie morale de Saint Thomas devant la pensée contemporaine.* Louvain: Publications Universitaires, 1955.

MEHL, R. *De l'autorité des valeurs. Essai d'éthique Chrétienne.* Paris: Presses Universitaires de France, 1957.

MELONI, A. *La Morale naturale nella morale Christiana.* Chieri: Moderna, 1962.

NABERT, J. *Eléments pour une éthique.* Paris: Aubier, 1962.

POLETTI, Vincenzo. *Introduzione per la ricerca del fondamento della morale.* Firenze: Fratelli Lega, 1959.

ROSMINI, A. *Antropologia in servizio della scienza morale.* Milano: Fratelli Bocca, 1954.

SCHUSTER, J. B. *Philosophia moralis.* Friburgi: Herder, 1953.

SPENCER. H. *Qu'est-ce-que la morale?* Paris: Costes, 1955.

VAGORIC, Stefano. *Etica Comunista.* Roma: Pontificia Universita Gregoriana, 1959.

WINKLER, P. *Les sources mystiques des concepts moraux de l'Occident.* Paris: Editions de Trévise, 1958.

ANTONELLI, M. J. "Il concetto di imperativa della norma," *Thomistica Morum Principia*, I (1961), 15-23.

DANIELOU, J. "La morale au service de la personne," *Etudes*, CCCXVII (1963), 145-53.

FINANCE, J. de. "Réflexions sur la notion philosophique du mérite," in *La philosophie et ses problèmes.* Lyons: Vitte, 1960. Pp. 283-300.

ELORDUY, E. "La metafísica del bien moral," *Pensamiento*, XIV (1958), 65-70.

FUCHS, J. "Ethique objective et éthique de situation," *Nouvelle Revue Théologique*, LXXVIII (1956), 798-818.

HAMEL, E. "Valeur et limites de la casuistique," *Sciences Ecclésiastiques*, XI (1959), 148-73.

HIPPEL, Ernst von. "Zur Ontologie des Rechts," *Studium Generale*, XII (1959), 69-76.

HURTH, F. "Hodiernae conscientiae problemata metaphysica, psychologica, theologica," *Problemi scelti di teologia contemporanea, Analecta Gregoriana*, LXVIII (1954), 393-410.

JANNACCONE, C. "Il fondamento psicologico della morale e del diritto in S. Tommaso," *Thomistica Morum Principia*, I (1960), 103-9.

JANSSEN, A. "Pour l'histoire de la théologie morale," *Ephemerides Theologicae Lovanienses*, XXXIII (1957), 736-44.

KORINEK, A. "Identitas entis et fundamentum moralis," *Thomistica Morum Principia*, I (1961), 110-19.

LASO, J. A. "Puede decirse, según Santo Tomás, que el valor infinito del hombre sea el fundamento de la moralidad?," *Thomistica Morum Principia*, II (1960), 118-20.

LE BLOND, J. M. "Sincérité et vérité. A propos de la morale de la situation," *Etudes*, CCXCII (1957), 238-55.

MEHL, R. "Ethique des valeurs ou éthique de la parole de Dieu," *Revué de Théologie et Philosphie*, V (1956), 81-92.

MUZIO, G. "Il fondamento ontologico e psicologico della moralità secondo S. Tommaso," *Palestra del Clero*, XL (1961), 51-57.

PASTORE, A. "Dalla morale della legge alla morale dell'amore e del lavoro," *Sophia*, LVI (1956), 549-83.

PETRUZELLIS, N. "Sul fondamento critico della morale," *Thomistica Morum Principia*, II (1961), 24-43.

PINCKAERS, S. "La structure de l'acte humain suivant Saint Thomas," *Revue Thomiste*, LV (1955), 393-412.

RAEYMAEKER, L. de. "Le sens et le fondement de l'obligation morale," *Revue Philosophique de Louvain*, LVIX (1961), 76-91.

RAHNER, K. "Uber die Frage einer Formalen Existentialethik" in *Schriften zur Theologie.* Einsiedeln: Benziger, 1955. Vol. II, pp. 227-46.

SCIACCA, M. F. "Intelligenza morale e ragione etica," *Studia Patavina,* II (1955), 243-54.

STEVAUX, A. "L'idée-mère de la morale chrétienne," *Revue Dioc. Tournai,* XII (1957), 171-75.

URDANOZ, T. "El problema del orden moral y sus normas según Santo Tomás," *Ciencia Tomista,* LXXXI (1954), 241-76.

VAN MUNSTER, D. "Das Prinzip der Ethik. Eine Kierkegaardsche Annäherung," *Wissenschaft und Weisheit,* XXVI (1963), 197-205.

VANNI ROVIGHI, S. "Natura e moralità nell'etica di S. Tommaso D'Aquino," *Rivista di Filosofia Neoscolastica,* XLIX (1957), 201-12.

ZALBA, M. "Inquietudes metodológicas en teología moral," *Arbor,* XXX (1955), 357-75.

D. LAW

AQUINAS, St. Thomas. *Treatise on Law.* Chicago: Regnery, 1949.

BARTH, M. *Christ and Law.* Geneva: Student World, 1961.

BEGIN, R. F. *Natural Law and Positive Law.* Washington, D.C.: Catholic Univ. of America Press, 1959.

DALY, C. B. *Morals, Law and Life.* Dublin: Clonmore and Reynolds, 1962.

DAVITT, E. *The Elements of Law.* New York: Little, Brown, 1959.

———. *The Nature of Law.* St. Louis: Herder, 1951.

ELLUL, J. *The Theological Foundation of Law.* London: S.C.M. Press, 1961.

FREIDRICH, C. J. *The Philosophy of Law in Historical Perspective.* London: Cambridge Univ. Press, 1958.

HAGERSTROM, Axel A. T. *Inquiries into the Nature of Law and Morals*. Stockholm: Almqvist and Wiksell, 1956.

HERRON, M. *The Binding Force of Civil Laws*. Paterson, N.J.: St. Anthony Guild Press, 1958.

HOOK, Sidney. (ed.) *Law and Philosophy*. New York: New York Univ. Press, 1964.

INAGAKI, Bernard R. *Elements of Thomistic Jurisprudence*. Washington, D.C.: Catholic Univ. of America Press, 1953.

KANTORAWICZ, H. *The Definition of Law*. London: Cambridge Univ. Press, 1958.

KATZ, W. G. *Fulfillment of the Law*. Geneva: The Student World, 1961.

KELSEN, Hans. *Politics, Ethics, Religion and Law*. Berlin: de Gruyter, 1963.

KEULARD, P. B. *Religion and the Law*. Chicago: Aldine, 1962.

NORTHROP, Filmer S. C. *The Complexity of Legal and Ethical Experience; Studies in the Method of Normative Subjects*. Boston: Little, Brown, 1959.

PETRAZHITSKII, Lev Iosifovish. *Law and Morality*. Cambridge: Harvard Univ. Press, 1955.

SHUMAN, Samuel I. *Legal Positivism, Its Scope and Limitations*. Detroit: Wayne State Univ. Press, 1963.

ST. JOHN-STEVAS, Norman. *Law and Morals*. New York: Hawthorn, 1964.

VECCHIO, Giorgio del. *General Principles of Law*. Portland: Boston Univ. Press, 1958.

————. *Philosophy of Law*. Washington, D.C.: Catholic Univ. of America Press, 1953.

WRIGHT, John J. *The Christian and the Law*. Notre Dame: Fides, 1962.

BUNN, E. "A Transcendental View of Law," *Jurist*, XXIII (1963), 320-26.

CARNES, J. R. "Why Should I Obey the Law?" *Ethics*, LXXI (1960), 14-26.

COLLINS, J. "Law and the Common Good," *Irish Theological Quarterly*, XXIV (1957), 132-43.

CORBISHLEY, T. "Law, Morals and Religion; Three Levels of One Fundamental Reality," *Wiseman Review*, CCXXXV (1961), 291-302.

DWYER, R. J. "Law as Wisdom," *Jurist*, XVI (1957), 339-44.

FRANCISCO, V. A. "Man, Human Rights and Law," *Unitas*, XXVI (1953), 50-63, 272-91.

HEDENIUS, Ingemar. "On Law and Morals," *The Journal of Philosophy*, LVI (1959), 117-25.

HOPKINS, Vincent. "The Supremacy of Law: Idea and Ideal," *Thought*, XXXIV (1959), 25-53.

JENKINS, J. "The Matrix of Positive Law," *Natural Law Forum*, VI (1961), 1-50.

KAUFMANN, A. "Ontological Structure of Law," *Natural Law Forum*, VIII (1963), 79-96.

KENEALY, W. "Law and Morals," *Catholic Lawyer*, IX (1963), 200-16.

KNOWLES, David. "The Limits of Law," *Blackfriars*, XXXVII (1956), 402-12.

LUMB, R. D. "Law, Reason, Will," *Philosophical Studies*, X (1960), 179-89.

―――. "The Scholastic Doctrine of Law," *Linacre Quarterly*, XXVIII (1961), 87-88.

LYNCH, J. J. "Moral Law and Civil Legislation," *Theological Studies*, XXII (1961), 234-38.

MacGUIGAN, M. "St. Thomas and Legal Obligation," *Catholic Lawyer*, VII (1961), 323-24.

MESSNER, J. "Law in Economics and in Ethics," *Review of Social Economy*, XIII (1955), 91-99.

NAKHNIKIAN, G. "Contemporary Ethical Theories and Jurisprudence," *Natural Law Forum*, XI (1957), 4-40.

O'CONNELL, D. P. "Human Rights and the State," *Month*, XXVII (1962), 101-8.

200   MORAL PHILOSOPHY

OSSOWSKA, MARIA. "Moral and Legal Norms," *The Journal of Philosophy*, LVII (1960), 251-58.

PASSERIN d'ENTREVES, Alexander. "Legality and Legitimacy," *Review of Metaphysics*, XVI (1963), 687-762.

REALE, S. "Traditional Morality Obsolete?" *Nuntius Aulae*, XL (1958), 125-34.

ROSHWALD, Mordecai. "The Concept of Human Rights," *Philosophy and Phenomenological Research*, XIX (1958-59), 355-79.

ST. JOHN-STEVAS, N. "The Law and Christian Morals," *Catholic Mind*, LIX (1961), 230-35.

STEVENS, G. "Relation of Law and Obligation," *Proceedings of the American Catholic Philosophical Association*, XXIX (1955), 195-205.

VAN DER VEN, J. J. "The Philosophy of Law," *World Justice*, II (1961), 357-72.

WARD, L. R. "Nature as Law," *Ethics*, LXVII (1957), 294-300.

WEGMANN, R. A. "The Nobility of the Law," *Jurist*, XVIII (1958), 18-39.

WHITE, R. J. "Law in the Image of God," *Jurist*, XVII (1957), 1-8.

WRIGHT, J. J. "The Law and the Person," *Jurist*, XXIII (1963), 314-20.

BUDZIK, G. *De conceptu legis ad mentem Johannis Duns Scoti.* Burlington, Wisc.: Franciscan Printery, 1954.

CESARINI, Sforza. *Filosofia del diritto.* Milano: Giuffrè, 1958.

GALLONI, G. *La interpretazione della legge.* Milano: Giuffrè, 1955.

LACHANCE, Louis. *Le droit et les droits de l'homme.* Paris: Presses Universitaires de France, 1959.

LEVI, Alessandro. *Scrittori minori di filosofia del diritto.* Padova: CEDAM, 1957.

LOTTA, S. *Il concetto di legge nella "Summa Theologiae" di San Tommaso d'Aquino.* Torino: Giappichelli, 1955.

OPOCHER, Enrico. *Lezioni di filosofia del diritto.* Padova: CEDAM, 1957.

PALAZZOLO, Vincenzo. *Scienza e epistemologia giuridica.* Padova: CEDAM, 1957.

PIOVANI, P. *Linee di una filosofia del diritto.* Padova: CEDAM, 1958.

RUIZ-GIMENEZ CORTES, Joaquin. *Derecho y vida humana: reflexiones a la luz de santo Tomas.* Madrid: Inst. de Estudios Políticos, 1944.

SERTILLANGES, Antonin G. *La philosophie des lois.* Paris: Alsatia, 1946.

VECCHIO, Giorgio del. *L'état et le droit.* Paris: Dalloz, 1964.

——. *Sui principi generali del diritto.* Milano: Giuffrè, 1958.

GENNARO, A. "De obligatione legis," *Perfice Munus,* XXXII (1957), 151-52.

KURELLA. A. "Zur Theorie der Moral. Eine alte Polemik mit Ernest Bloch," *Deutsche Zeitschrift für Philosophie,* VI (1958), 599-621.

LHOIR, J. "De conciliatione legis cum libertate christiana," *Collectanea Mechliniensia,* XXX (1960), 522-24.

LINTAUF, J. D. "Des lois, pourquoi faire?," *Lumière et Vie,* XII (1963), 131-47.

LOTTIN, O. "Loi naturelle, droit naturel et raison naturelle," *Doctor Communis,* X (1957), 105-17.

MOLITOR, A. "Pouvoir de fait, pouvoir de droit," *Revue Nouvelle,* XXVI (1957), 467-71.

PLAGNIEUX, J. "Le Chrétien en face de la loi, d'après le DE SPIRITU ET LITTERA de S. Augustin," in *Theologie in Geschichte und Gegenwart.* Hrsg. J. Auer und H. Volk. München: Zink, 1957. Pp. 725-54.

SORIA, C. "La esencia de la ley según Santo Tomás," *Estudios Filosóficos,* V (1956), 131-58.

VAN CRAENENBROECK, J. "De primatu caritatis et obligatione legis in elaboratione theologiae moralis," *Collectanea Mechliniensia,* XXVII (1957), 377-79.

E. NATURAL LAW

BEGIN, Raymond F. *Natural Law and Positive Law.* Washington, D.C.: The Catholic Univ. of America Press, 1959.

BROWN, B. F. *The Natural Law Reader.* New York: Oceana, 1960.

COGLEY, John. *Natural Law and Modern Society.* Cleveland: World, 1963.

FISHER, Ronald A. *Creative Aspects of Natural Law.* Cambridge: Univ. Press, 1950.

MARITAIN, Jacques. *The Rights of Man and the Natural Law.* New York: Scribner's, 1943.

PASSERIN d'ENTREVES, A. *Natural Law; an Introduction to Legal Philosophy.* New York: Hutchinson's Univ. Library, 1951.

RUSSELL, Robert P. *The Natural Law in the Philosophy of Thomas Hobbes.* Roma: Pont. Univ. Gregoriana, 1939.

TOLAND, Terrence J. *The Unjustified Man and Natural Law Observance.* Roma: Pontificia Universita Gregoriana, 1956.

WRIGHT, Benjamin F. *American Interpretation of Natural Law.* New York: Russell, 1962.

WU, John C. H. *Fountain of Justice, A Study in the Natural Law.* New York: Sheed and Ward, 1959.

ANAN, S. "Some Trends of Legal Thought or Natural Law Study in Japan," *Natural Law Forum,* VII (1962), 109-19.

BARRETT, E. "Natural Law and the Lawyer's Search for a Philosophy of Law," *Catholic Lawyer,* I (1955), 128-42.

BAUM, G. "Protestants and Natural Law," *Commonweal,* LXXIII (1961), 427-30.

BOURKE, V. "Two Approaches to Natural Law," *Commonweal,* LXIV (1956), 562-63.

BROWN, B. "Natural Law Norms," *Catholic Lawyer,* IX (1963), 57-62.

CARLEY, F. J. "The American Proposition and Natural Law: Murray and Douglas," *Social Justice*, LIII (1961), 375-77.

CAUCHY, A. "A Defense of Natural Ethics," *Proceedings of the American Catholic Philosophical Association*, XXIX (1955), 206-18.

CAVANAGH, J. "The Natural Law," *Guild of Catholic Psychiatrists*, VIII (1961), 1-2.

COGLEY, J. "Natural Law and Modern Society," *Commonweal*, LXXVII (1963), 37-38.

CONSTABLE, G. "The False Natural Law: Prof. Goble's Straw Man," *Natural Law Forum*, I (1956), 97-103.

————. "Who Can Determine What the Natural Law Is?" *Natural Law Forum*, VII (1962), 54-83.

CROWE, M. B. "Human Nature, Immutable or Mutable?" *Irish Theological Quarterly*, XXX (1963), 204-31.

————. "The Irreplaceable Natural Law," *Studies (Dublin)*, LI (1962), 268-85.

DORE, E. S. "Today's Climate of Opinion: Order, the Philosophic Basis of Natural Law," *Fordham Law Review*, XXIV (1955), 519-34.

FARRELL, P. M. "Sources of St. Thomas' Concept of Natural Law," *Thomist*, XX (1957), 237-94.

FASSO, G. "On Natural Law as the Basis of Democracy," *Natural Law Forum*, VII (1962), 97-108.

FAY, C. "Natural Moral Law in the Light of Cultural Relativism and Evolutionism," *Anthropology*, XXXIV (1961), 177-91.

FULLER, L. I. "Human Purpose and Natural Law," *Natural Law Forum*, III (1958), 68-104.

GALE, Richard M. "Natural Law and Human Rights," *Philosophy and Phenomenological Research*, XX (1959-60), 521-31.

GOBLE, G. W. "Dilemma of the Natural Law," *Catholic Lawyer*, II (1956), 226-36.

HAMMETT, I. "A Lawyer's View of the Natural Law," *Blackfriars*, XLII (1961), 370-77.

HERBERG, W. "Conservatives, Liberals and the Natural Law, I" *National Review*, XII (1962), 407-22, 438-58.

KATZ, W. G. "Natural Law and Human Nature," *Catholic Lawyer*, I (1955), 70-73.

KENEALY, W. "Whose Natural Law?" *Catholic Lawyer*, I (1955), 259-66.

LECLERCQ, J. "Natural Law the Unknown; Immutability and the Development of Knowledge," *Natural Law Forum*, VII (1962), 1-15.

————. "Suggestions for Clarifying Natural Law," *Natural Law Forum*, II (1957), 64-87.

LINDBECK, G. A. "Natural Law in the Thought of Paul Tillich," *Natural Law Forum*, VII (1962), 84-96.

LLOYD, A. C. "Natural Justice," *Philosophical Quarterly*, XII (1962), 218-27.

LOTTEN, O. "Natural Law and Right and Reason," *Philosophy Today*, III (1959), 10-18.

McKINNON, H. R. "Natural Law and the Gentiles: Some Observations on the Denial of Natural Law in Modern Times," *Catholic Univ. Law Review*, V (1955), 1-9.

MEAD, M. "Some Anthropological Considerations Concerning Natural Law," *Natural Law Forum*, VI (1961), 51-64.

MESSNER, J. "The Postwar Natural Law Revival and its Outcome," *Natural Law Forum*, IV (1959), 101-5.

MURPHY, C. "Augustinian Natural Law," *Univ. of Detroit Law Journal*, XXXIX (1963), 650-59.

NIELSEN, K. "Examination of the Thomistic Theory of Natural Moral Law," *Natural Law Forum*, IV (1959), 44-71.

OAKLEY, F. "Medieval Theories of Natural Law: William of Ockham and the Significance of the Voluntarist Tradition," *Natural Law Forum*, VI (1961), 65-83.

PALMER, B. W. "Natural Law and Pragmatism," *Catholic Lawyer*, II (1956), 150-60.

PASSERIN d'ENTREVES, A. "The Case for Natural Law Reexamined," *Natural Law Forum*, I (1956), 5-52.

PIUS XII. "Church and the Natural Law," *Homiletic and Pastoral Review*, LV (1955), 592-94.

PLATTEL, M. G. "Personal Response and the Natural Law," *Natural Law Forum*, VII (1962), 16-37.

"The Problem of Our Age: The Technological Revolution and the Role of Natural Law," *America*, CVI (1962), 676-77.

ROMMEN, H. A. "Genealogy of Natural Rights," *Thought*, XXIX (1954), 403-25.

———. "Natural Law: Man and Society," *Fordham Law Review*, XXIV (1955), 128-40.

ROONEY, M. "Philosophy of Natural Law of St. Thomas," *Catholic Lawyer*, II (1956), 22-30.

RUMBLE, L. "New Interest in Natural Moral Law," *Homiletic and Pastoral Review*, LVII (1957), 1105-13.

SELZNICK, P. "Sociology and Natural Law," *Natural Law Forum*, VI (1961), 84-108.

STANLIS, P. "Dr. Wu and Justice Holmes: A Reappraisal on Natural Law," *Univ. of Detroit Law Journal*, XVIII (1955), 249-70.

SUY, E. "Legality, Morality and Natural Law," *World Justice*, IV (1962), 351-62.

VAWTER, Bruce. "Natural Law and the Tradition of Reason in the Bible," *Catholic Messenger*, LXXIX (1961), 7-8.

VON LEYDEN, W. "John Locke and Natural Law," *Philosophy*, XXXI (1956), 23-25.

WARD, L. R. "The Natural Law Rebound," *Review of Politics*, XXI (1959), 114-30.

———. "Nature as Law," *Ethics*, LXVII (1957), 294-300.

WEISS, Paul. "The Nature and Locus of Natural Law," *Journal of Philosophy*, LIII (1956), 713-21.

WU, J. C. H. "Christianity, the Natural Law and the Common Law," *American Benedictine Review*, VI (1955), 133-47.

DELHAYE, Philippe. *Permanence du droit naturel*. Louvain: Nauwelaerts, 1960.

FUCHS, Joseph. *Le droit naturel: essai théologique.* Tournai: Desclée, 1960.

HAMEL, Edward. *Loi naturelle et loi du Christ.* Paris: Desclée, 1964.

KELSEN, H. *Le droit naturel.* Paris: Presses Universitaires de France, 1959.

LOTTIN, Odon. *Le droit naturel chez Saint Thomas d'Aquin et ses prédécesseurs.* Bruges: Beyaert, 1931.

MESSNER, J. *Das Naturrecht.* Innsbruck: Tyrolia, 1958.

SCHMÖLZ, Franz. *Das Naturgesetz und Seine Dynamische Kraft.* Freiburg, Breisgau: Paulusverlag, 1959.

TAPARELLI D'AZEGLIO, L. *Saggio teoretico di diritto naturale.* Roma: Civiltà Cattolica, 1962.

WELZEL, Hans. *Naturrecht und Materiale Gerechtigheit.* Göttingen: Vandenhoeck und Ruprecht, 1955.

ANTOINE, P. "Conscience et loi naturelle," *Etudes,* CCCXVII (1963), 162-83.

BERTRAMS, W. "Siensethic und Naturrecht Heute," *Stimmen der Zeit,* CLVII (1955),11-20.

DELEHAYE, P. "Courte notice sur le droit naturel," *Studio Montis Regis,* V (1962), 215-27.

DIEZ-ALEGRIA, J. "¿Qué piensa Molina sobre el fundamento de la obligatoriedad de la ley natural?," *Pensamiento,* XXXVIII (1954), 189-95.

HAMEL, E. "Loi naturelle et loi du Christ," *Sciences Ecclésiastiques,* X (1958), 49-76.

LAZURE, Jacques. "La loi naturelle en philosophie morale," *Revue de l'Université d'Ottawa,* XXVIII (1958), 5-30.

LOTTIN, Odon. "Loi naturelle, droit naturel et raison naturelle," *Doctor Communis,* X (1957), 105-17.

PIWOWARSKI, W. "Principes sociaux fondamentaux du droit naturel," *Roczmiki Filozoficzne,* II (1963), 111-21.

PIZZORRI, Reginaldo M. "Legge morale, diritto naturale e libertà," *Thomistica Morum Principia; Communicationes V Congressus Thomistici Internationalis,* Romae: Officium Libri Catholici, 1960. I, 430-41.

———. "Principali precetti della legge e del diritto naturale," *Sapienza,* X (1957), 91-101.

VAN OVERBEKE, P. M. "La loi naturelle et le droit naturel selon S. Thomas," *Revue Thomiste,* LIV (1957), 53-78.

CHAPTER VIII

Teaching Philosophy

This chapter comprises selected books and articles since 1934 relating to the teaching of philosophy, especially Christian philosophy. It presupposes the above materials concerning the nature of this philosophy and its work on the contemporary problems of technology and religious renewal. The concern of this chapter is rather with the mode of the teaching process itself. The materials are divided as follows:

A. Teaching Philosophy

B. Teaching Christian Philosophy

C. The Church on Teaching Philosophy.

This division allows for an initial presentation of all possible views on the teaching of philosophy. This is followed by more particular considerations concerning the teaching of Christian philosophy, and the orientations provided by the Church in its concern for that philosophy.

A. TEACHING PHILOSOPHY

GARRETT, Leroy. (ed.) *Philosophy in High School.* Jacksonville, Ill.: MacMurray College, 1960.

GILSON, E. *History, Philosophy and Philosophical Education.* Milwaukee: Marquette Univ. Press, 1948.

———, and PEGIS, A. *Truth and the Philosophy of Teaching.* West Hartford, Conn.: St. Joseph's College, 1955.

GREENE, Theodore. *Religious Perspectives of College Teaching in Philosophy.* New Haven: Hazen, 1950.

McLEAN, George F. (ed.) *Philosophy and the Integration of Contemporary Catholic Education.* Washington, D.C.: The Catholic Univ. of America Press, 1962.

MELZER. John H. *Philosophy in the Classroom: a Report.* Lincoln: Univ. of Nebraska Press, 1954.

The Proceedings and Addresses of the Conference on the Teaching of Philosophy. Edited by Frederick P. Harris. Cleveland: Western Reserve Univ. Press, 1950.

Theology, Philosophy, and History as Integrating Disciplines in the Catholic College of Liberal Arts. Edited by Roy J. Deferrari. Washington, D.C.: The Catholic Univ. of America Press, 1953.

ADLER, Mortimer J. "Controversy in the Life and Teaching of Philosophy," in *Proceedings of the American Catholic Philosophical Association,* XXX (1956), 16-35.

ASHLEY, Benedict M., O.P. "The Role of the Philosophy of Nature in Catholic Liberal Education," in *Proceedings of the American Catholic Philosophical Association,* XXX (1956), 62-85.

BERENDA, C. W. "The Liberal Arts Function of Philosophy," *Journal of Philosophy,* LIV (1957), 19-20.

BLACK, Max. "The Training of Teachers of Philosophy," *Journal of Higher Education,* XIV (1943), 19-24.

BLANSHARD, Brand. "Excerpts from Letters Received by the Commission on the Function of Philosophy in Liberal Education of the American Philosophical Association," *Philosophical Review,* LIV (1945), 197-260.

BRADY, Leo. "Dialogue with the Artist," in *Philosophy and the Integration of Contemporary Catholic Education.* Edited by G. McLean, O.M.I. Washington, D.C.: The Catholic Univ. of America Press, 1962. Pp. 193-204.

CAMERON, J. M. "The Scope of Philosophy in the University," *Universities Quarterly,* VI (1951-52), 225-34.

CANNABRAVA, Euryalo. "What is Scientific Philosophy?" in *Atti XII Congresso internazionale di filosofia,* V, (1960), 93-99.

CONZE, Edward. "Philosophers and Techniques," *Hibbert Journal*, LV (1956-57), 14-19.

DE KONINCK, Charles. "Philosophy in University Education," *Laval Théologique et Philosophique*, VIII (1952), 123-29.

DU LAC, Henri. "The Role of Logic in a Catholic Liberal College," in *Proceedings of the American Catholic Philosophical Association*, XXX (1956), 36-47.

FIELD, G. C. "The Teaching of Philosophy," in *Knowledge and Foreknowledge, Proceedings of the Aristotelian Society*, XVI, Suppl. (1937), 1-19.

FOLEY, Leo. "The Empirical Method and Speculative Presuppositions" in *Philosophy and the Integration of Contemporary Catholic Education*. Edited by G. McLean, O.M.I. Washington, D.C.: The Catholic Univ. of America Press, 1962. Pp. 118-29.

GALLIE, W. B. "Philosophy in Modern Universities," *Universities Quarterly*, VIII (1954), 153-62.

GARVEY, Edwin D. "The Role of Metaphysics in a Catholic Liberal College," in *Proceedings of the American Catholic Philosophical Association*, XXX (1956), 85-102.

GREENWOOD, T. "Philosophy in the Schools," *The Philosopher*, XII (1934), 49-55.

GUTHRIE, Hunter. "Some Suggestions for Revision of the Philosophy Curriculum," in *Proceedings of the American Catholic Philosophical Association*, XXXII (1958), 226-29.

GUZIKOWSKI, Max. "Discussion in Teaching Philosophy" in *Teaching Thomism Today*. Edited by G. McLean, O.M.I. Washington, D.C.: The Catholic Univ. of America Press, 1963. Pp. 194-98.

HAHN, Lewis E. "Philosophy as Comprehensive Vision," *Philosophy and Phenomenological Research*, XXII (1961-62), 16-25.

HENLE, Robert. "The Modern Liberal University: Reflective Intelligence versus Tradition," *Confluence*, VI (1957), 184-95.

————. "Philosophy and Liberal Education" in *Teaching Thomism Today*. Edited by G. McLean, O.M.I. Washington, D.C.: The Catholic Univ. of America Press, 1962. Pp. 259-65.

HESBURGH, Theodore M. "The University and Philosophy," in *Proceedings of the American Catholic Philosophical Association*, XXVII (1953), 12-16.

HILL, Walker H. "A Report to Teachers of Philosophy," *Journal of Philosophy*, XL (1943), 214-20.

HUGHES, W. H. "Philosophy and General Education," *School Review*, L (1942), 356-61.

KEVANE, Eugene. "Philosophy and the Unity of the Curriculum," in *Philosophy and the Integration of Contemporary Catholic Education*. Edited by G. McLean, O.M.I. Washington, D.C.: The Catholic Univ. of America Press, 1962. Pp. 228-48.

KNOX, T. M. "Two Conceptions of Philosophy," *Philosophy*, XXXVI (1961), 289-308.

LARRABEE, H. A. and BALZ, A. G. "Philosophy and Education—Union Now?" *School and Society*, LVI (1942), 4-9.

LECHNER, Robert F. "The Practice of Philosophy: a Call to Contemplation," in *Proceedings of the American Catholic Philosophical Association*, XXXIV (1960), 1-10.

MELZER, John H. "On the Teaching of Aesthetics," *Personalist*, XXXVII (1956), 136-46.

MOORE, Asher. "Two Methods of Philosophy" in *Atti XII Congresso internazionale di Filosofia*, V (1960), 419-25.

MULLANEY, James V. "Problems in the Teaching of Contemporary Philosophy," *Modern Schoolman*, XXXIV (1956-57), 105-19.

NEMETZ, Anthony "The Problem of Philosophic Communication" in *International Philosophical Quarterly*, I (1961), 193-213.

NIEMEYER, Sr. M. Fredericus. "Philosophy and the Personal Formation of the Student" in *Philosophy and the Integration of Contemporary Catholic Education*. Edited by G. McLean, O.M.I. Washington, D.C.: The Catholic Univ. of America Press, 1962. Pp. 249-58.

PERRY, C. M. "The Place of Philosophy in Universities," *Journal of Higher Education*, XIII (1942), 463-70.

PRUFER, Thomas. "What Is Philosophy," in *Teaching Thomism Today*. Edited by G. McLean, O.M.I. Washington, D.C.: The Catholic Univ. of America Press, 1962. Pp. 127-49.

ROEMER, W. F. "The Teaching of Logic. Logic Taught as a Liberal Art," in *Proceedings of the American Catholic Philosophical Association*, XIII (1937), 171-72.

SASTRI, P. S. "The Study of Philosophy," *Prabuddha Bharata*, LVII (1952), 459-62 and 496-500.

SMITH, Gerard. "The Position of Philosophy in a Catholic College," in *Proceedings of the American Catholic Philosophical Association*, XXIX (1955), 20-40.

SMITH, Vincent E.; HART, Charles A.; DILLON, David; and DU LAC, Henri. "Philosophy as a Way of Life," in *Proceedings of the American Catholic Philosophical Association*, XXVII (1953), 168-76.

TOULMIN, Stephen. "The Place of Philosophy in Other Honours Courses," *Universities Quarterly*, VI (1951-52), 235-43.

WALLACE, William. "Natural Philosophy and the Physical Sciences," in *Philosophy and the Integration of Contemporary Catholic Education*. Edited by G. McLean, O.M.I. Washington, D.C.: The Catholic Univ. of America Press, 1962. Pp. 130-57.

WOJCIECHOWSKI, J. A. "Philosophy in the Science Curriculum," *Culture*, XXII (1961), 55-61.

WOLTER, Allan B. "Towards a Theory of Real Knowledge," in *Philosophy and the Integration of Contemporary Catholic Education*. Edited by G. McLean, O.M.I. Washington, D.C.: The Catholic Univ. of America Press, 1962. Pp. 44-74.

WRIGHTMAN, W. P. D. "Note on the Teaching of History and Philosophy of Science," *British Journal for the Philosophy of Science*, XI (1960-61), 336.

BORTIGNON, Girolamo. *Insegnamento della filosofia e educazione cristiana*. Padova: Gregoriana, 1953.

CASOTTI, Mario. *L'insegnamento della filosofia*. Brescia: La Scuola, 1946.

L'enseignement de la philosophie. Recherches et Débats, XXXVI (1961).

L'enseignement de la philosophie. Une enquête internationale de l'Unesco. Paris: Unesco, 1953.

HUISMAN, D. and REVAULT D'ALLONNES, O. *Guide de l'étudiant en philosophie*. Paris: Presses Univ. de France, 1956.

PIEPER, J. *Was heisst philosophieren? Vier Vorlesungen*. München: Kösel, 1948.

PIRLOT, Jules. *L'enseignement de la métaphysique. Critiques et suggestions*. Louvain: Nauwelaerts, 1950.

RICHARD, T. *Comment étudier et situer saint Thomas*. Paris: Lethielleux, 1938.

SALMAN, Dominique. *La place de la philosophie dans l'université idéale*. Montréal: Inst. d'Etudes Médiévales, 1954.

AGAZZI, Evandro. "Sulla scientificità della filosofía," in *Atti XII Congresso Internazionale di Filosofia*, V (1960), 1-7.

AGOGLIA, Rudolfo M. "La cientificidad de la filosofía," in *Atti XII Congresso Internazionale di Filosofia*, V (1960), 9-16.

ALTHUSSER, L. "L'enseignement de la philosophie," *Esprit*, XXII (1954), 858-64.

AMERIO, Franco. "Criticità e crisi nell'insegnamento della filosofia," *Filosofia e Vita*, I (1960), 28-33.

BÉNÉZÉ, G. "La classe de philosophie et les sciences humaines," *Revue de l'Enseignement Philosophique*, X (1960), 39-44.

BETTAZZI, Luigi. "Note sull'insegnamento della filosofia," *Filosofia e Vita*, I (1960), 15-19.

BORNE, Etienne. "La passion de la vérité," in *L'enseignement de la philosophie. Recherches et Débats*, XXXVI (1961), 182-94.

BOYER, Carlo, " 'Nolite timere' vale anche per lo studio della filosofia," *Filosofia e Vita*, I (1960), 15-17.

BRES, Yvon. "Les sciences humaines dans l'enseignement de la philosophie," in *L'enseignement de la philosophie. Recherches et Débats*, XXXVI (1961), 103-12.

BRUAIRE, Jean-Claude. "L'enseignement de la métaphysique dans les classes scientifiques," in *L'enseignement de la philosophie. Recherches et Débats*, XXXVI (1961), 83-86.

CANGUILHEM, Georges. "La signification de l'enseignement de la philosophie," in *L'enseignement de la philosophie*. Paris: Unesco, 1953. Pp. 111-30.

CARROI, M. A. "L'enseignement de la philosophie dans les lycées et collèges," *Revue Universitaire*, XLIII-XLIV (1945), 145-54.

CECCATO, Silvio. "Comment ne pas philosopher," in *Actes du XIᵉ Congrès International de Philosophie*, I (1953), 99-105.

CHAMBON, E. "Le problème de Dieu dans la classe de philosophie: compte rendue d'une enquête," *Bulletin des Facultés Catholiques de Lyon*, LXXVI (1954), 37-44.

CICINATO, Dante. "Difficoltà nell'insegnamento della filosofia," *Rassegna di Pedagogia*, VI (1949), 191-205.

CIRELLI, Alberto D. "Metodologia de la enseñanza de la filosofía desde el punto de vista antropológico," in *Actas del Primer Congreso Nacional de filosofíá*, Mendoza, Argentina, Marzo 30—Abril 9, 1949. Tomo III. Mendoza: Universidad Nacional de Cuyo, 1949. Pp. 1777-83.

COLIN, Pierre. "Rôle de l'enseignement de la philosophie dans l'évolution psychologique et spirituelle des adolescents," in *L'enseignement de la philosophie. Recherches et Débats*, XXXVI (1961), 135-45.

COMPOSTA, Dario. "Saggio di didattica della storia della filosofia," *Filosofia e Vita*, I (1960), 58-64.

"Conclusions de l'enquête et suggestions en vue du développement et du perfectionnement de l'enseignement de la philosophie," in *L'enseignement de la philosophie*. Paris: Unesco, 1953. Pp. 195-225.

CROISSANT, Jeanne. "Principes et méthodes d'un enseignement non-confessionnel de la morale," *Revue de l'Université de Bruxelles*, VIII (1955-56), 375-90.

CRUZ HERNANDEZ, Miguel. "El problema de la estructura y método de la enseñanza de la filosofía en la universidad," *Revista de Educación*, II (1952), 107-12.

DANIÉLOU, Jean. "La crise du sens de la vérité," in *L'enseignement de la philosophie. Recherches et Débats*, XXXVI (1961), 146-62.

DERISI, Octavio N. "Visión y conceptualización de la verdad en filosofía. Importancia de la formación filosófica," *Sapientia*, XVI (1961), 23-28.

DEVAUX, André A. "Brèves notes sur l'enseignement philosophique en propédeutique," in *L'enseignement de la philosophie. Recherches et Débats*, XXXVI (1961), 44-50.

DOZO, L. A. "La enseñanza de la filosofía," *Revista de Educación*, IV (1959), 313-15.

FERRY, G. "L'enseignement philosophique devant le développement des sciences humaines," *Revue de l'enseignement philosophique*, X (1960), 45-49.

FOREST, A. "La recherche philosophique," *Revue Thomiste*, XLIII (1937), 51-77.

FOUGEYROLLAS, Pierre. "Les journées pour la coordination des enseignements de la philosophie et de l'histoire," *Pensée*, XLVII (1953), 139-43.

FRANCHINI, Raffaello. "Limiti di una concezione della filosofia come scienza," in *Atti XII Congresso Internazionale di Filosofia*, VII (1960), 105-12.

GEMELLI, Agostino. "Dopo il convegno per la riforma degli studi filosofici," *Rivista di Filosofia Neo-Scolastica*, XXXIV (1942), 6-17.

GODIN, Guy. "L'admiration, principe de recherche philosophique," *Laval Théologique et Philosophique*, XVII (1961), 213-42.

GOUIRAN, Emilio. "La enseñanza de la filosofía," *Estudios de Filosofía* (1942), 5-12.

GRASSI, Ernesto. "La filosofia nella tradizione umanistica," in *Actas del Primer Congreso Nacional de filosofia*, Mendoza, Argentina, Marzo 30—Abril 9, 1949. Tomo I. Mendoza: Universidad Nacional de Cuyo, 1949. Pp. 212-20.

INNOCENTI, Umberto Degl'. "L'ordine didattico dei vari trattati della filosofia," *Filosofia e Vita*, I (1960), 37-44.

JASPERS, Karl. "La Universidad y la razón," *Alcalá* (n. 47-48, 1954), pp. 1-2.

JOLIVET, Jean. "Du contenu possible d'un cours de philosophie," in *L'enseignement de la philosophie. Recherches et Débats*, XXXVI (1961), 71-74.

JOULIA, Pierre. "Savoir, réflexion et sagesse," in *L'enseignement de la philosophie. Recherches et Débats*, XXXVI (1961), 163-81.

JURON, Robert. "Quelle méthode adopter pour enseigner la philosophie?" *Bulletin des Facultés Catholiques de Lyon*, LXXVI (1954), 33-36.

KRUSE, Beda. "A Faculdade de Filosofia, factor imprescindível de cultura—O problema de especialização," *Paideia*, I (1954), 12-27.

LA BONNARDIERE, X. "Présentation du problème de Dieu," *Bulletin des Facultés Catholiques de Lyon*, LXXVI (1954), 45-54.

LECLERQ, Jacques. "Comment enseigner la morale chrétienne en notre temps?" *Collectaneo Mechliniensia*, XXXVI (1951), 560-68.

MAINO, Girolamo. "Filosofia e scuola di lettere formativa," *Filosofia e Vita*, II (1961), 11-19.

MAUBLANC, R. "La classe de philosophie, son présent et son avenir," *Cahiers Rationalistes*, CLXXIX (1959), 102-31.

———. "Remarques sur l'enseignement de la philosophie," *Pensée*, LII (1953), 101-10.

MILLET, Louis. "Classe de philosophie et sens de la vérité," in *L'enseignement de la philosophie. Recherches et Débats*, XXXVI (1961), 51-70.

MORFAUX, L.-M. "La philosophie dans les classes terminales," in *L'enseignement de la philosophie. Recherches et Débats*, XXXVI (1961), 32-43.

MÜLLER, Giovanni. "Via inventionis come metodo didattico in filosofia," *Filosofia e Vita*, IV (1963), 18-25.

PADOVANI, Umberto A. "L'insegnamento della filosofia nei licei classici," *Rivista di Filosofia Neo-Scolastica*, XXXIV (1942), 166-70.

"Pela manutenção do ensino da filosofia no curso secundário," *Estudios*, XIX (1959), 39-49.

PELLÉ-DOUEL, Yvonne. "Réflexions sur l'enseignement de la philosophie," *Archives de Philosophie*, XXI (1958), 483-503.

PETRUZZELLIS, Nicola. "Le scienze dello spirito e la filosofia come scienza rigorosa," *Sapienza*, XIV (1961), 5-30.

PICCOLI, G. "L'insegnamento della filosofia," *Città di Vita*, VII (1952), 671-75.

PIGNOLONI, Emilio. "Filosofia, storia della filosofia, didattica filosofica," *Rivista Rosminiana di Filosofia e di Cultura*, LI (1957), 176-80.

PONFERRADA, Gustavo. "La enseñanza de la metafísica," *Sapientia*, VI (1951), 222-29.

POPPI, Antonino. "Impostazione dello studio filosofico nei licei," *Filosofia e Vita*, II (n. 8, 1961), 76-83.

POZZI, Lorenzo. "Filosofia e religione negli Istituti cattolici," *Filosofia e Vita*, II (n. 7, 1961), 7-13.

PRA, Mario dal. "Per il nuovo ordinamento della Facoltà di Lettere e Filosofia," *Rivista Critica di Storia della Filosofia*, XVI (1961), 240-54.

———. "Su una proposta di nuovi programmi per l'insegnamento della filosofia nei Licei," *Rivista Critica di Storia della Filosofia*, XVII (1962), 345-51.

QUEIROZ, Amaro X. de. "Cocação e destino das faculdades de filosofia," *Kriterion*, IX (1956), 1-16.

QUILES, Ismael. "Educación católica y filosofía actual," *Latinoamérica*, LXVIII (1954), 369-72.

REDANO, Ugo. "Esperienza e filosofia," in *Attualità filosofiche. Atti del III Convegno di studi filosofici cristiani*. Padova: Ed. Liviana, 1948. Pp. 77-88.

ROBIN, L. "La formation de l'esprit philosophique," *Actes du VIIIe Congrès International*, à Prague, 2-7 Sept., 1936. Pp. 1003-10.

ROMERO, F. "Sobre la condicion y el estudio de la filosofía," *Studium*, III (1959), 269-79.

SACRA CONGREGAZIONE DEI SEMINARI E DELLE UNIVERSITA. "Insegnamento della filosofia negli Istituti medi superiori," commento di Raimondo Spiazzi, *Filosofia e Vita*, I (1960), 75-79.

SANTUCCI, Antonio. "Una prospettiva metodologica della filosofia," in *Atti XII Congresso Internazionale di Filosofia*, V, 481-89.

SCIACCA, Michele F. "Educazione ed insegnamento della storia della filosofia," *Filosofia e Vita*, I (1960), 6-14.

STEFANI, S., GUZZO, A., ABBAGNANO, N., GEMELLI, A., and ALIOTTA, A. "Per una riforma della facoltà di filosofia," *Rivista di Filosofia Neo-Scolastica*, XXXIII (1941), 243-61.

THIEL, M. "Moderne Hemmnisse des Philosophierens," *Divus Thomas* (Fr.), XXVI (1948), 271-90.

TITONE, Renzo. "Il valore formativo dellò studio filosofico." *Filosofia e Vita*, I (1960), 18-27.

TOCCAFONDI, E. T. "La filosofia comme scienza dell' universalità e necessità dell' ordine," *Angelicum*, XIX (1942), 3-38.

VAN STEENBERGHEN, F. "Réflexions sur la systématisation philosophique," *Revue Néoscolastique de Philosophie*, XLI (1938), 185-216.

VERSIANI VELLOSO, Arthur. "A filosofia como matéria de ensinança," *Kriterion*, IV (1951), 15-16.

VIALATOUX, Joseph. "La tâche du professeur de philosophie," *Bulletin des Facultés Catholiques de Lyon*, LXXVI (1954), 55-65.

VILLENEUVE, Suzanne. "Diagnostic sans pronostic. Quelques réflexions sur la classe de philosophie," in *L'enseignement de la philosophie. Recherches et Debats*, XXXVI (1961), 17-31.

ZARAGÜETA BENGOECHEA, Juan. "Plan de ensenanza de la filosofía en la universidad," *Revista de Educación*, X (1953), 128-34.

B. TEACHING CHRISTIAN PHILOSOPHY

BEALES, A. C. F. *The Function of Teaching: Seven Approaches to Purpose, Tradition and Environment.* London: Faber & Faber, 1959.

BRAUER, T. (ed.) *Thomistic Principles in a Catholic School.* St. Louis: Herder, 1943.

McLEAN, George F. (ed.) *Teaching Thomism Today.* Washington, D.C.: The Catholic Univ. of America Press, 1963.

WHEELER, M. C. *Philosophy and the* SUMMA THEOLOGICA *of Saint Thomas Aquinas.* Washington, D.C.: The Catholic University of America Press, 1956.

ASHLEY, Benedict M., and BONDI, Eugene. "The College Philosophy Course" in *Teaching Thomism Today.* Edited by G. McLean, O.M.I. Washington, D.C.: The Catholic Univ. of America Press, 1963. Pp. 339-49.

BACHHUBER, A. W. "Sense Lines: A Technique for Teaching the Text of St. Thomas," *Modern Schoolman,* XXXV (1957), 62.

BIRD, O. "How to Read an Article of the SUMMA," *New Scholasticism,* XXVII (1953), 129-59.

BOAS, George. "The Misuse of Scholasticism," in *St. Louis Studies in Honor of St. Thomas Aquinas,* I (1943), 43-44.

BOURKE, Vernon J. "Natural Law and the Contemporary Mind" in *Teaching Thomism Today.* Edited by G. McLean, O.M.I. Washington: The Catholic Univ. of America Press, 1963. Pp. 307-29.

COLLINS, James. "For Self-Examination of Neoscholastics," *The Modern Schoolman,* XXI (1943-44), 225-34.

FOLEY, Leo A. "On Using the Texts of St. Thomas" in *Teaching Thomism Today.* Edited by G. McLean, O.M.I. Washington, D.C.: The Catholic Univ. of America Press, 1963. Pp. 199-209.

GALLUP, A. "St. Thomas and the Hurdles," *Dominicana,* XXXVII (1952), 168-80.

HESS, M. W. "Modern Philosophy and the Apostolate," *Thomist,* XXIII (1960), 345-61.

KLUBERTANZ, George P. "Metaphysics and Theistic Convictions" in *Teaching Thomism Today.* Edited by G. McLean, O.M.I. Washington, D.C.: The Catholic Univ. of America Press, 1963. Pp. 271-306.

———. "The Teaching of Thomistic Metaphysics," *Gregorianum,* XXXV (1954), 187-205.

McCORMICK, John F. "The Student and his Philosophy," *The Modern Schoolman,* XVII (1939-40), 51-53.

McNICHOLAS, John T. "The Present Opportunity of Scholastic Philosophy," in *Proceedings of the American Catholic Philosophical Association,* XIV (1938), 89-95.

MILTNER, C. C. "Objectives in Teaching Philosophy," *New Scholasticism,* XI (1937), 350-57.

"Philosophy and the Catholic Student," in *The Life of the Spirit* (Supplement to *Blackfriars*), I (n. 11, 1945), 3-14.

RYAN, John K. "What St. Thomas Asks of Us" in *Teaching Thomism Today.* Edited by G. McLean, O.M.I. Washington, D.C.: The Catholic Univ. of America Press, 1963. Pp. 118-24.

SMITH, Ignatius. "The Place of Philosophy in the University Curriculum," in *Proceedings of the American Catholic Philosophical Association,* XII (1936), 11-17.

SMITH, Vincent E. "On Using the Logic Course" in *Teaching Thomism Today.* Edited by G. McLean, O.M.I. Washington, D.C.: The Catholic Univ. of America Press, 1963. Pp. 233-46.

STEENBERGHEN, F. Van. "The Reading and Study of St. Thomas," *Theology Digest,* IV (1956), 166-69.

WALLACE, William A. "The Thomistic Order of Development in Natural Philosophy" in *Teaching Thomism Today.* Edited by G. McLean, O.M.I. Washington, D.C.: The Catholic Univ. of America Press, 1963. Pp. 247-70.

WHITE, Victor. "Tasks for Thomists," *Blackfriars*, XXV (1944), 93-117.

BARBEDETTE, D. *Manière d'enseigner la philosophie scolastique.* Paris: Berche et Pagis, 1936.

Enchiridion clericorum. Documenta sacrorum alumnis instituendis. Roma: Vaticana, 1938.

MASNOVO, A. SUMMA THEOLOGICA *sancti Thomae.* Appunti delle lezioni di filosofia teoretica. Milano: Vita e Pensiero, 1947.

SAINTONGE, F. *Sciences ecclésiastiques.* Montréal: l'Immaculée-Conception, 1948.

BAUR, L. "Die Form der wissenschaftlichen Kritik bei Thomas von Aquin," in *Aus der Geisteswelt des Mittelalters.* Hrsg. v. A. Lang, J. Lechner, und M. Schmaus. Münster: Aschendorff, 1935. Pp. 688-709.

BERTI, Conradus M. "Methodus docendi perennem philosophiam," *Divus Thomas* (Pi.), LVIII (1955), 147-51.

BRETON, Stanislas. "L'acte philosophique et sa recherche d'unité," in *L'existence de Dieu. Cahiers de l'actualité religieuse,* No. 16. Paris: Casterman, 1961. Pp. 251-65.

CHENU, M.-D. "L'étude historique de saint Thomas," *Revue Philosophique de Louvain,* XLIX (1951), 735-43.

GIACON, Carlo. "La filosofia di S. Thommaso e i Seminari," *Rivista di Filosofia Neo-Scolastica,* XXXI (1939), 341-57.

GRABMANN, M. "Das Ethos der wissenschaftlichen Wahrheitserkenntnis nach dem hl. Thomas von Aquin," *Jahresbericht d. Görres-Gesellschaft.* Köln: Bachem in Komm., 1937. Pp. 38-58.

GUINDON, Roger. "Quelques réflexions sur l'enseignement de la morale chrétienne," *Revue de l'Université d'Ottawa,* XXI (1951), 61*-68*.

LAMARCH, C. A. "La jeunesse intellectuelle et la philosophie thomiste," *Documentation Catholique,* XXXII (1934), 893-95.

MARITAIN, J. "Notes pour un programme d'enseignement de la philosophie de la nature et d'enseignement des sciences dans une faculté de philosophie," *Bollettino Filosofico*, I (1935), 15-31.

PIERROT, M. "Pour la lecture de la SOMME THÉOLOGIQUE," *Bulletin Joseph Lotte*, VI (1934-35), 67-75; 406-14.

ROESLE, Maximilian. "Die neuscholastische Haltung vor der modernen Philosophie," *Schweizerische Kirchenzeitung*, CX (1942), 133-35; 150-53; 161-62.

SALMAN, D. H. "L'enseignement de la philosophie aux jeunes d'après Aristote, saint Thomas et M. E. Gilson," *Laval Théologique et Philosophique*, XI (1955), 9-24.

SCOTTI, Pietro. "Scienza e filosofia nei Seminari," *Rivista di Filosofia Neo-Scolastica*, XXXI (1939), 519-25.

SILY, P. J. "Discípulos de Santo Tomás," *Ciencia y Fe*, V (1949), 127-31.

STEENBERGHEN, F. Van. "La lecture et l'étude de saint Thomas. Réflexions et conseils," *Revue Philosophique de Louvain*, LIII (1955), 301-20.

TITONE, Renzo. "Alcune riflessioni sul valore del 'metodo scolastico,'" *Filosofia e Vita*, II (1961), 9-17.

C. THE CHURCH ON TEACHING PHILOSOPHY

ASHLEY, Benedict M. "Thomism and Ecclesiastical Approbation" in *Teaching Thomism Today*. Edited by G. McLean, O.M.I. Washington, D.C.: The Catholic Univ. of America, 1963. Pp. 97-110.

CROWLEY, T. "HUMANI GENERIS and Philosophy," *Irish Theological Quarterly*, XIX (1952), 25-32.

DULAC, Henri. "Commentary on 'The Authority of St. Thomas in Philosophy' by James V. Mullaney," in *Proceedings of the American Catholic Philosophical Association*, XXV (1951), 147-51.

GARCÍA MARTÍNEZ, F. "The Place of St. Thomas in Catholic Philosophy," *Cross Currents*, (1958), 43-66.

HARVANEK, Robert F. "The Church and Scholasticism," in *Proceedings of the American Catholic Philosophical Association*, XXXII (1958), 215-25.

———. "Philosophical Pluralism and Catholic Orthodoxy," *Thought*, XXV (1950), 21-52.

LEE, Anthony D. "Thomism and the Council," *Thomist*, XXVII (1963), 451-92.

MULLANEY, James V. "The Authority of St. Thomas in Philosophy," in *Proceedings of the American Catholic Philosophical Association*, XXV (1951), 141-47.

MOHAN, Robert P. "Philosophical Implications of HUMANI GENERIS," *The American Ecclesiastical Review*, CXXVI (1952), 425-31; CXXVII (1952), 58-66.

PELSTER, Franz. "The Authority of St. Thomas in Catholic Schools and the Sacred Sciences: an Opinion Regarding Two Recent Articles," *Franciscan Studies*, XIII (1953), 1-26.

RAMIREZ, Santiago. "The Authority of St. Thomas," *The Thomist*, XV (1952), 1-109.

WOLTER, Allan B. "Thomism and Ecclesiastical Approbation," in *Teaching Thomism Today*. Edited by G. McLean, O.M.I. Washington, D.C.: The Catholic Univ. of America Press, 1963. Pp. 111-17.

CARLINI, Armando. *Cattolicesimo e pensiero moderno*. Brescia: Morcelliana, 1953.

Commentarios a la encíclica HUMANI GENERIS. Primera Semana de Estudios Teológicos de la Diócesis de Bilbao. Bilbao: Publicaciones del Obispado de Bilbao, 1952.

EHRLE, Franz K. *Zur Enzyklika* AETERNI PATRIS. Text und Kommentar. Roma: Storia e Litteratura, 1954.

La encíclica HUMANI GENERIS. XI Semana Española de Teología, 17-22 sept., 1952. Madrid: C.S.I.C., 1952.

Filosofia e formazione ecclesiastica. Città del Vaticano: Tipografia Poliglotta Vaticana, 1960.

GARCIA MARTINEZ, Fidel. *De l'authenticité d'une philosophie à l'intérieur de la pensée chrétienne*. Oña, Burgos: Sociedad Internacional "Franciso Suarez," 1955.

224 TEACHING PHILOSOPHY

GILLET, Martin S. *Lettre encyclique sur l'enseignement de saint Thomas à l'heure présente.* Citta del Vaticano: Tipografia Poliglotta Vaticana, 1943.

GRENET, P. B. *Les 24 thèses thomistes: de l'évolution à l'existence.* Paris: Téqui, 1962.

HAYEN, A. *Saint Thomas et la vie de l'Eglise.* Paris: Desclée de Brouwer, 1952.

JULLIEN, A. *Études ecclésiastiques dans la lumière de Rome.* Paris: Alsatia, 1958.

LAMBERTUS a MATRE DEI. *Parvum catholici philosophi enchiridion,* continens selecta auctoritativa praesidia ab Ecclesia oblata studio rationis naturalis. Alwaye (Kerala, India): St. Joseph's Apostolic Seminary, 1961.

MULLER, C. *L'encyclique* HUMANI GENERIS *et les problèmes scientifiques.* Louvain: Nauwelaerts, 1951.

OROMI, Miguis, and SANCHES-MARIN, Faustino. *La filosofía escolástica y el intelectual católico.* Madrid: Nacional, 1955.

TÖTH, P. De. *Della preminenza, in sè e secondo le dichiarazioni dei Sommi Pontefici Leone XIII, Pio X, Benedetto XV e Pio XI, della filosofia e teologia tomistica, a proposito di un opusculo su* LA SCOLASTICA E I SUOI COMPITI ODIERNI. Aquapendente: "La Commerciale," 1936.

ALEJANDRO, J. "Inconciliabilidad del inmanentismo, del idealismo, del materialismo histórico y dialético y del existencialismo con el dogma católico," in *Comentarios a la Encíclica* HUMANI GENERIS. Primera Semana de Estudios Teológicos de la Diócesis de Bilbao. Bilbao: Publicaciones del Obispado de Bilbao, 1952.

BALIC, C. "L'autorité de l'Église par rapport au thomisme et aux autres écoles catholiques," *Bogoslovska Smotra,* XXVI (1938), 186-94.

BALUJA, J. M. "Doctrina católica y sistemas filosofico-teológicos," *Estudios,* XXVII (1953), 533-41.

———. "Sobre la obligación de seguir a Santo Tomás," *Ciencia y Fe,* X (1954), 67-85.

BANDERA, Armando. "Pío XII y Santo Tomás," *Ciencia Tomista*, LXXVIII (1951), 483-543.

BARALE, Paolo. "Il tomismo delle encicliche e quelle dei tomisti," *Rivista Rosminiana di Filosofia e di Cultura*, XLVII (1953), 110-16.

BOYER, C. "Réflexions sur la constitution DEUS SCIENTIARUM DOMINUS," *Gregorianum*, XVII (1936), 159-75.

CANILLERI, N. "Pensiero e magistero nella disciplina della cultura cattolica secondo l'enciclica HUMANI GENERIS di S.S. Pio XII," *Salesianum*, XIII (1951), 273-99.

CIAPPI, Luigi. "S.S. Pio XII e S. Tommaso d'Aquino," *Sapienza*, VIII (1955), 124-42.

CONGRÉGATION DES ETUDES. "Instruction sur la méthode de l'enseignement de la philosophie dans les établissements catholiques." Circulaire du 1er juillet, 1958. *Doctor Communis*, LVI (1959), 399-403.

CORDOVANI, M. "Da Leone XIII a Pio XII; nel 60° della enciclica AETERNI PATRIS," *Angelicum*, XVI (1939), 301-304.

CROSIGNANI, G. "Aspetti della personalità e dell'opera di Pio XII. Pio XII e S. Tommaso," *Divus Thomas* (Pi.), LXII (1959), 9-15.

DE ANDREA, M. "L'enciclica HUMANI GENERIS e il ritorno alla ragione," *Sapienza*, IV (1951), 5-26.

DERISI, Octavio. "In memoriam. La reconquista de la verdad científica en todos sus aspectos y su reintegración en la unidad sapiencial de la filosofía y de la teología y de la vida cristiana en la mente de Pío XII," *Sapientia*, XIV (1959), 3-7.

DONDEYNE, A. "Les problèmes philosophiques soulevés dans l'encyclique HUMANI GENERIS," *Revue Philosophique de Louvain*, XLIX (1951), 5-56; 141-88; 293-356.

ECHARRI, J. "Pío XII y la filosofía perenne ante las ciencias," *Salmanticensis*, III (1956), 321-49.

FABRAT, A. "Ideas filosóficas expuestas por SS. Pío XII," *Pensamiento*, VIII (1952), 75-86.

FABRO, Cornelio, "L'assoluto nel tomismo e nell'esistenzialismo: à propos de l'encyclique HUMANI GENERIS," *Salesianum,* XIII (1951), 185-201.

————. "Attualità perenne del tomismo nel Magistero pontificio," *Euntes Docete,* I-II (1951), 149-61.

————. "L'80° della AETERNI PATRIS," *Osservatore Romano,* August 6, 1959.

FUENTE, Alberto G. "Un discurso de SS. Pío XII sobre las relaciones entre experiencia científica y filosofía," *Estudios Filosóficos,* IV (1955), 335-37.

————. "Filosofía actual y filosofía de Santo Tomás a la luz de la HUMANI GENERIS," *Estudios Filosóficos,* I (1951-52), 27-43.

GALLEGOS ROCAFULL, José Matía. "Pio XII y la filosofía moderna," *Latino-américa,* III (1951), 151-52.

GARRIGOU-LAGRANGE, R. "De actualitate litterarum encyclicarum AETERNI PATRIS ab hinc annos septuaginta quinque datarum," *Angelicum,* XXXII (1955), 209-19.

————. "L'encyclique HUMANI GENERIS et la doctrine de saint Thomas," *Rivista di Filosofia Neo-Scolastica,* XLIII (1951), 41-48.

————. "L'encyclique HUMANI GENERIS et le relativisme," *Doctor Communis,* X (1957), 31-38.

GEMELLI, Agostino. "Gli insegnamenti nell' enciclica HUMANI GENERIS e le scienze," *Doctor Communis,* IV (1951), 24-25.

GEURTSEN, Henri. "La philosophie dans l'Eglise," in *Mélanges J. Maréchal.* Vol. I. Bruxelles: Universelle, 1950. Pp. 169-79.

GHELLINCK, J. De "Algunas particularidades de la constitución DEUS SCIENTIARUM DOMINUS," *Estudios Eclesiásticos,* XIV (1935), 289-309.

GILLIO-TOS, M. T. "Disciplina e libertà nel campo neoscolastico," *Criterion,* IV (1936), 32-41.

GILSON, Etienne. "La paix de la sagesse," *Aquinas,* III (1960), 28-46.

————. "Sur deux thèmes de réflexion," *Doctor Communis,* X (1957), 155-64.

GRENET, Paul. "La philosophie du Pape," *Bulletin du Cercle Thomiste* (Caen), VII (1950-51), 7-16; X (1951), 2-4; XI (1952), 5-10.

GUERRERO, Eustaquio. "La libertad del filósofo católico en un discurso del Papa," *Razon y Fe,* CIXL (1954), 443-54.

HAYEN, A. "L'encyclique HUMANI GENERIS et la philosophie," *Nouvelle Revue Théologique,* LXXIII (1951), 113-37.

HELLIN, José. "Alocución de Su Santidad Pío XII en el cuarto centenario de la fundación de la Pontificia Universidad Gregoriana," *Pensamiento,* X (1954), 89-95.

———. "Sana libertad de la filosofía escolástica en la encíclica HUMANI GENERIS y en otros documentos eclesiásticos," *Pensamiento,* VIII (1952), 53-73.

INNOCENTI, U. Degl'. "Pio XII e San Tommaso," *Divinitas,* IV (1959), 758-74.

———. "Valore della ragione umana nella dimostrazione dell'esistenza di Dio," *Euntes Docete,* I-II (1951), 162-71.

ITURRIOZ, J. "Tendencias filosóficas modernas no católicas y su influencia en algunos pensadores católicos," in *Comentarios a la Enciclica* HUMANI GENERIS. Bilbao: Publicaciones del Obispado de Bilbao, 1952.

JELICIC, V. "Nostra philosophico-theologica studia iuxta vigentem legislationem ecclesiasticam," *Collectanea Franciscana Slavica,* I (1937), 395-425.

JOANNES XXIII. "De momento thomisticae doctrinae oratio," *Aquinas,* III (1960), 5-7.

MALET-YVONNET, N. "Les implications philosophiques de la théologie antimoderniste," *Revue d'Historie et de Philosophie Religieuse,* XXXVIII (1958), 344-59.

MARROU, H. "HUMANI GENERIS. Du bon usage d'une encyclique," *Esprit,* XVIII (1950), 562-70.

MAYDIEU, A.-J. "N'appelez personne votre maître," *Vie Intellectuelle,* XXXI (1934), 224-27.

MIANO, Vincenzo. "Pio XII e lo studio della filosofia," *Salesianum,* XXI (1959), 482-503.

MIRGELER, Albert. "Philosophie, Geschichte und Katholizität," *Philosophisches Jahrbuch*, LXVIII (1959), 279-89.

"Die moderne Philosophie im Lichte von HUMANI GENERIS," *Herder Korrespondenz*, VI (1952), 471-76.

MORANDINI, F. "Filosofia ed apostolato nell'enciclica HUMANI GENERIS," *La Civiltà Cattolica*, CI (1950), 159-72.

MUNOZ, J. "Panorama de las reacciones filosóficas provocadas por la encíclica HUMANI GENERIS," *Pensamiento*, VII (1951), 603-11.

OROMI, M. "El filósofo católico frente a los errores filosóficos modernos según la HUMANI GENERIS," *Verdad y Vida*, IX (1951), 425-46.

PAGGIARO, Luigi. "La libertà di pensare del filosofo cattolico," *Rivista Rosminiana di Filosofia et di Cultura*, XLVIII (1954), 144-48.

PETERS, J. "Die Akkomodationsfrage im Lichte der Enzyklika HUMANI GENERIS," in *Missionswissenschaftliche Studien*. Hrsg. J. Rommerskirchen und N. Kowalsky. Metz: Aichin, 1952. Pp. 102-17.

PETRUZZELLIS, Nicola. "La filosofia nell' enciclica HUMANI GENERIS," *Doctor Communis*, IV (1951), 15-23.

PIEMONTESE, F. "Il tradizionalismo filosofico e l'enciclica HUMANI GENERIS," *Studium*, XLVII (1951), 59-74.

PIUS XII. "Fragen der Philosophie und der Naturwissenschaften." Ansprache anlässlich des IV Internationalen thomistischen Kongresses in Rom, 14 Sept., 1955. *Schweizerische Kirchenzeitung*, CXXIII (1955), 495-96, 507-8.

————. "La última alocución de tema filosófico, pronunciada por Pío XII," *Espíritu*, VIII (1959), 47-49.

————. "Sermo ad alumnos Seminariorum, Collegiorum et Institutorum in Urbe, die 24ª junii, 1939," *Acta Apostolicae Sedis*, XXXI (1939), 245-51.

POLESTRA, G. "Pio XI e la dottrina di San Tommaso," *Memorie Domenicane*, LVI (1939), 162-70.

POMPEI, Alfonso. "Il cattolico di fronte alla crisi contemporanea secondo l'enciclica HUMANI GENERIS," *Miscellanea Francescana*, LI (1951), 21-38.

RAMIREZ, Jacobus. "S. Thomas studiorum dux," *Aquinas*, III (1960), 11-27.

ROIG GIRONELLA, J. "Progreso y relativismo. Reflexiones a propósito de la encíclica HUMANI GENERIS," *Giornale di metafisica*, VII (1952), 180-88.

————. "Relativismo y metafísica absolutamente verdadera. A propósito de la encíclica HUMANI GENERIS," *Pensamiento*, VII (1951), 553-82.

SILY, Jorge. "Sobre la obligación de seguir a Santo Tomás," *Ciencia y Fe*, X (1954), 67-85.

STIRNIMANN, Heinrich. "Non 'tutum'—toto tutius? Zur Lehrauthorität des hl. Thomas," *Freiburger Zeitschrift für Philosophie und Theologie*, I (1954), 420-33.

VISSER, J. "Lex naturalis et intellectus humanus, valores fundamentales in scientia morali," *Euntes Docete*, I-II, (1951), 172-79.

XIBERTA, Bartholomaeus M. "De duabus phasibus humanae congitionis quae prae oculis habendae sunt in encyclica HUMANI GENERIS vindicanda," *Doctor Communis*, VI (1953), 29-33.

APPENDIX

This appendix lists the doctoral dissertations in philosophy presented at Catholic universities of the United States and Canada. They reflect the direction of philosophic research at different periods of the past and often offer useful analyses of particular problem areas. Those most pertinent to the theme of this bibliography have been annotated in the companion volume, *An Annotated Bibliography of Philosophy in Catholic Thought*, by the same editor. The sequence of the universities listed below is:

A. The Catholic University of America, Washington, D.C.

B. Fordham University, New York, New York

C. Georgetown University, Washington, D.C.

D. Laval University, Quebec, Canada

E. Loyola University, Chicago, Illinois

F. Marquette University, Milwaukee, Wisconsin

G. Notre Dame University, South Bend, Indiana

H. Pontifical Institute of Mediaeval Studies, Toronto, Ontario, Canada

I. St. John's University, Jamaica, New York

J. Saint Louis University, St. Louis, Missouri

K. Studium Generale of Saint Thomas, River Forest, Illinois

L. University of Montreal, Quebec, Canada

M. The University of Ottawa, Ottawa, Ontario, Canada

A. THE CATHOLIC UNIVERSITY OF AMERICA
WASHINGTON, D. C.

1895   LUCAS, George. *Agnosticism and Religion: An Analysis of Spencer's Religion of the Unknowable.*

1903   O'CONNOR, Maurice J. *The Idea of Responsibility: Its Foundation, Nature, and Extent.*

1905   DUBRAY, Charles A. *Theory of Dispositions.*

SCHUMACHER, Matthew. *The Knowableness of God: Its Relation to the Theory of Knowledge in St. Thomas.*

1911   HAGERTY, Cornelius. *The Problem of Evil.*

1912   CUNNINGHAM, William. *The Basis of Realism: A Study in the Metaphysics of the Concept Relation.*

1915   KNAPKE, Othmar. *A History of the Theory of Sensation from St. Augustine to St. Thomas.*

SMITH, H. Ignatius. *Classification of Desires in St. Thomas and in Modern Sociology.*

1918   MICHEL, Virgil. *The Critical Principles of Orestes A. Brownson.*

1921   MURPHY, Edward F. *St. Thomas' Political Doctrine and Democracy.*

O'CONNOR, William P. *The Concept of the Human Soul According to St. Augustine.*

ROLBIECKI, John J. *The Political Philosophy of Dante Alighieri.*

1924   BENDER, Joseph E. *The Relation between Moral Qualities and Intelligence According to St. Thomas Aquinas.*

1925   BRENNAN, Edward. *The Theory of Abnormal Cognitive Processes According to the Principles of St. Thomas Aquinas.*

1926   McKEOGH, Michael J. *St. Thomas' Theory of "Rationes Seminales."*

1927   CALLAHAN, Leonard. *A Theory of Esthetics According to the Principles of St. Thomas Aquinas.*

1929   MULLANE, Donald T. *Aristotelianism in St. Thomas.*

WARD, Leo. *St. Thomas' Theory of Moral Values.*

1930   BAUER, Joachim. *The Modern Notion of Faith.*

HART, Charles A. *The Thomistic Theory of Mental Faculties.*

1931   McMAHON, Francis E. *The Humanism of Irving Babbitt.*

O'LEARY, Conrad. *The Substantial Composition of Man According to St. Bonaventure.*

1932   COADY, Sr. Mary Anastasia. *The Phantasm According to St. Thomas.*

TALBOT, Edward. *Knowledge and Object.*

1933   RYAN, John K. *Modern War adn Basic Ethics.*

1934   KILLEEN. Sr. Mary Vincent. *Man in the New Humanism.*

McAULIFFE, Sr. Agnes Theresa. *Some Modern Non-Intellectual Approaches to God.*

MARLING, Joseph. *The Order of Nature in the Philosophy of St. Thomas Aquinas.*

REILLY, George C. *The Psychology of St. Albert the Great.*

1935   CRONIN, John F. *Cardinal Newman: His Theory of Knowledge.*

1936   CASEY, Joseph T. *The Primacy of Metaphysics.*

LUCKS, Henry A. *The Philosophy of Athenagoras: Its Sources and Value.*

SLAVIN, Robert J. *The Philosophical Basis for Individual Differences.*

1937   LINEHAN, James C. *The Rational Nature of Man.*

O'DONNELL, Clement M. *The Psychology of St. Bonaventure and St. Thomas Aquinas.*

RAGUSA, Thomas J. *The Substance Theory of Mind and Contemporary Functionalism.*

ROONEY, Miriam T. *Lawlessness, Law and Sanction.*

1938   McFADDEN, Charles J. *The Metaphysical Foundations of Dialectical Materialism.*

WOLFE, Sr. Mary Joan of Arc. *The Problem of Solidarism in St. Thomas.*

1939 CAHILL, Sr. Camilla. *The Absolute and the Relative in St. Thomas and in Modern Philosophy.*

DADY, Sr. M. Rachel. *The Theory of Knowledge of St. Bonaventure.*

FRIEL, George Q. *Punishment in the Philosophy of St. Thomas Aquinas and Among Some Primitive Peoples.*

GERRITY, Bro. Benignus. *The Relation between the Theory of Matter and Form and the Theory of Knowledge in the Philosophy of St. Thomas Aquinas.*

HOBAN, James H. *The Thomistic Concept of Person and Some of Its Social Implications.*

KILLEEN, Sylvester M. *The Philosophy of Labor According to St. Thomas Aquinas.*

KREILKAMP, Karl. *The Metaphysical Foundations of Thomistic Jurisprudence.*

McALLISTER, Joseph B. *The Letter of St. Thomas Aquinas:* DE OCCULTIS OPERATIONIBUS NATURAE AD QUENDAM MILITEM ULTRAMONTANUM.

McDONALD, William J. *The Social Value of Property According to St. Thomas Aquinas. A Study in Social Philosophy.*

MIRON, Cyril H. *The Problems of Altruism in the Philosophy of St. Thomas: a Study in Social Philosophy.*

O'BRIEN, Sr. Consilia. *The Antecedents of Being: an Analysis of the Concept "de nihilo" in the Philosophy of St. Thomas Aquinas. A Study in Thomistic Metaphysics.*

O'CONNOR, Edward M. *Potentiality and Energy.*

OSTHEIMER, Anthony L. *The Family: a Thomistic Study in Social Philosophy.*

SULLIVAN, James B. *An Examination of First Principles in Thought and Being in the Light of Aristotle and Aquinas.*

TALLON, Hugh J. *The Concept of Self in British and American Idealism.*

1940   MEEHAN, Francis X. *Efficient Causality in Aristotle and St. Thomas.*

RICHEY, Sr. Francis Augustine. *Character Control of Wealth According to St. Thomas Aquinas.*

SLEVA, Victor. *The Separated Soul in the Philosophy of St. Thomas Aquinas.*

1941   BRENNAN, Sr. Rose Emmanuella. *The Intellectual Virtues According to the Philosophy of St. Thomas.*

DOUGHERTY, George V. *The Moral Basis of Social Order According to St. Thomas Aquinas.*

HARVEY, Rudolf. *The Metaphysical Relation between Person and Liberty, and Its Application to Historical Liberalism and Totalitarianism.*

JOUBERT, Gerard R. *The Qualities of Citizenship in St. Thomas.*

LE CLAIR, Sr. M. St. Ida. *Utopias and the Philosophy of St. Thomas Aquinas.*

LEDVINA, Jerome P. *A Philosophy and Psychology of Sensation, with Special References to Vision According to the Principles of St. Thomas Aquinas.*

MULLEN, Sr. Mary Dominica. *Essence and Operation in the Teaching of St. Thomas and in Some Modern Philosophies.*

UDELL, Sr. Mary Gonzaga. *A Theory of Criticism of Fiction in Its Moral Aspects According to Thomistic Principles.*

1942   BENKERT, Gerald F. *The Thomistic Conception of an International Society.*

FERGUSON, Sr. Jane Frances. *The Philosophy of Equality.*

FERREE, William. *The Act of Social Justice: an Analysis of the Thomistic Concept of Legal Justice with Special Reference to the Doctrine of Social Justice Proposed by His Holiness Pope Pius XI in His Encyclicals* QUADRA-GESIMO ANNO *and* DIVINI REDEMPTORIS, *to Determine the Precise Nature of the Act of This Virtue.*

HAYES, Sr. Mary Dolores. *Various Group Mind Theories Viewed in the Light of Thomistic Principles.*

KINNEY, Sr. Cyril Edwin. *A Critique of the Philosophy of George Santayana in the Light of Thomistic Principles.*

PENTA, Clement D. *Hope and Society: A Thomistic study of Social Optimism and Pessimism, a Study in Social Philosophy.*

SHIRCEL, Cyril L. *The Univocity of the Concept of Being in the Philosophy of John Duns Scotus.*

1943   BENNETT, Owen. *The Nature of Demonstrative Proof According to the Principles of Aristotle and St. Thomas Aquinas.*

COX, John F. *A Thomistic Analysis of the Social Order.*

FISHER, Luke. *A Philosophy of Social Leadership According to the Principles of St. Thomas Aquinas.*

KERINS, James. *The Social Role of Self-Control.*

McSWEENEY, Alan. *The Social Role of Truth According to St. Thomas Aquinas.*

MAGUIRE, John J. *Selfishness and Social Order: a Study in Thomistic Social Philosophy.*

1944   DUZY, Bro. F. Stanislaus. *Philosophy of Social Change According to the Principles of St. Thomas.*

GRAJEWSKI, Maurice J. *The Formal Distinction of Duns Scotus: a Study in Metaphysics.*

GUSTAFSON, Gustaf J. *The Theory of Natural Appetency in the Philosophy of St. Thomas Aquinas.*

HORRIGAN, Alfred F. *Metaphysics as a Principle of Order in the University Curriculum.*

KLEINZ, John P. *The Theory of Knowledge of Hugh of St. Victor.*

O'TOOLE, Christopher. *The Philosophy of Creation in the Writings of St. Augustine.*

POUSSON, Lyon B. *The Totalitarian Philosophy of Education.*

SCHEU, Sr. Marina. *The Categories of Being in Aristotle and St. Thomas.*

VARGAS, Alfonso. *Psychology and Philosophy of Teaching According to Traditional Philosophy and Modern Trends.*

1945   DUFFY, John A. *A Philosophy of Poetry Based on Thomistic Principles.*

BUCKLEY, George. *The Nature and Unity of Metaphysics.*

DeBENEDICTUS, Mathew M. *The Social Thought of St. Bonaventure.*

FOLEY, Leo A. *A Critique of the Philosophy of Being of Alfred North Whitehead in the Light of Thomistic Philosophy.*

HUGHES, Sr. Mary Cosmas. *The Intelligibility of the Universe.*

SPELTZ, George H. *The Importance of Rural Life According to the Philosophy of St. Thomas Aquinas.*

WOLTER, Allan B. *The Transcendentals and Their Function in the Metaphysics of Duns Scotus.*

1947   COLLINS, James D. *The Thomistic Philosophy of Angels.*

SMITH, Sr. E. *The Goodness of Being in Thomistic Philosophy and Its Contemporary Significance.*

SMITH, Vincent F. *The Philosophical Frontiers of Physics.*

1948   DeCOURSEY, Sr. Mary Edwin. *The Theory of Evil in the Metaphysics of St. Thomas and Its Contemporary Significance.*

MOHAN, Robert P. *A Thomistic Philosophy of Civilization and Culture.*

SATTLER, Henry V. *A Philosophy of Submission: A Thomistic Study in Social Philosophy.*

TYRRELL, Francis M. *The Role of Assent in Judgment: A Thomistic Study.*

1949   ALLUNTIS, Felix. *The Problem of Expropriation.*

PORRECO, Rocco F. *The Place of Economics in the Philosophical Hierarchy.*

RZADKIEWICZ, Arnold. *The Philosophical Basis of Human Liberty.*

SCHUMACHER, Leo S. *The Philosophy of the Equitable Distribution of Wealth: a study in Economic Philosophy.*

SHEPPARD, Vincent F. *Religion and the Concept of Democracy: a Thomistic Study in Social Philosophy.*

VEGA, Francis J. De La. *Social Progress and Happiness in the Philosophy of St. Thomas Aquinas and Contemporary American Sociology.*

1950   BENARD, Edmund D. *The Problem of Belief in the Writings of John Henry Newman, William James, and St. Thomas Aquinas.*

BODE, Roy R. *A Philosophy of Courage.*

BRENNAN, Sr. Mary Alethea. *The Origin of the Rational Soul According to Saint Thomas Aquinas.*

BUEHLER, Walter E. *The Role of Prudence in Education.*

CRONAN, Edward P. *The Dignity of a Human Person.*

DELEHANT, Sr. M. Dunstan. *The Role of Quality in the Philosophy of St. Thomas Aquinas.*

FONTAINE, Raymond G. *Subsistent Accident in the Philosophy of St. Thomas and in His Predecessors.*

FRANZ, Edward Q. *The Thomistic Doctrine on the Possible Intellect.*

GIGUERE, Robert J. *The Social Value of Public Worship According to Thomistic Principles.*

GUZIKOWSKI, Max F. *A Philosophy of Liberalism in the Light of Thomistic Principles.*

HUNT, Ben B. *The Nature and Significance of the One that Follows Being in the Philosophy of St. Thomas Aquinas.*

KANE, Sr. Anne Virginia. *Truth and Political Freedom.*

LAKY, John J. *A Study of George Berkeley's Philosophy in the Light of the Philosophy of St. Thomas Aquinas.*

McQUADE, Francis P. *A Philosophical Interpretation of the Contemporary Crisis of Western Civilization.*

NAUGHTON, E. Russell. *Freedom in Education.*

ROSENBERG, Jean R. *The Principle of Individuation: A Comparative Study of St. Thomas, Scotus, and Suarez.*

1951   BAGEN, John J. *The Brotherhood of Man in the Philosophy of St. Thomas Aquinas.*

CANGEMI, Dominic. *The Thomistic Concept of the "Vis cogitativa."*

DOUGHERTY, Kenneth F. *The Subject, Object and Method of the Philosophy of Nature According to Saint Thomas Aquinas.*

HOGAN, Joseph E. *The Virtue of Prudence in the Social Philosophy of St. Thomas.*

MALONEY, William. *Individualism: Extreme and Moderate.*

MORAN, Lawrence P. *Permanence and Progress: A Philosophical Investigation into the Foundations of the Law of Energy Conservation.*

NIEMEYER, Sr. M. Fredericus. *The One and the Many in the Social Order.*

NOONAN, John T. *Banking and the Early Scholastic Analysis of Unity.*

SAVARIA, Sr. Madeline Gabrielle. *Etienne Gilson's Concept of the Nature and Scope of Philosophy.*

WAGSTAFF, Sr. M. Joseph. *The Thomistic Philosophy of Culture and the Virtue of Art.*

1952   BREEN, Joseph S. *Religion and Secularism in the Light of Thomistic Thought.*

DECHERT, Charles R. *Thomas More and Society: A Study in Renaissance Thought.*

HARRINGTON, John. *The Contemporary Philosophy of Security in the Light of Scholastic Theory of Divine Providence.*

HARKENRIDGE, Edward W. *The Relation of the Virtue of Justice to Personality.*

O'BRIEN, James F. *The Concept of Nature in Philosophy and Physics.*

SCHEURER, Marcelius. *Philosophy of Man in Communism.*

SLATTERY, Kenneth F. *The Thomistic Concept of the Virtue of Temperance and Its Relation to the Emotions.*

WEISWURM, Alcuin A. *The Nature of Human Knowledge According to St. Gregory of Nyssa.*

1953   ANDERSON, Sr. M. Evangeline. *The Human Body in the Philosophy of St. Thomas.*

HORRIGAN, Sr. Anita. *Moral Standards and Social Organization.*

KEATING, James W. *The Function of the Philosopher in American Pragmatism.*

LYNAM, Gerald J. *The Good Political Ruler According to St. Thomas Aquinas.*

NOLAN, Paul F. *St. Thomas and the Unconscious Mind.*

O'CONNOR, John J. *Philosophical Aspects of Communication.*

PETRITZ, Margaret M. *The Philosophy of Anger and the Virtues.*

REUTEMANN, Bro. Charles. *The Thomistic Concept of Pleasure as Compared with Hedonistic and Rigoristic Philosophies.*

SIMEC, Sr. M. Sophie. *Philosophical Basis for Human Dignity and Chance in Thomistic and American Non-Thomistic Philosophy.*

1954   BONANSEA, Bernardino M. *The Theory of Knowledge of Tommaso Campanella: Exposition and Critique.*

COGGIN, Walter A. *The Role of the Will in Personality Development.*

FELD, Norbert R. *The Persistence of Realism in the Modern Scientific Interpretation of Nature.*

FLECKENSTEIN, Norbert J. *A Critique of John Dewey's Theory of the Nature and the Knowledge of Reality in the Light of the Principles of Thomism.*

FREDRICKSON, Owen P. *The Psychology of Ownership.*

TOON, Mark. *The Philosophy of Sex According to St. Thomas Aquinas.*

WARTHER, Mary A. *The Transcendental Notion of Supposit with Special Reference to the Material Supposit and Its Quality in Thomistic Metaphysics.*

1955   BURROUGHS, Joseph A. *Prudence Integrating the Moral Virtues According to Saint Thomas Aquinas.*

DOHERTY, John J. *The Concept of Man in Communist Philosophy.*

INAGAKI, Bernard. *The Constitution of Japan and the Natural Law.*

MASIELLO, Ralph. *The Intuition of Being According to the Metaphysics of St. Thomas Aquinas.*

MYERS, Joseph R. *Social Distance According to St. Thomas Aquinas.*

PAPARELLA, Benedict A. *Sociality and Sociability: a Philosophy of Sociability According to St. Thomas Aquinas.*

RAMIREZ, Augustine. *Unconscious Drives and Human Freedom in Freud's Psychoanalysis.*

SUMMERS, James J. *St. Thomas and the Universal.*

1956   ELBERT, Edmund J. *A Thomistic Study of the Psychology of Human Character.*

FOLEY, Sr. M. Thomas Aquin. *Authority and Personality Development According to St. Thomas Aquinas.*

HEATH, Thomas R. *Aristotelian Influence in Thomistic Wisdom: a Comparative Study.*

McCALL, Robert E. *The Reality of Substance.*

O'HARA, Sr. M. Kevin. *The Connotations of Wisdom According to St. Thomas Aquinas.*

O'SHEA, Robert S. *Truth of Being Through Knowledge by Connaturality.*

SHEEHAN, Robert J. *The Philosophy of Happiness According to Saint Thomas Aquinas.*

TAMME, Sr. Anne Mary. *A Critique of John Dewey's Theory of Fine Art in the Light of the Principles of Thomism.*

WHEELER, Mother Mary C. *Philosophy and the* SUMMA THEOLOGICA *of St. Thomas Aquinas.*

ZAMOYTA, Bro. Casimir Stanislaus. *The Unity of Man: St. Thomas's Solution to the Body-Soul Problem.*

1957   MAJCHRZAK, Coleman J. *A Brief History of Bonaventurianism.*

1958   CONLAN, F. Allan. *A Critique of the Philosophy of Religion of Henry Nelson Wieman in the Light of Thomistic Principles.*

DALY, Sr. Jeanne Joseph. *The Metaphysical Foundations of Free Will as a Transcendental Aspect of the Act of Existence in the Philosophy of St. Thomas Aquinas.*

GALLAGHER, Thomas A. *The Contemporary Status of the Notion of Existence and Its Limitation in Thomistic Metaphysics.*

KANE, William J. *The Philosophy of Relation in the Metaphysics of St. Thomas.*

LYONS, Lawrence F. *Material and Formal Causality in the Philosophy of Aristotle and St. Thomas.*

McLEAN, George F. *Man's Knowledge of God According to Paul Tillich: A Thomistic Critique.*

MANN, Jesse A. *Existential Import and the Aristotelian Syllogistic.*

TWOMEY, John E. *The General Notion of the Transcendentals in the Metaphysics of Saint Thomas Aquinas.*

1959   ASPELL, Patrick J. *Thomistic Critique of Transsubjectivity in Recent American Realism.*

CASE, Edward M. *A Critique of the Formative Thought Underlying Francis Suarez's Concept of Being.*

KINZEL, Sr. Margaret Mary. *The Metaphysical Basis of Certain Principles of the Religious Life in the Light of Thomistic Principles.*

1960   BURT, Donald X. *The State and Religious Toleration: Aspects of the Church-State Theories of Four Christian Thinkers.*

CUNNINGHAM, Sr. Miriam Ann. *Certitude and the Philosophy of Science.*

DOUGHERTY, Jude P. *Recent American Naturalism: An Exposition and Critique.*

FITTS, Sr. Mary Pauline. *John Locke's Theory of Meaning: An Exposition and Critique.*

PRESTON, Robert A. *Causality and the Thomistic Theory of Knowledge.*

PUTNAM, Mother Caroline Canfield. *Beauty in the Pseudo-Denis.*

SCHALDENBRAND, Sr. Mary Aloysius. *Phenomenologies of Freedom: An Essay on the Philosophies of Jean-Paul Sartre and Gabriel Marcel.*

1961   NUGENT, James B. *The Fundamental Theistic Argument in the Metaphysical Doctrine of St. Thomas Aquinas.*

QUINN, John M. *The Doctrine of Time in St. Thomas Aquinas: Some Aspects and Applications.*

1962   ARBUCKLE, Gilbert B. *A Critique of the Thomistic Doctrine of Definition.*

BRADY, Sr. Marian. *The Philosophical Basis of Human Values According to Thomistic Principles.*

COOK, Edward M. *The Deficient Cause of Moral Evil According to St. Thomas.*

Di NARDO, Ramon. *The Unity of the Human Person.*

JOLY, Ralph. *The Human Person in a Philosophy of Education.*

KEVANE, Eugene. *An Augustinian Philosophy of Education for American Catholic Schools.*

TOUGAS, Sr. Miryam. *The Relation of Existence to the Subject of Metaphysics in the Philosophy of St. Thomas.*

1963 BROUSSARD, Joseph. *Eternity in Greek and Scholastic Philosophy.*

FOX, Robert J. *Limitation of Warfare According to the Just War Theory.*

HALPIN, Sr. Marlene. *The Origin of the First Principle.*

NARDONE, Henry F. *St. Thomas Aquinas and the Condemnation of 1277.*

STEPELEVICH, Lawrence S. *Henri Bergson's Concept of Man: an Exposition and a Critique.*

WILKERSON, Jerome F. *The Concept of Friendship in the* NICOMACHEAN ETHICS *of Aristotle.*

1964 DARNOI, Dennis N. *Edward von Hartmann's Metaphysics of the Unconscious.*

DRISCOLL, John M. *Situation Ethics and the Practical Validity of Universal Moral Principles.*

GIGLIO, Charles J. *Freedom of Self-Determination in Saint Thomas and Contemporary Western Thought.*

HAY, Gerald C. *Maritain's Theory of Poetic Knowledge: a Critical Study.*

SESEK, Raphael A. *Leibniz's Proofs of God.*

1965 SULLIVAN, Emmanuel F. *The Analogy of Instrumental Causality in Thomistic Metaphysics.*

YARDAN, John L. *Demonstration of Fact in Philosophy and Science.*

1966 CANTWELL, Peter W. *Towards a Psychology of Real Knowledge.*

DESHARNAIS, Richard P. *The History of the Distinction between God's Absolute and Ordained Power and Its Influence on Martin Luther.*

DRAGHI, Robert A. *The Negative Judgment.*

MARCIL, George. *Efficient Causality in the Philosophy of Duns Scotus.*

B. FORDHAM UNIVERSITY
NEW YORK, N. Y.

1939   McGUIGAN, Sr. St. George, *Nominalism and Realism in Abelard.*

1940   LOFTUS, Arthur A. *The Works and the Mystical Theology of William of St. Thierry.*

1941   McCALL, Raymond J. *Necessity, Analogy and the Histoical Position of Spinoza.*

1943   O'CONNOR, William R. *Saint Thomas Aquinas and the Natural Desire for God.*

1944   CAFFREY, Mary C. *Realism and Knowledge According to William of Auvergne.*

HARVANEK, Robert F. *The Philosophy of Creation of Saint Gregory of Nyssa.*

1945   BRADY, Mary L. *John Dewey: Philosophy as a Methodology.*

FLYNN, John V. *The Development of Kant's Theory of Sensation.*

KENDZIERSKI, Lottie H. *The Aristotelian Physics and the Problem of Creation in the Thirteenth Century.*

MURRAY, Michael V. *The Theory of Distinctions in the Metaphysics of Francis Suarez.*

VOGEL, Mural R. *The Philosophy of Father Claude Buffier, S.J.*

1946   CORCORAN, Albert C. *Godefredi de Fontibus:* QUAESTIONES DISPUTATAE DE VIRTUTIBUS.

WOLZ, Heinrich G. *The Role of the Will in the Philosophy of René Descartes.*

1947   McMANUS, Charles, *The Notion of Being According to Thomas de Vio Cajetan.*

O'MAHONY, Timothy J. *Individuation in the Philosophy of Nicholaus Cusanus.*

ZEDLER, Beatrice H. *St. Thomas' Critique of Avicennianism in the* DE POTENTIA DEI.

1948 GLEASON, Robert W. *The Objective Good for the Person.*

O'CALLAGHAN, Louis T. *The Function of Reflection in the Psychology of Saint Thomas Aquinas.*

PROBST, Joseph S. *Reason, Experience, and Natural Law.*

1949 JOURDAIN, Alice. *The Role of Created Goods in the Philosophy of St. Augustine.*

O'HARA, Christopher E. *The Relationship Between Philosophy and Theology in the Ontologism of Vincenze Gioberti.*

1950 BURNS, John V. *Dynamism in the Cosmology of Christian Wolff.*

JACKLIN, Edward G. *The Problem of Individuation in Saint Thomas Aquinas.*

REDDING, James F. *The Virtue of Prudence in the Writings of St. Thomas Aquinas.*

SPARGO, Sr. Emma Jane Marie. *The Category of the Aesthetic in the Philosophy of Saint Bonaventure.*

1951 BRADY, Mother Gertrude V. *Basic Principles of the Philosophy of Jonathan Edwards.*

DAY, Francis T. *The Concept of Being in the Metaphysics of Suarez.*

1952 CONWAY, James. *The Nature of Cartesian Realism.*

HUETTER, Norbert. *The Eidetic Existentialism of Saint Thomas.*

KELLY, Bro. Pascal. *An Analysis of the Proper Senses in the Philosophy of Saint Thomas Aquinas.*

MacGREGER, Philip S. *Spinoza and Religious Philosophy.*

MARRA, William A. *Our Knowledge of Objects Through Themselves and as Themselves.*

O'NEILL, Reginald. *The Meaning of Our World as Seen by Saint Bonaventure in the Light of Exemplary Causality.*

OWENS, Thomas J. *The Problem of Interpersonal Relations as Posed in Contemporary Thought.*

1953   BRADY, Mother Cora. *The Philosophy of Creation in Saint Bonaventure's* COMMENTARY ON THE SENTENCES.

ELEASAR, Jose M. *Xavier Zubiri: His Fundamental Moral Concepts.*

ERLINGHAVEN, Helmut. *Moral, Personal Responsibility: Its Conditions and Limitations.*

KLAUDER, Francis J. *The Intrinsic Nature of Good and Evil According to Saint Bonaventure.*

1954   HOULIHAN, Sr. Elizabeth Marie. *Metaphysical Necessity in Saint Thomas and Its Historical Foundations.*

MULLANEY, James V. *The Natural, Terrestrial End of Man.*

NOONE, John B. *The Form and Meaning of Knowledge in Mathematical Physics.*

ROUSSEAU, Edward. *The Distinction between Essence and Supposit in the Angel According to Saint Thomas.*

SOMERVILLE, James M. *Bond in Being.*

WASSMER, Thomas. *A Phenomenological Study of the Guilt Experience in the Light of Modern Ethics and Value Theory.*

1955   CLARK, Mother Mary. *Augustine: First Philosopher of Freedom.*

DALY, John Emmanuel. *Orestes Brownson and the Transcendentalists.*

DENEEN, Gerard F. *The Vision of Truth in the Doctrine of Saint Augustine.*

FARLEY, Mother Elizabeth. *The Efficacy of Secondary Causes in the Doctrine of Saint Thomas Aquinas.*

MITROS, Joseph. *The Philosophy of Religion of Edgar Sheffield Brightman.*

APPENDIX

250

DRISCOLL, Leo. *Methodology of Charles Sanders Peirce.*

GRONTKOWSKI, Raymond. *Descartes and Galileo: New Views on the Philosophy of Nature.*

McGRATH, Charles. *Gregory of Nyssa's Doctrine on Knowledge of God.*

SMITH, Mother Frances A. *Louis Lavelle's Philosophy of Man: Self-Creation through Consent to Participation.*

1965 ESTRADA, Charles. *Freedom and the Personality in the Thought of André Gide, Albert Camus, and Fyodor Dostoevsky.*

LANGLEY, Raymond J. *Hume's Logic of the Imagination.*

STENGREN, George L. *Human Intellectual Knowledge of the Material Singular According to Francis Suarez.*

1966 CHEN, Ellen Marie. *Tao, Nature, Man: A Study of the Key Ideas in the Tao Te Ching.*

COUSINS, Ewert Hilary. *The Notion of the Person in the* DE TRINITATE *of Richard St. Victor.*

HOLLOWAY, Alvin J. *The Transformation of Stoic Themes in St. Augustine.*

IORIO, Dominick A. *The Notion of Intelligible Extension in Nicolas Malebranche.*

KREEFT, Peter John. *A Study of Wonder in Plato and Augustine.*

C. GEORGETOWN UNIVERSITY
WASHINGTON, D. C.

1930 BRADY, Francis I. *Certitude: The Complete Doctrine Evolved from the Conclusions of the Various Branches of Philosophy Which Bear Upon the Subject.*

1945 DENECKE, Charles. *The Role and Importance of Sel Existence in the Science of Metaphysics.*

1948 AXER, Engelbert. *The Knowledge of Reality and G According to Nicholas Berdyaev.*

SPONGA, Edward J. *The Problem of Transcendence-Immanence in Blondel's Philosophy of Action in Terms of Hegel's Dialectic.*

1956 BROWNE, Joseph W. *An Analysis and Evaluation of Berkeley's Doctrine on Abstraction.*

CALLAHAN, Francis F. *Philosophical Method in Maurice Blondel.*

DOWD, Mother Ruth. *Saint Bernard's Contribution to Philosophy.*

FLYNN, Thomas J. *Empirical and Metaphysical Proofs for the Immortality of the Human Soul.*

GILLIGAN, Bernard B. *Philosophy and Psychiatry.*

JAVIER, Benjamin P. *The A Priori Factor in the Logic and Psychology of Maréchal's Critical Philosophy.*

McCOOL, Gerald A. *The Historical Sources of the Image and Likeness of God in the Anthropology of Saint Augustine.*

McGANN, Thomas F. *Suarez and Personalism.*

1957 BYRNE, James W. *Religious Toleration: Its Background in the Philosophy of John Locke.*

FONTINELL, Eugene. *The Participation Theory of Being in the Philosophy of Josiah Royce.*

LADEMAN, William D. *Nietzsche's Philosophy of the Free Spirit.*

MACKEY, Robert R. *The Role of Prudence in the Act of Obedience According to St. Thomas.*

O'BRIEN, Thomas S. *The Principle of Finality in the Philosophy of St. Thomas Aquinas.*

PAPAY, Joseph L. *The Concept of Non-Being in Plato and in his Contemporaries and Predecessors.*

REILLY, William L. *Metaphysical Abstraction according to Joseph Maréchal, S.J.*

1958 BUSHINSKI, Edward A. *An Introduction to the Natural Theology of John of St. Thomas.*

DOMBRO, Richard J. *The Two Supreme Newmanic Realities.*

GALLAGHER, Kenneth T. *The Philosophical Method of Gabriel Marcel.*

MARTIN, Stuart B. *The Notion of Error in Descartes' Theory of the Embodied Self.*

NAVICKAS, Juozas-Leonas. *The Moral Philosophy of Lossky.*

PEPPER, George B. *The Concept of Man in Anthropological Theory.*

WALSH, Joseph M. *The Principle "Bonum est diffusivum sui" in St. Bonaventure: Its Meaning and Importance.*

1959   DRENNEN, Donald A. *The Oppositionist Character of Nicholas Berdyaev's Philosophy.*

FERRIOLS, Roque. *The "Psychic Entity" in Aurobindo's* THE LIFE DIVINE.

GERRY, Joseph. *Kierkegaard: The Problem of Transcendence: an Interpretation of the Stages.*

HETZLER, Florence M. *An Introduction to the Philosophy of Nature: the Commentary of St. Thomas Aquinas on Book One of the* PHYSICS *of Aristotle.*

McDERMOTT, John J. *Experience is Pedagogical: The Genesis and Essence of the American Nineteenth Century Notion of Experience.*

O'TOOLE, Edward Joseph. *The Mind-Body Problem in Contemporary Schools of Language Analysis.*

1960   CARPINO, Joseph James. *A Study of Negation in Hegel.*

SULLIVAN, Arthur F. *Religion in Santayana's Philosophy of the Spirit.*

1960   TWOHILL, Sr. M. Dominic. *The Background of St. Thomas Aquinas' Reading of the* DE DIVINIS NOMINIBUS.

1961   BRENNAN, Bernard. *The Moral Implications of James'* PRAGMATISM.

DOWNEY, Bro. Leo Robert. *Life, Reason, and History in the Philosophy of Ortega y Gasset.*

LYNCH, John J. *The Metaphysical and Epistemological Presuppositions of H. Weyl's Conception of Mathematics.*

MACHO, Thomas. *Freedom and Necessity in St. Augustine.*

REILLY, William F. *The Pragmatism of William James as a Religious Philosophy.*

ROTH, Robert J. *The Conditions of Self-realization in the Philosophy of John Dewey.*

1962   KEATING, Sr. Mary William. *The Relation between the Proofs for the Existence of God and the Real Distinction of Essence and Existence in St. Thomas Aquinas.*

LONG, Jerome. *Dewey and Pragmatism: Towards a True Conception of Values in Process.*

MICELI, Vincent P. *The Life of Communion and Community in the Philosophy of Gabriel Marcel.*

MORAN, John H. *Ludwig Wittgenstein's Philosophical Therapy.*

SWEENEY, Robert D. *Material Value in Max Scheler's Ethics: an Exposition and Critique.*

1963   TRANT, Edward J. *The Ethical Realism of G. E. Moore.*

BARRAL, Mary R. *Merleau-Ponty: The Significance of the Body in Interpersonal Relations.*

BARRY, Robert M. *The Epistemology of Talcott Parsons.*

DILWORTH, David. *Whitehead's Philosophy of Organism as a Development of American Pragmatism.*

GIOSCIA, Victor. *Plato's Image of Time.*

HASHIMOTO, Rentaro. *Process and Finality in Hegel.*

HENNESSY, James. *The Background, Sources, and Meaning of Divine Infinity in St. Gregory of Nyssa.*

MURPHY, Richard T. *Phenomenology and the Dialectic: A Study of Pre-Reflexive Consciousness in the Phenomenological Theories of Husserl, Sartre and Merleau-Ponty.*

1964   ANSBRO, John. *Kierkegaard's Critique of Hegel: An Interpretation.*

BLAIR, George. *"Entelecheia" and "Energeia" in Aristotle.*

1949 WILSON, Russell. *The Modes of Abstraction According to St. Thomas Aquinas.*

CARNEY, William J. *Agent Intellect and Phantasm: Their Relationship in the Teaching of St. Thomas and His Commentators.*

1950 AQUINO Y PAULINO, Conrado. *Conflicting Concepts of Man and Philosophies of Education in Relation to the Philippines.*

SAYEGH, Fayez, A. *Existential Philosophy: A Formal Examination.*

1951 POWELL, Francis de Sales. *A Thomistic Evaluation of James Wilson and Thomas Reid.*

TOMEH, George J. *Reason and Revelation in Islam with Particular Reference to Al-Chazzali and Averroes.*

1953 KOHLS, Henry H. *Some Factors in our Knowledge of Existence Compared with Teachings of Aquinas.*

SAENZ DE SANTA MARIA, Carmelo. *A History of the Organization of Philosophical Studies in Guatemala, 1577-1769.*

1955 ADDERLEY, Bertram R. *Ownership and Natural Right: Being an Exposition of the Relationship of Private Property Rights and Natural Law.*

OWENS, Francis X. *A Study of Natural and Humanistic Motivations in Thirteen Cases of Religious Conversion.*

1956 SCOTT, Frederick J. *The Pragmatism of Maurice Blondel: The Problem of Knowledge in the Perspective of Action.*

SULLIVAN, Henry J. *The New Psychology.*

1958 FITZGIBBON, John P. *The Philosophy of Poetic Symbolism: Medieval and Modern.*

GOODWIN, Robert P. *The Metaphysical Pragmatism of Charles Sanders Peirce.*

1959 CONNOR, Joseph G. *The Jesuit College and Electivism: a Study in the Philosophy of American Education.*

KANDA, John R. *Certain Intellectual Operations and the Neo-Scholastic Manuals.*

KLINE, Robert R. *The Present Status of Value Theory in the United States.*

1960   PETERSON, Forrest H. *A Study of Power in the Philosophies of Hegel and Marx.*

1961   NYS, Pierre E. *Body and Soul: the Center of Metaphysics? A Comparison of the Philosophy of Gabriel Marcel with the Philosophy of Saint Thomas.*

SULLIVAN, Paul R. *Ontic Aspects of Cognition in Poetry.*

1962   BALTAZAR, Eulalia R. *A Critical Examination of the Methodology of the* PHENOMENON OF MAN.

1963   SCHAEFER, Thomas E. *The Meaning of Chun Tzu in the Thought of Mencius.*

1964   OWEN, William A. *Whitehead's Philosophy of Science and the Concept of Substance.*

1965   MIHALICH, Joseph C. *The Notion of Value in the Existentialism of Jean-Paul Sartre.*

MUNOZ-COLBERG, Magda. *An Evaluation of Auguste Comte's Theory of Inequality.*

1966   DE BRABANDER, Rene Firmin. *Immanent Philosophy and Transcendent Religion: Henry Dumery's Philosophy of Christianity.*

D. LAVAL UNIVERSITY
QUEBEC, CANADA

1936   ROBERT, Patrice. *Hylémorphisme et devenir chez saint Bonaventure.*

1940   DORVAL, Georgette. *Expositio definitionis pulchri a S. Thoma traditae.*

1941   GONZALES, M. Crescentius. *Imperfectio et peccatum veniale.*

GUTIERREZ, Florentino. *De republica secundum Franciscum de Vitoria.*

OESTERLE, J. *Two Essays on the Problem of Meaning.*

SUPPLE, J. M. *Dialectics and Experimental Biology.*

1942   LOCKWELL, Bro. Clement. *La génération temporelle de la sagesse chez les poètes-théologiens et les premiers physiologues.*

1943   HAMMOND, Francis. *La conception psychologique de la société selon Gabriel Tarde.*

JETTE, Emile. *Etude comparative de la sensation chez Bergson et saint Thomas.*

LALOR, Juvenal. *The Notion of Limit.*

LEGAULT, Henri. *Le marxisme et la critique de la religion.*

1944   MARCOTTE, Normand. *Matter and Knowledge.*

OTIS, Louis-Eugène. *La doctrine de l'évolution.*

1945   CANTIN, Stanislas. *Henri Bergson et le problème de la liberté.*

KEARNEY, Francis W. *Cassirer's Mirandola.*

KELLY, Sr. Marie-de-Jésus. *Adam Smith's Theory of Moral Sentiments.*

MALONEY, James R. *The Formal Constituent of a Sin of Commission.*

MORENCY, Robert. *L'action selon Jean de Saint-Thomas.*

REITH, Herman. *The Marxist Dialectics of Nature.*

1946   CONWAY, Pierre H. *Essays on Immortality in Relation to the Emancipation of Man.*

GAREY, Sr. Mary Jocelyn. *Measure in the Eternity of God and in Created Durations.*

HOLLENCAMP, Charles. *Causa causarum.*

KOCOUREK, Roman A. *Rationalization in Mathematics.*

MARIE-DE-LOURDES, Sr. *Essai de commentaire critique de l'* ENQUIRY CONCERNING HUMAN UNDERSTANDING *de David Hume.*

MULLAHY, Bernard J. *Thomism and Mathematical Physics.*

SMITH, Bro. Sixtus R. *A Thomistic Theory of the Liberal Arts.*

1947   DORAN, Sr. Mary Verda Clare. *On the Goodness of Created Things.*

DUFAULT, Wilfred. *L'apriorisme dans les termes de la science expérimentale.*

MARTIN, Vincent M. *Nicolas of Cusa on God and the Creature.*

TAYLOR, Joseph C. *The Aristotelian Concept of Natural Philosophy.*

VACHON, Louis-Albert. *Les preuves naturelles de l'existence des substances séparées.*

1948   DOLAN, Bro. S. Edmund. *The Resolutive and Compositive Modes.*

DURAND, Anthony. *Shelley on the Nature of Poetry.*

HEBERT, Thomas. *La connaissance du singulier matériel selon Jean de Saint-Thomas.*

LAROCHELLE, Joseph. *La solidarité humaine selon l'enseignement des derniers Souverains Pontifes.*

SIMARD, Emile. *L'hypothèse.*

1949   BAUMGAERTNER, William. *A Study of Definition.*

DILLON, David A. *An Inquiry Into the Notion of Christian Philosophy.*

DULAC, Henri. *The Modal Enunciation.*

GRIFFIN, John J. *The Interpretation of the Two Thomistic Definitions of Certitude.*

LANGLOIS, Jean. *La délectation.*

LYONS, John T. *The Signification of Being.*

OUELLET, Henri R. *Les présupposés d'une théorie de l'imitation dans l'art d'après Platon.*

1950   DROUIN, Paul-Emile. *Etude comparée de saint Thomas d'Aquin et de Suarez sur la question de l'entitatif et de l'intentionnel.*

1951   CAULFIELD, Joseph. *Practical Ignorance in Moral Actions.*

CONNELL, Richard J. *An Exposition of a Treatise Written b ySt. Albert the Great, Entitled* DE NATURA LOGICAE.

CUNNINGHAM, Robert L. *The Aristotelian Notion of Nature.*

GERMAIN, Paul, *La génération et la corruption des mixtes.*

GURNAN, Sr. Saint Michael. *On Love.*

O'BRIEN, Sr. Julia Marie. *Self-love and Human Society.*

OTTO, John A. *The Commentary of St. Thomas on the* ETHICS *of Aristotle, Book I.: Introductory Study and Translation.*

SULLIVAN, Richard H. *Custom and Authority in Education.*

WEST, Charles M. *The Aristotelian Conception of Intellect.*

1952   BEACH, John D. *Necessitas quae est ex materia.*

LABRIE, Robert. *Commentaire du traité du temps d'Aristote.*

McARTHUR, Ronald. *The "universale in praedicando" and the "universale in causando."*

McCOY, Charles. *Ludwig Feuerbach and the Formation of the Marxian Revolutionary Idea.*

WOJCIECHOWSKI, Jerzy. *Le problème du mouvement.*

1953   SLAFKOSKY, Alexander L. *The Best Form of Government.*

WARREN, John D. *Natura agit propter finem.*

1954   CLEMENT, André. *La conception du hasard chez Lévy-Bruhl et la critique qu'en fit Bergson.*

McINERNY, Ralph. *The Existential Dialectic of Søren Kierkegaard.*

O'FLYNN, Sheila. *The First Two Meanings of* "rational process" *According to the* EXPOSITIO IN BOETHIUM DE TRINITATE.

SCHWARTZ, Charleen. *Neurotic Anxiety.*

1955   LAVERE, Georges J. *The Political Principles of John Locke.*

ROBINSON, Andrew H. *Contingency and the Modern Scholastics.*

SAINT-EDOUARD, Sr. *Quelques problèmes sur la qualité.*

1956   McGOVERN, Thomas. *The Division of Logic.*

1957   CREM, Theresa. *A Commentary on the* RHETORIC *of Aristotle.*

FERRARI, Leo. *The Origin of the State According to Plato.*

MacLELLAN, Thomas. *The Moral Virtues which Rectify the Exercise of the Speculative Life.*

1958   CHABOT, Sr. Marie-Emmanuel. *Le concept de nature chez Cicéron.*

DOLAN, Joseph V. *Natural Law and Modern Jurisprudence.*

EAST, Simon-Pierre. *La méthode en biologie selon le premier livre du* DE PARTIBUS ANIMALIUM *d'Aristote.*

McMAHON, Georges J. *The Order of Procedure in the Philosophy of Nature.*

PHAM-VAN-LONG, Joseph. *Les preuves de l'immortalité de l'âme humaine.*

ROYAL, Peter E. *The Coercion of the Intellect by Its Object.*

1959   McDONALD, Joseph B. *The Art of Agriculture According to the Teachings of Saint Thomas.*

McNAMARA, Vincent J. *The Personalism of Nicholas Berdyaev.*

1961   AUGUSTIN, Gabriel. *La matière intelligible.*

CHEN, Joseph. *Piété filiale et religion dans la tradition chinoise.*

COTE, André, *La logique de la première opération.*

1962   NEUMAYR, John. *Plutarch, Aristotle, and the Nature of Poetry.*

SCHOLZ, Donald F. *Aristotle's Definition of Place.*

1963   GALLUP, John R. *The Primary Meanings of the Latin Word "Modus."*

KELLY, Cornelius J. *St. Thomas on the Division of Speculative Knowledge.*

1964   BERQUIST, Duane H. *Descartes and the Way of Proceeding in Philosophy.*

BLAIS, Martin. *La colère.*

DONALDSON, James. *Hegel's Dialectic and the Motion of Motion.*

PROULX, Sr. Saint-Jean-Elzéar. *Le Marxisme et la rapport de la pensée à l'être.*

SAINT-MARTIN-DE-TOURS, Sr. *Sur le "proemium" de la* POLITIQUE.

1965   BLANCHETTE, Oliva. *The Perfection of the Universe in the Philosophy of Saint Thomas Aquinas.*

BROUILLETTE, Gerarda. *Appétit et locomotion ou l'âme comme principe du mouvement local d'après le traité de l'âme d'Aristote.*

FEELEY, Thomas. *The Function of Touch.*

GOSSELIN, Marcelle. *Le droit naturel.*

LAMBERT, Roger. *La voie d'invention dans les* PHYSIQUES *d'Aristote.*

MacDONALD, Charles. *The Role of Negation in Knowledge.*

SAMSON, André. *Sensation et intellection des présocratiques à Aristote.*

STROMBERG, James S. *An Essay on Experimentum.*

1966   BLANCHET, Louis-Emile. *Deux enseignements sur l'infini.*

PICARD, Guy. *La causalité accidentelle dans la nature.*

E. LOYOLA UNIVERSITY
CHICAGO, ILLINOIS

1939   SUTFIN, Edward J. *The Mind of St. Anselm of Canterbury: A Study in Early Scholasticism.*

1940   McKIAN, John D. *The Limits of Natural Knowledge According to the Doctrine of Saint Thomas Aquinas.*

1941   MARTIN, Hugh. *St. Augustine's Political Theory.*

ROYCE, James E. *A Glossary of* QUAESTIONES DISPUTATAE DE VERITATE, I.

1947   ROEMER, Lawrence J. *The Political Philosophy of Orestes Brownson.*

1948   TSEU, Augustinus. *The Moral Doctrine of Mo-Tze.*

1950   POWERS, William E. *Plato's Philosophy of Participation with a Critical Evaluation According to the Basic Principles of Thomism.*

F. MARQUETTE UNIVERSITY
MILWAUKEE, WISCONSIN

1930   RIEDL, John O. *The Life and Philosophy of Orestes A. Brownson.*

1938   BOGDANSKI, Augustine. *The Significance of Clement Baeumker in Neo-Scholastic Philosophy.*

1939   GARVEY, Sr. Mary Patricia. *Saint Augustine: Christian or Neo-Platonist? From His Retreat at Cassiacum Until His Ordination at Hippo.*

1941   MAYNARD, Sr. M. Francis. *The Structure of the Human Act According to Saint Thomas Aquinas.*

1943   ROGERS, Mother Vera. *Saint Thomas's Argument from Motion and Its Critics.*

1944   GALLAGHER, Donald A. *The "Scio me esse" of Saint Augustine and the "Cogito ergo sum" of Rene Descartes.*

1963   GALLAGHER, Idella J. *Moral Obligation in the Philosophy of Henri Bergson.*

        LINDGREN, John R. *Adam Smith's Theory of the Ultimate Foundations of Commercial Society.*

1965   CRITELLI, Ida Jo Ann. *The Political Good in the Philosophy of John Locke.*

        O'MALLEY, Joseph J., *Material Being and Scientific Knowledge According to Pierre Duhem.*

        PULS, Sister Mary Sarto. *The Personalistic Theism of Borden Parker Bowne.*

1966   ANDERSON, Thomas C. *The Object and Nature of Mathematical Science in Aristotle and St. Thomas Aquinas.*

        CHARRON, William C. *An Exposition and Analysis of William James' View on the Nature of Man.*

        KEANE, Helen V. *Knowledge by Connaturality in St. Thomas Aquinas.*

        LEWIS, John Underwood. *Man's Natural Knowledge of the Eternal Law.*

        LUTHER, Arthur R. *Existence as Dialectical Tension: A Study of the Philosophy of W. E. Hocking.*

G. NOTRE DAME UNIVERSITY
SOUTH BEND, INDIANA

1934   EGGLESTON, Sr. Mary Frederick. *Some Effects of the Theory of Evolution on the Philosophy of Religion.*

1940   McMORROW, George J. *A Metaphysical Study of the Individual and the Person.*

1941   BAKER, Richard R. *The Thomistic Theory of the Passions and Their Influence on the Will.*

        CZAJKOWSKI, Casimir J. *The Theory of Private Property in the Political Philosophy of John Locke.*

RAGO, Henry. *The Philosophy of Esthetic Individualism.*

1942   FLYNN, Frederick E. *Wealth and Money in the Economic Philosophy of St. Thomas.*

JACOBY, Paul J. *Common Sense in Epistemology.*

SCHORSCH, Robert S. *The Psychology of Play.*

1944   BABIN, Arthur E. *The Theory of Opposition in Aristotle.*

JUNKERSFELD, Sr. M. Julienne. *The Aristotelian-Thomistic Concept of Chance.*

1946   DONOVAN, Sr. Mary Annice. *The Henological Argument for the Existence of God in the Works of St. Thomas.*

PACHECO, Armando C. *Plato's Conception of Love.*

1948   GERHARD, William A. *Infra-Rational Knowledge and the Intellectual Virtue of Prudence.*

1949   O'CONNELL, Sr. M. Marguerite. *The Relation between Solitude and Social Action as Lived and Taught by St. Bernard.*

VELEZ, Jaime S. *The Doctrine of the Common Good in the Works of St. Thomas Aquinas.*

1950   GLANVILLE, John J. *Verification in the Philosophy of Nature.*

1951   EVANS, Joseph W. *Development of Thomistic Principles in Jacques Maritain's Notion of Society.*

GANGULY, Theotonius A. *Purush and Prakrti (Self and Nature) a Philosophical Appraisal of Patanjala-Samkhya-Yoga.*

MORRISON, John J. *A Definition of Mathematics.*

1952   SIMMONS, Edward D. *The Thomistic Doctrine of Intellectual Abstraction for the Three Levels of Science: Exposition and Defense.*

1953   BOBIK, Joseph. *Materia Quantitate Signata: the Thomistic Principle of the Individuation of Corporeal Substance.*

1955   HOLLENHORST, George D. *Consciousness.*

1956   CROSSON, Frederick J. *Presence and Subjectivity.*

FITZGIBBON, John F. *The Origin of Ideas in the Latin-Avicennian Tradition.*

KAHN, Journet D. *A Thomistic Theory of Emotion.*

LANIGAN, Joseph F. *An Investigation into the Human Knowledge of the Singular.*

1957   HACHEY, Sr. M. Mercedes. *An Investigation and Evaluation of Two Interpretations of St. Thomas' Doctrine on the Objectivity of the Concept.*

MATTINGLY, Basil. DE PRINCIPIIS NATURAE *of St. Thomas Aquinas: Critical Edition.*

1958   FRANCOEUR, Bro. Robert A. *The People in the Social Role of the Church according to Lamennais.*

PERILLAT, Robert J. *St. Thomas Aquinas on the Meaning of Subsistence.*

SIKORA, Joseph J. *Object and Method in the Philosophy of Nature and in Physical Science.*

1959   HADDOX, John H. *Reasons for the Importance of a Philosophical Study of Some of the Basic Principles of the Living World.*

KEEGAN, Francis L. *The Development of Jacques Maritain's Conception of Christian Philosophy: 1910-1929.*

O'GRADY, Donald A. *A Metaphysics of Beauty.*

1960   BASEHEART, Sr. Mary Catharine. *The Encounter of Husserl's Phenomenology and the Philosophy of St. Thomas in Selected Writings of Edith Stein.*

HOLLENBACH, Sr. Mary William. *The Nature of the Intellectual and Moral Virtues and Their Various Relationships.*

SCHRYNEMAKERS, Arthur H. *Descartes' Philosophical, Psychological, and Moral Views on* THE PASSIONS OF THE SOUL.

WEIHER, Charles F. *Foundations of An Abstractionist Theory of Natural Number.*

1961   FAIRBANKS, Matthew J. *C. S. Peirce and Nineteenth Century Positivism.*

GRUENENFELDER, John B. *Plato's Theory of Scientific Knowledge in the Later Dialogues.*

HERX, Fredrick C. *The Problem of Illumination in St. Bonaventure and St. Thomas Aquinas: During the Period 1250-1259.*

NELSON, Ralph C. *Jacques Maritain's Conception of Moral Philosophy Adequately Considered.*

NUGENT, Francis R. *The Nature and Properties of Immanent Action.*

1962   GRAHAM, Joseph M. *Secondary Causal Influx According to St. Thomas Aquinas.*

KELLY, Sr. M. James Therese. *An Examination of Eric Gill's Philosophy of Art.*

PAX, Clyde V. *The Approach to God in the Thought of Gabriel Marcel.*

RYAN, Michael T. *The Notion and Uses of Dialectic in St. Thomas Aquinas.*

1963   BEIS, Richard H. *Modern Ethical Relativism and the Natural Law Theory of St. Thomas Aquinas.*

HAMPSCH, George H. *Some Aspects of the Marxist Notion of Classless Society.*

KELLY, Mathew J. *The Interpretation of St. Thomas Aquinas of 191a7-8: the Underlying Nature is Known by Analogy.*

KENNEDY, Samuel J. *Conscience: Its Nature and Role in Moral Activity According to St. Thomas Aquinas.*

WOJCIECHOWSKI, Edward C. *Vladimir Soloviev's Doctrine of the Absolute.*

1964   CAVANAGH, Patrick E. *The Doctrine of Assent of John Henry Newman.*

COULSON, William R. *Client-Centered Therapy and The Nature of Man.*

FRANCIS, Richard P. *The Doctrine of Natural Selection in John Dewey's Value Theory.*

MURPHY, Laurence T. *The Role of Nature and Connaturality in Moral Philosophy According to St. Thomas Aquinas.*

TURLEY, Robert S. *Determinism in Freudian Psychoanalytic Theory.*

1965   CAMPBELL, James Ian. *Logical Positivism and Religious Discourse.*

ERPENBECK, James Richard. *The Relation of Pragmatism and Realism in the Philosophy of C. S. Peirce.*

GEORGE, Richard J. *The Role of Points in Hume's Analysis of Space.*

GERVASI, Julian Anthony. *The Philosophy of Michele Sciacca.*

KEANE, Sr. Ellen Marie. *The Equation of Truth and Subjectivity in Kierkegaard's* POSTSCRIPT.

KEARLEY, Carroll J. *Ortega y Gasset's Non-Eleatic Concept of Being.*

KING, Edward George. *Spiritual Substance in the Empiricist Philosophy of George Berkeley.*

LARKIN, Sr. Miriam Therese. *A Study of Language in the Philosophy of Aristotle.*

1966   ASHMORE, Robert B. *The Analogical Notion of Judgment in St. Thomas Aquinas.*

BEATTY, Richard D. *The Logical Foundations of Peirce's Categories, 1867-85.*

BRUZINA, Ronald C. *Logos and Eidos: A Study in the Phenomenological Meaning of "Concept" according to Husserl and Merleau-Ponty.*

BUCKLEY, Joseph A. *The Dimensions of the Real According to Jacques Maritain.*

CARANDANG, Amado I. *Jean-Paul Sartre and His Atheism.*

GAMBATESE, Angelus. *The Commentary of William of Ockham on Aristotle's* PERIHERMENEIAS.

H. PONTIFICAL INSTITUTE OF MEDIAEVAL STUDIES [1]

TORONTO, CANADA

1931   PEGIS, Anton C. *The Problem of the Soul in the Thirteenth Century.*

1932   POLLOCK, Robert C. *St. Anselm's Doctrine of Rectitude.*

1933   O'MEARA, William J. *The Unity of Duns Scotus' Thought.*

1934   CHAPMAN, Emmanuel. *St. Augustine's Philosophy of Beauty.*

       WALSH, Daniel C. *The Metaphysics of Ideas According to Duns Scotus.*

1935   KIRBY, Gerald J. *Law in the Writings of John of Salisbury and St. Thomas Aquinas.*

1936   MORRIS, Daniel J. *The "Liberum arbitrium" According to St. Thomas Aquinas.*
       SMITH, Gerard. *Freedom in Molina.*

1937   GARVEY, Edwin C. *A Study of St. Thomas' Interpretation of Aristotle on the Question of Creation and God.*

1938   BOURKE, Vernon J. *The Perfecting of Potency by "Habitus" in the Philosophy of St. Thomas Aquinas.*

1938   JOHNSTON, Herbert L. *Mediaeval Teachings on the Morality of Usury.*

       MILLER, Robert G. *The Notion of the Agent Intellect in St. Albert the Great.*

       MULLER-THYM, Bernard J. *The Establishment of the University of Being in the Doctrine of Meister Eckhart of Hochheim.*

---

[1] These dissertations were directed by staff members of the Institute in their capacity as professors of the University of Toronto. The dissertation of Joseph Owens was submitted for the Doctorate in Mediaeval Studies at the Institute of Mediaeval Studies.

MUNDAY, Daniel P. *The Theory of Knowledge of Godfrey of Fontaines.*

1939 BIRD, Otto. *Mediaeval Philosophic Thought as Reflected in the* CANZONE D'AMORE *of Calvalcanti, according to the* COMMENTARY *of Dino del Garbo.*

O'NEIL, Charles. *The Structure and Foundation of Prudence in Aristotle.*

1940 ANDERSON, James F. *Analogy, a Study in Thomistic Metaphysics.*

HUNT, DeRay. *The Relations Between Descartes and Locke.*

LYNCH, Lawrence E. *The Doctrine of the Non-Coeternity of the Ideas in John the Scot.*

THOMPSON, Richard J. *The Ethics of Abelard.*

1941 BARATH, Désiré. *Thomas Aquinas' Natural Science and the New Sciences.*

HEISER, Basil H. *The Status of Metaphysics according to John Duns Scotus.*

TURNER, Walter. *The Concept of Casus in the Philosophy of St. Thomas Aquinas.*

1943 BREZIK, Victor. *Friendship and Society: A Study in Thomistic Social Philosophy.*

1944 BURBACH, Maur R. *The Theory of Beatitude in Latin-Arabian Philosophy and Its Initial Impact on Christian Thought.*

KOSSEL, Clifford G. *Relation in the Philosophy of St. Thomas Aquinas.*

SMYTH, Sr. Mary Marcia. *The Nature and Role of Prudence According to the Philosophy of St. Thomas Aquinas.*

1945 LEMIEUX, Albert A. *The Theory of Knowledge According to Francesco Suarez.*

1946 CASSASSA, Charles H. *The Political Thought of Francisco de Vitoria.*

HOLMES, Bernard G. *The Anselmian Problem, Its Various Interpretations and a Suggested Solution.*

KALBERER, Augustine. *St. Thomas' Notion of Order.*

MacDONALD, Ralph J. *Gregory of Rimini and "Notitia simplex": An Edition of Gregory of Rimini* IN I SENT., D. III, *with Introduction and Notes.*

O'DONNELL, J. Reginald. *The* DE BONO ET MALO *of William of Auvergne: Text, Introduction and Brief Analytical Studies.*

SWAN, Peter. *The Equality of Man in the Philosophy of St. Thomas Aquinas.*

1947   KLUBERTANZ, George, P. *"Vis Cogitativa" according to St. Thomas Aquinas: Sources and Doctrine.*

MAURER, Armand. *Ockham's Interpretation and Criticism of the Formalism of Duns Scotus.*

ROWAN, John P. *St. Thomas' Doctrine of Peace.*

SCHMIDT, Robert. *The Domain of Logic According to St. Thomas Aquinas.*

WALTON, William M. *The Person in the Writings of St. Thomas Aquinas.*

1948   BRADY, Ignatius. The LIBER DE ANIMA *of William of Vauroullon, with an Introduction.*

CAIRD, Alfred. *The Doctrine of Quiddities and Modes in Francis of Meyronnes.*

FAGIN, Charles. *The Doctrine of the Divine Ideas in the* SUMMA DE BONO *of Ulrich of Strasbourg.*

NASH, Peter. *"Esse Actuale": The Problem of Existence and Individuality in Giles of Rome.*

OWENS, Joseph. *The Doctrine of Being in the Aristotelian* METAPHYSICS.

REGAN, Sr. Frances Carmel. *A Study of the* LIBER DE SPIRITU ET ANIMA: *Its Doctrine, Sources and Historical Significance.*

THRO, Linus J. *The Critique of St. Thomas in the* REPORTATA PARISIENSIA *and the Orientation of the Scotistic Metaphysics.*

1949   HEIMAN, Ambrose J. *The "Esse" of Creatures in the Doctrine of Jean Quidort: Study and Texts.*

LESCOE, Frank J. *The Theory of the First Principle in the* SUMMA DE BONO *of Ulrich of Strasbourg: a Philosophical Study and Text.*

O'CALLAGHAN, Jeremiah, J. *Walter of Chatton's Doctrine of Intuitive and Abstractive Knowledge: Study and Text.*

1951 GARVEY, Charles M. *Substance and Being in Books IV and V of the* SAPIENTIALE *of Thomas of York: Study and Texts.*

MANLEY, Michael F. *God, His Nature and Existence, According to the* SAPIENTIALE *of Thomas of York: Study and Text.*

REILLY, James P. *The Divisions of Being in Thomas of York: Study and Text.*

SULLIVAN, Edward J. *The Divine Ideas According to William of Ockham: Study and Text.*

1952 COLLINGWOOD, Francis J. *The Theory of Being in* SUMMA DE BONO (Book II) *of Ulrich of Strasbourg: Study and Text.*

GRASSI, Carlo A. *The Doctrine of Creation in the* SAPIENTIALE *of Thomas of York: Study and Text.*

PRZEZDZIECKI, Joseph J. *The Passivity of the Possible Intellect According to Thomas of Sutton: Study and Text.*

SYNAN, Edward A. *The* LOGICA *Attributed to Richard of Campsall: Study and Texts.*

TONER, Jules J. *The Notion of Spiritual Nature According to St. Thomas Aquinas.*

1953 DAY, Abyann. *The* CONCORDANTIA VERITATIS *Attributed to Benedict of Assignano: Text and Study.*

DUNPHY, William B. *The Doctrine of Causality in the* QUAESTIONES IN METAPHYSICAM *of Peter of Auvergne.*

GROSSER, Elmer J. *St. Thomas Aquinas and the* POLITICS *of Aristotle.*

MICHENER, Norah W. *The Integral Humanism of Jacques Maritain as Related to his Philosophy of the Person.*

MONAHAN, Arthur P. *The Doctrine of Being in the* QUAESTIONES IN METAPHYSICAM *of Peter of Auvergne.*

MONAHAN, Edward J. *The Doctrine of Human Liberty and Free Will in John Buridan's* QUAESTIONES SUPER DECEM LIBROS ETHICORUM ARISTOTELIS AD NICOMACHUM.

MORTON, Edmund W. *Doctrine of "Ens commune" in St. Thomas Aquinas.*

ROBB, James H. *The Nature of the Human Soul in the* QUAESTIONES DE ANIMA (Q. 1-3) *of St. Thomas Aquinas: Text and Study.*

SCHMITZ, Kenneth L. *The Problem of the Immortality of the Human Soul in the Works of Cajetan.*

1954   GELINAS, Elmer T. *The Relation between Life and Existence: A Study of "Vivere viventibus est esse" as found in Thomas Aquinas.*

HENLE, Robert J. *Saint Thomas and Platonism. A Study of the Plato and Platonici Texts in the Writings of Saint Thomas.*

LINDON, Luke J. *The Notion of Human Virtue According to St. Thomas Aquinas.*

SWEENEY, Charles L. *Divine Infinity in the Writings of St. Thomas Aquinas.*

WESTLEY, Richard J. *The Doctrine of Individuation in the Philosophy of Gilbert de la Porrée.*

1955   BYRNE, Paul M. *The Doctrine of the Soul in the* SAPIENTIALE *of Thomas of York: Study and Text.*

CARLO, William E. *The Doctrine of Creation in Giles of Rome: A Study of the Relation of Essence and Existence in the Creative Act.*

WELLS, Norman J. *The Distinction of Essence and Existence in the Philosophy of Francis Suarez.*

1956   GRIESBACH, Marcellus F. *The Relationship between Temporal and Spiritual Powers in John of Paris and James of Viterbo.*

1957   LAPIERRE, Michael J. *The Objective Concept: A Study in the Poetical Theory of Gabriel Vasquez.*

        MacGUIGAN, Mark R. *The Best Form of Government in the Philosophy of St. Thomas Aquinas.*

1958   ALLEN, Elliott B. *The Notion of Being in Hervaeus Natalis.*

        KENNEDY, Leonard A. *Abstraction and Illumination in the Doctrine of St. Albert the Great.*

1960   DECK, John. *Nature as Contemplation in Plotinus.*

        O'REILLY, Peter. *Saint Thomas Aquinas'* Expositio super Librum Boetii De Hebdomadibus: *An Edition and Study.*

        RIORDAN, Joseph. *Form and Intellect in Averroes.*

        SCULLY, John P. *Reality and Truth in Thomas of York. Study and Text.*

1961   STOKES, Thomas J. *William of Ockham's Doctrine of Science.*

1962   GATTO, Edo P. *The Doctrine in the Opusculum,* De natura generis *Attributed to St. Thomas Aquinas.*

        STRASSER, Michael W. *Saint Thomas' Critique of Platonism in the* Liber de causis.

1965   CATAN, John R. *The Relation Between Soul and Separate Mind in Aristotle.*

        CUNNINGHAM, Stanley B. *The Significance of St. Albert the Great's* De bono *in Early Thirteenth-Century Moral Philosophy.*

        LYNCH, John E. *The Theory of Knowledge of Vital du Four.*

        McCARTHY, Donald. *Free Choice and Liberty According to Thomas Bradwardine.*

McLAUGHLIN, Robert J. *Abstraction as Constitutive of Science According to Aristotle and Saint Thomas Aquinas.*

SCHNEIDER, Richard. *Eckhart's Doctrine of the Transcendental Perfections in God and Creatures.*

YEE, Richard. *Pietro Ponpanazzi's Doctrine of the Soul.*

1966   DOYLE, John P. *The Metaphysical Nature of the Proofs for God's Existence According to Francis Suarez, S.J.*

QUINN, John. *St. Bonaventure and the Notion of Christian Philosophy in Modern Scholarship: an Introduction to St. Bonaventure and the Divine Immutability.*

TETREAU, Richard D. *The Agent Intellect in Meister Dietrich of Freiberg.*

WINGELL, Albert E. *The Relationship of Intellect and Will in the Human Act According to St. Thomas Aquinas.*

I. ST. JOHN'S UNIVERSITY
JAMAICA, NEW YORK

1962   CATALANO, Joseph S. *The Eduction of Substantial Forms According to Saint Thomas Aquinas.*

1963   KELLY, James P. *The Continuation Between the Human Sense Powers and the Human Speculative Intellect According to Saint Thomas Aquinas.*

1964   LaCENTRA, Walter J. *Freedom and Society in Jacques Maritain.*

1965   TRAINOR, Sr. Mary Rosaleen. *Thomas Jefferson on Freedom of Conscience.*

J. SAINT LOUIS UNIVERSITY
ST. LOUIS, MISSOURI

1930   McWILLIAMS, James A. *The Bearing of the Integral Composition on the Essential Composition of Bodies.*

1931 ENGLES, Sr. Mary Francisca. *The Evaluation of the Standard of Morality in Modern Ethical Theories.*

1932 MULVIHILL, Josephine F. *The American New Realist Concept of Substance with Special Reference to the Substantiality of the Self or Ego.*

1933 KEELER, Leo W. *The Problem of Error from Plato to Descartes.*

RUEVE, Stephen J. *Suarez and the Natural Moral Law.*

1934 DOLLARD, Stewart E. *Bergsonian Metaphysics and God.*

McCUE, Edward C. *Theophany: a Study of the Nature of God and His Manifestations from the Works of Joannes Scotus Eriugena, Ninth Century Philosopher.*

1935 WADE, William L. *A Comparison of the* DE MAGISTRO *of Saint Augustine with the* DE MAGISTRO *of St. Thomas.*

1936 KENNEDY, Paul V. *A Philosophical Appraisal of the Modernist Gnosticism of Nicholas Berdyaev.*

LEFEBVRE, Reginald R. *Lenin's Materialism: An Evaluation of the Philosophical Basis of Russian Communism.*

1937 LEMMER, Jerome G. *The Problem of the Plurality of Substantial Forms in a Compound as Treated by St. Albert the Great.*

1945 WOLF, Theodore J. *The Function of Qualities in Substantial Change According to St. Thomas Aquinas.*

1947 BUSHMAN, Sr. Rita Marie. *Right Reason in Stoicism and in the Christian Moral Tradition up to Saint Thomas.*

1949 BRADY, Jules. *The Function of the Seminal Reasons in St. Augustine's Theory of Reality.*

1950 DAVITT, Thomas E. *The Relation between the Concept of Law and the Philosophy of Intellect and Will.*

MARTINEZ, Mother Marie Louise. *"Recta Ratio" according to Saint Thomas Aquinas.*

1951 PENET, Sr. Mary Emil. *Property and Right in Representative Catholic Moralists of the Thirteenth to Seventeenth Centuries.*

1952   GANNON, Sr. Mary Ann Ida. *The Active Theory of Sensation in Plotinus and St. Augustine.*

1953   BREIDENBACH, Francis J. *The Meaning of Nature in Aristotle.*

MONTAGUE, Michael J. *Secondary Causality in the Act of Will-to-end in the Writings of St. Thomas Aquinas.*

1954   BLACKWELL, Richard J. *Aristotle's Theory of Predication.*

HECHT, Francis T. *Self-evidence of God's Existence in Some Theologians, 1650-1750.*

TILLMAN, Stanley C. *The Principle of Contiguity—Its Meaning and Value as Applied by St. Thomas to the Powers of Man.*

1955   ADELMANN, Frederick J. *The Rational Appetite in the* DE FIDE ORTHODOXA *of St. John Damascene.*

GURR, John E. *The Principle of Sufficient Reason in Some Scholastic Systems, 1750-1900.*

HAYES, Justin D. *Moral Conscience in the Thought of Saint Bonaventure.*

McTIGHE, Thomas P. *God and Physics.*

ROCKEY, Palmer L. *The Moral Philosophy of Giambattista Vico.*

1956   FAY, Charles. *St. Thomas' Modification of Boethius' Doctrine on Being, Goodness, and Participation.*

MARIEN, Francis J. *God in the Personalism of Borden Parker Bowne.*

1957   BURLAGE, Carl J. *The Proper Object of Metaphysics in the Latin Text of Averroes.*

KAUFMANN, Leo B. *Predication and Reality in Plato.*

SCHNEIDER, Sr. Mary Monica. *Augustinian Citations in St. Bonaventure's Formal Treatment of Knowledge.*

1958   LAUER, Rosemary Z. *Voltaire's Constructive Deism.*

MATHEWS, Paul L. *A Study of the Literary Background and the Methodology of St. Thomas'* COMMENTARY ON THE POSTERIOR ANALYTICS *of Aristotle.*

1959   CATANIA, Francis J. *Divine Infinity According to Albert the Great's Commentary on Lombard's* SENTENCES.

DELANEY, Howard R. *The Doctrine of Four Term Analogy in Aristotle.*

HAYMOND, William S. *Hume's Theory of Sense Perception.*

KENNEY, W. Henry. *John Locke and the Oxford Training in Logic and Metaphysics.*

KOENER, Sr. Jane. *Human Operations and Their Finalities in St. Thomas Aquinas.*

KRAUS, Donald W. *Toward a Realistic Theory of Moral Value: a Constructive Study of Perry, Vivias, and T. V. Smith.*

LAWLER, Ronald D. *The Moral Judgment in Contemporary Analytic Philosophy.*

REILLY, Francis E. *The Method of the Sciences According to Charles Sanders Peirce.*

1960   CHILDRESS, Marianne. *The Morally Good as Ontologically Perfective.*

DONOHUE, Thomas C. *Warfare and Justice in Fifteenth Century Scholasticism.*

DOYLE, Sr. Mary Antoinette. *Nature and Naturalism in George Santayana.*

HUNGERMAN, Sr. Marie Gabriel. *Berkeley and Newtonian Natural Philosophy.*

LANGLEY, Wendel E. *Berthier's* MEMOIRES DE TREVOUX *(1745-1762): Fideism and the Problem of Method.*

REAGAN, James T. *The Material Substrate in the Platonic Diologues.*

STOKES, Walter E. *The Function of Creativity in the Metaphysics of Whitehead.*

VOLKOMENER, Sr. Mary Theophane. *Thomistic Ethics and Anthropological Data: Some Possible Contributions of Empirical Materials to Moral Science.*

1961   MANIER, August E. *The Meaning of "Nature" in the Philosophy of Leibniz.*

REILLY, John P. *Cajetan's Notion of Existence.*

ROULEAU, Sr. Mary Celeste. *The Place of Love and Knowledge in Human Activity According to Selected Texts of St. Thomas Aquinas.*

VAN DOMELEN, Sr. Mary Ermelinda. *The Philosophical Method of Edgar Sheffield Brightman.*

1962   CONNELLY, George E. *The Existence and Natures of God in the Philosophy of Alfred North Whitehead.*

ELLIS, Frank R. *Hume's Theory of Nature.*

FRENCH, Sr. Mary Anne. *Creation in Saint Thomas: a Metaphysical Study.*

GOROSPE, Vitaliano R. *Moral Obligation in John Dewey's Ethical Naturalism.*

LLAMZON, Benjamin S. *Esse As First Actuality in Bañez.*

OPPENHEIM, Frank M. *Royce's Mature Idea of General Metaphysics.*

REIF, Sr. Mary Richard. *Natural Philosophy in Some Early Seventeenth Century Scholastic Textbooks.*

ROWLAND, Sr. Mary Joyce. *The Acts of the Mind in Newman's Theory of Assent.*

1963   BILL, Thomas I. *The Theory of Nature in John Stuart Mill.*

ERMATINGER, Charles J. *The Coalescent Intellective Soul in Post-Thomistic Debate.*

DAMHORST, Donald E. *Social Norms and Protestant Ethics: The Ethical Views of Reinhold Niebuhr and H. Richard Niebuhr.*

HASSEL, David J. *Method and "Scientia" in St. Augustine: A Study of Books VIII to XV in his* DE TRINITATE.

HOPKINS, John M. *Urban on the Form of Philosophical Intelligibility.*

McMAHON, Mary Roberta. *"Separatio" in Recent Thomism.*

PUNZO, Vincent C. *Royce on the Problem of Individuality.*

ST. HILLAIRE, Sr. Mary Georgeta. *Precepts of Natural Law in St. Thomas.*

1964   FLANIGAN, Sr. Thomas Marguerite. *Collingwood on the Nature of Metaphysics.*

RANLY, Ernest W. *Scheler's Phenomenology of Community.*

1965   FELT, James W. *Whitehead's Early Theory of Scientific Objects.*

McMAHON, John J. *The Concept of Matter in the Metaphysics of Henri Bergson.*

STEVENS, Edward V. *G. H. Mead on the Moral Self.*

1966   DUNN, Sr. Dorothy Ann. *The Problem of Dualism in John Dewey.*

CORR, Charles A. *Order and Method in Christian Wolff's Speculative Philosophy.*

MORKOVSKY, Sr. Theresa Clare. *Henri Bergson's Doctrine of Freedom.*

K. STUDIUM GENERALE OF SAINT THOMAS

RIVER FOREST, ILLINOIS

1947   KENNY, John P. *A Philosophical Study of the International Military Tribunal.*

1949   ALMEIDA, Enrique D. *Sto. Tomas de Aquino y el Problema Psicologico de la Union del Alma con el Cuerpo.*

SULLIVAN, Robert P. *The Thomistic Concept of the Natural Necessitation of the Human Will.*

1950   FARAON, Michael J. *The Metaphysical and Psychological Principles of Love.*

UBEDA, Manuel. *A Contribution to the Psychophysiology of Sensory Cognition.*

1951   FLYNN, Thomas V. *The Cogitative Power According to Saint Thomas and His Commentators.*

SHEEHAN, Thomas D. *The Morality of the Restrictive Covenant.*

1952   ERWIN, James M. *An Analysis of the Virtue of Patience According to Saint Thomas.*

NADEAU, Louis V. *Role of Final Causality in Self-Adaptation of Living Things to Their Environment, in Particular with Regard to the Organs of Vision.*

SCULLION, Matthew R. *A Thomistic Critique of the Jurisprudence of Oliver Wendell Holmes.*

1955   GARCIA, Leovigildo. *Mathematics' Foundations in Aristotle.*

GLUTZ, Melvin A. *The Manner of Demonstrating in Natural Philosophy.*

1956   CONLAN, Pius. *The Theological Meaning of History According To Saint Thomas.*

1959   MORENO, Antonio. *Science and Philosophy.*

KINSELLA, Arthur L. *The Meritorious Act of Meekness.*

1960   KANDARAPALLY, Joseph. *A Study of Some of the Basic Philosophical Concepts in the Bhagavad Gita.*

1961   VEERKAMP, Theodore M. *An Inquiry into the Study of Language in Its Relations to Society.*

1962   RUSH, Vincent E. *A Phenomenological Response to Existential Ethics.*

TENSING, Robert H. *A Critical Analysis of the Philosophy of Brand Blanshard.*

1964   RODRIGUEZ, J. F. *An Analysis of the Social Value of Wealth and the Distributive System of.Wealth in Spain.*

ROENSCH, F. J. *The Unicity of Substantial Form and Its Implications in the Early Thomistic School.*

1965   STRUIK, L. *Wonder: The Beginning of Wisdom.*

1966   FREEMAN, Hilary. *The Problem of Chance.*

L. UNIVERSITY OF MONTREAL
MONTREAL, QUEBEC, CANADA

1922   TOUPIN, Charles. *Le mariage indissoluble de droit naturel.*

JASMIN, Louis D. *La propriété privée et les systèmes opposés.*

1933 GINGRAS, Jules A. *Le problème des raisons éternelles dans la connaissance intellectuelle.*

1935 BANHAM BRIDGES, Katharine M. *Emotional Development in the Young Child.*

1937 MARTIN, Jean. *Le problème expérimental de l'intelligence.*

1938 PELLAND, Laurence. *Etude comparée de la psychologie féminine chez saint Thomas d'Aquin et chez les Modernes.*

1939 SAINT-HILAIRE, C. A. *L'union objective du connaissant à l'être.*

1940 PETIT, Gérard. *La métaphysique thomiste et la doctrine sociale de l'Eglise en regard des erreurs contemporaines.*

1941 ETHIER, Wilfrid. *Nos secondes natures: recherche expérimentale de la notion d'habitude.*

1942 PÉTRIN, Jean. *La finalité du savoir humain.*

1943 DESLAURIERS, Augustin M. *La théorie de la participation chez Plotin.*

1945 MARCOTTE, Marcel. *Le problème des origines dans la philosophie de Bergson.*

WALSH, John G. *The Argument of Authority.*

1947 BLANCHARD, Yvon. *Le problème de la définition de l'âme chez Aristote.*

DENBURG, Chaim N. *Matter and Form in Maimonides.*

1947 CAUCHY, Venant. *Le scepticisme grec surtout d'après Sextus Empiricus.*

MARIE-DE-BON-SECOURS, Sr. *La formation de l'esprit par la conquête du savoir: notions de psychologie pédagogique.*

VANIER, Paul. *Les influences néoplatoniciennes et aristotéliciennes dans l'élaboration du concept thomiste.*

1948 TESSIER, Hector. *L'Unité de la vie morale d'après saint Thomas d'Aquin.*

1949   BERNIER, Robert. *L'autorité politique internationale.*

DEMPSEY, Peter. *The Psychology of Jean-Paul Sartre.*

1950   ANGERS, William P. *Modern Irreligion and the Problem of Human Happiness.*

DÉCARIE, Vianney. *Aristote, PHYSIQUE, I: traduction et commentaire.*

ERCILLA, José De. *La causalité du phantasme dans la philosophie de saint Thomas.*

GENDREAU, Bernard. *La certitude selon saint Thomas d'Aquin.*

MARSCHALL, Mathias. *La doctrine de l'intelligence chez Alexandre d'Aphrodise d'après saint Albert le Grand.*

NEWBOLD, Thomas M. *The Problem of the "Affections of Soul" in the Noetic of Aristotle.*

1951   GIRNIUS, Juozas. *La métaphysique existentielle de Karl Jaspers.*

1952   LAVIGNE, Jacques. *L'inquiétude humaine.*

1953   BÉRUBÉ, Jean-François. *La personne humaine chez saint Thomas d'Aquin.*

MIGNAULT, Richard. *Genèse, nature et engagements d'une métaphysique vécue.*

1954   REID, Jean-L. *Aperçu sur la philosophie de Louis Lavelle.*

1955   MURIN, Charles. *Moral Being According to St. Thomas Aquinas.*

1956   HOUDE, Roland. *On the Methodology of the Syllogism: a Comparative Essay.*

1957   MARIE-DE-MASSABIELLE, Sr. *La philosophie de l'education chez saint Thomas d'Aquin.*

PERREAULT, Aimon-M. *Les echelles de mesure en psychologie de la sensation.*

PRUCHE, Benoît. *Existant et acte d'être: essai de philosophie existentielle.*

1958   LEWIS, Hebert. *The Notion of Contemplation in Aristotle's* ETHICS.

1959   BRODEUR, Claude. *Itinéraire de l'esprit humain dans sa rencontre de l'amour au coeur de l'être.*

DALCOURT, Gérard J. *The Methods of Moral Philosophy.*

ELDERS, Léon. *Aristotle's Theory of Principles, A Commentary on Book X of the* METAPHYSICS.

POHIER, Jacques-M. *Essai d'epistémologie comparée de la pensée religieuse et de la pensée de l'enfant.*

1960   GASTONGUAY, Jacques-M. *La psychologie de la mémoire selon saint Thomas d'Aquin: sources et doctrines.*

LÉVESQUE, Claude. *Processus de socialisation et construction de la personnalité: essai de psychologie comparée.*

URUSOV, Andrei. *Essai sur l'aspect humain ou les racines psycho-philosophiques de la puissance du communisme à travers une typologie.*

1961   WATERS, Raphaël T. *Participation as a Key to Thomistic Epistemology.*

1962   ABIMRAD-MAALOUF, Nouhad. *Le témoignage chrétien de Kierkegaard: essai analytique.*

CARDASH, M. Yehuda. *On Aristotle's Intelligences as Compared to Those of Maimonides' Angelology.*

MAALOUF, M. Nayet. *La place du verbe dans la pensée arabe.*

1963   MARIE-ST-JEAN-FRANCOIS, Sr. *L'homme ne naît pas libre, il le devient.*

1965   HELAL, Georges. *La Structure de l'intentionnalite de la philosophie de la nature de A. N. Whitehead.*

JETTE, Jacqueline. *L'interpretation de l'argument cartésien dans la philosophie de Louis Lavelle.*

1966   SERRE, Jacques. *Thomas d'Aquin et le concept de la totalité.*

M. THE UNIVERSITY OF OTTAWA
OTTAWA, ONTARIO, CANADA

1938   TREMBLAY, Jean-Jaques. *Patriotisme et nationalisme.*

1939   CLEMENT, Laurent. *Le droit de propriété privée d'après saint Thomas.*

MANNING, Thomas. *Corporative Organization of Society.*

1941   BEAUCHAMP, Maurice. *Méthode thomiste de la théologie naturelle.*

1942   TAYLOR, John Edward. *An Essay on the Philosophy of John Dewey.*

1944   CARRIERE, Gaston. *La condition humaine dans la philosophie de Plotin.*

1945   BLANCHETTE, Arthur. *An Introduction to Psychoanalysis.*

OSTIGUY, Roland. *La philosophie du droit selon saint Thomas.*

WESSEL, Stephen. *Cubberley's Educational Principles.*

1949   LÉVESQUE, Jean-Claude. *La nature et les limites de la connaissance intuitive selon Jean-de-Saint-Thomas.*

MAZIARZ, Edward. *The Nature of Mathematical Abstraction.*

O'GRADY, Francis Thomas. *The Theory of Good in the Philosophy of John Dewey.*

1950   GRATTON, Henri. *Problèmes de la biologie contemporaine: étude bio-philosophique.*

1951   KREYCHE, Robert J. *The Naturalism of Roy Wood Sellars.*

1952   AUGER, Georges-Albert. *Le triomphe de la liberté dans le personnalisme thomiste.*

BÉRUBÉ, Georges. *La méthode thomiste en philosophie.*

CROTEAU, Jacques. *Individu et personne dans le personnalisme de Maritain.*

DUMONT, Richard Edward. *An Historical Sketch of the "Cogitative Force" in the Middle Ages: Its Transition Through the Orient and the Occident.*

SMITH, Edward T. *The Nature of Life in Saint Thomas Aquinas and Some Modern Biologists.*

1953   PIERZCHALSKI, Raymond J. *Existence and Faith in the Philosophy of Kierkegaard.*

1954   ANTAL, John. *The Epistemology and Religion of Lord Herbert of Cherbury.*

HAKIM, Albert B. *The Meaning of Man in St. Augustine.*

1955   BECKER, Ralph. *The Philosophy of Charles Augustus Strong.*

PATRY, Marcel. *La nature de la logique dans l'école thomiste.*

1956   KREYCHE, Gerald Francis. *Kierkegaardian Existentialism: a Thomistic Critique.*

1957   BOH, Ivan. *An Examination of the Emotive Theory of Value Judgments.*

GOLEBIEWSKI, Casimir. *The Truth of Judgment in St. Augustine's* DE MAGISTRO.

PLAMONDON, Paul. *La preuve augustinienne de l'existence de Dieu.*

TISZAI, Paul. *Maoism: the Political Philosophy of Mao Tse-Tung: the Third Theoretician of Marxism.*

1958   CARROLL, Owen. *An Introductory Essay to the History of the Development of Metaphysics in the* COMMENTARY ON PETER LOMBARD'S SENTENCES *by Thomas Aquinas.*

FORD, John H. *An Evaluation in the Philosophy of Art of Lewis Mumford.*

1959   JALBERT, Guy. *Nécessité et contingence chez saint Thomas d'Aquin et chez ses prédécesseurs.*

1960   ROESCH, Eugene. *Inevitableness of Totalitarianism in a Society Founded on a Philosophy of Individualism: as Seen in Hobbes and Rousseau.*

1961   KILEY, John F. *The Metaphysical Foundations of the Epistemology of Albert Einstein.*

SCHUBERT, Robert J. *On Wonder in Chesterton.*

1962   PETRAROJA, Sergio. *Karen Horney's Theory of Neurosis: an Aristotelian-Thomistic Critique with an Introduction to the School of Interpersonal Relations.*

1963   BECKA, Richard. *Human Knowing in the Psychology of Jung.*

MUTH, Edward. *African Philosophy and Applications to Basutoland Politics.*

1965   DOOLEY, William. *The World State: A Necessary Condition for World Peace.*

MAJOR, Jean-Louis. *Dialectique existentielle de Saint-Exupéry.*

SCHUETZINGER, Caroline E. *The Gnoseological Transcendence in Nicolai Hartmann's Metaphysics of Cognition.*

1966   KRAUS, John L. *Locke's Theory of Universals and its Relation to the Question of a "Science of Physical Things."*

O'MANIQUE, John T. *The Theory of Orthogenesis in the Synthesis of Teilhard de Chardin.*

SAINDON, Sr. Saint-Georges-Etienne. *Univocité et analogie en rapport avec la démonstration en logique traditionnelle.*

INDEX

Abbagnano, Nicola, 19, 61, 176, 180, 218
Abimrad-Maalouf, Nouhad, 279
Achtemeier, Paul, 161
"Actualidad y perennidad del tomismo," 26
Adalbertus a Postioma, 94
Adamczyk, S., 26
Adams, James, 124, 127
Adderley, Bertram, 251
Adelmann, Frederick, 272
Adler, Mortimer, 21, 108, 123, 140, 173, 190, 209
Agazzi, Evandro, 213
Agoglia Rudolfo, 213
Aguirre Beltrán, Gonzalo, 68
Aja, Pedro, 8
Albanese, Francesco, 24
Albert, Ethel, 184
Albo, X., 138
Alcorta, José, 180
Aldwinckle, R., 168
Alejandro, José, 63, 180, 224
Alexander, W., 112
Alfaro, Juan, 148
Alimwrung, M., 22
Aliotta, Antonio, 218
Allen, Elliott, 269
Allen, Francis, 67
Allers, Rudolf, 61
Alluntis, Felix, 236
Almeida, Enrique, 26, 275
Almeida, Paulo de, 26
Alston, William, 91
Althusser, L., 213
Altizer, Thomas, 111, 112, 124, 152, 161, 167
Alvarez Turienzo, S., 108
Alves de Campos, A., 44
Amerio, Franco, 94, 213

Ames, Van Meter, 75
Amore, Benedetto D', 8, 26, 180
Analytic Philosophy, 45
Anan, S., 202
Anderson, D., 136
Anderson, Harold, 60
Anderson, James, 22, 91, 265
Anderson, Sr. M. Evangeline, 239
Anderson, Thomas, 259
Angers, William, 125, 278
Annan, N., 136
Annice, Sr. Mary, 91
Ansbro, John, 249
Anscombe, G., 191
Anshen, Ruth, 173
Antal, John, 281
Antoine, P., 206
Antoine, R., 108
Antonelli, M., 129, 195
Antweiler, A., 178
Anz, W., 8
Apalek, John, 118
Aquinas, Thomas, see Thomas Aquinas
Aquino Y Paulino, Conrado, 251
Arata, Carlo, 94, 180
Arbuckle, Gilbert, 242
Ardley, G., 21
Arenhoevel, D., 148
Arévalo Bilbao, Pedro-José, 8
Armatas, P., 165
Armstrong, A., 1, 21
Armstrong, C., 112
Arnold, Magda, 76
Arvon, Henri, 75
L'ascèse chrétienne, 102
Ashley, Benedict, 3, 22, 209, 219, 222
Ashley, Montague, 83
Ashmore, Robert, 263
Aspell, Patrick, 241

L'attualità dei filosofi classici, 18
Aubert, Roger, 94, 102, 105, 150
Aubrey, Edwin, 50
Auer, Alfons, 128, 130, 139
Auger, Georges-Albert, 280
Augustin, Gabriel, 257
Augustin, Hermann, 122
Augustine, St., 173
Austin, J., 45
Avelino, Andrés, 123
Averill, Lloyd, 148
Axer, Engelbert, 250
Ayer, A., 45
Ayers, Robert, 168
Ayres, C., 67

Babin, Arthur, 260
Babin, P., 146
Babolin, A., 116
Bachhuber, A., 219
Baden, Hans, 68
Bagen, John, 238
Bahm, Archie, 190
Baier, Kurt, 190
Baillie, John, 156
Baker, A., 108
Baker, Richard, 259
Balic, C., 26, 27, 224
Ballard, E., 112
Baltazar, Eulalia, 252
Balthasar, Hans von, 71, 79, 110, 118, 134
Baluja, J., 224
Balz, A., 211
Bandera, Armando, 225
Banerjee, N., 160
Bangerter, O., 72
Banham Bridges, Katherine, 277
Barale, Paolo, 8, 24, 225
Baranski, Leo, 65
Barath, Désiré, 265
Barbedette, D., 221
Barbuy, H., 188
Bardet, Gaston, 63
Barion, J., 19
Baron, Roger, 9
Barral, Mary, 249
Barrett, Donald, 184
Barrett, E., 202
Barry, Robert, 249
Bars, Henry, 146, 150
Barth, Karl, 6, 9, 120, 146, 152

Barth, M., 197
Barthel, P., 171
Bartisch, H., 167
Bartolomei, T., 9, 24
Bartolone, Filippo, 178
Baruk, H., 79
Basabe, Fernando de, 27
Baseheart, Sr. Mary Catherine, 261
Basili de Rubí, B., 9
Bastable, J., 22
Battaglia, Felice, 75
Baudoux, B., 9
Bauer, Joachim, 232
Bauhofer, Oscar, 69
Baum, Gregory, 103, 120, 202
Baumer, F., 111
Baumer, W., 160
Baumgaertner, William, 254
Baumgartner, M., 27
Baur, L., 221
Bausani, A., 157
Bavinck, J., 147
Bayley, John, 83
Beach, John, 255
Beales, A., 219
Beardslee, William, 125
Beatty, Richard, 263
Beauchamp, Maurice, 280
Becka, Richard, 282
Becker, A., 9
Becker, Ralph, 281
Bednarsky, J., 41
Bedoyère, Michael de la, 99
Begin, Raymond, 197, 202
Beis, Richard, 191, 262
Beker, E., 120
Bell, Bernard, 111
Bell, D., 54
Bell, George, 103
Belmond, S., 27
Benard, Edmund, 237
Bendall, K., 45, 147
Bender, Joseph, 231
Bendiek, J., 95, 156
Bénézé, G., 213
Benkert, Gerald, 234
Bennett, Owen, 235
Benoit, Hubert, 83
Bense, Max, 59
Benson, Purnell, 127
Bérard, Léon, 68
Berdiaev, Nikolai, 62, 83, 89, 174

Berenda, C., 209
Berger, Gaston, 188
Berggren, D., 168
Bergson, Henri, 174
Bernard, A., 50
Bernier, Robert, 278
Berquist, Duane, 257
Berrigan, D., 131
Berthelemy, J., 178
Berti, Conradus, 221
Bertocci, Peter, 76, 85, 108, 186
Bertrams, W., 206
Bérubé, Georges, 280
Bérubé, Jean-François, 278
Besanceney, P., 191
Beschin, Giusèppe, 9
Best, Ernest, 131
Betancur, Cayetano, 9
Bettazzi, Luigi, 9, 213
Betts, J., 36
Bevan, Edwin, 167
Bévenot, M., 101, 161
Bianca, Omero, 62
Bianco, Franco, 170
Bigger, C., 161
Bill, Thomas, 274
Binkley, L., 161
Birault, Henri, 118
Bird, Otto, 219, 265
Birou, A., 129
Biser, E., 114, 116, 131
Bismarck, K. Von, 162
Black, Max, 209
Blackham, H., 134
Blackstone, W., 45
Blackwell, Richard, 272
Blair, George, 249
Blais, Martin, 257
Blake, J., 152
Blanchard, Yvon, 277
Blanchet, Louis-Émile, 258
Blanchette, Arthur, 280
Blanchette, Oliva, 257
Blanshard, Brand, 209
Blehl, V., 176
Blewett, J., 49, 50
Blic, J. de, 9
Blomme, Robert, 112
Blondel, Maurice, 6, 19, 36, 52, 131
Boas, George, 219
Bobik, Joseph, 91, 260
Bochenski, Innocentius, 51, 160

Bode, Roy, 237
Böhner, Philotheus, 6, 9, 22
Bogdanski, Augustine, 258
Bogliolo, Luigi, 6
Boh, Ivan, 281
Bohlmann, R., 158
Bohm, Anton, 140
Boisset, J., 6
Bon, H., 95
Bonafede, Giulio, 27
Bonansea, Bernardino, 239
Bond, Charles, 158
Bondi, Eugene, 219
Bonet, A., 24
Bonhoeffer, D., 139, 147
Bontadini, Gustavo, 27, 180
Bontemps, C., 178
Bordoni, M., 159
Bordoy-Torrents, P., 27
Borne, Etienne, 74, 93, 95, 111, 116, 213
Boros, L., 122
Bortignon, Girolamo, 212
Bortolaso, G., 27, 180
Bosio, G., 36, 38
Bosley, Harold, 17
Boudier, F., 56
Boughton, J., 191
Bouillard, Henri, 44
Bouillard, M., 154
Boulding, Kenneth, 186
Bourassa, F., 180
Bourg d'Ire, Marie-Benoît du, 134
Bourke, Vernon, 91, 121, 191, 202, 219, 264
Bouthillier, Yves, 52
Bouyer, Louis, 103, 134
Bovis, André de, 72
Bower, William, 125
Boyer, Charles, 9, 27, 105, 213, 225
Brady, Mother Cora, 246
Brady, Francis, 250
Brady, Mother Gertrude, 245
Brady, Ignatius, 266
Brady, Jules, 271
Brady, Leo, 209
Brady, Sr. Marian, 184, 242
Brady, Mary, 244
Braithwaite, R., 45, 49
Brancaforte, Antonio, 156
Brauer, Theodore, 22, 219
Braun, Herbert, 152

Bredow, Gerda, 178
Breen, Joseph, 238
Breidenbach, Francis, 272
Brennan, Bernard, 248
Brennan, Edward, 231
Brennan, Martin, 36
Brennan, Sr. Mary Alethea, 237
Brennan, R., 22
Brennan, Sr. Rose Emmanuella, 234
Brès, Yvon, 214
Breton, Stanislas, 41, 43, 44, 52, 85, 188, 221
Breton, V., 27
Brezik, Victor, 265
Brien, A., 148
Brightman, E., 77
Brinkmann, Donald, 62, 63
Broad, C., 22
Brodeur, Claude, 279
Broglie, Guy de, 148
Brophy, Thomas, 3
Brouillette, Gerardo, 257
Broussard, Joseph, 243
Brown, B., 202
Brown, E., 136
Brown, James, 39
Brown, R., 104
Browne, Joseph, 247
Bruaire, Jean-Claude, 214
Bruce, Michael, 152
Brugger, Walter, 95
Bruin, P. de, 59
Bruneau, A., 87, 88
Brunello, Bruno, 103
Bruni, G., 9
Brüning, W., 81
Brunner, August, 36, 63, 69, 80
Brunner, Emil, 71, 130
Brunner, Heinrich, 147
Brushovsky, Meyer, 65
Bruzina, Ronald, 263
Buber, Martin, 77, 83, 147, 152
Buchenbacher, Hans, 6
Buckler, R., 83
Buckley, George, 236
Buckley, Joseph, 263
Budzik, G., 200
Buehler, Walter, 237
Bulle, G., 59
Bulnes, J., 194
Bultmann, Rudolf, 99, 126, 130, 140, 147, 167, 168

Bunn, E., 198
Burbach, Maur, 265
Burch, George, 3
Burchard, John, 65
Burckhardt, Georg, 56
Burgelin, Pierre, 10
Burke, Eugene, 3
Burkhardt, Frederick, 66
Burkill, T., 41, 107, 125
Burlage, Carl, 272
Burlingame, Roger, 67
Burns, John, 245
Burr, Nelson, 51, 123
Burroughs, Joseph, 240
Burt, Donald, 242
Burtt, E., 152
Busa, Roberto, 95
Buschmann, W., 125, 128
Bushinski, Edward, 247
Bushman, Sr. Rita Marie, 271
Busij, J., 65
Bustamento, J., 180
Busti, M., 86
Byrne, James, 247
Byrne, Paul, 268

Cadier, J., 106
Caes, P., 180
Caffrey, Mary, 244
Cahill, Sr. Camilla, 233
Cahill, J., 168
Cahill, P., 148
Caird, Alfred, 266
Cairns, Dorion, 41, 113
Caldin, E., 67
Callahan, D., 100, 140
Callahan, Francis, 247
Callahan, Leonard, 231
Callens, L., 156
Callus, D., 22
Calvetti, Carla, 180
Camelot, T., 180
Cameron, Bruce, 131
Cameron, J., 209
Campbell, James, 263
Campo, Mariano, 10
Camporeale, Ignazio, 95
Camus, Albert, 113
Canal Gómez, M., 10
Canfield, F., 51
Cangemi, Dominic, 238

Canguilhem, Georges, 214
Canilleri, N., 225
Cannabrava, Euryalo, 209
Cantin, Stanislas, 253
Cantwell, Peter, 243
Capizzi, Antonio, 123
Capocaccia, Antonio, 63
Caporale, V., 88
Caracciolo, Alberto, 171
Carandang, Amado, 263
Carbonara, Cleto, 81
Cardahi, Choucri, 194
Cardash, M., 279
Carley, F., 203
Carlini, Armando, 10, 27, 223
Carlo, William, 268
Carnes, J., 198
Carney, William, 251
Carpentier, R., 88
Carpino, Joseph, 248
Carr, A., 191
Carrière, Gaston, 280
Carroi, M., 214
Carroll, Owen, 281
Carrouges, M., 86
Caruso, Igor, 63
Cary-Elwes, Columba, 83
Casas, M., 25
Case, Edward, 241
Casel, Odo, 81
Casey, Joseph, 232
Casotti, Mario, 27, 213
Cassassa, Charles, 265
Casserley, Julia, 130, 133, 169
Cassirer, Ernst, 167
Castelli, Enrico, 10, 155, 170, 171
Casula, M., 95
Catalino, Joseph, 270
Catan, John, 269
Catania, Francis, 273
Caton, C., 45
Cauchy, Vinant, 203, 277
Caulfield, Joseph, 255
Caussimon, J., 27
Cavanagh, J., 203
Cavanagh, Patrick, 262
Cayré, Fulbert, 93, 95
Ceccato, Silvio, 19, 214
Cecchini, Augusto, 38
Celestin, G., 131
Ceriani, G., 10
Cesari, Paul, 187

Cesarini, Sforza, 200
Chabot, Sr. Marie-Emmanuel, 256
Chakravarti, K., 62
Chamberlin, Edward, 184
Chambon, E., 214
Chapman, Emmanuel, 264
Chapman, R., 162
Charlesworth, M., 45, 47, 162
Charmot, F., 81
Charron, William, 259
Chauchard, Paul, 62
Chauvin, Remy, 71, 134, 159
Chen, Ellen, 250
Chen, Joseph, 257
Chenu, Marie, 10, 25, 28, 50, 72, 113, 128, 221
Cherbonnier, E., 155
Chevallier, Louis, 56, 73
Chiavacci, Gaetano, 10
Childress, Marianne, 273
Chiseri, S., 10
Chopard, Edmond, 62
Christian, William, 125, 158, 160
Christian Humanism, 71
Chubb, J., 3
Ciappi, Luigi, 225
Cicinato, Dante, 214
Cilento, V., 28
Cirelli, Alberto, 214
Cirne-Lima, C., 148, 150
Clagett, Marshall, 54
Clark, Mother Mary, 152, 174, 181, 246
Clark, Merlin, 128
Clarke, B., 162, 169
Clarke, T., 131, 140
Clarke, W., 47, 50, 62, 101, 136, 162
Clement, André, 255
Clément, Laurent, 280
Coady, Sr. Mary Anastasia, 232
Cobb, John, 109, 155, 161
Cochet, L., 10
Coffy, R., 114
Coggin, Walter, 239
Cogley, John, 141, 202, 203
Cohen, M., 1
Cohen, Robert S., 55
Coleburt, Russell, 185
Colen, Remy, 35
Colin, Pierre, 159, 214
Collier, K., 67, 148
Collingwood, Francis, 267

Collins, James, 3, 17, 22, 36, 47, 52, 89, 91, 104, 108, 148, 153, 199, 219, 236
Collins, Joseph, 91
Colombo, C., 10, 47, 110, 159
Colombo, Giusèppe, 95
Colomer Pous, Eusébio, 10
Colonnetti, G., 64
Combés, Joseph, 187
Comes, Salvatore, 73
Commentarios a la encíclica HUMANI GENERIS, 223
Composta, Dario, 214
Compton, John, 186
Comte-Lime, V., 28
Conant, James, 60, 62
"Conclusions de l'enquète l'enseignement de la philosophie," 214
Confort et technocratie, 68
Congar, Yves, 100, 106
Congrégation des Etudes, 225
Conlan, F., 241
Conlan, Pius, 276
Connell, Francis, 72
Connell, Richard, 255
Connelly, George, 274
Connolly, Frederick, 57
Connolly, Thomas, 91
Connor, Joseph, 251
Conrad-Martius, H., 28
Conradie, Anna, 1
Constable, G., 203
Conway, James, 245
Conway, John, 103
Conway, Pierre, 253
Conze, Edward, 210
Cook, Edward, 242
Cope, Gilbert, 169
Copleston, F., 3, 18, 51, 52, 79, 113, 148, 162
Corbett, J., 18
Corbishley, T., 5, 121, 141, 154
Corcoran, Albert, 244
Cordovani, M., 225
Corkey, R., 3, 131
Corr, Charles, 275
Corts Grau, J., 10
Corvez, M., 95, 119, 138
Costabel, Pierre, 59
Coté, André, 257
Cottier, M., 95, 116

Coulson, Charles, 100, 134
Coulson, William, 262
"Council and the Problems of the Age," 109
Courthial, P., 123
Courtois, R., 119
Cousins, Ewert, 250
Cowley, R., 104
Cox, Harvey, 139, 141
Cox, John, 235
Cranston, M., 174
Creaven, John, 41
Creegan, Robert, 75
Crem, Theresa, 256
Crémer, P., 72
Creus Vital, L., 95
Cristaldi, Giusèppe, 119, 181
Cristaldi, Mariano, 19, 95
Critelli, Ida, 259
Croce, Benedetto, 19
Croissant, Jeanne, 214
Cronan, Edward, 60, 77, 237
Cronin, John, 74, 232
Crosignani, G., 225
Crosson, Frederick, 261
Croteau, Jacques, 81, 134, 280
Crowe, M., 203
Crowley, T., 222
Cruz Hernández, Miguel, 215
Cruz, Tomas de la, 86
Crystal, David, 160
Cuesta, Salvador, 181
Cunningham, G., 22, 23
Cunningham, Justin, 131
Cunningham, Sr. Miriam Ann, 242
Cunningham, Robert, 255
Cunningham, Stanley, 269
Cunningham, William, 231
Curnow, A., 148
Cushing, R., 85
Cuskelly, E., 77
Czajkowski, Casimir, 259

Dady, Sr. M. Rachel, 233
Daffara, M., 93
Dagonet, F., 68
Dainville, Francois, 69
Dalcourt, Gérard, 279
Dalencour, F., 178
Dalmau, José, 81
Daly, C., 47, 91, 192, 197

Daly, Sr. Jeanne Joseph, 241
Daly, John, 246
Damhorst, Donald, 274
Daniélou, Jean, 18, 35, 50, 89, 91, 100, 101, 103, 110, 120, 157, 169, 171, 195, 215
Darby, J., 141
D'Arcy, Eric, 174, 176, 190
D'Arcy, Martin, 83, 89, 108, 120, 147
Darnoi, Dennis, 243
Daujat, Jean, 53, 133
Daumas, Maurice, 56
Daval, Roger, 187
Davenport, Russell, 81
Davie, D., 136
Davis, H., 23
Davitt, E., 197
Davitt, Thomas, 271
Dawson, Christopher, 71, 123, 127, 136, 139, 141
Day, Abyann, 267
Day, Francis, 245
De Andrea, M., 225
DeBenedictus, Matthew, 236
De Brabander, René, 252
Debuisson, Damien, 82
Decarie, Vianney, 278
Dechert, Charles, 238
Deck, John, 269
Deckers, H., 181
Decloux, S., 123
DeCoursey, Sr. Mary Edwin, 236
Deferrari, Sr. T. M., 83
Defever, Joseph, 93
DeGeorge, R., 79, 155
De Koninck, Charles, 39, 210
Delaney, Howard, 273
Delanglade, Jean, 110
Delehant, Sr. M. Dunstan, 237
Delhaye, Philippe, 194, 205, 206
Delesalle, Jacques, 159, 170, 178, 187
Deman, T., 194
Demonque, M., 64
Demos, Raphael, 162
Dempf, Alois, 6, 11, 176
Dempsey, Peter, 278
Denburg, Chaim, 277
Denecke, Charles, 250
Deneen, Gerard, 246
Denis, Paul, 38
Dennes, William, 134

Deploige, Simon, 74
Derisi, Octavio, 6, 11, 19, 20, 25, 28, 43, 81, 82, 96, 215, 225
Desan, Wilfrid, 35, 39, 77
Desch, Paul, 3, 91
Descoqs, P., 25
Desharnais, Richard, 243
Deslauriers, Augustin, 277
Desmarais, Marcel, 81
Dessauer, Friedrich, 56, 59, 68
Deurinck, G., 101
Devauh, L., 64
Devaux, André, 215
De Waelhens, A., 42
Dewey, John, 49, 134, 174
DeWulf, M., 25
"Dialogue Between Catholics and Communists," 136
Diaz, J., 44
Dickinson, R., 158
Dietrich, S., 100
Dieu, 93
Díez Alegría, José, 11, 206
Diggs, B., 83
Dilley, Frank, 158, 160
Dillon, David, 212, 254
Dilworth, David, 249
DiNardo, Ramon, 242
Dingle, Herbert, 2
Dippel, C., 138
Diseit, Shrinewas, 176
Doberstein, J., 130
Dodds, E., 2
Dodson, E., 136
Doherty, John, 240
Doherty, Richard, 60
Doig, James, 156
Dolan, Bro. S. Edmund, 254
Dolan, Joseph, 256
Dollard, Stewart, 271
Dombro, Richard, 247
Donaldson, James, 257
Donceel, J., 23, 176
Doncoeur, P., 171
Dondeyne, Albert, 2, 39, 51, 53, 73, 116, 128, 132, 181, 225
Donohue, Thomas, 273
Donovan, Sr. Mary Annice, 260
Doolan, A., 21, 36
Dooley, William, 282
Dooyeweerd, Herman, 6, 11, 138, 156

Doran, Sr. Mary Verdas Clare, 254
Dore, E., 203
Dorval, Georgette, 252
Doty, W., 103
Dougherty, George, 234
Dougherty, Jude, 52, 109, 134, 192, 242
Dougherty, Kenneth, 238
Dowd, Mother Ruth, 247
Downey, Bro. Leo Robert, 248
Doyle, John, 270
Doyle, Sr. Mary Antoinette, 273
Dozo, L., 215
Dracaulides, N., 64
Draghi, Robert, 243
Drennen, Donald, 248
Driscoll, John, 243
Driscoll, Leo, 250
Drouin, Paul, 28, 254
Drucker, Peter, 67
Duba, A., 161
Dubarle, Dominique, 66, 69, 134
Dubay, T., 176
Dubray, Charles, 231
Ducasse, C., 47
Ducasse, P., 59
Ducasse, S., 148
Ducatillon, V., 64
Duchet, René, 68
Dufault, Wilfred, 254
Duff, E., 104
Duffus, R., 125
Duffy, John, 236
Dufrenne, Mikel, 20
Duhrssen, Alfred, 79
DuLac, Henri, 210, 212, 222, 254
Dumas, André, 145
Duméry, Henry, 43, 108, 154, 171
Duméry, Nicholas, 96
Dumont, Christopher, 103
Dumont, Richard, 281
Duncan, Paul, 55
Dunlop, John, 55
Dunn, Sr. Dorothy Ann, 275
Dunphy, William, 267
Duponchel, P., 25
Dupréel, E., 189
Duquesne, M., 82
Duquesne Univ. Symposium on Evolution, 35
Durand, Anthony, 254
Durfee, Harold, 3

Duzy, Bro. F. Stanislaus, 235
Dwyer, R., 199

Earle, William, 113, 176
East, Simon-Pierre, 256
Easton, Burnet, 192
Ebbinghaus, Julius, 181
Ebeling, G., 119, 150, 166
Ebert, Hermann, 136
Echarri, J., 225
Ecole, J., 110
Edel, Abraham, 49
Edie, James, 109, 113
Edwards, David, 109, 120
Edwards, J., 174
Egan, J., 23
Eggleston, Sr. Mary Frederick, 259
Eglise et la liberté, 178
Eglise et le monde, 129
Ehrle, Franz, 223
Ehrlich, Walter, 188
Eickelschulte, D., 166
Elbers, Gerald, 55
Elbert, Edmund, 240
Elders, Léon, 279
Eleasar, José, 246
Eliade, Mircea, 123, 139, 167, 168
Eliot, T., 127
Ellis, Oliver, 141
Ell, J., 28
Elliott, F., 37
Ellis, Frank, 274
Ellis, J., 101
Ellul, Jacques, 55, 68, 197
Elorduy, E., 195
Elswijk, H. Van, 28
Enchiridion clericorum, 221
Enciclica HUMANI GENERIS, 223
Engelhardt, Wolf von, 62
Engels, Friedrich, 135
Engels, Sr. Mary Francisca, 271
Englebardt, Stanley, 55
Enseignement de la philosophie, 213
Entenza-Escobar, P., 192
Entmythologisierung und Interpretation, 171
Ercilla, José, 278
Erlinghaven, Helmut, 246
Ermatinger, Charles, 274
Ernst, C., 121, 192
Erpenbeck, James, 263
Erwin, James, 276

Essays in the Science of Culture, 66
Esser, G., 192
Estrada, Charles, 250
Etcheverry, A., 116, 136
Ethics and Other Knowledge, 190
Ethier, Wilfrid, 277
Eustace, C., 104
Evans, Donald, 132, 161
Evans, Joseph, 260
Ewing, J., 35, 37
Existence and Nature of God, 89
Existence de Dieu, 119
Eyken, Albert, 61

Fabrat, A., 225
Fabro, Cornelio, 11, 28, 29, 44, 60, 82, 110, 115, 116, 226
Fackenheim, Emil, 109
Fagin, Charles, 266
Fagothey, A., 186, 190
Fairbanks, Matthew, 262
Faraon, Michael, 83, 275
Farber, Marvin, 39
Farley, Edward, 120
Farley, Mother Elizabeth, 246
Farré, L., 189
Farrell, P., 203
Farrer, Austin, 111, 174
Fasso, G., 203
Fay, Charles, 79, 192, 203, 272
Fazio-Allmayer, Vito, 11, 96
Febrer, M., 20
Feeley, Thomas, 257
Feibleman, James, 162
Feld, Norbert, 239
Fellermeier, Jakob, 11, 119
Felt, James, 275
Fennell, William, 113, 141
Fenton, J., 169
Ferguson, J., 185
Ferguson, Sr. Jane Frances, 234
Fernández Alonso, Aniceto, 11
Ferrari, Leo, 256
Ferré, Fred, 45, 147, 161, 162
Ferré, Nels, 3, 121, 128, 130, 158
Ferree, William, 234
Ferriols, Roque, 248
Ferry, G., 215
Fessard, G., 29
Feuerbach, Ludwig, 135
Feynman, Richard, 72
Fichter, Joseph, 128, 139

Fiebleman, James, 55
Field, G., 210
Filiasi Carcano, Paolo, 20, 96
Filosofia e cristianesimo, 6
Filosofia e formazione ecclesiastica, 223
Finance, Joseph de, 29, 69, 79, 88, 181, 189, 195
Finch, James, 55
Findlay, J., 192
Finili, Antonius, 91
Firkel, E., 51
Fisher, Luke, 235
Fisher, Ronald, 202
Fitch, F., 162
Fitch, R., 91
Fitts, Sr. Mary Pauline, 242
Fitzgibbon, John F., 261
Fitzgibbon, John P., 111, 251
Flaceliere, R., 88
Flanigan, Sr. Thomas Marguerite, 275
Fleckenstein, Norbert, 240
Fleming, D., 128
Flew, Antony, 45
Flores D'Arcais, Giusèppe, 96
Fluke, Otto, 110
Flynn, Frederick, 260
Flynn, John, 244
Flynn, Thomas J., 247
Flynn, Thomas V., 275
Foi et réflexion philosophique, 6
Foley, G., 123
Foley, Leo, 57, 210, 219, 236
Foley, Sr. M. Thomas Aquinas, 77, 240
Folliet, Joseph, 102
Folz, R., 181
Font Puig, P., 29
Fontaine, Raymond, 237
Fontinell, Eugene, 153, 247
Forbes, R., 61
Ford, J., 192
Ford, John, 281
Ford, Lewis, 121
Forest, Aimé, 11, 189, 215
Forster, E., 136
Forti, Edgard, 56
Foster, K., 42
Foster, M., 47
Foster, P., 125
Fougeyrollas, Pierre, 215
Fourastié, Jean, 55, 73

Fowler, William, 185
Fox, M., 155
Fox, Robert J., 243
Fox, Robert W., 186
Forti, Edgard, 82
Fraile, Guillermo, 11
Franchini, Raffaello, 68, 215
Francis, Richard, 262
Francisco, V., 199
Francoeur, Bro. Robert, 35, 37, 261
Frank, Philipp, 49, 58
Frankel, Charles, 61
Franklin, R., 125
Franz, Edward, 237
Fredrickson, Owen, 240
Freeman, David, 4, 153
Freeman, Hilary, 276
Freidrich, C., 197
French, Sr. Mary Anne, 274
Freyer, Hans, 59
Friedman, M., 169
Friedmann, Georges, 68, 73
Friedrick, Lawrence, 57
Friel, George, 233
Friend, J., 118
Fries, H., 171
Fromm, Erich, 39, 135, 174
Fromme, Allan, 83
Frondizi, Risieri, 188, 189
Fuchs, Joseph, 196, 206
Fudalla, Siegfried, 68
Fuente, Alberto, 226
Fuentes Castellanos, F., 29
Fues, E., 151
Fuller, L., 203
Fullman, Christopher, 85
Funk, R., 162
Funke, G., 166
Furstenberg, E., 115

Gabriel, Leo, 43
Gaede, Erwin, 190
Gahringer, R., 125
Gale, Richard, 203
Gallagher, Donald, 104, 259
Gallagher, Idella, 259
Gallagher, Kenneth, 39, 248
Gallagher, Thomas, 241
Gallegos Rocafull, José, 226
Gallie, W., 210
Galloni, G., 200
Gallucci, G., 29

Gallup, A., 220
Gallup, John, 257
Gambatese, Angelus, 263
Gambra Ciudad, R., 20
Ganguly, Theotonius, 260
Gannon, Sr. Mary Ann Ida, 272
Ganser, Geoffrey, 117
Garaudy, R., 115
García Asensio, Pedro, 20, 29
García, Leovigildo, 276
García López, J., 160
García Martínez, Fidel, 6, 19, 23, 29,
    222, 223
Garey, Sr. Mary Jocelyn, 253
Gariepy, Benoît, 20
Garnett, A., 85, 123, 185
Garrard, L., 136
Garrett, Leroy, 208
Garrigou-Lagrange, Réginald, 11, 21,
    25, 29, 93, 226
Gasson, J., 76
Gastonguay, Jacques, 279
Gatto, Edo, 269
Garvey, Charles, 261
Garvey, Edwin, 210, 264
Garvey, Sr. Mary Patricia, 258
Gayo, F., 11
Gebsattel, Viktor, 133
Geertz, C., 169
Geffré, C., 82
Geiger, G., 49
Geiger, Louis, 6, 29, 80, 86, 123, 181
Gelber, S., 136
Gelbmann, Frederick, 174
Gelinas, Elmer, 268
Gelinas, J., 25
Gellner, Ernest, 168
Gemelli, Agostino, 215, 218, 226
Gendreau, Bernard, 278
Gennaro, A., 201
Gentile, Marino, 11
George, André, 64
George, Richard, 263
Gerber, William, 18
Gerhard, William, 260
Germain, Paul, 56, 255
Gerrity, Bro. Benignus, 233
Gerry, Joseph, 248
Gervasi, Julian, 263
Guertsen, Henri, 226
Gewirth, Alan, 192
Gex, M., 138

Ghellinck, J., 226
Giacon, Carlo, 25, 60, 73, 96, 181, 221
Giannini, Giorgio, 12, 29, 172
Giardini, Fabio, 88
Gibbs, Y., 137
Gibson, A., 125, 148
Giglio, Charles, 243
Giguere, Robert, 237
Gilkey, Langdon, 113, 139, 141, 162
Gill, J., 162
Gilleman, G., 84
Gillet, Martin, 224
Gilligan, Bernard, 247
Gillio-Tos, M., 226
Gillon, Ludovico, 12
Gilson, Etienne, 2, 4, 6, 12, 21, 29, 84, 89, 108, 119, 130, 208, 226
Gingras, Jules, 277
Gioscia, Victor, 249
Girardeau, Émile, 62
Girardi, Jules, 116, 156
Girnius, Juozas, 278
Giszter, W., 30
Giuliano, Balbino, 119
Glanville, John, 260
Glasgow, W., 91, 158
Gleason, Robert, 85, 117, 157, 192, 245
Glockner, H., 181
Glutz, Melvin, 276
Goble, G., 203
Godin, Guy, 215
Godsey, John, 139
Gogarten, F., 138, 145
Goldbrunner, J., 77
Goldmann, Lucien, 157
Golebiewski, Casimir, 281
Gollwitzer, Helmut, 117, 172
Gómez Caffarena, José, 172
Gómez Nogales, Salvador, 44, 189
Gonseth, Ferdinand, 25, 64
Gonzales, M. Crescentius, 252
Gonzales, P. A., 149
Gonzalez F. Cordero, Francisco, 182
Gonzáles Rios, Francisco, 69
Goodwin, Robert, 251
Goossens, W., 12
Gornall, T., 108
Gorospe, Vitaliono, 274
Gorres, Ida, 149
Gosselin, Marcelle, 257
Gouhier, H., 12, 134

Gouirán, Emilio, 215
Goulet, D., 42
Grabau, R., 169
Grabmann, M., 30, 221
Graham, Aelred, 84, 100
Graham, Angelus, 185
Graham, Joseph, 262
Grajewski, Maurice, 235
Grassi, Carlo, 267
Grassi, Ernesto, 64, 215
Gratton, Henri, 280
Gray, D., 132
Greeley, Andrew, 89, 100, 101, 169
Green, Clifford, 141
Green-Armytage, A., 92
Greene, Theodore, 190, 208
Greenwood, T., 210
Grégoire, Franz, 12, 96, 194
Gregory, C., 160
Gregory, T., 162
Grenet, Paul, 30, 224, 227
Grenier, Jean, 178
Griesbach, Marcellus, 47, 269
Griffin, John, 254
Grimsley, R., 176
Grindel, C., 174
Grisez, Germain, 4, 104
Grison, M., 156
Grontkowski, Raymond, 250
Grosser, Elmer, 267
Gruber, Frederick, 185
Gruenenfelder, John, 262
Gualtieri, A., 162
Guardini, Romano, 51, 64, 70, 74, 81, 89, 96, 100, 126, 127, 174
Guelluy, Robert, 120
Guérin, P., 12, 126
Guerrero, Eustaquio, 227
Guinan, A., 137
Guindon, Roger, 221
Guitton, Jean, 84, 85, 86, 93, 96, 133, 150
Gulian, C., 189
Gunther, G., 7
Gurnan, Sr. St. Michael, 255
Gurr, John, 272
Gusdorf, Georges, 171, 178
Gustafson, G., 186, 235
Gustafson, James, 137
Gutierrez, Florentino, 253
Gutierrez de los Monteros, César, 189
Guthrie, Hunter, 4, 210

Guzikowski, Max, 210, 237
Guzzo, Augusto, 57, 70, 96, 218

Haas, W., 102
Hachey, Sr. M. Mercedes, 261
Hadas, Moses, 125
Haddox, John, 261
Häberlin, Paul, 12
Haecht, L., 166
Häcker, Theodor, 81
Häring, Bernhard, 174, 194
Hagerstrom, Axel, 124, 198
Hagerty, Cornelius, 231
Hahn, Lewis, 210
Hahn, W., 145
Haidant, Paul, 62
Hakim, Albert, 281
Hall, A., 55
Hall, Everett, 185
Hall, R., 163
Halpern, B., 67
Halpin, Sr. Marlene, 243
Hamel, Edward, 196, 206
Hamelin, O., 96
Hamilton, F., 147
Hamilton, Kenneth, 111, 132
Hamilton, William, 111, 141, 142, 158
Hamm, Johann, 87
Hammett, I., 203
Hammond, Francis, 253
Hammond, Guyton, 108
Hammond, Phillip, 125
Hampsch, George, 262
Hampshire, S., 176
Handy, Rollo, 186
Hanell, P., 105
Hanley, T., 137
Hantel, Erika, 69
Hardon, John, 100
Hardwick, E., 142
Hare, R., 163
Harkenridge, Edward, 239
Harmon, John, 137
Harnack, Adolf, 130
Haroutunian, Joseph, 4
Harrington, John, 238
Harris, Flavian, 186
Harrison, F., 158
Hart, Charles, 92, 212, 232
Hartman, Robert, 186, 188
Hartmann, Albert, 19, 178

Hartshorne, Charles, 47, 49, 52, 89, 97, 121, 153, 157, 158, 163
Harvanek, Robert, 23, 47, 223, 244
Harvey, Rudolf, 234
Harvey, V., 149
Hashimoto, Rentaro, 249
Hassel, David, 274
Hassett, J., 42
Hatchett, Marion, 132
Havard, R., 178
Hawkins, Denis, 52, 89, 92, 190
Hay, Gerald, 243
Hayek, F. A., 174
Hayen, A., 224, 227
Hayes, Justin, 272
Hayes, Sr. Mary Dolores, 235
Haymond, William, 273
Hazelton, Roger, 132
Heard, Gerald, 61
Hearings on Automation, 55
Heath, Thomas, 240
Hebert, Thomas, 254
Hecht, Francis, 272
Hedenius, Ingemar, 199
Heer, F., 113, 151
Heidegger, Martin, 39, 70
Heim, Karl, 129
Heiman, Ambrose, 266
Heinemann, F., 18, 42, 56, 149
Heinrich, Fries, 172
Heiser, Basil, 265
Helal, Georges, 279
Hellín, José, 227
Henderson, Edgar, 18, 52
Henderson, Ian, 168
Henle, P., 163
Henle, R., 210, 268
Hennemann, Gerhard, 7
Hennessy, James, 249
Hennig, Johannes, 12
Henrich, D., 110
Henry, André, 12, 190
Henry, C., 129, 147
Henry, François, 74
Henry, Paul, 77
Hepburn, Ronald, 46, 90
Herberg, W., 39, 142, 204
Hering, H., 12
Hering, Jean Von, 182
Héris, C., 87
Hernanz, Francisco, 30
Herron, M., 198

Hertzberg, Arthur, 113
Herx, Frederick, 262
Hesburgh, Theodore, 211
Heschel, L., 42
Hess, M., 42, 220
Hessen, Johannes, 25, 188
Hetzler, Florence, 248
Heuvel, A., 121
Hibbert, Giles, 153
Hick, John, 46, 47, 149
Hilckman, A., 12
Hildebrand, Dietrich Von, 44, 62, 77, 186, 192
Hill, Edmund, 153
Hill, Walker, 211
Hinners, Richard, 18
Hippel, Ernst Von, 196
Hirsch, E., 133
Hoban, James, 233
Hocking, William, 89
Hodgson, Leonard, 100, 163
Hoffman, E., 7
Hogan, Joseph, 238
Holbrook, Clyde, 135
Holcomb, Harmon, 132, 142
Holland, J., 121
Hollenbach, J., 43, 195
Hollenbach, Sr. Mary William, 261
Hollencamp, Charles, 253
Hollenhorst, George, 261
Hollon, Ellis, 109
Holloway, Alvin, 250
Holmer, Paul, 47, 163
Holmes, Arthur, 4
Holmes, Bernard, 265
Holmes, Frank, 155
Holte, R., 195
Hook, Sidney, 49, 89, 124, 174, 198
Hopkins, John, 274
Hopkins, Vincent, 37, 199
Hopko, T., 121
Horosz, W., 125
Horrigan, Alfred, 235
Horrigan, Sr. Anita, 239
Horvath, Alexander, 94
Hoselitz, Bert, 66
Hostie, R., 171
Houde, Roland, 278
Houlihan, Sr. Elizabeth Marie, 246
Hourdin, G., 151
Hovda, R., 102
Howell, C., 105

Hoyt, R., 142
Hubbeling, H., 130
Huetter, Norbert, 245
Hufnagel, A., 20
Hug, Pacific, 4
Hughes, H., 58
Hughes, Sr. Mary Cosmas, 236
Hughes, W., 211
Huisman, D., 213
Humanismus und Technik, 62
Hungerman, Sr. Marie Gabriel, 273
Hunt, Ben, 237
Hunt, DeRay, 265
Hurth, F., 196
Husserl, Edmund, 39, 40
Hutchison, J., 161
Huxley, Julian, 35, 135
Hytten, E., 190

Imbs, P., 166
Inagaki, Bernard, 198, 240
Incardona, Nunzio, 7
Innocenti, Umbertus Degl', 12, 30, 82, 97, 216, 227
"Inquietud del filósofo católico," 30
Intellectuelles dans la chrétienté, 102
Iorio, Dominick, 250
Iriarte, Joaquín, 12, 13
Isasi, J., 138
Isaye, G., 156
Iturrioz, J., 227
Iwand, H., 151

Jacklin, Edward, 245
Jacobson, N., 132
Jacoby, Paul, 260
Jalbert, Guy, 281
James, F., 2
James, William, 49, 124
Jannaccone, C., 196
Jansen, B., 13
Janssen, A., 196
Janssens, L., 179
Jarrett-Kerr, Martin, 135, 139, 163
Jarvis, J., 193
Jasmin, Louis, 277
Jaspers, Karl, 7, 61, 77, 168, 216
Javier, Benjamin, 247
Javillier, Maurice, 64
Jeannière, Abel, 113
Jelicic, V., 227
Jellema, D., 109

Jenkins, Daniel, 100, 109
Jenkins, David, 121
Jenkins, J., 199
Jenson, R., 125
Jérôme, J., 88
Jerphagnon, Lucien, 179
Jersild, P., 132
Jetté, Emile, 253
Jetté, Jacqueline, 279
Jiménez Fernández, Manuel, 30
Johann, R., 37, 84, 85, 86, 137, 149, 176
John XXIII, 71, 84, 227
Johnson, Frederick, 168
Johnston, Herbert, 264
Jolif, Jean, 116
Jolivet, Jean, 30, 216
Jolivet, Régis, 13, 40, 43, 44, 81, 89, 92, 94, 152, 156
Joly, Ralph, 242
Jonas, Hans, 110
Jones, Howard, 56
Jones, I., 121
Joravsky, David, 58
Jorgensen, Carl, 193
Joubert, Gerard, 234
Joulia, Pierre, 216
Jourdain, Alice, 245
Journet, Charles, 89
Jouve, Raymond, 102
Juchen, Aurel Von, 115
Jugnet, J., 25
Juhos, Béla, 188
Jullien, A., 224
Jungmann, Joseph, 100, 125
Junkersfeld, Sr. M. Julienne, 260
Juron, Robert, 216

Kahn, Jean-Louis, 70
Kahn, Journet, 261
Kalberer, Augustine, 266
Kanda, John, 251
Kandarapally, Joseph, 276
Kane, Sr. Anne Virginia, 237
Kane, William, 241
Kantorawicz, H., 198
Kaplan, Max, 66
Karisch, R., 151
Karrer, Otto, 106, 108
Kattsoff, Louis, 193
Katz, W., 198, 204
Kaufman, Gordon, 121, 125, 147

Kaufmann, A., 199
Kaufmann, Leo, 272
Kaufmann, Walter, 2, 124, 152
Kautz, Heinrich, 70
Kayayan, A., 116
Keane, Sr. Ellen Marie, 263
Keane, Helen, 259
Kearley, Carroll, 263
Kearney, Francis, 253
Keating, James, 239
Keating, Sr. Mary, 58
Keegan, Francis, 261
Keeler, Leo, 271
Keilbach, Wilhelm, 97, 126
Kelley, Alden, 142, 163
Kelly, Cornelius, 257
Kelly, G., 192
Kelly, James, 4, 270
Kelly, Sr. M. James Therese, 262
Kelly, Sr. Marie-de-Jésus, 253
Kelly, Matthew, 262
Kelly, Bro. Pascal, 245
Kelsen, Hans, 198, 206
Kemp, J., 193
Kendzierski, Lottie, 244
Kenealy, W., 199, 204
Kennedy, Leonard, 193, 269
Kennedy, Paul, 271
Kennedy, Samuel, 262
Kenney, W., 273
Kennick, William, 47, 92, 163
Kenny, A., 47
Kenny, John, 275
Kerenyi, C., 169
Kerins, James, 235
Kerr, F., 163
Kerr, H., 130
Keulard, P., 198
Kevane, Eugene, 211, 242
Kierkegaard, S., 40
Kiley, John, 282
Killeen, Sr. Mary Vincent, 232
Killeen, Sylvester, 74, 233
Kimmerle, Heinz, 167
Kimpel, Benjamin, 46, 89, 168
King, Edward, 263
King-Farlow, John, 149
Kinney, Sr. Cyril Edwin, 235
Kinsella, Arthur, 276
Kinzel, Sr. Margaret Mary, 242
Kirby, Gerald, 264
Kircher, Paul, 67

Kircher, V., 179
Kirchhoff, R., 151
Kitchanova, I., 30
Klamp, Gerhard, 13
Klauder, Francis, 246
Kleinke, E., 163
Kleinz, John, 235
Klemke, E., 132
Klemm, Friedrich, 55
Kline, Robert, 252
Klubertanz, George, 92, 220, 266
Kluckholn, C., 186
Knapke, Othmar, 231
Knevels, W., 172
Knight, Thomas, 176
Knowles, David, 199
Knox, John, 168
Knox, Ronald, 71, 84
Knox, T., 211
Kobeile, A., 139
Koch, Hans, 111
Kocourek, Rowan, 253
Koener, Sr. Jane, 273
Kohler, R., 160
Kohler, Wolfgang, 185
Kohls, Henry, 251
Kohn, H., 139
Kolbe, H., 149
Konvitz, Milton, 185
Korinek, A., 196
Korner, S., 163
Kossel, Clifford, 265
Kössler, P., 57
Koyré, A., 58
Kraft, C., 129
Kraus, Donald, 273
Kraus, John, 282
Kreeft, Peter, 250
Kreilkamp, Karl, 233
Kreyche, Gerald, 23, 40, 52, 281
Kreyche, Robert, 108, 280
Krikorian, Yervant, 49, 135
Krikowski, Johannes, 110
Kroeber, A., 36
Kroner, Richard, 127
Krook, D., 190
Kruger, G., 182
Kruithof, B., 142
Kruse, Beda, 216
Kuhn, Oskar, 38
Küng, Hans, 100
Künneth, W., 122

Kurella, A., 201
Kurth, Edmund, 56
Kurtz, Paul, 49, 193
Kwant, Remy, 40, 57, 74, 161

La Bonnardière, X., 216
Labourdette, M., 102
Labrie, Robert, 255
LaCentra, Walter, 270
Lachance, Louis, 200
Lachs, John, 109
Lacombe, Olivier, 7, 13, 20
Lacroix, Jean, 81, 87, 111, 115
Lademan, William, 247
Ladrière, Jean, 60, 137
La Farge, J., 51
Laffoucriere, Odette, 134
Lagaz y Lacambra, Luis, 97
Laguna, Grace de, 67
Laird, John, 185
Lais, Hermann, 145
Laky, John, 238
Lalande, André, 57, 189
Lalor, Juvenal, 253
Laloup, Jean, 62
Lamarch, C., 221
Lambert, Roger, 257
Lambertus a Matre Dei, 224
Lambilliotte, M., 160
Lamont, C., 137
Lamont, William, 185
Lamprecht, Sterling, 49
Landgrebe, Ludwig, 13
Langan, Thomas, 40
Lange, Joseph, 130
Langer, Susanne, 168
Langley, Raymond, 250
Langley, Wendel, 273
Langlois, Jean, 254
Langmead Casserley, J., 2
Lanigan, J., 80, 261
Lapierre, Michael, 269
La Pira, G., 188
Larkin, Sr. Miriam Thérèse, 263
Larochelle, Joseph, 254
Larrabee, H., 211
Laso, J., 196
Lauer, Quentin, 40, 43, 77, 193
Lauer, R., 177, 272
Laurenco de Faria, E., 182
Lauretano, Bruno, 182
Lavelle, L., 86, 188

Lavere, Georges, 256
Lavigne, Jacques, 278
Lawler, R., 48, 190, 273
Lawlor, Monica, 77
Lawson, W., 23
Lazure, Jacques, 206
Lazzarini, Renato, 97
Leander, Folke, 135
Lebacqz, J., 179
Le Blond, J., 110, 113, 196
Lechner, Robert, 211
Le Clair, Sr. M. St. Ida, 234
Leclerc, Joseph, 103
Leclercq, Jacques, 70, 77, 97, 101, 102,
    151, 195, 204, 216
Lecomte du Nouy, M., 151
Ledvina, Jerome, 234
Lee, Anthony, 223
Lee, Robert, 124, 139
Leeming, Bernard, 103
Leese, K., 138
Leeuw, G. van der, 43
Leeuwen, A., 127
Lefebvre, Reginald, 271
Legault, Henri, 253
Lehmann, Paul, 142
Lehrer, Keith, 177
Leibrecht, W., 127
Lemaître, G., 87
Lemieux, Albert, 265
Lemmer, Jerome, 271
Lenz, Joseph, 30, 43, 193
Léon, Philip, 48, 125
Léonard, Augustine, 80, 102, 119
Leonardi, P., 38
Leoni, B., 174
Lepley, Ray, 185
Lepp, Ignace, 43, 84, 111, 133
Leprince-Ringuet, Louis, 64
Leroi-Gourhan, André, 57, 62
Lersch, Philipp, 63, 64
Lescoe, Frank, 267
Le Senne, R., 159, 187, 188
Levard, G., 64
Lévesque, Claude, 279
Lévesque, Jean-Claude, 280
Levi, Alessandro, 200
Levie, Jean, 149
Lewis, C., 61, 84
Lewis, Clarence, 185
Lewis, Ford, 158
Lewis, Hebert, 278

Lewis, Hywell, 46, 90, 117, 157
Lewis, John, 71
Lewis, John U., 259
Lewis, John W., 149
Leyvraz, J., 151
Lhoir, J., 201
Lichnerowicz, André, 70
Liebhart, L., 97
Liégé, P., 149, 151
Lilje, Hanns, 112
Lillie, W., 142
Lindbeck, G., 204
Lindgren, John, 259
Lindon, Luke, 268
Lindsay, Alexander, 71
Linehan, James, 92, 118, 232
Linera, A. de, 20
Linssen, Robert, 87
Lintauf, J., 201
Litt, Theodor, 63, 69
Little, Arthur, 21
Little, David, 142
Llamzon, Benjamin, 274
Lloyd, A., 204
Lobato, Abelardo, 182
Lochet, Louis, 101, 160
Lochman, J. J., 142
Lochman, J. M., 121
Lockwell, Bro. Clement, 253
Löwith, Karl, 128, 151
Loftus, Arthur, 244
Lombardi, R., 20, 77
Lonergan, Bernard, 149
Long, Jerome, 249
López Salgado, Cesáreo, 97
Lossier, Jean, 73
Lossky, Vladimir, 157
Lotta, S., 200
Lottin, O., 97, 182, 201, 204, 206
Lotz, Giovanni, 97
Lotz, J., 116, 160
Lovell, Bernard, 66
Lowry, Charles, 72
Lubac, Henri de, 13, 90, 94, 103, 115,
    157
Lucas, George, 231
Lucks, Henry, 232
Luijpen, William, 40, 88, 112
Lumb, R., 199
Lusignani, Gildo, 81
Luther, Arthur, 259
Luyster, Robert, 169

Luyten, Norbert, 80
Lynam, Gerald, 239
Lynch, J., 193
Lynch, John E., 269
Lynch, John J., 199, 248
Lynch, Lawrence, 265
Lynch, William, 177
Lyon, Mary, 163
Lyonnet, S., 182
Lyons, John, 254
Lyons, Lawrence, 241

Maalouf, M., 279
McAllister, Joseph, 233
McArthur, Ronald, 255
McAuliffe, Sr. Agnes, 232
McCall, Raymond, 244
McCall, Robert, 240
McCarthy, Donald, 177, 269
McCollough, T., 153
McCool, Gerald, 18, 80, 247
McCormick, J., 4, 220
McCoy, Charles, 255
McCue, Edward, 271
McDermott, John, 248
MacDonald, Charles, 257
McDonald, H., 126
McDonald, Joseph, 256
MacDonald, Ralph, 266
McDonald, William, 233
McEachran, F., 121
McFadden, C., 232
McGann, Thomas, 247
McGill, V., 177
McGinnis, R., 84
McGlynn, J., 48, 155, 163, 190
McGovern, Thomas, 256
McGrath, Charles, 250
MacGregor, Geddes, 135
MacGregor, Philip, 245
MacGuigan, M., 199, 269
McGuigan, Sr. St. George, 244
Macho, Thomas, 249
McInerny, R., 153, 255
MacIntyre, A., 45, 46, 90, 153
McKenzie, John, 101
McKeogh, Michael, 231
Mackey, Robert, 247
McKian, John, 258
McKinney, Richard, 67
MacKinnon, D., 190
McKinnon, H., 204

MacLagen, W., 193
McLaughlin, J., 113
McLaughlin, P., 90, 118, 164
McLaughlin, Robert, 270
McLean, George, 18, 23, 169, 209, 219, 241
MacLellan, Thomas, 256
McLelland, J., 169
McMahon, Francis, 232
McMahon, Georges, 256
McMahon, John, 275
McMahon, Mary, 274
McManus, Charles, 244
McMullen, E., 48, 72
MacMurray, John, 36, 61, 77, 175
McMorrow, George, 259
McNally, R., 102
McNamara, Vincent, 257
McNeil, H., 4
McNicholas, John, 220
McNicholl, A., 42
McPherson, Thomas, 92, 164, 169
McQuade, Francis, 238
MacQuarrie, John, 50, 153
McSweeney, Alan, 235
McTigh, Thomas, 121, 272
McWilliams, J., 92, 270
Madariaga, Bernardo, 7, 20
Madden, H., 157
Madicke, Horst, 156
Madinier, Gaston, 87
Maguire, J., 105, 235
Mailloux, Noël, 177
Maino, Girolano, 216
Majchrzak, Coleman, 241
Major, Jean-Louis, 282
Malcolm, Norman, 48
Malet, A., 167
Malet-Yvonnet, N., 227
Malevez, L., 4, 13, 39, 103
Malone, E., 101
Maloney, James,, 253
Maloney, William, 238
Man in Contemporary Society, 61
Manier, August, 273
Manley, Michael, 267
Mann, J., 23, 42, 241
Mann, W., 164
Manning, Thomas, 280
Manno, M., 172
Manser, G., 13, 25
Marc, André, 30, 82, 102

Marcel, Gabriel, 40, 63, 66, 88, 92, 114, 137
Marcesca, M., 25
Marchello, Giusèppe, 179, 188
Marcil, George, 243
Marcotte, Marcel, 277
Marcotte, Normand, 253
Marcozzi, V., 133
Margolis, Joseph, 187
Marian, Sr Dolores, 78
Marías Aguilera, Julian, 20, 25, 155
Marie-de-Bon-Secours, Sr., 277
Marie-de-Lourdes, Sr., 253
Marie-de-Massabielle, Sr., 278
Marie-St-Jean François, Sr., 279
Marien, Francis, 272
Maritain, Jacques, 2, 7, 30, 52, 90, 114, 115, 126, 129, 157, 175, 202, 222
Mark, J., 169
Markovics, R., 25
Markus, R., 1
Marle, René, 172
Marling, Joseph, 232
Marra, William, 245
Marrou, H., 227
Marschall, Mathias, 278
Martano, Giusèppe, 81
Martí del Castillo, Rubén, 60
Martin, C., 46
Martin, Hugh, 258
Martin, J., 164, 277
Martin, Stuart, 248
Martin, Vincent, 254
Martindale, C., 109
Martínez, Elías, 13
Martínez, Mother Marie L., 271
Martini, A., 30
Marty, M., 108, 112, 124, 132, 147
Marx, Karl, 135
Marz, F., 151
Mascall, E., 46, 135, 139
Masi, Giusèppe, 97
Masi, Roberto, 13, 73, 97
Masiello, Ralph, 240
Masih, Y., 164
Maslow, Abraham, 185
Masnovo, Amato, 7, 13, 26, 30, 31, 221
Masterson, Patrick, 123
Matczak, Sebastian, 157
Mathews, Paul, 272

Mathieu, Vittorio, 98
Mathrani, G., 51, 187
Matson, Wallace, 112, 117, 170
Matteucci, B., 126
Mattingly, Basil, 261
Maublanc, René, 216
Mauchaussat, Gaston, 179
Maurer, Armand, 266
Mauris, E., 115
May, Rollo, 168
May, W., 193
Maycock, H., 122
Maydieu, A. J., 227
Maydieu, J. J., 13
Maynard, Sr. M., 258
Maziarz, Edward, 280
Mazzantini, C., 14, 19, 20
Mazzarella, P., 31
Mazzei, Alfredo, 90, 117
Mead, Margaret, 128, 204
Meadows, Paul, 66
Means, Blanchard, 193
Meehan, Francis, 234
Mehl, Roger, 7, 14, 84, 130, 188, 195, 196
Mehta, Ved, 152
Mekkes, J., 7
Meland, B., 18, 126, 137
Meloni, A., 195
Melsen, Andrew, 57
Melsen, H., 67
Melzer, John, 209, 211
Men and Machines, 61
Menasce, Giovanni de, 191
Mensch und Technik, 63
Merleau-Ponty, M., 14, 41
Meserve, H., 137
Messenger, Ernest, 36
Messner, Johannes, 102, 199, 204, 206
Metz, Johannes, 142, 149
Meurers, Joseph, 159
Meyer, Hans, 14, 21, 31
Meyer, Hermann, 59
Miano, V., 14, 154, 182, 227
Miceli, Vincent, 249
Michalson, C., 431, 122, 149
Michel, Virgil, 74, 231
Michener, Norah, 268
Micklem, P., 140
Miegge, Giovanni, 140
Miéville, Henri, 87
Mignault, Richard, 278

Mihalich, Joseph, 41, 252
Millard, Richard, 76
Miller, David, 142, 170
Miller, Joseph, 112
Miller, R., 164, 264
Miller, S., 149
Millet, Louis, 216
Miltner, C., 200
Minear, Paul, 103
Miquel i Macaya, J., 14
Miranda, D., 14
Mirgeler, Albert, 228
Miron, Cyril, 233
"Misión perenne y misión actual de
    la filosofía," 20
Mitchell, B., 46, 147, 153
Mitros, Joseph, 246
Mitterer, A., 31
Mitton, C., 122
"Moderne Philosophie im Lichte von
    HUMANI GENERIS," 228
Moeller, Charles, 106, 129, 132
Moeller, J., 52, 94, 151
Mohan, Robert, 57, 223, 236
Molitor, A., 201
Moll, Jan Van, 58
Monahan, Arthur, 268
Monahan, Edward, 268
Monde moderne et sens de Dieu, 53
Montague, Michael, 272
Montull, T., 116
Moore, Asher, 211
Moore, K., 193
Moore, T., 191
Moran, John, 249
Moran, Lawrence, 238
Morandini, F., 228
More, P., 147
Moré-Pontigibaud, Charles de, 94,
    159
Moreau, C., 44
Moreau, J., 98
Moreau, Jules, 161
Morency, Robert, 253
Moreno, Antonio, 276
Moretti-Costanzi, Teodorico, 189
Moreux, Théophile, 57
Morfaux, L., 216
Morkovsky, Sr. T., 275
Morón Arroyo, Ciriaco, 31
Morra, Gianfranco, 98
Morris, Bertram, 58

Morris, David, 264
Morris, Herbert, 175
Morris, Leon, 112
Morris, Louis, 185
Morris, V., 48
Morrison, C., 23
Morrison, J., 37, 260
Morton, Edmund, 268
Moschetti, A., 98
Motte, A., 14
Mould, D., 102
Moulton, Warren, 114
Mounier, E., 78, 175
Mourgue, G., 129
Mouroux, Jean, 61, 90
Muellner, J., 142
Müler-Schwefe, H., 115
Müller, Camille, 224
Müller, G., 116
Müller, O, 154
Müller, Giovanni, 216
Müller-Thym, B., 4, 264
Mullahy, Bernard, 254
Mullane, Donald, 232
Mullaney, James, 23, 211, 223, 246
Mullaney, Thomas, 80
Mullen, Sr. M., 234
Mulvihill, Josephine, 271
Mumford, L., 66, 67
Munby, D., 140
Munday, Daniel, 265
Munk, W., 155
Muñoz, J., 228
Muñoz Alonso, Adolfo, 7, 31, 44, 98,
    117
Munoz-Colberg, Magda, 252
Munsterberg, Hugo, 185
Murchland, Bernard, 143
Murciego, Pablo, 182
Murin, Charles, 278
Murphy, C., 204
Murphy, Edward, 231
Murphy, Joseph, 130
Murphy, Lawrence, 263
Murphy, Richard, 249
Murray, Desmond, 36
Murray, J., 51, 78, 108, 109, 137, 177,
    182
Murray, Michael, 244
Murry, John, 84
Muth, Edward, 282
Muzio, G., 24, 41

Myers, C. K., 142
Myers, C. M., 164
Myers, Gerald, 155
Myers, Joseph, 240

Nabert, Jean, 98, 195
Nade, S., 133
Nadeau, Louis, 276
Nakhnikian, G., 164, 193, 199
Napoleon, I., 84
Nardone, Henry, 243
Nash, Peter, 92, 118, 266
Naud, André, 7, 134
Naughton, E., 238
Navickas, Juozas, 248
Navratil, Michel, 98
Nédoncelle, Maurice, 2, 87, 98, 131, 179
Neill, S., 131
Neill, Thomas, 58, 71, 128
Neilsen, K., 177
Nell-Breuning, Oswald von, 74
Nelson, Everett, 126
Nelson, J., 78
Nelson, Ralph, 262
Nemetz, A., 48, 211
Neumann, Erich, 78
Neumayr, John, 257
Newbigin, L., 126
Newbold, Thomas, 278
New Essays in Philosophical Theology, 90
Nichols, James, 140
Nicolas, J., 154
Niebuhr, H., 128
Niebuhr, Reinhold, 124, 128, 164
Nielsen, H., 164
Nielsen, Kai, 4, 132, 158, 164, 193, 204
Nielsen, N., 153
Niemeyer, Sr. M. Fredericus, 211, 238
Nieto Arteta, Luis, 82
Nittel, J., 182
Noak, H., 166
Noël, L., 14
Nogar, Raymond, 37, 122
Nolan, Paul, 239
Noller, G., 171
Nolte, Fred, 66
Noonan, John, 238
Noone, John, 246
Novak, Michael, 143, 147, 150

Norris, Richard, 109
North, R., 37
Northrop, Filmer, 198
Noth, M., 140
Nothomb, D., 88
Nugent, Francis, 262
Nugent, James, 242
Nussbaum, J., 165
Nuttin, Joseph, 183
Nygran, Anders, 84
Nys, Pierre, 252

Oakley, F., 204
Obéissance et la religieuse, 179
Obert, Elisa, 64
O'Brien, Sr. Consilia, 233
O'Brien, Ignatius, 158
O'Brien, James, 86, 239
O'Brien, John, 36
O'Brien, Sr. Julia Marie, 255
O'Brien, Thomas C., 117, 158
O'Brien, Thomas S., 247
O'Callaghan, Jeremiah, 267
O'Callaghan, Louis, 245
O'Connell, David, 175, 199
O'Connell, F., 51
O'Connell, J., 92
O'Connell, Sr. M. Marguerite, 260
O'Connell, Robert, 143
O'Connor, Edward, 233
O'Connor, John, 230
O'Connor, Maurice, 231
O'Connor, William P., 231
O'Connor, William R., 244
O'Dea, Thomas, 52, 105, 143
O'Doherty, E., 80
O'Donnell, Clement, 232
O'Donnell, J., 266
O'Donovan, Leo, 143
Oesterle, J., 191, 253
O'Flynn, Sheila, 256
O'Gara, J., 102
Ogden, Schubert, 143, 147, 150
Ogiermann, Helmut, 160
Ogletree, Thomas, 143
O'Grady, Daniel, 24
O'Grady, Donald, 261
O'Grady, Francis, 280
O'Hara, Christopher, 245
O'Hara, Sr. M. Kevin, 240
Olbricht, T., 150
O'Leary, Conrad, 232

Oleschtschuk, F., 115
Olford, J., 129
Olgiati, Francesco, 14, 31
Oliva, Antonio, 38
Olson, Robert, 193
O'Mahony, Timothy, 244
O'Malley, F., 102
O'Malley, Joseph, 259
O'Manique, John, 282
O'Meara, William, 264
O'Neil, Charles, 177, 265
O'Neill, Reginald, 246
Ong, Walter, 36, 50, 129
Opocher, Enrico, 201
Oppenheim, Felix, 175, 274
Oppenheimer, Robert, 68
O'Rahilly, Alfred, 191
Oraison, M., 84
O'Reilly, Peter, 158, 269
Orestano, F., 21
Oromí, Miguis, 26, 224, 228
Ortega y Gasset, José, 52, 63, 78, 84
Osborn, R., 164
O'Shea, Robert, 241
Ossowska, Maria, 200
Ostheimer, Anthony, 233
Ostiguy, Roland, 280
Otis, Louis, 38, 253
O'Toole, Christopher, 235
O'Toole, Edward, 248
Ottensmeyer, Hilary, 87
Otto, John, 255
Ouellet, Henri, 254
Ouwerkerk, C., 87
Overholser, James, 124
Owen, William, 252
Owens, Francis, 251
Owens, John, 150
Owens, Joseph, 266
Owens, Thomas, 246

Pacheco, Armando, 260
Paci, Enzo, 172
Padovani, Umbertó, 7, 14, 31, 217
Padovano, Anthony, 114
Page, Robert, 120
Paggiaro, Luigi, 98, 133, 228
Paissac, Hyacinthe, 98
Palazzolo, Vincenzo, 201
Palmer, B., 204
Panneberg, W., 110
Pap, A., 164

Paparella, Benedict, 240
Papay, Joseph, 247
Pappi, A., 193
"Para el desarrollo de la filosofía
    cristiana," 14
Parente, P., 31
Pareyson, Luigi, 82
Paris, Carlos, 63
Parker, De Witt, 187
Parker, Francis, 110
Parkin, Vincent, 170
Parsons, Howard, 5, 126, 153
Passerin d'Entrèves, Alexander, 200,
    202, 204
Passeri Pignoni, Vera, 44
Pasteur, Valléry-Radot, 68
Pastore, Annibale, 73, 196
Paton, H., 108
Patry, Marcel, 281
Patte, D., 115
Patterson, Robert, 5
Paul, R., 137
Pax, Clyde, 262
Peacocke, A., 137
Pearl, Leon, 143
Pears, D., 46
Pearson, R., 147
Pécantet, J., 31
Pégis, Anton, 2, 208, 264
"Pela manutenção do ensino da filo-
    sofia no curso secundário," 217
Pelland, Lawrence, 277
Pellé-Douël, Yvonne, 217
Pellegrino, Ubaldo, 14
Pelster, Franz, 15, 223
Pelz, Werner, 112
Pende, Nicolas, 81
Penelhum, Terrence, 5, 48
Penet, Sr. Mary E., 271
Penido, M., 15
"Pensiero cristiano e pensiero meta-
    fisico," 15
Penta, Clement, 235
Pépin, Adrien, 87
Pepin, J., 172
Pepper, George, 248
Pepper, Stephen, 185
Pera, Ceslao, 31
Percy, J., 150
Pérez Ballestar, Jorge, 179
"Perfection de Dieu," 98
Perillat, Robert, 261

Perini, Giusèppe, 15
Perreault, Aimmon, 278
Perrier, J., 21
Perrin, R., 64
Perriollat, C., 7
Perroux, François, 70, 73
Perry, C., 212
"Personnalité," 82
Perticone, Giacomo, 183
Pesce, Dominico, 154
Peters, Thomas, 15, 228
Peterson, Forrest, 252
Petit, Gerard, 277
Petraroja, Sergio, 282
Petrazhitskii, Lev, 198
Petrin, Jean, 277
Petritz, Margaret, 239
Petruzzellis, Nicola, 32, 196, 217, 228
Petter, Dominique de, 119
Peursen, C. van, 15, 87
Pfaffenwimmer, Georgius, 183
Pfeil, H., 114, 115
Pham-Van-Long, Joseph, 256
Picard, Max, 65
Philipp, Wolfgang, 154
Philippe de la Trinité, 98, 183
Philips, Gérard, 106
Phillips, J., 112
Philosophie chrétienne, 7
Philosophies chrétiennes, 7
"Philosophy and the Catholic Student," 220
Philosophy in a Pluralistic Society, 17
"Physical Science and Human Values," 75
Picard, Guy, 258
Picard, Max, 65, 90
Piccoli, G., 217
Piemontese, Filippio, 15, 98, 228
Pieper, J., 15, 21, 24, 32, 42, 66, 84, 105, 129, 147, 151, 213
Pierrot, M., 222
Piersol, Wesley, 188
Pierson, M., 150
Pierzchalski, Raymond, 281
Pignoloni, Emilio, 217
Pinckaers, S., 196
Piovani, P., 201
Pirlot, Jules, 119, 213
Pius, XII, 56, 86, 94, 99, 205, 228
Pius XII and Technology, 71

Piwowarski, W., 206
Pizzorni, Reginaldo, 32, 183, 207
Plagnieux, J., 201
Plamondon, Paul, 281
Plantinga, Alvin, 147, 164
Platt, David, 118
Plattel, M., 205
Platzeck, Erhard, 8
Plé, Albert, 86, 175
Plotzke, U., 151
Pohier, Jacques, 279
Pohl, Heinrich, 60
Poirier, René, 60
Pokrovsky, G., 55
Polyani, M., 153
Polestra, G., 228
Poletti, Vincenzo, 195
Pollock, Robert, 264
Pollock, S., 150
Pompa, K., 21
Pompei, Alfonso, 229
Ponferrada, Gustavo, 217
Pontet, M., 37
Pontifex, Mark, 92, 175
Poppi, Antonino, 217
Porreco, Rocco, 18, 227
Poteat, William, 165
Pousson, Lyon, 235
Powell, Francis, 251
Powers, William, 258
Pozzi, Lorenzo, 217
Pozzo, Gianni, 73, 74, 82
Pra, Mario del, 32, 217
Pratt, O., 137
Prentice, Robert, 84
Prestige, G., 2
Preston, Robert, 242
"Presupposti filosofici di un Concilio ecumenico," 15
Preuse,, C., 183
Price, H., 150
Prini, Pietro, 32, 117
"Problem of Our Age," 205
Problema del valore, 188
Problemi filosofici del mondo moderno, 53
Probst, Joseph, 245
Proceedings: Conference on the teaching of Philosophy, 209
Proulx, Sr. Saint-Jean-Elziar, 257
Pruche, Benoit, 32, 111, 278
Prufer, Thomas, 212

Przezdziecki, Joseph, 267
Przywara, Eric, 15, 32, 94, 154, 172
Pucelle, Jean, 188
Puls, Sister Mary Sarto, 259
Puntel, L., 32
Punzo, Vincent, 274
Putnam, Mother Caroline, 242

Qadir, C., 126
Quadri, Goffredo, 82
Quaestio de philosophia christiana, 8
Queirolo, A., 32
Queiroz, Amaro, 217
Qu'est-ce que l'homme?, 81
Questiaux, F., 15
Quiles, Ismael, 15, 26, 32, 43, 217
Quinn, E., 153
Quinn, Francis, 74
Quinn, John, 242, 270
Quinn, Thomas, 177
Quito, E., 86

Rabbitte, Erwin, 177
Rabut, Oliver, 73
Rademacher, Arnold, 124
Rae, John, 56
Raeymaeker, Louis de, 15, 32, 99, 175, 196
Rago, Henry, 260
Ragusa, Thomas, 232
Rahner, Karl, 5, 8, 24, 90, 101, 111, 129, 143, 152, 197
Ralea, Mihail, 57
Ramírez, Augustine, 240
Ramírez, J., 88, 229
Ramírez, Santiago, 223
Ramsey, Arthur, 133, 140
Ramsey, Ian, 46, 137, 154, 161, 175
Ramsey, P., 114
Randall, John, 50
Ranly, Ernest, 275
Rast, M., 94
Rathenou, Walter, 56
Reagan, James, 273
Reale, S., 200
Reardon, B., 154, 170
Reatz, A., 32
Recaséns Siches, Luis, 189
Redanò, Ugo, 99, 111, 217
Redding, James, 245
Reding, M., 115

Reed, L., 143
Reese, William, 49, 89, 165
Regan, Sr. Frances, 266
Regina, G., 87
Régnéll, Hans, 8
Reid, Jean, 278
Reif, Sr., Mary R., 274
Reilly, Francis, 273
Reilly, George, 24, 232
Reilly, James, 267
Reilly, John, 274
Reilly, William, 247
Reilly, William F., 249
Reiner, Hans, 44
Reinhardt, Kurt, 5
Rein'l, Robert, 18
Reisman, David, 78
Reisner, E., 15
Reith, Herman, 253
Religione e filosofia, 8
Religious Experience and Truth, 46
Renard, Henri, 42, 194
Resan, J., 80
Reutemann, Bro. Charles, 239
Revault D'Allonnes, O., 213
Ricard, L., 45
Richard, T., 213
Richardson, W., 42
Richey, Sr. Francis A., 234
Richman, H., 114
Ricoeur, Paul, 41, 80, 88, 179
Rideau, Emile, 65, 117
Riedl, John, 258
Rieger, Ladislau, 70
Riessen, I. H. van, 57, 60
Riet, Georges Van, 154
Riniker, H., 119
Rintelen, Fritz, 99, 189
Rio, Manuel, 179
Riordan, Joseph, 269
Rivetti, Barbo, 99
Robb, James H., 268
Robert, Jean, 99, 119
Robert, Patrice, 252
Roberts, David, 5, 41
Roberts, Louise, 187
Roberts, T. A., 133
Roberts, T. D., 179
Robilliard, J., 82
Robin, L., 217
Robinson, A., 256
Robinson, C., 137

Robinson, James, 140, 161
Robinson, John, 108, 120, 131
Robinson, Richard, 112
Robles, Lawrence, 16
Rock, J., 92
Rockey, Palmer, 272
Rodriguez, J., 276
Rodríguez, José, 183
Rodríguez-Bachiller, A., 32
Roemer, Lawrence, 258
Roemer, W., 212
Roensch, F. J., 276
Röpke, Wilhelm, 57
Roesch, Eugene, 281
Roesle, Maximilian, 222
Roger, Aubert, 106
Roger, H., 41
Rogers, Carl, 78
Rogers, Mother Vera, 258
Roig Gironella, Juan, 16, 183, 229
Rolbiecki, John, 231
Role of the Christian Philosopher, 2
Rolland, E., 160
Romero, F., 218
Romeyer, B., 16
Rommen, H., 205
Ronco, Albino, 82
Rooney, Miriam, 205, 232
Ropp, Theodore, 74
Roqueplo, P., 120
Rorty, R., 48
Rosanas, J., 26
Rose, M., 165
Roshwald, Mordicai, 200
Rosmini, A., 195
Ross, J., 48, 165
Ross, W., 165
Rossi, Opilio, 16
Rossi, P., 16
Rossman, Kurt, 60
Rostenne, Paul, 69, 99
Rotenstreich, N., 105, 135
Roth, Paul, 65
Roth, Robert, 37, 50, 51, 249
Rotureau, Gaston, 73
Rougemont, Denis de, 85
Rouleau, Sr. Mary A., 274
Rousseau, Edward, 246
Routley, E., 120
Rovasenda, E. Di, 74
Rowan, John, 266
Rowland, Sr. Mary, 274

Royal, Peter, 256
Royce, James, 258
Royce, Joseph, 124
Rubenstein, Richard, 143, 170
Rubert Candau, José, 45
Ruch, E., 5
Rüfner, V., 83
Ruether, R., 129
Rueve, Stephen, 65
Ruffini, E., 36
Ruiz-Gimenez Cortes, Joaquin, 201
Rumble, L., 205
Rush, Vincent, 276
Rushdoony, R., 129
Russell, Bertrand, 66
Russell, John, 37, 58
Russell, Robert, 202
Russo, François, 16, 50, 57, 69, 70
Ryan, Columba, 92, 122, 165
Ryan, John, 5, 74, 86, 220, 232
Ryan, M., 110
Ryan, Michael, 262
Ryle, Gilbert, 46, 93
Rzadkiewicz, Arnold, 175, 237

Sacra Congregazione dei Seminari, 218
Sáenz de Santa Maria, Carmelo, 251
Saindon, Sr. Saint-Georges-Etienne, 282
Saint-Edouard, Sr., 256
Saint-Hilaire, C., 277
Saint-Hilaire, G., 177, 194
St. Hilaire, Sr. Mary, 275
St. John, Henry, 104, 105
St. John-Stevas, Norman, 198, 200
Saint-Martin-de-Tours, Sr., 257
Saintonge, F., 221
Saitta, G., 26
Salamucha, J., 93
Salisbury, W., 143
Salman, Dominique, 213, 222
Salmon, W., 164
Salvinien, J., 70
Samson, André, 257
Samuel, Herbert L., 2
Samuel, Otto, 69
Sánchez, J., 32
Sánchez-Marin, Faustino, 26, 224
Santamaria, Carlos, 160
Santayana, George, 135
Santero, L., 183

Santinello, Giovanni, 45
Santos, P. dos, 32
Santucci, Antonio, 218
Sarton, George, 18, 135
Sartory, Thomas, 106
Sastri, P., 212
Sattler, Henry, 236
Sauerbruch, Ferdinand, 65
Savaria, Sr. Madeline, 238
Sayegh, Fayez, 251
Schadewaldt, Wolfgang, 59
Schaefer, Thomas, 252
Schaldenbrand, Sr. Mary Aloysius, 242
Schall, James, 143
Scharl, E., 179
Schatz, O., 127
Scheler, Hermann, 65
Scheler, Max, 78, 85
Schelling, F., 175
Schelsky, H., 67
Schepers, Maurice, 101
Scheu, Sr. Marina, 236
Scheurer, Marcelius, 239
Schillebeeckx, E., 101, 123, 126, 138
Schilpp, Paul, 66
Schindler, A., 111
Schlemmer, H., 72
Schlette, H., 145
Schlipp, Paul, 58
Schmidt, Gerhart, 167
Schmidt, Hermann, 106
Schmidt, Paul, 68, 158
Schmidt, Robert, 266
Schmitz, Kenneth, 268
Schmölz, Franz, 206
Schneemelcher, W., 166
Schneider, E., 143
Schneider, Herbert, 2, 50
Schneider, J., 133
Schneider, Sr. Mary M., 272
Schneider, Richard, 270
Schneiderman, Leo, 187
Scholz, Donald, 257
Schopenhauer, A., 175
Schorsch, Robert, 260
Schrag, C., 37, 159
Schrag, O., 5
Schröder, E., 70
Schröter, M., 59
Schruers, P., 123, 160
Schrynemakers, Arthur, 261

Schubert, Robert, 282
Schuetzinger, Caroline, 282
Schuhl, Pierce, 65
Schultz, N., 86
Schumacher, Leo, 237
Schumacher, Matthew, 231
Schuster, J., 195
Schuter, Dietrich, 156
Schwartz, Charleen, 256
Schwarz, Baldwin, 78, 186
Schwarz, Ernest, 63
Schwarzschild, Steven, 143
Sciacca, Michele, 19, 53, 72, 83, 94, 110, 183, 197, 218
Science and Life in the World, 66
Science peut-elle former l'homme?, 63
Scimé, S., 16
Scott, Frederick, 251
Scotti, Pietro, 33, 222
Scullion, Matthew, 276
Scully, John, 269
"Secularism in America," 143
Sellers, J., 150
Selvaggi, Filippo, 99
Selznick, P., 205
Semmelroth, Otto, 81, 145
Serre, Jacques, 279
Sertillanges, A., 8, 26, 33, 87, 201
Sesek, Raphael, 243
Sesonski, Alexander, 191
Sever de Montsonís, 16
Sferrazza, A., 183
Sheed, W., 37
Sheehan, Robert, 241
Sheehan, Thomas, 275
Sheen, Fulton, 90, 175
Sheerin, John, 37, 144
Sheppard, Vincent, 237
Shideler, Emerson, 122
Shiner, Larry, 144
Shircel, Cyril, 235
Shuman, Samuel, 198
Shwayder, D., 194
Siegmund, G., 94
Siewerth, Gustav, 166, 183
Sikes, Walter, 154, 155
Sikora, Joseph, 261
Sillem, Edward, 5, 90, 93, 118, 157
Silva-Tarouca, Amadeo, 26, 94
Sily, Jorge, 229
Sily, P., 222
Simard, Emile, 254

Simard, G., 33
Simec, Sr. M. Sophie, 78, 239
Simmons, Edward, 260
Simon, Yves, 16, 105, 175, 179, 194
Simoncioli, F., 179
Simondon, G., 65
Sineux, R., 188
Singer, Charles, 55
Sirchia, Franco, 16
Slafkosky, Alexander, 255
Slattery, Kenneth, 239
Slattery, M., 170
Slavin, Robert, 232
Sleeper, R., 138, 165, 187
Sleva, Victor, 234
Sloyan, Gerard, 101
Smart, J., 118
Smart, Ninian, 90, 150
Smith, Alan, 66
Smith, E., 129
Smith, Edward, 281
Smith, Sr. Enid, 236
Smith, F., 51
Smith, F. J., 86
Smith, Mother Frances, 250
Smith, Gerard, 175, 177, 212, 264
Smith, H., 122
Smith, Ignatius, 220, 231
Smith, J. MacDonald, 93, 144
Smith, John E., 51, 157, 159
Smith, Joseph, 159
Smith, Raymond, 150
Smith, Roger, 165
Smith, Ronald, 135, 140, 144
Smith, Bro. Sixtus, 254
Smith, Vincent, 36, 38, 212, 220, 236
Smylie, James, 144
Smyth, Sr. Mary Marcia, 265
Söhngen, Gottlieb, 171
Solages, B. de, 33
Solie, Dorothée, 115
Somerville, James, 246
Sontag, F., 5, 154, 165, 170
Soria, C., 201
Soucy, Claude, 60
Soukup, L., 81
Spaemann, H., 151
Spargo, Sr. Emma Jane Marie, 245
Speltz, George, 236
Spencer, H., 195
Spiazzi, Raimundo, 73

Spico, C., 87
Spiegelberg, Herbert, 41, 42
Spilka, B., 165
Spinks, G., 150
Spirito, Ugo, 69, 183
Sponga, Edward, 247
Squadrini, I., 16
Staab, Giles, 78
Stace, W., 124
Stackhouse, Max, 144
Staffa, Dino, 33
Stakemeier, E., 152
Stallknecht, Newton, 177
Stanlis, P., 205
Stauffer, Robert, 67
Staunton, J., 21
Steele, George, 67
Steenberghen, Fernand van, 16, 33,
    94, 99, 119, 120, 220, 222
Stefani, S., 218
Stefanini, Luigi, 16, 83
Stein, E., 43
Steiner, K., 22
Stengren, George, 250
Stepelevich, Lawrence, 243
Stephenson, A., 105
Stevaux, A., 197
Stevens, Edward, 275
Stevens, G., 80, 200
Stevenson, J., 110
Still, Joseph, 67
Stirnimann, Heinrich, 229
Stock, M., 38, 80
Stokes, M., 154
Stokes, Thomas, 269
Stokes, Walter, 52, 122, 273
Strasser, Michael, 269
Strasser, Stephen, 43, 78
Strawson, P., 46
Streiker, L., 122
Streng, F., 170
Stromberg, James, 257
Structures et liberté, 179
Stucki, Pierre-André, 167
Struik, L., 276
Studies in Ethical Theory, 191
Studies in Ethics, 191
Suenens, Léon, 87, 104
Sullivan, Arthur, 248
Sullivan, Edward, 267
Sullivan, Emmanuel, 243

Sullivan, Henry, 251
Sullivan, James, 233
Sullivan, John, 78
Sullivan, Paul, 252
Sullivan, Richard, 255
Sullivan, Robert, 275
Summers, James, 240
Summers, Robert, 194
Supple, J., 253
Susinos, Francisco, 65
Sutfin, Edward, 258
Suy, E., 205
Swan, Peter, 266
Sweeney, Charles, 268
Sweeney, Robert, 249
"Symposium on God and Philosophy," 48
"Symposium on the Concept of God," 48
Synan, Edward, 267
Szczesny, G., 115, 148, 151

Talbot, Edward, 232
Tallon, Hugh, 233
Taner, J., 86
Tannenbaum, Frank, 75
Taparelli d'Azeglio, L., 206
Taube, Mortimer, 55
Taubes, S., 118, 122
Tavard, Georges, 104, 105, 133, 138
Taylor, John, 280
Taylor, Joseph, 254
Taylor, Paul, 194
Taylor, Sherwood, 104
Taylor, W., 165
Teilhard de Chardin, Pierre, 36, 38
Tello, B., 183
Temi e problemi di filosofia classica, 19
Temple, William, 24, 124
Tensing, Robert, 276
Terán, S., 19
Terrier, H., 38
Tessier, Hector, 277
Tester, S., 138
Tétreau, Richard, 270
Teucher, W., 70
Thalhammer, D., 105
Theology, Philosophy, and History, 209
Theubet, Louis, 65

Theunis, F., 171, 172
Thibeaud, Henri, 8, 159
Thibon, Gustave, 175
Thiel, A. Van, 161
Thiel, M., 16, 69, 218
Thielicke, Helmut, 114, 117
Thier, E., 117
Thils, G., 131
Thiry, A., 17
Thomas Aquinas, 83, 178, 197
Thomas, O., 126
Thompson, Richard, 265
Thomson, J., 191
Thonnard, F., 33, 127
Thorman, D., 104
Thro, Linus, 266
Thum, B., 152
Thum, Beda, 189
Thurneysen, E., 152
Tiberghien, P., 102
Tillman, Stanley, 272
Tillich, Paul, 17, 41, 85, 124, 126, 131, 148, 154, 170
Tinello, Francesco, 17
Tiszai, Paul, 281
Titone, Renzo, 218, 222
Toccafondi, Eugenio, 17, 33, 218
Todd, J., 79, 104, 176
Töth, P. de, 224
Toland, Terrence, 202
Tomeh, George, 251
Toner, Jules, 267
Toon, Mark, 240
Torrance, T., 165
Tougas, Sr. Miryam, 243
Toulmin, Stephen, 90, 212
Toupin, Charles, 276
Tournier, Gilbert, 65
Tournier, P., 79
Tout, T., 24
Towers, B., 38
Toynbee, A., 69
Trainor, Sr. Mary Rosaleen, 270
Trant, Edward, 249
Tremblay, Jean, 280
Tresmontant, Claude, 2, 8, 90, 94, 133, 151, 155, 156, 157, 159
Trethowan, Illtyd, 3, 48, 93, 118, 122, 148, 154, 159, 165
Trinité, see Philippe de la Trinité
Troisfontaines, Roger, 41

Troquer, R. le, 79
Trotter, F., 114, 122
Tseu, Augustinus, 258
Tucker, Robert, 135
Turley, Robert, 263
Turner, Vincent, 176
Turner, Walter, 265
Twohill, Sr. M. Dominic, 248
Twomey, John, 241
Tyrrell, Francis, 236
Tyrrell, N., 61
Tyson, Ruel, 144

Ubeda, Manuel, 275
Udell, Sr. Mary Gonzaga, 234
Underwood, Richard, 165
Upton, Cyril, 58
Urdánoz, T., 178, 184, 197
Urmeneta, F., 33
Urmson, J., 46
Urusov, Andrei, 279

Vachon, Louis, 254
Vagoric, Stefano, 195
Vahanian, Gabriel, 112, 114, 128, 133, 170
Valensin, A., 184
Valori, Paolo, 8, 33, 172, 184
Van Ackeren, Gerald, 5
Van Buren, Paul, 114, 129, 140, 144, 165, 166
Vancourt, R., 8, 43, 117, 130
Van Craenenbroeck, J., 201
Van der Ven, J., 88, 200
Van Domelen, Sr. Mary Ermelinda, 274
Van Dusen, H., 131
Vanier, Paul, 277
Van Kaam, A., 80
Van Munster, D., 197
Vann, Gerald, 191
Vanni Rovighi, Sofia, 33, 197
Van Overbeke, P., 207
Van Peurson, C., 42
Van Roo, William, 166
Van Steenberghen, Fernand, 24, 218
Vansteenkiste, Clemente, 33
Vargas, Alfonso, 236
Vassler, Karl, 166
Vawter, Bruce, 205
Vazquez, Juan, 70

Vecchio, Giorgio del, 198, 201
Veerkamp, Theodore, 276
Vega, Francis, 237
Velez, Jaime, 260
Vennes, Gaston, 179
Verga, Leonardo, 184
Vergote, A., 172
Verità e libertà, 179
Verneaux, R., 17, 115
Versiani Velloso, Arthur, 218
Veuillot, M., 115
Via, Vincenzo, La, 17
Vialatroux, J., 73, 218
Viglino, C., 8
Villain, Maurice, 104, 106
Villeneuve, J., 33, 34
Villeneuve, Suzanne, 218
Visser, J., 229
Vleeschauwer, J. de, 34
Vogel, Arthur, 131, 138, 157
Vogel, Cornelia de, 17, 80
Vogel, Mural, 244
Volk, Hermann, 87
Volkomener, Sr. Mary Theophane, 273
Vollert, Cyril, 38, 150
Vonessen, F., 171
Von Leyden, W., 205
Vries, J. de, 17

Wach, J., 126
Wade, Francis, 178
Wade, William, 271
Waelhens, Alphonse de, 43, 44, 167
Waelkens, R., 19
Wagers, Herndon, 3, 154
Wagstaff, Sr. M. Joseph, 238
Walch, J., 127
Walgrave, J., 167
Wallace, William, 38, 58, 59, 72, 212, 220
Walsh, Daniel, 264
Walsh, John G., 277
Walsh, John V., 86
Walsh, Joseph, 248
Walters, Sr. Annette, 78
Walton, William, 266
Walz, H., 144
Ward, Barbara, 176
Ward, Leo, 71, 187, 200, 205, 232
Warnach, V., 87

Warnock, G., 48
Warren, John, 255
Warther, Mary, 240
Wasmuth, E., 65
Wassmer, F., 187
Wassmer, Thomas, 246
Waters, Raphael, 279
Watts, A., 155
Weber, J., 166
Wébert, J., 26
Wedel, T., 138
Wegmann, R., 200
Weigel, G., 90, 104, 157, 170, 178
Weiher, Charles, 261
Weiler, Gershon, 150
Weisheipl, James, 58
Weiss, Paul, 5, 118, 205
Weissman, Hans, 178
Weiswurm, Alcuin, 239
Weitz, Morris, 48
Weizsacker, C., 135
Welch, Claude, 144
Wells, Donald, 157
Wells, Norman, 268
Wells, R., 166
Welty, Eberhard, 191
Welzel, Hans, 206
Wendland, H., 138
Wenzl, Aloys, 59
Werkmeister, W., 155, 187
Werner, Charles, 179
Wessel, Stephen, 280
West, Charles C., 144
West, Charles M., 255
Westermann, C., 117
Westfall, Richard, 71
Westley, Richard, 268
Wheeler, A., 170
Wheeler, Mother Mary, 219, 241
White, H., 136
White, R., 200
White, Victor, 90, 93, 94, 104, 159, 221
Whitehead, Alfred, 67, 136, 168
Whittaker, Edmund, 71, 118
Whyte, William, 79
Wicker, B., 144
Wickham, E., 144
Widart, Henri, 184
Widmer, Gabriel, 127
Wieman, Henry, 157

Wiener, Norbert, 55, 61
Wild, John, 122, 154, 176, 194
Wilder, Amos, 43
Wilhelmsen, Frederick, 51, 85
Wilkerson, Jerome, 243
Williams, Boniface, 114
Williams, C., 48, 93, 166
Williams, Leo, 165
Willman, Hermann, 184
Wilson, John, 46, 124
Wilson, Russell, 251
Wingate, M., 61
Wingell, Albert, 270
Winkler, P., 195
Winn, J., 132
Winter, G., 140
Winters, F., 93
Wittgenstein, Ludwig, 46
Wisse, S., 171
Woelfel, James, 166
Woestyne, Z. Van de, 34
Wojciechowski, Edward, 262
Wojciechowski, Jerzy, 212, 255
Wolf, E., 152
Wolf, Theodore, 271
Wolfe, Sr. Mary Joan of Arc, 233
Wolfson, H., 124
Wolter, Allan, 24, 212, 223, 236
Wolz, Heinrich, 244
Woodbridge, F., 50
Wright, Benjamin, 202
Wright, John J., 105, 198, 200
Wrightman, W., 212
Wu, John, 5, 68, 202, 205
Wust, Peter, 34, 44
Wylleman, Andre, 189

Xiberta, Bartholomaeus, 229

Yardan, John, 243
Yarnold, G., 136
Yee, Richard, 270
Yela, Mariano, 184
Young, William, 136
Younger, George, 144

Zalba, M., 197
Zamboni, Giusèppe, 21
Zamoyta, Bro. Casimir Stanislaus, 241

Zaragüeta Bengoechea, Juan, 17, 26, 184, 218
Zavalloni, Roberto, 79, 180, 184, 194
Zebeeh, F., 48
Zedler, Beatrice, 245
Zehrer, Hans, 61

Zilboorg, Gregory, 79
Zachimmer, E., 59
Zubiri, Xavier, 130
Zundel, Maurice, 91, 151
Zuurdeeg, Willem, 47, 166
Zvorikine, A., 56